D1535340

OXFORD STUDIES IN AFRICAN AFFAIRS

BRITAIN, THE SAHARA,
AND THE WESTERN SUDAN
1788–1861

BRITAIN,
THE SAHARA, AND
THE WESTERN SUDAN
1788-1861

BY

A. ADU BOAHEN

LECTURER IN HISTORY
IN THE UNIVERSITY OF GHANA

CLARENDON PRESS · OXFORD
1964

Oxford University Press, Amen House, London E.C.4

GLASGOW NEW YORK TORONTO MELBOURNE WELLINGTON
BOMBAY CALCUTTA MADRAS KARACHI LAHORE DACCA
CAPE TOWN SALISBURY NAIROBI IBADAN ACCRA
KUALA LUMPUR HONG KONG

© *Oxford University Press, 1964*

PRINTED IN GREAT BRITAIN

TO THE MEMORY OF
MY MOTHER

Preface

THIS is a study of the British penetration into the Sahara and the western Sudan which began with the systematic exploration of the interior and ended with the attempts to develop trade with the Sudan across the Sahara and to abolish the trans-Saharan slave trade. An effort has been made to bring out what the reaction of the African rulers to these European explorers and traders was and a picture of the commercial and political conditions in the interior in the nineteenth century has been presented. These latter subjects have, however, been dealt with mainly in Chapters V, VIII, and in the Appendixes IV and V (which should be regarded as a composite part of the work). Until the masses of Arabic material being collected in Nigeria have been organized and made available to scholars, any attempt at a detailed study of social, economic, and political conditions in the Sahara and western Sudan in the eighteenth and nineteenth centuries will be premature. On the other hand, the sources available now do make a full study of the activities of the British in the Sahara and the western Sudan during the period 1788 to 1861 not only feasible but even long overdue. And it is on this theme that I have mainly focused my attention in this work.

That the theme of British activities in the hinterland of the Barbary states and the Guinea and forest regions has been almost neglected by historians cannot be doubted. Though books exist on the exploration of the interior of Africa, such questions as why the systematic exploration of the continent did not begin until the 1780's, what were the objects of the expeditions and who were the men behind them, have never received serious attention. Even less known are the activities of the British in the Sahara during the first half of the nineteenth century. In his introduction to *The People of the Veil*, published in 1926, Francis Rodd, now Lord Rennell, wrote:

Few people in this country or abroad realise how great was the influence of Great Britain in the Sahara during the lifetime and after the death of that remarkable man, Colonel Hanmer Warrington, H.M. Consul of Tripoli from 1814–1846. Apart from the fact that he virtually governed Tripoli, our influence and interests may be gauged by the existence of the

Vice-Consulates and Consulates, not only along the coast at Khoms and Misurata, but far in the interior at Ghadames and Murzuk.'

It is indeed doubtful whether the number of such people has increased since 1926. Rodd himself does not tell us anything else about Warrington, or when the posts were established in the Sahara, what the vice-consuls did and with what results, and when and why these posts were withdrawn. Neither in his *Caravans of the Old Sahara* (1933) nor, more surprisingly still, in his new edition of it under the title *The Golden Trade of the Moors* (1958), does Bovill mention the vice-consular posts at Murzuk and Ghadames. French writers are equally silent on British activities in the Sahara. Duveyrier, Gautier, Chudeau, Rey, Bernard and Lacroix say nothing of the posts. Although Vuillot in his detailed *L'Exploration du Sahara* even mentioned the name of the Vice-Consul at Murzuk, he simply described him as the European Consul and tactfully forgot to state which European country he represented. Finally, though the abolition of the slave trade on the west and east coasts of Africa, in Egypt, and in the Sudan has been exhaustively dealt with by H. A. Wyndham, Coupland, C. Lloyd, E. Shukri, and Gray, there is no work on the trans-Saharan slave trade and the attempts made by the British to abolish it. Not even in general works on the anti-slavery campaign such as those by Coupland, Mathieson, and Gaston-Martin is there any reference to the British campaign against the trans-Saharan slave trade. There is thus a hiatus in our knowledge of British activities in Africa during this period, and it is essentially this that the author attempts to fill.

The main sources for this work have been the unpublished material in the Public Record Office, the private papers of Sir Joseph Banks in the British Museum (Natural History) in Kensington and at Kew Gardens, the papers of the British and Foreign Anti-Slavery Society at Rhodes House, Oxford, the minutes of the African Association in the Library of the Royal Geographical Society, London, and the published journals of the explorers. The material in the Public Record Office on which I have principally drawn consists of the correspondence between the various Government Departments, especially the Admiralty and the Colonial and Foreign Offices, between the Government and the explorers before and after their departure from England, and between the consular agents in Barbary and the Foreign Office.

A glance at the footnotes will also reveal how heavily I have drawn on Barth's journal. The detail and scientific accuracy of his observations stand unexcelled in the annals of the exploration of Africa. It is indeed one of the paradoxes of the history of African exploration that the greatest of the explorers has hitherto been the most neglected by modern historians. It is gratifying to see that British and African scholars are now rectifying this gross injustice to Barth. In commemoration of his centenary, for instance, Dr. A. Mansell Prothero read a paper on his mission to the Royal Geographical Society and Mr. A. H. M. Kirk-Greene contributed two articles on him to the journal, *West Africa*. Dr. Prothero, I am told, is writing a full biography of Barth, and Mr. Kirk-Greene has recently published extracts from his journals and biographical memoir under the title *Barth's Travels in Nigeria* (1962). I hope my chapter on the Central African Mission will also contribute to the rescue of this eminent and talented scholar-explorer from the obscurity in which he has been for so long confined.

This book is based on the thesis which I submitted to the University of London in June 1959 for the Ph.D. degree. I am grateful to Mr. H. C. F. Smith, Professor G. W. Irwin, and my friend and colleague Dr. C. C. Ifemesia, all of whom made suggestions as to the lines along which the thesis could be revised for publication, to Dr. J. D. Fage and Dr B. G. Martin for reading through the revised edition, and making very useful comments, to the Institute of African Studies of the University of Ghana for a grant to meet the cost of preparing the manuscript, and to the University of Ghana for granting me a return passage to the United Kingdom in July 1962 in connexion with the revision of the thesis. Finally I wish to acknowledge my indebtedness to Dr. Roland Oliver of the School of Oriental and African Studies, who originally drew my attention to the subject, supervised my post-graduate work, and encouraged and inspired me to revise the manuscript for publication. Finally, may I record my thanks to the staff of the Public Record Office, the Secretary and Librarian of the Royal Geographical Society, the Librarian of the Royal Society, the Librarian of Kew Gardens, and the Warden and Librarian of Rhodes House for their assistance and co-operation.

A. A. B.

Department of History,
University of Ghana,
Legon,
Ghana.

Contents

List of Maps

CHAPTER I

The African Association, 1788-1805

ONE striking feature of European activities in western Africa from the late fifteenth to the late eighteenth centuries was their obvious limitation in scope and objective. These activities were confined entirely to the coastal periphery, and their purpose was economic—the tapping of the human and mineral resources of the country. The non-intervention in the interior is not difficult to understand. There were no compelling reasons for penetrating into the hinterland, for the minerals and the slaves required by the European merchants were easily obtained on the coast, and fortified castles and trading hulks, as well as the political power of the coastal rulers, afforded them adequate protection. Thus confined to the coast, the Europeans could not but remain ignorant of the interior. Nothing illustrates the profundity of this ignorance better than the fact that although they had been trading to the rivers of the Bight of Biafra for over three centuries, they did not know that these rivers were the outlets of the Niger. It was not until the last two decades of the eighteenth century that the first steps were taken towards ending this ignorance. At a meeting of a dining club—The Saturday's Club—held in St. Alban's Tavern in London on 9 June 1788, the twelve members present unanimously resolved to constitute themselves into 'an Association for promoting Discovery of the Inland parts of Africa'.[1] From that date till 1805 it was this Association that spearheaded the drive into the interior of western Africa—that is, into the Sahara and the western Sudan. And in order to find out why the exploration of the interior began in 1788, it will be necessary to examine the nature of the Association and the circumstances leading to its inauguration.

Conflicting accounts have been given by different schools of thought. The most popular school, two of whose earliest exponents were Sir Harry Johnston and Sir Reginald Coupland, describes the Association as 'a creation of the humanitarian movement', a philan-

[1] C.U.L. MS. Add. 7086/1-2, minutes of the Saturday's Club, 9 June 1788.

thropic body formed to promote the exploration of Africa as a pre-
requisite for the abolition of the slave trade through the development
of legitimate trade.[1] Some recent historians, including J. H. Plumb,
Jack Simmons, and Margery Perham, admit the existence of other
motives—scientific, commercial, and strategic—behind the exploring
activities, but maintain that these were important only at the beginning, and that from the time of Park's first journey (1795-7) African
exploration was dominated by the abolition movement.[2] A second
school, whose greatest champions are the Nigerian historian Kenneth
Dike and the German scholar Heinrich Schiffers, sees African
exploration as nothing but the inevitable response to the exigencies of the Industrial Revolution and the loss of the North American
export outlets.[3] A third group of historians describe the Association as a geographical body primarily dedicated to the solution of
the problem of the source and termination of the Niger. These historians, notably W. H. Hewitt and R. H. Mill, see African exploration as a by-product not of the abolition movement but rather
of the discoveries of Captain Cook in the South Seas and the
explorations of James Bruce in Abyssinia between 1768 and
1771.[4]

Although all these authorities agree—though for very different
reasons—that the first concern of the African Association was to find
the source and mouth of the Niger, they provide ample evidence of
conflicting views of the motives underlying the commencement of the
exploration of Africa in 1788. Some of these views cannot bear close
analysis, others are only partially true.

It is true that, led by the Quakers, the movement for the abolition
of the slave trade was growing steadily from about the end of the
seventeenth century and gathered momentum when the famous

[1] H. H. Johnson, *The Opening Up of Africa* (London, 1911), pp. 216-17.
R. Coupland, *The British Anti-Slavery Movement* (London, 1933); see also
Andrew Cohen, *British Policy in Changing Africa* (London, 1959), pp.
8-9.
[2] J. H. Plumb, 'The Niger Quest', *History Today*, Apr. 1952; *West African
Explorers* (London, 1951), pp. 6-7; M. Perham and J. Simmons, *African Discovery*
(Oxford, 1942), p. 25.
[3] K. O. Dike, *Trade and Politics in the Niger Delta 1830-1885* (Oxford, 1956),
pp. 15-16; H. Schiffers, *The Quest for Africa* (Eng. translation, London, 1957),
p. 285.
[4] Hewitt calls the Association the first Geographical Society in Britain; W. H.
Hewitt, *Mungo Park* (London, 1923), p. 20; H. R. Mill, *The Records of the Royal
Geographical Society 1830-1930* (London, 1930), p. 6.

Mansfield judgement of June 1772 established that any slave who set foot in the British Isles became free. Fifteen years later sufficient converts had been won for the cause to justify the formation of the Society for the Abolition of the Slave Trade (May 1787). It is also true that the African Association was formed only a year later. The two movements were therefore not only contemporaneous but also both interested in Africa. However, there is no evidence to justify the view that the second was an offshoot of the first.

Had the abolition movement been responsible for the formation of the Association, one would have expected to find among its foundation members a large number of the members of the anti-slave-trade Society. On the contrary, only two of the original twelve members of the Association were members of that Society, whereas ten were members of the Royal Society.[1] The two were Henry Beaufoy, the first Secretary of the Association, and the Bishop of Llandaff. Indeed, the Bishop of Llandaff was no other than Professor Richard Watson, who until his appointment as Regius Professor of Divinity in 1771 was Professor of Chemistry at Trinity College, Cambridge.[2] What is more, at the time of the formation of the Association he had retired from the University and had taken up farming and the improvement of waste lands. Henry Beaufoy was also a keen student of geographical discoveries, as is evident from the plan of the Association he drew up. It seems very probable, therefore, that both Beaufoy and the Bishop of Llandaff joined the Association for scientific rather than anti-slavery reasons. Had such well-known abolitionists as Wilberforce, Clarkson, Granville Sharp, and Henry Thornton been found on the list of the foundation members of the Association, the case of the abolition school might be acceptable. But they were not. Furthermore, if the first secretary of the Association was an abolitionist, Sir Joseph Banks, its main founder, and Bryan Edwards and Sir William Young, the successors of Henry Beaufoy from 1797 to 1807, were all convinced anti-abolitionists; as Members of Parliament, the two last vigorously and consistently

---

[1] Seven of these were keenly interested in natural history. They were Sir Joseph Banks, President, Sir John Sinclair, Sir William Fordyce, Lord Rawdon, the Bishop of Llandaff, General Conway, and William Putteney. Banks, Fordyce, and Putteney were indeed the leading botanists of the day.

[2] N. Sykes, *Church and State in the Eighteenth Century* (London, 1934), pp. 332–78; E. Stock, *The History of the Church Missionary Society* (London, 1899), i, 33–34; *D.N.B.*

opposed Wilberforce's motions for abolition.[1] The very fact that the first secretary of the Association was an abolitionist but his two immediate successors were convinced supporters of the slave trade invalidates Plumb's contention that the Association became gradually dominated by humanitarian considerations.

If the original membership of the Association does not corroborate the views of the first school of historians, neither do the proceedings of the Association nor the instructions issued to the explorers. Nowhere in the minutes of the committee of the Association still extant from 1788 to 1809, nor in those of its annual general meetings throughout its existence from 1788 to 1831, was either legitimate trade or the abolition of the slave trade mentioned.[2] Moreover, in spite of the assumption of responsibility for African exploration by the British Government in 1805, it was not until the second Clapperton mission in 1825 (as will be seen in Chapter III) that the possible abolition of the slave trade was mentioned for the first time in instructions issued to explorers. Surely if abolition had been such an important motive in the drive into the interior, it would have been raised long before 1825.

Moreover, the African Association was not concerned with Africa alone. It was equally interested in the exploration of Australia. This is borne out by the fact that at the general meeting of the Association in 1798 it was decided that Park should be recommended to the Government to be 'employed in exploring the interior of New Holland [i.e. Australia]'. At the meeting in the following year the Secretary reported that Park's services had been accepted by the

[1] Among the reasons which Banks gave for his opposition to the abolition of the slave trade were that negroes who had been liberated never took to manual labour but lived by petty traffic and that there was nothing in the Bible to show that it was sinful to employ slaves (Rhodes House, Br. Emp. MSS, r. 2). Bryan Edwards, the Secretary of the Association from 1797–1801, was the famous West Indian planter and historian who came to England in 1792 specifically to obtain a seat in Parliament with a view to opposing the abolition of the slave trade (*D.N.B.*). In his speech in the Commons in 1805 against Wilberforce's motion for abolition, Sir William Young, then Secretary of the Association, said, 'In promoting this measure, you are not doing an act of humanity to the negroes themselves, . . . you are doing the highest injustice to the colonists, . . . you are neglecting your revenue and putting a great part of it in the greatest hazard and therefore forgetting the interests of your country. . . . I have the greatest hope that the House will view the question in its proper light and concur with me in a decided opposition to the second reading of this Bill' (Hansard, vol. III, pp. 625–53). The House did concur with him and the Bill was rejected.

[2] C.U.L. MSS. Add. 7085 and 7087, Minutes of the Committee and of the Annual General Meetings of the Association.

Government.[1] Again, while Park and Hornemann were scouring the interior of Africa, Flinders and Bass, both sponsored by Joseph Banks, were exploring the east coast of Australia.[2] What connexion, one might ask, had Australia with the slave trade?

Finally, if the Association had been pursuing a predominantly abolitionist policy, it would probably have been amalgamated with the Anti-Slavery Society formed in 1823. On the contrary, and rather significantly, it was merged in the Royal Geographical Society of London in 1831.[3]

Thus the African Association was not the product of the anti-slave-trade movement. It is true that in the course of time anti-slavery considerations began to play an influential part in the drive into the interior. No one can adequately explain the Niger expedition of 1841, or the travels of James Richardson in the Sahara,[4] or the work of David Livingstone in Central Africa, without considering the abolition motive. But this motive was definitely absent at the beginning and did not appear until the mid-twenties.

While the views of the anti-slavery school are not borne out by the available evidence, those of the other two schools by and large are. Dike's contention of the need for markets and raw materials, a need whose acuteness increased with the progress of the Industrial Revolution, is indisputable. That the loss of the American colonies in 1783 immediately caused alarm in commercial and industrial circles in Britain and further intensified the urgency of the problem of new markets cannot be denied. Moreover, as early as its meeting in August 1789 the Committee of the Association noted that a less hazardous and less difficult intercourse with Timbuctu might 'eventually prove of the greatest importance to the commercial interests of Britain'.[5] Again in 1790, 1793, and 1799 the Association sent memoranda to the British public and Government pointing out the commercial opportunities awaiting Britain in the interior and

[1] Banks to King, 15 May 1798, printed in *Historical Records of New South Wales*, iii, 382–3; Proceedings of the African Association, 1798. Park did not leave for Australia on 26 May 1798 or 25 May 1799, owing to last-minute disagreement about his remuneration.

[2] H. C. Cameron, *Sir Joseph Banks* (London, 1952), p. 92.

[3] Minutes of the Council of the Royal Geographical Society, 23 July 1831; C.U.L. MS. Add. 7087/240–4, Minutes of the Subscribers, 9 July 1831.

[4] See below, pp. 74–89, 174–9.

[5] C.U.L. MS. Add. 7085/25–30, Minutes of the Committee of the Association, 6 Aug. 1789.

urging that steps should be taken to exploit them.[1] The members of the Association were obviously alert to the economic needs of the time and fully conscious of the practical application of their discoveries. Economic considerations clearly form an important background to the exploring activities in Africa. Indeed, they came to dominate it from the beginning of the nineteenth century.

Geographical considerations were equally important in the formation of the Association. The eighteenth century was not only the age of the Industrial, American, and French Revolutions. It was also the century which saw the exploration of the interior of most of the continents. The Jesuit missionaries led by H. Desideri were exploring the interior of Southern Asia in the 1720's and 1730's.[2] In North America the French were pushing up the St. Lawrence, and by the close of the century the Americans had opened up the country as far as the Mississippi. The far north of Canada was being scanned under the auspices of the Hudson Bay Company. In South America the basins of the Amazon, the Paraguay, and the Parana were being explored. In Europe the first scientific expeditions went to Siberia, and the drive into the hinterland of Australia began with its colonization in the 1780's. By the 1780's then it was only the interior of the continent of Africa that was not being subjected to the scrutiny of explorers, and Sir Adam Ferguson, another foundation member of the Association who was keenly interested in geographical discovery, may also have felt this neglect. In the plan of the Association drafted by Beaufoy, the work of exploration which had been going on throughout the world was reviewed. Cook's voyages round the world were referred to, and mention was made of the progress that had been made and was still being made in Asia and America. But the map of the interior of Africa, it was pointed out, was 'still but a wide extended blank, on which the geographer, on the authority of Leo Africanus, and of Xeriff Edrissi, the Nubian author, has traced with a hesitating hand, a few names of unexplored rivers and of uncertain nations'. The unknown rise, course, and termination of the Niger was specifically referred to. Such ignorance was described in the plan as 'a degree of reproach upon the present age', and the Association was formed to remove it.[3]

[1] See below, pp. 15–16, 18, 24–25.
[2] A. Wolf, *A History of Science, Technology and Philosophy in the Eighteenth Century* (London, 1938), p. 414; Sir Percy Sykes, *A History of Exploration* (3rd edition, London, 1950), pp. 162–3.
[3] Proceedings, Plan of the Association, i, 2–8.

However, if these economic and geographical considerations had been by themselves decisive, the systematic exploration of the interior of Africa would have begun long before the 1780's. After all, the problems of the interior of Africa and especially of the Niger had been haunting and puzzling scholars ever since the time of Herodotus, Pliny, and Ptolemy (450 B.C.–A.D. 150), and the need for markets and raw materials was not new. A perusal of the plans put forward in the 1770's for the colonization of Australia shows how pressing the need for markets was. Yet it is interesting to note that in spite of the great commercial prospects conjured up by the advocates of Australian colonization, what immediately decided the issue, as is evident from the Colonial Secretary's letter to the Treasury sanctioning the colonization scheme, was the acute convict problem in Britain.[1] Similarly, for the impulse of the formation of the African Association and the initiation of the systematic exploration of the interior of Africa, we must turn not to Wilberforce and Clarkson but to Sir Joseph Banks and Carl Linnaeus, not to humanitarianism, commerce, and geography but to botany and natural history.

The African Association of 1788 owed its birth and inspiration to Banks. The first three and many subsequent meetings of the Committee set up to carry on the day-to-day business of the Association took place in his house in Soho Square, and nearly all the explorers who served the Association were selected on his personal recommendation.[2] It should also be remembered that Banks did not patronize exploration only in Africa and Australia. While Ledyard and Lucas were trying to forge their way through the Sahara, Captain Bligh, a protégé of Banks, was heading towards the South Seas in the *Bounty*. While Major Houghton was pushing on along the Gambia, Mackenzie and Menzies, also nominees of Banks, were respectively sailing up the St. Lawrence and examining the coast of North America. A common denominator must then be found in the forces propelling all these activities, and this was Banks's interest in botany and natural history.

This, his biographies agree, began at Eton at the age of fifteen, when he was converted 'from a boy interested only in sports and

---

[1] *Historical Records of New South Wales*, vol. i, Part 2, pp. 1–84; Lord Sydney to the Treasury, 18 Aug. 1786 (p. 14).

[2] C.U.L. MS. Add. 7085/7–18, Minutes of the Committee, 13, 17, 26 Jan. 1788. Banks's work in connexion with African exploration has not as yet been recognized. His biographer, E. Smith, dismissed it in a few pages, and H. C. Cameron (op. cit.) mentions it only in a footnote.

games, to a worshipper of Nature and thereafter her devotee'. He
was so impressed by some flowers which he saw one fine summer
evening that he exclaimed, 'How beautiful! Would it not be far more
reasonable to make me learn the nature of these plants than the
Greek and Latin I am confined to?'[1] By the time he left Eton for
Oxford he had become so engrossed in botany that when he found
that lectures were not being given on that subject at the University,
he sought for permission to recruit a lecturer. This was granted on
condition that the students paid the lecturer themselves. Coming as
he did from a very rich home, Banks accepted this condition, and he
found the man he wanted at Cambridge—Israel Lyons.[2] With the
help of this lecturer and relying heavily on the works of the greatest
living authority on the subject, Carl Linnaeus, Professor of Medicine
and Natural History at the University of Uppsala, he continued his
studies. Later he established regular correspondence with Linnaeus,
who had made the garden at Uppsala the Mecca of botanists, and
had initiated the practice of sending people to all parts of the world
to collect objects of natural history for his herbarium.[3] When Banks
completed his studies at Oxford, he was determined, as a true apostle
of Linnaeus, to extend his knowledge in botany and natural history,
to build up a herbarium for himself, and finally to make the gardens
at Kew the equal of those at Uppsala. Two years after leaving Oxford
he went to Newfoundland; in 1767 he visited North Wales; in 1769-
70 he accompanied Captain Cook on his celebrated first voyage
round the world, and in 1772 he visited Iceland.

From these travels, some historians, including Mill and Plumb,
have described Banks as a geographer. But this is quite wide of the
mark, for what he was concerned with in his travels was natural
history. John Barrow, Banks's personal friend, states that Banks
went to Newfoundland 'to enrich his collection of plants, fishes and

[1] E. Smith, *The Life of Sir Joseph Banks* (London, 1911), p. 6.
[2] Smith, ibid., pp. 7-8.
[3] In 1746 Linnaeus sent Christopher Tarnstrom to Spain and thence to South
Africa, Java, and China; in 1752 Pehr Osbeck, his pupil, went to Canton and
Java, while Peter Kalm made collections in the regions of New York, Phila-
delphia, and the Great Lakes in Canada. Between 1746 and 1776 Linnaeus also
dispatched collectors to Egypt, Tripoli, Tunis, West Africa, and South Africa.
The greatest of these collectors was Peter Thunberg, who began his journey in
1770, stayed in South Africa for three years, then in East Africa, Japan, and
Ceylon, and returned to Sweden nine years later with a very rich cargo of plants
and animals. For further details see R. E. Fries, *A Short History of Botany in
Sweden* (Uppsala, 1950) and W. I. Stearn, *Carl Linnaeus* (London, 1958).

insects with those of the northern region'.[1] And his equipment for his voyage with Cook leaves no doubt at all as to what his interests were; it included a fine library of natural history, all sorts of machines for catching and preserving insects, different kinds of nets, trawls, drags, and hooks for coral fishing, and many cases of bottles with stoppers; his staff included draughtsmen, painters, and 'several volunteers who had a tolerable notion of natural history'.[2] Banks is said to have spent the huge sum of £10,000 on his equipment. This turned out to be a good investment, since he brought back as many as a hundred new genera and a thousand new species, which even Linnaeus described as a 'matchless and truly astonishing collection such as never had been seen before nor may ever be seen again'.[3] Furthermore, in his unpublished journal of this voyage Banks gave a detailed account of the tattooing, ornaments, religion, and the structure of the languages of the aborigines of Tahiti and Australia[4] —positive evidence that his interest in natural history extended to human beings. Finally, that Banks was a botanist and what we may call an ethnologist rather than a geographer is amply demonstrated by his refusal to accompany Cook on his second voyage, when the Navy Board did not allow him sufficient accommodation on the vessels for his rather cumbersome scientific equipment.[5]

After these voyages, which enabled him to deepen his knowledge of natural history and to build a herbarium which soon acquired world fame, Banks embarked on turning Kew into both a plant quarantine station and the botanists' and naturalists' Mecca which it is today. From 1772 till his death in 1820 he assumed the post of 'unpaid director of Kew Gardens'.[6] In the pursuit of his aim he introduced, *inter alia*, the typical Linnaean practice of sending collectors to various parts of the world in search of plants of aesthetic, botanical, or economic value for Kew.[7] This has since become an

---

[1] J. Barrow, *Sir Joseph Banks* (London, 1845), p. 17.

[2] This description was given in a letter written by Ellis, a Fellow of the Royal Society, to Linnaeus and quoted by Cameron, op. cit., p. 15.

[3] Linnaeus to Ellis, quoted by J. H. Maiden, *Sir Joseph Banks, the Founder of Australia* (London, 1909), p. 31; Fries, op. cit., p. 15.

[4] Maiden, op. cit., pp. 12–18.

[5] Cameron, op. cit., pp. 48–56.

[6] G. S. Boulger, 'The connection of Kew with the history of Botany', a paper read before the South-East Union of Scientific Societies, 1915; *The Times*, 3 Mar. 1958.

[7] The other important practice which Banks introduced was the establishment in different parts of the British Empire of botanical gardens in which possibilities

accepted practice at Kew; it was also to trigger off the penetration into the interior of Africa.

Francis Masson, the first of the long line of collectors to be sent out from Kew, left in 1772. By the 1780's Banks had collectors in Portugal, Canada, the Americas, the West Indies, China, Siam, India, and Australia, as well as Africa.[1] Masson, the first of his collectors, went to South Africa, where he remained for three years before leaving for Portugal, the West Indies, and Canada. Banks also corresponded with James Bruce, the explorer of Abyssinia and the sources of the Nile, and received from him a collection of Nubian and Egyptian seeds and other objects of natural history.[2] To obtain specimens of the flora and fauna of the west coast of Africa, Banks secured the post of clerk in the service of the African Company for W. Brass, who was a keen botanist. Brass arrived in Cape Coast in October 1780 and three months later sent to Banks a good consignment of plants and seeds.[3] The most conclusive evidence that Banks was focusing his attention on Africa in the eighties, however, was the fact that in 1786 he secured the post of consul-general in Morocco for his protégé James Matra. Matra arrived in Tangiers in May 1787, and from then until his retirement seventeen years later he not only sent plants, seeds, and old coins to Banks but also became one of his foremost advisers on African exploration.[4]

It is clear then that by 1787 Banks's agents had operated or were still operating along the northern, western, and southern coasts of Africa, and it was almost a foregone conclusion that the hinterland would be invaded sooner or later by these intrepid collectors. Some of them even drew their patron's attention to this virgin field and suggseted ways and means of entering it. In March 1783, for example,

of acclimatizing exotic plants might be tested. Between 1770 and 1800 Banks established or assisted in the establishment of botanical gardens in India, Australia, Jamaica, St. Vincent, and Sierra Leone. It may be noted that it was while Captain Bligh, a protégé of Banks, was conveying bread-fruit to Jamaica from Tahiti in 1788 that the famous mutiny on the *Bounty* occurred. See Maiden and Smith, op. cit.

[1] Maiden, op. cit., pp. 52, 116–38; B.M. Add. MSS. 8094/112–13, Sparrman to Banks, 22 July 1776; Kew B.C. 1/205 Ponthieu to Banks, 27 Sept. 1785; B.M. Add. MSS. 8096/331–2, Isert to Banks, 13 Jan. 1785.
[2] Kew B.C. 6/45, Bruce to Banks, 5 July 1778.
[3] Kew B.C. 1/100, Brass to Banks, 21 Dec. 1780.
[4] B.M. Add. MSS. 33978/9, Matra to Banks, 23 Sept. 1786; D.T.C. 6/33–37, Matra to Banks, 24 June 1788; B.M. Add. MSS. 33978/228–9, Matra to Banks, 13 Feb. 1789; B.M. Add. MSS. 33980/231–2, Banks to Matra, 4 Apr. 1800; D.T.C. 8/48–51, Matra to Banks, 5 Aug. 1793.

Henry de Ponthieu, his agent in Antigua, mooted the question and pointed out that three or four of the negroes in the West Indies might be educated in England and sent back to Africa as explorers. He suggested that the cost of the scheme could be defrayed 'by subscription amongst a few men of fortune and of a curious turn [of mind] at home'.[1] Two years later Banks's attention was drawn to the interior of Africa by Paul Isert, a German then employed as physician to the Danish fort at Accra. In his letter to Banks,[2] Isert mentioned his own interest in 'Natural Philosophy' and the number of objects he had been able to collect since his arrival in Accra. He suggested that if he were given a salary of £500 per year, he could undertake a journey from Christiansborg castle through Akwapim and Akim to Ashanti and thence northwestward to the Senegal and the Gambia. After waiting patiently but vainly for a year for a reply, he wrote a reminder.[3] In 1787 Thomas Thompson informed Banks of his impending visit to Sierra Leone, asked for advice about equipment, and promised to add to his collections.[4]

Banks did not ignore these suggestions—indeed it was in 1786 that he arranged for Matra's appointment to North Africa. His main problem was how to implement them. In countries where there were either political or commercial British establishments, Banks could easily secure posts for some of his collectors in those establishments. This he did for Matra in Morocco, Brass in West Africa, Sir George Staunton in China, and Dr. William Roxburgh in India.[5] In the interior of Africa, where these facilities were not available, there were only two alternatives: either the British Government could take up exploration, or Banks could do so himself as suggested by Ponthieu. Preoccupied with more pressing economic and social problems at home and fully absorbed at this time in the colonization of Australia, the Government was apathetic. There is no evidence to support Plumb's view that in the 1780's 'the Government, too, was willing to give a strong support to African exploration'.[6] The dispatch of the first two missions of the Association was made possible by a volun-

---

[1] Kew B.C. 1/131, Ponthieu to Banks, 29 Mar. 1783.
[2] B.M. Add. MSS. 8096/331-2, Isert to Banks, 13 Jan. 1785.
[3] B.M. Add. MSS. 8096/333-4, Isert to Banks, 13 Jan. 1786.
[4] B.M. Add. MSS. 33978/97, Thomas Thompson to Banks, 23 Jan. 1787.
[5] In 1776 Banks arranged for Roxburgh to be appointed surgeon in the service of the East India Company. He remained in India for thirty years and his monumental work, *Flora Indica*, was published posthumously. Staunton, who made some valuable collections for Banks in China, was Secretary to Lord Macartney's embassy to China in 1793.　　[6] Plumb, 'The Niger Quest', op. cit.

tary contribution of fifty guineas by each of the members of the Committee,[1] and the cost of the subsequent ones was borne out of members' subscriptions. Even as late as 1800 the Government was still refusing to give the Association the necessary financial assistance.[2] It was not until 1805 that, for reasons to be dealt with in the next chapter, the Government assumed responsibility for exploring the interior of Africa. Meanwhile Banks had recourse to the other alternative. Luckily for him, there were in his dining club the few men of a 'curious turn of mind' who could help him to launch the Association.

Though the Niger problem was mentioned in the plan, its solution was not, as is generally supposed, the first concern of the Association. It was not particularly emphasized in the instructions given to John Ledyard, the first explorer sent out by the Association.[3] He was asked to traverse the continent of Africa 'as nearly as possible in the direction of the Niger' and to make himself acquainted with that river and the towns and countries on its banks. In the directions issued to Lucas, the second explorer, the Niger was not even mentioned. He was to proceed directly to Fezzan, transmit by way of Tripoli whatever intelligence respecting the inland regions of the continent the people might give him, and return to England via the Gambia or the Guinea coast.[4] Major Houghton and Mungo Park, the next two explorers, were certainly asked to find the course and the mouth of the Niger. But although Park unravelled only one of the knots in the Niger tangle, namely the course of the river, it was unanimously decided at the general meeting of the Association in 1798 that 'it appears to this meeting expedient for the present to suspend any attempt at further discoveries in the direction of the Niger'.[5] And if the Niger problem was mentioned in the instructions to the two previous explorers, it was not raised in those given to Hornemann, Weald, and Nicholls, the last explorers dispatched to Africa during the period under review. The instructions given to the last two are

[1] MS. Add. 7085/11–12, Minutes of the Committee, 17 June 1788.

[2] Banks informed Matra of the Government's attitude, and Matra replied, 'Your Society can want so little considered as a national sum that it is a shame for Government not to step forward to your assistance' B.M. Add. MS. 33980/231–2, Matra to Banks, 4 Apr. 1800; D.T.C. 12/28–31, Banks to Matra, 4 Feb. 1800.

[3] C.U.L. MS. Add. 7085/15–18, Minutes of the Committee, 26 June 1788.

[4] Proceedings, i, 21.

[5] C.U.L. MS. Add. 7087/38–42, Minutes of the Subscribers of the Association, 26 May 1798.

particularly noteworthy. In 1800 Weald was asked to visit 'those nations called the Tippoo [Tibu] who live beyond the great desert to the west of Fezzan; it is said that there are in that direction indigenous people whose manners would be a curious discovery.'[1] Nicholls left for Africa in 1804, with orders to start from Calabar on the Guinea coast, because the Association had as yet gained 'no very clear and satisfactory intelligence respecting the aboriginal people of Africa'. The Association contended that in all the areas hitherto visited by its explorers, the habits and institutions of the Africans had been greatly influenced by Islamic culture and beliefs, but that '. . . starting from the Bite [sic] of Benin, and pursuing his travels to the north-east, in his way towards the interesting cities of the Niger, he will have to pass an unexplored country, probably covered with intermediate nations of the "vera Nigritia", the Negro aborigines of Africa; and have subject to his observation African manners, mind, and temper, in social life and in policy and government native and genuine.'[2]

Moreover, the explorers were instructed, either privately by Banks or officially, to make botanical and zoological collections. Indeed, one of the reasons why Park was selected by the Association in 1795 was that he was 'not unacquainted with natural history', and he himself pointed out that his main aim in going to Africa was 'to examine the productions of a country so little known and to become experimentally acquainted with the modes of life, and character of the natives'.[3] And to render Hornemann more useful for the purposes of the Association, he was sent to Göttingen University for a year to study not only Arabic, astronomy, and mathematics, but also natural history.[4] Most of the explorers brought back zoological and botanical collections. Lucas, for instance, delivered to Banks seeds and plants 'of a curious nature' which he collected at or near Tripoli. Park and Hornemann sent similar collections.[5] It is evident from the

[1] D.T.C. 12/28–31, Banks to Matra, 4 Feb. 1800; B.M. Add. MSS. 33980/231–2, Banks to Matra, 4 April 1800. Weald changed his mind at the last minute and went to the West Indies.
[2] Proceedings, ii, 347.
[3] M. Park, Travels in the Interior Parts of Africa (London, 1799), p. 2.
[4] C.U.L. MS. Add. 7085/153–64, Minutes of the Committee, 3 June 1796; B.M. Add. MSS. 8093/313, Blumenbach to Banks, 7 Sept. 1796.
[5] Kew B.C. 1/353, Lucas to Banks, 3 June 1789; Park, Travels, pp. 8–10, 99–100, 352; D.T.C. 10 (2)/166–7, Banks to Hornemann, 16 Jan. 1798. In reply to Hornemann's letter containing a description of some plants, Banks wrote, 'You say in your last letter that the Dura is the Lea Mays of Linnaeus; pray inquire

instructions given to these explorers that what interested the Association was not the Niger problem *per se*, but the acquisition of general information about the indigenous peoples, their manners, cultures, and institutions, as well as about the plants and animals—in short, the natural history in the widest sense of the term—of the country to be explored.

Both Bovill and Plumb have criticized the Association for its 'curiously unimaginative approach' to African exploration. According to them, the Association started its work by making exhaustive inquiries about the interior from British consuls and traders in Africa, and it was only after it realized 'the futility of these inquiries' that it wisely decided to send out explorers.[1] There is absolutely no justification for this criticism, for though the Association did send out questionnaires to the consuls in Barbary, it did not wait for replies before it sent out its explorers. Indeed, only three weeks after its inauguration its first explorer left London for Africa, and the second explorer followed two months after the first.[2] The first choice of the Association, John Ledyard, was a protégé of Banks, under whose auspices he had travelled, between 1786 and 1788, through Germany, Sweden, and Russia as far as Oczakov on the Kamchatka Sea.[3] He entered Cairo on 19 August 1788. Two months later he sent to the Association the information he had collected about the interior, and in particular about Wangara, which, he wrote, 'is talked of here as a place producing much gold'.[4] Unfortunately, in

into that matter; the Botanists who have visited Egypt before you consider Dura as the generic name for several species of Holcus.'

[1] E. W. Bovill, *The Golden Trade of the Moors* (London, 1958), p. 208; Plumb, *West African Explorers*, p. 9.

[2] C.U.L. MS. Add. 7085/15-18, Minutes of the Committee, 26 June 1788; Proceedings, i, 20-24. In fact only James Matra appears to have replied to that circular, and his letter was dated 13 Feb. 1789 and cannot have reached the Association until a month later at the earliest (B.M. Add. MSS. 33978/228-9, Matra to Banks, 13 Feb. 1789).

[3] John Ledyard had planned to cross the continent of Europe and then go by sea to America, his homeland, and Banks established a subscription fund on his behalf. He managed to push on, at times on foot, as far as Oczakov before he was arrested by the Russian Government and deported to Poland. He returned to London only a few days after the formation of the African Association. Banks of course immediately introduced him to the Committee of the Association and he was selected. When the Committee asked him when he would be ready to set out he replied with characteristic impetuosity, 'Tomorrow morning'. For a fuller account of his interesting life see J. Sparks, *Memoirs of the life and travels of John Ledyard* (1828); Proceedings, i, 14-19.

[4] D.T.C. 6182, Beaufoy to Banks, 18 Oct. 1788; Proceedings, i, 24-40.

October 1788, shortly before his intended departure for the interior, he died in Cairo from a bilious complaint. Even before the news of Ledyard's death reached England the Association had dispatched to Africa Simon Lucas, a former British Vice-Consul in Morocco.[1] He arrived at Tripoli in October 1788 and was introduced by the British Consul, Tully, to the Pasha. His request for permission to go to Fezzan naturally took the Pasha's breath away, since it had never been made before by any European. It was, nevertheless, granted. But a rebellion which was raging against the Pasha in the southern districts of the Regency compelled Lucas to abandon his attempt after reaching Misurata, a hundred miles east of Tripoli.[2] He returned to London in July 1789.

Although Lucas did not make much headway, his journey was not such an unmitigated failure as to justify the scant attention paid to it by historians. He brought back some interesting information about the interior, strung together mainly from his conversations with the Shereef Mohammed Bensein Hassan Fouwad, who had travelled extensively in Bornu and Hausaland. Moreover, while Lucas was holding discussions with the Shereef, the Committee of the Association was interviewing Ibn 'Ali, a native of Morocco and a caravan trader, who was then in London. From these two sources a very illuminating picture of the political and commercial conditions of the Sahara and Western Sudan was presented to the people of England.[3] Fezzan appeared in these accounts as a small fertile oasis set in the desolate waste of the Sahara. The government, currency, commerce, and size of the two Sudanese kingdoms of Bornu and Katsina were described. Bornu was represented as more populous than Katsina and forty-five days' caravan journey south of Fezzan; it was said to have an elective monarchy and an army of a multitude of horsemen. Particularly detailed was the account of the caravan trade—the exports and imports involved and the size of the caravans.[4] But what is even more significant about these reports is the 'conclusions' which the Association drew from them for the consumption of the British public.[5] The attention of the 'philosopher' was drawn to the fact that the cowries used as currency in Katsina were the same as those used in Bengal. Fezzan was recommended to those thinking of

[1] C.U.L. MS. Add. 7085/7, Minutes of the Committee, 13 June 1788.
[2] Proceedings, i, 47–80.
[3] Proceedings, i, 81–189; D.T.C. 6/190–1, Beaufoy to Banks, 31 July 1789.
[4] Ibid., i, 181–91; see also Chapter V.   [5] Ibid., i, 196–205.

the 'usual excursions from Calais to Naples'. The lover of adventure was reminded of the powerful empires of Bornu and Katsina, and assured that 'the luxurious city of Timbuctoo whose severe police attract the merchants of the most distant states of Africa will unfold to him the causes of her vast prosperity'. To the geographer the mysterious Niger would disclose its unknown termination, while the naturalist could study the unknown flora and fauna of the regions. Finally, the enormous commercial opportunities were pointed out to the nation at large. Indeed, the Association canvassed the idea that if associations of Englishmen would form caravans and start from the last navigable reaches of the Gambia or from Sierra Leone, 'countries new to the fabrics of England, and probably inhabited by more than a hundred millions of people, may be gradually opened to her trade'.

Since the information from which these far-reaching and rather exaggerated conclusions were drawn was derived from secondary sources, it was natural that the Association should employ someone to test its validity. Further reports were also received from Matra in Morocco, and from Shabeni, another caravan trader who was then in London.[1] In Matra's report Timbuctu was represented as 'a very populous country full of large towns', and its capital, of the same name, as a general rendezvous, 'not only for the people of this country, [Morocco], but likewise for those of Algiers, Tunis and Tripoli, and its trade with Barbary'. Shabeni also gave a very spirited account of the Hausa Empire and its capital city called Hausa on the banks of the Niger. The population of the capital, in which he claimed to have lived for two years, was said to be equal to that of London or Cairo, its government was described as monarchical, justice was said to be administered according to written laws, and the art of writing was alleged to be very common. Shabeni said he was far more impressed by the wealth and grandeur of that empire than by those of any kingdom he had seen except England. It is not surprising that the Committee felt anxious 'to investigate the truth of these accounts; and impatient to explore the origin and course of a river that might possibly open to Britain a commercial passage to rich and populous nations;'[2] and even less so that it readily accepted the offer of Major Houghton, another ex-consul in

---

[1] B.M. Add. MSS. 33978/228-9, Matra to Banks, 13 Feb. 1789; F.O. 52/8, Matra to Sydney, 18 Nov. 1788.
[2] Proceedings, i, 241.

Morocco and a former fort-major at Goree, to proceed to Africa. On 16 October 1790 Houghton therefore left England with significant instructions 'to ascertain the course and if possible the rise and termination of that mysterious river', to visit 'the cities of Timbuctoo and Hausa', to report on the 'animal, vegetable or mineral productions of the inland countries of Africa', and finally to inquire into the central and provincial governments of the states, the religion, language, music, and manners of the peoples.[1] In the circumstances leading to Houghton's mission we see clearly the beginning of the principle of the solution of the Niger problem as the *sine qua non* for the extension of British commerce into the interior of Africa, a principle which was to provide the main impulse for Africa exploration after 1805.

Houghton arrived at the mouth of the Gambia in November 1790 and set off for the interior without delay. The last that was heard of him was in September 1791, when he was about to enter the Moorish kingdom of Waledomar. He seems therefore either to have been killed by the Moors, or, as Park heard later, to have perished of hunger after having been decoyed into the desert by them and abandoned.[2] Before his death, however, he sent home some description of the four kingdoms which he had already explored, namely, Wulli, Bondu, Bambuk, and Waledomar, all in the modern republics of Senegal and Mali (see Map 1, facing p. 19). He spoke highly of the first, whose capital, Medina, was 900 miles east of Bathurst, commented on the friendly attitude of the peoples of the first three kingdoms and their anxiety to trade with Europeans, and also emphasized the great economic possibilities in the Senegambia region. He reported, for instance, that 'gold, ivory, wax and slaves may at all times be had here for the most trifling articles; and a trade, the profit of which would be upwards of eight hundred per cent can be carried on . . . without the least trouble'.[3] He also sent information he had collected about the source and course of the Niger. From this the Association drew the correct conclusion that the river took its rise 'in a contrary direction from that of the Senegal and the Gambia' and flowed 'from the south and south west to the north and north east'.[4] It should be clear from this that Park's discovery four

[1] C.U.L. MS. Add. 7085/53-70, Minutes of the Committee, 18 Dec. 1790; Proceedings, i, 241.
[2] Park, *Travels*, p. 52.   [3] Proceedings, i, 318-22.
[4] C.O. 267/10, Memorandum of the Committee, 26 June 1793; Proceedings, i, 256; D.T.C. 7/213-15, Beaufoy to Banks, 28 Apr. 1791.

years later was not as revolutionary an event as historians have hitherto made it out to be.

Though Houghton's accounts confirmed the Association's hopes as to the possibility of establishing trade with the interior via the Gambia, the tragic outcome of the journey made it obvious that security and protection would have to be guaranteed by the British Government to any future pioneers before those hopes could be realized. Consequently in June 1793 the Committee of the Association submitted a long memorandum on the subject to the Government.[1] In this it mentioned the lucrative commerce existing between the Barbary states and the states on the Gambia and the Niger, the value of which was stated to be 'much underrated at a million pounds sterling per annum', and pointed out the ease with which that trade might be diverted westwards via the Gambia and the Senegal by British merchants acting in co-operation with the King of Wulli, 'who had expressed the strongest desire of establishing a commercial intercourse with the English'. It then emphasized the need for protection for the merchants, and concluded:

'The appointment of a consul to Senegambia would ensure that protection, and should instructions be given to him to proceed to Bambuk, would in all probability, establish a commerce that would soon transfer to Great Britain the trade which is now carried on by the Barbary States to the inland nations of the continent, and consequently super-add to her commerce a profitable export of much greater extent than the whole of her present traffic with the coasts and western rivers of Africa.'

This highly optimistic and apparently feasible suggestion was readily accepted by the British Government. The consular post was to be established at Fattatenda, about which Houghton had written in very glowing terms, and James Willis, a correspondent of J. G. Jackson, a British trader and writer resident in Morocco, was appointed to the post and authorized to make the necessary preparations.[2] The reasons for the Government's ready adoption of this scheme are evident from the instructions given to Willis. He was to endeavour 'by every means in his power to open and establish a regular communication between Great Britain and the countries on the Niger and Gambia for the purpose of traffic and barter and a free and mutual exchange of their respective commodities for the

[1] C.O. 267/10, Memorandum of the Committee, 26 June 1793.
[2] C.U.L. MS. Add. 7087, Minutes of the subscribers of the Association, 31 May 1794; C.O. 267/10, Willis to Huskisson, 18 Apr. 1795.

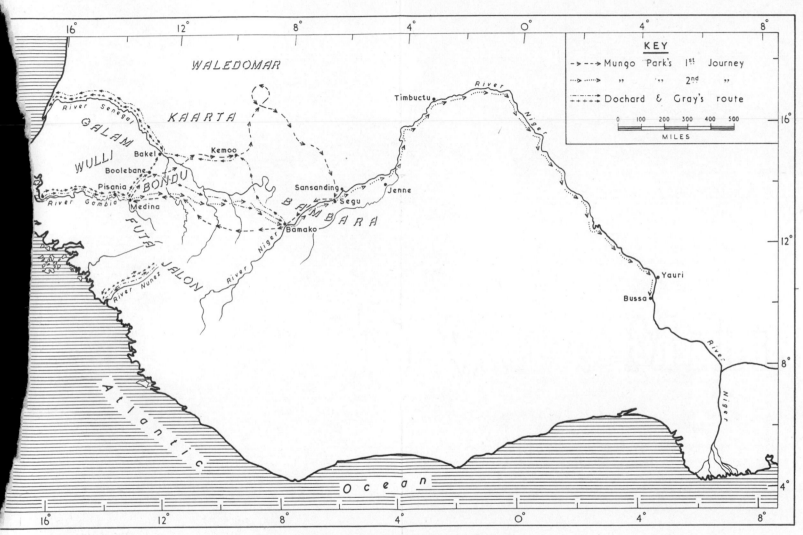

Map 1. Missions of Mungo Park, Gray, and Dochard

KEY

-➤---➤ Mungo Park's 1st Journey
➤······➤   "   "   2nd   "
+-+-+-+➤ Dochard & Gray's route

0   100   200   300   400   500

MILES

WALEDOMAR

KAARTA

GALAM

WULLI

Bakel

Kemoo

Boolebane

Pisania

BONDU

Medina

FUTA

JALON

River Senegal

River Gambia

River Nunez

River Niger

BAMBARA

Sansanding

Segu

Jenne

Bamako

Timbuctu

River Niger

Yauri

Bussa

River Niger

Atlantic

Ocean

merchandize and manufactures of this Kingdom.' With this in view, he was to cultivate the friendship of the Princes or Governments of the countries and to settle terms and conditions for carrying on trade and commerce with them.[1] But while these instructions were being drafted in London, the French were attacking the British traders on the Gambia. Therefore, acting on the advice of the Committee of the Association that the departure of Willis should be postponed till after the end of the war with France, the Government counter-manded the mission.[2]

While these negotiations with the Government were going on the Committee was looking for someone to continue the work of exploration. This search ended in the selection of Mungo Park. While a medical student at Edinburgh, Park had shown keen interest in botany. He was undoubtedly influenced by his brother-in-law, James Dickson, who was then a botanist of wide repute and had won the friendship of Banks.[3] It was through Dickson that Park was admitted to the circle of Banks's friends. After the completion of his medical course at Edinburgh, Park obtained, with the help of Banks, the post of assistant surgeon in the East India Company, and was sent out to Sumatra in 1792. He returned to England in 1795 at the very time when the Committee was looking for another man to send to Africa. Through Banks, he offered his services to the Association, and they were accepted after a short interview. He was asked to ascertain the course, and if possible the termination, of the Niger, and to visit the principal cities on its banks.[4]

With these brief instructions Park left Portsmouth in May 1795. A year later he set eyes on the Niger at Segu, where it was as 'broad as the Thames at Westminster'. He pushed down the river as far as Sillo, a place within two days' march of Jenne. The advanced state of the rainy season, the inadequacy of his means, and above all his fear of continuing any farther without being under the protection of some ruler or influential person, compelled him to return to the Senegal and then to England, where he arrived on Christmas Day

[1] C.O. 267/10, King to Willis, 31 Dec. 1795.

[2] C.O. 267/10, Report of the Committee, 13 Feb. 1796; C.O. 267/10, Willis to Dundas, 22 Feb. 1796.

[3] J. Thompson, *Mungo Park and the Niger* (London, 1889), p. 41; M. Park, *The Journal of a Mission to the Interior of Africa in the year 1805* (London, 1815), p. vi.

[4] C.U.L. MS. Add. 7085/75-28, Minutes of the Committee, 23 July 1794; Park, *Travels*, p. 3.

1797. His discovery of the course of the Niger was not a particularly exciting event for him. As he pointed out himself, 'the circumstances of the Niger's flowing towards the east and its collateral points did not, however, excite my surprise . . . more especially as I knew that Major Houghton had collected similar information in the same manner'.[1] In the opinion of the Association the real importance of Park's mission was in the valuable information which he brought back about the peoples, the institutions, the commerce and civilization, as well as the flora of the regions he visited.

His travels covered the area lying between latitudes 12° and 15°N. and longitudes 17° and 12° W. (i.e. the modern republics of Senegal and Mali). Ethnically, the area was occupied by three main groups of peoples, the Fulani,[2] the Moors, and the Negroes. The Moors inhabit the northern portions of the area traversed by Park. He described them as resembling the mulattoes of the West Indies in appearance. This is not inexplicable, since they were the product of miscegenation between the Negroes and the Berber tribes who were pushed down from northern Africa as a result of the Arab conquests between the seventh and eleventh centuries. He found them 'a subtle and treacherous race of people' and not unjustifiably held them responsible for most of the difficulties and delays he experienced *en route*.[3] Their hostile attitude was only natural, since they felt that Park's travels were a threat to their commercial monopoly of the area.

The Negroes were in a majority in the upper regions of the Senegal, the Gambia, and the Niger. They were, as Park discovered, sub-divided into four main groups, namely the Feloops (Felup), the Jaloffs (Jolofs or Wolofs), the Serawoollies (Serer), and the Mandingoes (the Wangarawa of Barth). The Felup, 'a wild, unsociable race of people with a peculiar language', occupied and still are found in the coastal areas south of the Gambia; while the Jolofs, 'active, powerful and warlike', who enjoy the reputation of being the blackest of the Negro peoples, dominated the area between the mouths of the Senegal and the Gambia.[4] The Mandingoes, numerically the largest and culturally and commercially the most important, were and still are spread over the region between the Atlantic and the upper Niger. Park described them as 'mild, sociable, and [of] obliging disposition', and throughout his journey found them exceedingly friendly, hospitable, and sympathetic. He was particularly astonished

---

[1] Park, *Travels*, p. 195.
[2] See below, pp. 240-1.
[3] Park, *Travels*, pp. 102, 111-15, 225-6.
[4] Ibid., pp. 15-16.

by the high standard of civilization attained by these people. He found, for instance, that not only was the weaving of cloth a very common occupation but that their loom was 'made exactly upon the same principle as that of Europe'.[1] When the cloth left the loom it was dyed by the women in a mixture of indigo and wood ash and the colour obtained was 'very beautiful with a fine purple gloss; and equal to the best Indian or European blue'. He also discovered that the Mandigoes knew how to smelt iron and gold for the making of implements and trinkets, and how to make gunpowder from nitre obtained from dried-up ponds and sulphur brought by the Arabs from the Barbary coast, how to make butter from the nuts of the shea tree—which to Park's palate 'was of a richer flavour than the best butter he ever tasted made from cow's milk'—and how to brew beer.[2] Park said that this beer tasted so much like the strong beer of his native Scotland that he was induced to inquire into its composition and learned 'with some degree of surprise' that it was actually made from corn which had been previously malted much as barley was malted in Great Britain.[3] Besides these manufactures, Park also found to his surprise, and undoubtedly to that of his contemporaries, that 'the belief of one God and of a future state of reward and punishment is entire and universal'; the Mandingoes believed that this deity was the creator and the preserver of all things and had appointed subordinate spirits to control the events of the world, and that these spirits could be influenced by certain ceremonies.[4]

Although ethnically the area visited by Park was shared among three main groups of peoples, politically it was divided into more than twice as many independent kingdoms. The most powerful of these were Bambara, Kaarta, Bondu, and Waledomar (see Map 1). Park was particularly impressed by Segu, the capital of Bambara, whose population he estimated at 30,000. 'The view of this extensive city,' he wrote, 'the numerous canoes upon the river; the crowded population, and the cultivated state of the surrounding country, formed altogether a prospect of civilization and magnificence, which I little expected to find in the bosom of Africa.'[5] Some of the peoples and tribes described dominated particular kingdoms. Bondu, for instance, was occupied almost wholly by the Fulani and Waledomar by the Moors. In some kingdoms, such as

---

[1] Park, *Travels*, pp. 281–2.   [2] Ibid., pp. 283–5, 116–17, 42.
[3] Ibid., pp. 42–43.   [4] Ibid., pp. 273–4.   [5] Ibid., p. 196.

Waledomar, the king was absolute; in others, such as Wulli, he was assisted by a council composed of the great officers of the state, without whose consent he could not, for example, declare war.[1]

Cutting across both ethnographical and political boundaries, as Park reported, was the Muslim religion. The Fulani and the Moors were Muslim; so also, though far less intolerant and fanatical, were some of the Negroes.[2] Islam, Park found, was not being propagated by the sword but rather 'by means abundantly more efficacious', namely by education. There were many schools open to all and sundry, and education consisted in teaching pupils to read the Koran and the commentaries on it in Arabic. This was not the end of their reading, for Park discovered that some of the educated Negroes had, among other works, the *Tawriya limūsa* (the Arabic version of the Pentateuch of Moses), the *Zabūr Dawūd* (the Psalms of David), and the *al-injīl li 'Isa* (the Gospel of Christ).[3] By a study of these books the convert was familiarized with the lives of Abraham and his sons, the story of Joseph and his brothers, the history of Moses, and the life and teaching of Christ. 'My surprise', Park wrote, 'was not greater on hearing these accounts from the lips of the Negroes, than theirs, on finding that I was already acquainted with them.'[4] Even in the kingdoms where the people were predominantly animistic, their social and judicial institutions were deeply impregnated with Muslim influences. For instance, Park observed that in all the courts of the Mandingo towns that he visited both civil and criminal jurisdiction were based on the *Koran* and the *Sharia*. On this he commented:

This frequency of appeal to written laws, with which the pagan natives are necessarily unacquainted, has given rise in their palavers to (what I little expected to find in Africa) professional advocates, or expounders of the

---

[1] Park, *Travels*, p. 35.
[2] That Islam was so widespread in the area explored by Park is nothing strange. One of the very first Muslim missionaries to the Sudan was the Berber Abdallah Ibn Yasin, who probably founded a monastery on an island in the Senegal in the eleventh century. It was from there that Islam began to spread westwards, a development which was accelerated by the conquest of Ghana by the Almoravid in 1076 and the conversion of the rulers of the Empires of Mali and Songhay. D. Westermann, *Islam in Western and Central Sudan* (London, 1920).
[3] Park, *Travels*, p. 314; *al-injil li-'Isa* is the Gospel of Christ and not the Book of Isaiah as Park thought. I am grateful to Mr. H. F. C. Smith for drawing my attention to this.
[4] Ibid., p. 315.

law, who are allowed to appear and to plead for the plaintiff or defendant, much in the same manner as counsel in the law courts of Great Britain. They are Mohammedan Negroes who have made, or affect to have made, the laws of the Prophet their peculiar study; and if I may judge from their harangues, which I frequently attended, I believe that in the forensic quali-fications of procrastination and cavil, and the arts of confounding and perplexing a cause, they are not always surpassed by the ablest pleaders in Europe . . .[1]

Equally illuminating were Park's accounts of the three main exports of the area: slaves, gold, and ivory. Park reported that gold could be found in considerable quantities throughout every part of the district of Manding, particularly around Bure. The gold of Manding was obtained in grains varying from 'a pin's head to that of a pea' by washing the sediments brought down from the neigh-bouring hills by the floods during the rainy season or by digging a deep pit and washing the earth in calabashes.[2] He was certain that if more scientific methods of mining were adopted there would be a great increase in output.

Botanical observations and collections were an important part of Park's work. He tells us, for instance, that while he waited at Pisania in Gambia to learn the Mandingo language, he went out 'on botanical excursions', and when it rained, amused himself with 'drawing plants in my chamber'.[3] In Masina, in the kingdom of Kaarta, he came across 'farinaceous berries of a yellow colour and delicious taste which I knew to be the fruit of the rhamnus of Linnaeus'; he observed the same species on the sandy soil of Wale-domar and the northern Bambara and was certain that it was the same as the lotus found in Tunis, which was said by Pliny to be the food of the Libyan Lotophagi.[4] He also examined the shea tree and classified it as belonging to the natural order of Sapotae.[5]

Although Park's first mission failed to throw any light on the age-old problem of the mouth of the Niger, it is nevertheless a landmark in the history of African exploration. His discoveries dispelled scepticism about the existence of the Niger and confirmed what had

[1] Park, Travels, p. 20.
[2] Ibid., pp. 299-304. As Bovill has shown, these areas were the Wangara of the Arabic writers and the main source of the gold which was sent across the Sahara from very ancient times. Gold is still being mined in the same area and by the same methods that were used in the days of Park (see Bovill, The Golden Trade, pp. 190-8; L. P. Carter and J. Scarisbrick, 'The Gold of Wangara', Ghana Notes and Queries, vol. v, 1961).
[3] Ibid., pp. 8-9.   [4] Ibid., pp. 99-100.   [5] Ibid., p. 352.

been surmised as to its course; they revealed its source and also those of the Gambia and the Senegal. His accounts of the gold of Manding may have tickled the cupidity of the industrial world. Instead of savages, barbarians, cannibals, or people with tails, as was generally believed in Europe and Britain at the time, he found perfectly normal human beings with their own music, arts, and manufactures, and even some learning. His botanical finds, such as the lotus and the shea tree, added to the knowledge of the flora of the interior.

As Houghton's discoveries led to the suggestion of a consular establishment in the Senegambia, the greater hopes evoked by Park's could not but revive that suggestion. This was, in fact, mooted by Banks at the general meeting of the Association in 1799. In expatiating on the advantages that could be derived from Park's discoveries, he declared that a great gate into the interior of Africa had now been found, 'into which it is easy for every nation to enter and to extend its commerce and discovery from the west to the eastern side of that immense continent'.[1] The meeting thereupon unanimously passed a resolution asking the Committee 'to take up again into consideration, the plan of appointing a consul to the district of Senegambia; and the sending there of sufficient force to take possession of a station on the banks of the Joliba [Niger], and from thence exploring the interior of Africa'.[2] In the letter forwarding the resolution to the Government, the Committee summarized the main discoveries of Park, reiterated that a prosperous trade could easily be established, and gave a warning that if the opportunity was neglected some rival nation would exploit it. Banks attached such importance to the project that he also wrote a personal letter to Lord Liverpool appealing to him to recommend it to other members of the Cabinet.[3] Since the Revolution and Napoleonic wars were still raging in Europe, nothing came of this suggestion.

While Park was pushing up the Gambia, the attention of the Association was turned again to the north. Once more through Banks, Frederick Hornemann, a German, was chosen to attempt to penetrate from that direction. He was asked to proceed to Cairo, where he was to remain until he had perfected his knowledge of

[1] C.U.L. MS. Add. 7087/38–48, Minutes of the meeting of subscribers, 25 May 1799.

[2] C.O. 2/1, Memorandum of the Association, 29 May 1799; D.T.C. 11/233–5, Banks to Liverpool, 8 June 1799.

[3] C.U.L. MS. Add. 7085/153–64, Minutes of the Committee, 3 June 1796.

Arabic and had become acquainted with the manners and customs of the Africans; he was then to proceed into the interior to explore Katsina in particular, and then return home, if possible via the Bight of Benin or through the Gold Coast. He was also asked to report on the animal, vegetable, and mineral productions of the inland countries.[1]

In September 1797 Hornemann landed in Cairo, where he remained for a year, in conformity with his instructions. On the eve of his departure, however, Napoleon arrived in Egypt and Hornemann was taken prisoner. But Napoleon's regard for science and his interest in the work of the Association was so strong that he released Hornemann, promised him protection, offered him money, and undertook to convey his letters to the Association.[2]

With the benevolent co-operation of Napoleon, Hornemann left Cairo in September 1798. Disguised as an Arab named Yasuf ibn 'Abdallah, and accompanied as interpreter by another German, Joseph Frendenburgh, who could speak Arabic and Turkish fluently, Hornemann arrived at Murzuk, the capital of Fezzan, in October 1798. He and Frendenburgh were the first Europeans to set foot in the oasis, about which the Association was already well informed. On their arrival they found that the Fezzaners and the Tuareg tribes were at war. As this ruled out any further penetration southwards, Hornemann decided to return to Tripoli to escape the climate of the region (to which Frendenburgh fell victim) and to await the departure of the next annual caravan to the Sudan. He reached Tripoli in October 1798 and from there dispatched his accounts of his travels. He did not leave Tripoli for the interior until a year later. He returned confidently to Fezzan in January 1800 and left there three months later, with the hope of proceeding first to Agades, then to Gobir, Katsina, and Nupe, and finally to Timbuctu.[3]

His letter to Banks in April 1800 informing him of his plans and departure from Fezzan was the last that was ever received from Hornemann. How far he was able to penetrate and what happened to him are problems as mystifying today as they were to his contemporaries. From the little information that trickled in

[1] B.M. Add. MSS. 8093/313, Blumenbach to Banks, 7 Sept. 1796; D.T.C. 10 (2)/25–26, Banks to Hornemann, 6 Jan. 1797.
[2] Proceedings, ii, 8–9.
[3] D.T.C. 11/265–74, Hornemann to Banks, 19 Aug. 1799; D.T.C. 11/293–6, Hornemann to Banks, 3 Oct. 1799; D.T.C. 12/32, Hornemann to Banks, 20 Feb. 1800; R.G.S. MSS. 408 (6), Hornemann to Banks, 6 April 1800.

spasmodically, it seems that Hornemann succeeded in reaching Katsina, where he died probably in 1804 or 1805.[1]

It was not until seven years after the departure of Hornemann in 1797 that the Association sent out another explorer. The first reason for this long period of inaction was Hornemann's advice that the Association should await his return before it sent out another traveller.[2] At the time he cherished the fond hope of returning to England by the beginning of 1802. The second and certainly the stronger reason was financial. As the Association depended entirely on the annual subscriptions of its members, whose number steadily declined, it was never strong financially. By May 1799 it had only fifty-seven paid-up members and its finances had reached their nadir. Since the Government was not prepared to aid the Association financially, the other alternative was to appeal to the public. But the Committee were uncompromisingly opposed to this. The Secretary asserted dogmatically that 'the Society cannot condescend to solicitation'. By 1804, however, such misgivings were entertained about Hornemann's survival as to justify another excursion into the interior, and the Secretary's report to the Annual General Meeting of May 1804 that the funds of the Association were in a flourishing state made such a journey possible.

Henry Nicholls was selected for the expedition. For reasons already given,[3] he was asked to proceed via the Guinea coast and to collect and note down every item of curious and interesting information respecting countries and peoples. He was to remain in Calabar until he had familiarized himself with the manners and language of the people and then proceed into the interior. Nicholls sailed from Liverpool in November 1804 and entered old Calabar in January 1805.[4] Unfortunately he succumbed to the climate of Calabar three months after his arrival, the sixth martyr in the cause of African exploration.

[1] Proceedings, ii, 363; C.U.L. MS. Add. 7087/208-9, Minutes of the meeting of the subscribers, 30 May 1818; C.O. 2/8, Ritchie to Hamilton, 20 Aug. 1819. A journal of Hornemann's mission was published by the Association in 1802, but this contains only the accounts of his journey from Cairo to Fezzan and the information which he gathered in Fezzan and dispatched to the Association during his visit to Tripoli. The main point of interest about the journal is that it contains the first eyewitness account of Fezzan, and in particular of the Tuareg and the Tibu, the principal inhabitants of the Sahara. (F. Hornemann, *The Journal of Hornemann's Travels from Cairo to Murzouk*, London, 1802.)
[2] D.T.C. 11/324-8, Hornemann to Banks, 29 Nov. 1799.
[3] See above, p. 13.
[4] C.U.L. MS. Add. 7087/119-54, Minutes of the meeting of the subscribers of the Association, 31 May 1806.

The death of Nicholls marks the end of the militant and relatively successful phase in the life of the African Association. Between 1805 and 1831, when it was amalgamated with the Royal Geographical Society, the Association sent out only two explorers, Burkhardt and A. Linant (1826-9), and sponsored two others, Captain Gordon (1821-2) and Lieutenant Welford (1830-1).[1]

However, the work of the Association up to 1805 is of far greater significance than has been generally recognized. Largely through its voluntary efforts, the interior of Africa, particularly the Sahara, the area between the mouths of the Gambia and the Senegal, and the sources of the Niger were for the first time correctly delineated. Swift, in his usual satiric style, had written:

> Geographers, in Afric maps,
> With savage pictures fill their gaps,
> And o'er inhabitable downs
> Place elephants for want of towns.[2]

A glance at the map of northern Africa drawn by Rennell in May 1798 from the information supplied by Browne, Lucas, Matra, Houghton, Park, and Hornemann is enough to convince one of the phenomenal advance made in the geography of the interior of the continent.[3] There were, of course, obvious blunders. The Niger was shown as terminating in Lake Chad, and Ghana was placed east of Hausaland. But the positions of Fezzan, Agades, and Timbuctu, and the sources of the Niger, the Gambia, and the Senegal were quite accurate. Secondly, a great deal of light was thrown by the discoveries on African peoples and their civilization and institutions, and some of the fantastic ideas entertained in Europe were thus dispelled. 'Christians and tailed men in the interior of Africa shall,

[1] C.U.L. MS. Add. 7087/214-15, Minutes of the meeting of the subscribers of the Association, 28 May 1822; Ibid., 7 June 1823, 16 June 1827, 31 May 1828, 19 June 1830. All these explorers were asked first to tackle the problem of the sources of the Nile and then proceed from there to Bornu. But not even one of them made any headway. After exploring Syria, Egypt, Damascus, and Nubia, Burckhardt died in 1818 on the eve of his departure for the interior. Gordon, who left England in 1821, got only as far as Wadi Halfa. Linant entered Cairo in 1826 and, in a boat provided by the Association, sailed up the river as far as the junction of the White and Blue Niles. Bad weather and unsettled political conditions compelled him to return to Cairo in 1829. Welford, who left England in April 1830, died in Sennar about a year later.

[2] Jonathan Swift, *On Poetry*.

[3] Proceedings, inserted between Vol. i, pp. 208 and 209.

as I suppose, never be found,' wrote Hornemann.[1] Thirdly, some knowledge of the flora and fauna of the continent had been gained by 1805. Lastly, but certainly most important for industrial England, the great economic possibilities awaiting exploitation were revealed. Without the formation of the African Association, the penetration into the interior would not have begun when it did, and without its memoranda and resolutions drawing attention to the possibility of opening up the area discovered to British commerce, the Government would probably not have assumed responsibility for the exploration of the African hinterland.

Whatever its achievements, however, it is clear that by 1805 the African Association had lost its drive. The financial revival which it experienced in the 1800's did not continue, and by the late 1820's its funds were very small. Indeed it had to refuse to renew Linant's contract when it expired in 1829; and prospects remained bleak since membership continued to dwindle. At the time of its amalgamation with the Royal Geographical Society, the Association had only fourteen members.[2] A new patron of African exploration was called for. Fortunately by 1805 the British Government was prepared, for reasons to be discussed in the next chapter, to assume this responsibility.

[1] D.T.C. 11/265-7, Hornemann to Banks, 19 Aug. 1799.
[2] C.U.L. MS. Add. 7087/240-4, Minutes of the meeting of the subscribers, 9 July 1831.

CHAPTER II

The British Government and The Niger Quest, 1805-18

THOUGH the original impulse for the systematic exploration of the interior of Africa in 1788 was scientific, the reports of the explorers as well as the memorandum of the Association had raised fervent hopes of lucrative commercial intercourse with the interior of Africa. In particular, Park's accounts of the gold industry of Manding had revived the traditional myths about Timbuctu, with its golden roofs and 'argent streets'. These hopes had, however, not been realized, first because the Revolutionary and Napoleonic wars had foiled the scheme of establishing a British consul in the Senegambia region and rendered impracticable the occupation of the area between the Gambia and the Niger as advocated by Banks. Secondly, a more direct route to Timbuctu and Katsina had still not been discovered. The Association had already convinced the British Government that the only obvious solution of this difficulty was to find the mouth of the Niger. Hence the Niger problem, which in 1788 was of mainly academic interest, had by the beginning of the nineteenth century become one of practical and national importance, and the main object of African exploration between 1805 and 1818. Its solution was officially considered as necessary for the establishment of commercial relations between Britain and the western Sudan. It was chiefly for this reason that the Government assumed responsibility for exploration of the interior of Africa from 1805 till 1830.

But even though the Government had by 1800 become convinced of the commercial importance of the drive into the interior of Africa, it would not have assumed the responsibility when it did but for the activities of the French in the Senegambia, which by 1800 were threatening to nip in the bud the great commercial hopes being entertained in England. It is quite evident from the circumstances leading to the dispatch of the first Government-sponsored mission into the interior of Africa that this fear of the French precipitated official action. Indeed this expedition was conceived of not, as is generally supposed, simply as a journey of exploration, but also as a British move to expel the French from the region of the Senegambia, or rather, to quote an official record, as 'a military and commercial expedition to the continent of Africa with a view to permanent establishment'.[1]

The expedition, which left England under Mungo Park in January 1805, had in fact been in preparation since August 1802. It was planned by John Sullivan, one of the Colonial Under-Secretaries, at the instance of Banks. In a letter to Sullivan, Banks drew his attention to a book written by a Frenchman with the intention of inducing the French Government to colonize the whole of the Senegambia, and ended with the warning:

His Majesty's Ministers should . . . hold in mind what will happen, which is, that whoever colonizes in that part of Africa with spirit will clearly be able to sell colonial products of all kinds in European markets at a cheaper price than any part of the West Indies or America can afford it.[2]

After further consultations with Zachary Macaulay, Major Rennell, Colonel Stevenson, and Mungo Park, the Under-Secretary drew up a plan for the expedition.[3] It was to have three wings, commercial, military, and naval. The first was to be headed by Mungo Park and was to consist of a detachment of 150 of the African Corps, 20 artificers, and 100 of the garrison at Goree. The military wing was to be composed of 1 battalion of 1,000 soldiers armed with 6 light three-pounders and 200 large pistols, and was to be under the command of Colonel Stevenson. The naval wing, to be commanded by three intelligent naval officers, was to consist of 1 small frigate, 1 sloop, 3 brigs, 4 gun-boats, 2 troop-ships, 1 hospital ship, and 1 store ship. A medical staff of a surgeon-general, 4 surgeons, and 8 assistants was to accompany the expedition.

The movements of the expedition were carefully worked out. The whole party was first to dislodge the French from their factories at Albreda on the Gambia and St. Joseph on the Senegal. Park and

[1] C.O. 2/1, Stevenson to Sullivan, 13 Jan. 1804.
[2] C.O. 2/1, Banks to Sullivan, 1 Aug. 1802, encl. in 'Memoranda on certain paragraphs contained in the *Moniteur* relative to the French establishments in Africa', by Sullivan. The book referred to by Banks was *Fragmen d'un voyage en Afrique*, by J. M. Golberry.
[3] C.O. 2/1, Rennell to Sullivan, 17 Oct. 1802; D.T.C. 14/61, Banks to Park, 10 Oct. 1803; C.O. 2/1, Stevenson to Sullivan, 13 Jan. 1804; C.O. 2/1, Macaulay to Sullivan, 4 Sept. 1802; Rennell to Sullivan, 12 Oct. 1802; Sullivan's memoranda and draft instructions to Park.

Stevenson were then to establish factories in Wulli and Bondu and to negotiate a tariff of duties with the kings of those states. From Bondu, Park, accompanied by his party, was to pay a goodwill visit to 'the Kings of Segu, Timbuctoo and Houssa' with a view to establishing 'a free and secure intercourse of trade with the natives'. Stevenson was to stay behind and employ his forces either in establishing other posts in Bambuk and in the gold-producing regions or in strengthening the lines of communication between Bondu and the coast. The naval wing of the expedition was to navigate and chart the rivers of the region.

This whole plan, which clearly illustrates the anti-French element in the motives behind the expedition, was approved by Lord Hobart, the then Colonial Secretary, and the departure of the expedition was fixed for February 1804. However, when all was set and part of the troops had even gone on board at Portsmouth, the expedition was suddenly countermanded.[1] Hard pressed abroad by the war with France and harassed at home by the attacks of Fox and Pitt, Addington's feeble cabinet was tottering. It was therefore deemed wiser to await the impending reshuffle of portfolios. The crash came in May 1804 and Lord Camden succeeded Hobart as Colonial Secretary. For reasons which were not stated but which may well have been financial, the new Colonial Secretary drastically revised the original plan after consultations with Banks and Park.[2] Park was to be accompanied by not more than forty-five soldiers and he was to proceed up the Gambia and then by land to the Niger. He was to pursue its course to its termination, to study the character and institutions of the people, and above all 'to discover and ascertain whether any, and what, commercial intercourse can be opened therein for the mutual benefit of the natives and of his Majesty's subjects'.[3] The expedition was now, as Camden described it to Banks, 'a journey of enquiry without any military attendance upon it' and the scramble for the Senegambia was thus postponed.

To Park, of course, natural history and the Niger problem were consuming passions. In a memorandum on the expedition which he submitted to Camden, he rejected the theory of Major Rennell, the leading arm-chair geographer in Britain, that the Niger ter-

---

[1] C.O. 26/18, Hobart to Fraser, 30 Mar. 1803; Park, *Journal*, p. xxxvii.
[2] D.T.C. 15/140-1, Camden to Banks, 28 Sept. 1804; Park, *Journal*, pp. xxxix–xlvii.
[3] Instructions to Park, 2 Jan. 1805, printed in Park, *Journal*, pp. liii–liv.

minated in an inland lake, and also that of J. G. Jackson, the British
trader and writer in Morocco, who thought it was identical with the
Nile. He preferred to identify it with the Congo.[1] This was not
originally Park's idea but was first advanced in 1804 by George
Maxwell, a friend of his, who once traded at the mouth of the Congo
and had made a survey of that part of the river.[2] This theory seems to
have won popular support in England, for not only Banks and
Barrow but also the *Quarterly Review* and the *Edinburgh Review*
lent it their weighty support. The *Quarterly Review*, for instance,
argued in the arm-chair fashion of the day:

There is in North Africa a great river of which nobody knows the end—
there is in South Africa another great river of which nobody knows the
beginning—the river of North Africa flows to the southward—the river in
South Africa comes from the northward. When to these facts are super-
added the singular phenomenon of the South African river being in a state
of flood for six months in the year, when no rain falls to the southward of
the line, and consequently can only be supplied from a country to the
northward of the line where in those six months the rains prevail; it will
hardly be denied that there are at least strong and rational grounds for
conjecture that the Niger and the Zayr (Congo) are one and the same river
. . .[3]

It may be added that these literary affrays over the Niger were not
confined to England. In 1808 a German geographer, M. Reichard,
advanced for the first time the hypothesis that the Niger entered the
Gulf of Guinea through the delta in the Bight of Biafra. Park was
therefore correctly interpreting prevailing ideas about the Niger
when he stated in his memorandum that 'considered in a commercial
point of view, it is second only to the discovery of the Cape of Good
Hope, and in a geographical point of view, it is certainly the greatest
discovery that remains to be made in the world'.[4]

Unfortunately, this carefully organized expedition ended disas-
trously. After leaving England in January 1805, Park set off from the
Gambia with a company of forty-four European soldiers in April.
But by the time he embarked on the Niger in November in a boat

[1] The memorandum is printed in full in Park, *Journal*, pp. xxxix–xlvii; D.T.C.
15/232–40.
[2] D.T.C. 15/7–9, Maxwell to William Keir, 20 July 1804; D.T.C. 15/148–56,
Maxwell to Parks, 12 Oct. 1804; D.T.C. 15/242, Memorandum by Banks, 8 Jan.
1805.
[3] *Quarterly Review*, vol. 13, p. 151; *Edinburgh Review*, vol. 24, pp. 487–90.
[4] Park's Memorandum.

built by himself, only four of them were alive and one was mentally deranged.[1] Park sailed down the Niger as far as Bussa, a town in the district of Yauri in the present-day Northern Nigeria, where his boat capsized in the rapids and he and all his colleagues perished.[2] However, considering the fact that Bussa is about 800 miles south-east of Timbuctu, it is inaccurate to write the expedition off as a total failure and a gross underestimate of the remarkable achievement of this intrepid explorer. His contemporaries made this mistake, as is evident from the map[3] illustrating his journey, on which Bussa is placed only about 100 miles east of Timbuctu. What does make the expedition tragic is the fact that Park's account of the area between Sansanding and Bussa, an area as yet unvisited by any European, perished with him. What is now known as the journal of Park's second mission in fact ends at Sansanding and therefore covers only the area he had previously traversed. This in itself would not have made it a less welcome addition to the growing literature on the interior of Africa. But unfortunately he had followed nearly the same route as on his return journey in 1797. Of the entire distance between Long. 17° and 7° W., the only new ground broken was between Long. 11° and 9° W. Moreover, he described this journal (in a letter to Camden) as a mere sketch of trifling incidents 'intended to recall to my recollection (if it pleased God to restore me again to my dear native land) other particulars illustrative of the manners and customs of the natives, which would have swelled this bulky communication to a most unreasonable size'.[4] The Journal therefore contains very little information that is new or detailed. It does, nevertheless, throw a glimmer of light on conditions at the time which should not be ignored.

The first impression one gets from reading the journal is of the apparently friendly attitude of the people and the chiefs and kings of villages and kingdoms through which Park passed between Kayee

[1] Park, *Journal*, pp. 141–2, 163–4.

[2] That Park perished at Bussa was confirmed both by the oral tradition collected by the Landers in 1830 and by a medium quarto book of logarithms of 564 pages with three pieces of paper containing notes in Park's handwriting which Lieutenant Glover received as a present in Nupe in 1858. Glover was told that the book was brought from Bussa to Nupe when Bussa was sacked and destroyed in a war in 1843. This book is now in the library of the Royal Geographical Society.

[3] See the map facing p. 1 of Park, *Journal*.

[4] Park to Camden, 17 Nov. 1805, Park, *Journal*, pp. lxxix–lxxx.

and Sansanding. Only on a single occasion was he on the point of fighting his way. And only once did he actually fire on an African to deter others from pilfering his goods. When the Africans came across any of the soldiers who had lost their way or had been inadvertently left behind, they often took the trouble to lead the stragglers back into the fold, and even buried them when they died. On many occasions the chiefs gave Park guides and presents. It should be emphasized, however, that this benevolence and co-operation had always to be purchased with presents carefully calculated and selected 'in proportion to the power and mischievous disposition of the chiefs'.[1] The single occasion when he was within an ace of resorting to arms was precipitated by the fact that the chief deemed the presents given him not commensurate with his dignity.

The report on the commercial side of the mission was far more encouraging. Park delivered a long lecture to the Prime Minister of Segu on the need for opening up direct trade between Bambara and England instead of obtaining goods through the Moors. This lecture appears to have gone down very well, for the King readily offered Park his assistance and protection and granted him permission to choose any port for the construction of his boat.[2] The shop which he opened 'in great style' and in which he displayed a choice assortment of European goods for wholesale or retail trade proved an instantaneous success. Indeed it attracted so many customers that he found himself at times compelled to employ 'three tellers at once to count my cash', which consisted of cowries, the currency found throughout the western Sudan as far as the western borders of Bornu.[3]

Darkening these prospects, however, was the effect of the climate on the Europeans. The members of the expedition had reached Saladoo without any casualties. But there the first rains broke on them on 8 June 1805. An epidemic of fever was the immediate consequence. Within three days of the first rains twelve of the soldiers were down with fever. From that day the soldiers began to die with astonishing rapidity, until at their embarkation on 17 November at Sansanding only five of the original contingent of forty-four Europeans remained. Well did Park describe the commencement of the rainy season as 'the beginning of sorrow'.[4] It is important to note that in spite of their encounters with wild animals, flooded rivers,

---

[1] Park, *Journal*, pp. 30–32, 87, 103, 113, 141, 148, 154; Ibid., pp. 151–5.
[2] Ibid., pp. 151–5.   [3] Ibid., pp. 158–9.   [4] Ibid., p. 54.

and other perils, not one of the thirty-nine victims died of any other cause than the fatal effect of the rainy season.

As he gazed a second time on the Niger rolling its immense streams, Park summed up the lessons of the second mission in the following words:

It however afforded me peculiar pleasure, when I reflected that in conducting a party of *Europeans*, with immense baggage, through an extent of more than five hundred miles, I had always been able to preserve the most friendly terms with the natives. In fact, this journal plainly demonstrates, 1st, that with common prudence any quantity of merchandize may be transported from the Gambia to the Niger without danger of being robbed by natives: 2ndly, that if this journey can be performed in the dry season, one may calculate on losing not more than three or at most four men out of fifty.[1]

Park seems to have been too optimistic in his conclusions. It is undoubtedly true that the death rate could have been drastically reduced in more clement weather. But he overlooked the fact that the apparently friendly attitude of the people arose not only from the presents lavished on them, but still more from the presence of the military escort. Could one be sure of a repeat performance when these two factors were removed? On the other hand, could sound business be built on continuing large presents to every chief on the trade route and on the maintenance of military escorts? Secondly, he seems to have discounted the opposition of the established traders, which was very real. He himself mentioned the intrigues of the people from Jenne, of the Moors, and of the merchants who offered bribes to Mansong, the King of Bambara, to seize his store and either kill him or send him out of the kingdom.[2] And political conditions were not reassuring. Bondu was then in the throes of civil war; and a very precarious peace existed between Kaarta and Bambara. In a state of such instability and internecine warfare, it was the height of folly to suppose that commerce could flourish. These points, at any event, never occurred to Park, nor to his contemporaries, who greedily devoured his journal. This is clearly illustrated by the fact that the learned journals of the day echoed his conclusions.

Unquestionably, the most important result of the journey [wrote the *Edinburgh Review*] is the proof it has afforded of the practicability of conducting a caravan of Europeans across that difficult country, which lies

---

[1] Park, *Journal*, p. 140.   [2] Ibid., p. 159.

between the Gambia and the Niger, provided the proper season be chosen, and the utter impossibility of succeeding in such an attempt during the rains.[1]

It was not until 1815 that another expedition left England. This does not mean that the attempts to forge commercial links between Britain and the interior were not continued. On the contrary, after the conquest of Senegal by English forces under Major Maxwell in July 1809 the hopes long cherished in Britain of opening commercial intercourse with Bambara came to life again. Liverpool, the Colonial Secretary, in sending reinforcements, informed Maxwell, whom he had appointed Lieutenant-Governor, that 'as the consequence of the settlement of Senegal must result from the opening it may afford for diffusing the manufactures of this country into the interior of Africa, it is to this point especially I am to direct your attention, as upon this consideration all future arrangements must be guided'.[2]

Maxwell endeavoured to execute his instructions. He first of all established friendly relations with the chiefs on the banks of the Senegal and encouraged traders to sail up the river as far as the old French post of St. Joseph. The first such trading expedition went up the river in September 1810. Though this was not very successful, Maxwell was optimistic about the future.[3] In June 1811, however, he was appointed Governor of Sierra Leone in succession to Columbine, and his post was filled by Charles MacCarthy.[4] MacCarthy continued Maxwell's policy with greater success. He established regular contact with the chiefs of Bondu and Kaarta and even helped to settle their differences. He also persuaded some British and African merchants to attempt a trading voyage to Galam. This proved a very lucrative venture. A fleet of 75 vessels brought back 3,000 barrels of corn, 1,000 sheep, 3 or 4 tons of ivory, and nearly £5,000 worth of gold. In reporting this to the Colonial Office, he expressed his conviction that the next voyage would be attended 'with much more advantage and open a channel for diffusing into the very interior of Africa the manufactures of Great Britain'.[5]

MacCarthy's work in this area was unfortunately brought to a

---

[1] *Edinburgh Review*, vol. 24, p. 486.
[2] C.O. 268/18, Liverpool to Maxwell, 3 Jan. 1810.
[3] C.O. 267/33, Maxwell to Liverpool, 3 Feb. 1811.
[4] MacCarthy was later promoted to be Governor of Sierra Leone and the Gold Coast. In 1819 he was knighted for his services, but was killed in the Gold Coast in 1824 during the third Ashanti invasion of the Fantis.
[5] C.O. 267/38, MacCarthy to Liverpool, 21 Feb. 1814.

premature end when in May 1814 he was appointed to succeed Max-well as the Governor of Sierra Leone. On the eve of his departure he wrote to the Colonial Office to emphasize the commercial importance of the Senegal and strongly recommended its retention by Britain.[1] The same opinion was expressed by Matthew Forster, a prominent British merchant who had appreciable interests in West Africa. Had this advice been accepted, the history of the Senegambia might have been different. But at that date British interests in West Africa (and elsewhere) were being sacrificed to the demands of foreign policy. The British Foreign Secretary, Lord Castlereagh, dominated by his desire to restore the Bourbons to a not too humiliated throne, agreed to surrender many French colonies, including Senegal, which had been captured by Britain during the late war.[2] To make up for the loss of Senegal, MacCarthy advocated the establishment of a British trading factory at Galam. But this suggestion was also rejected by the Colonial Office on the ground that it was necessary to reduce the expense of the existing British settlements in West Africa.[3]

The restoration of Senegal and the reluctance of the Government to occupy Galam brought to a final conclusion the efforts of the British to develop trade with the interior via Senegambia. Another gateway had therefore to be found to the fabled markets of the central Sudan. Not unexpectedly, attention was once again turned to the Niger. Even before the echoes of the battle cries and the booms of the guns of the Napoleonic Wars had completely subsided, two attempts to discover the course and termination of the river were planned: one, organized by the Colonial Office, by land under Major Peddie, the other by water under Captain Tuckey, under orders from the Admiralty.

That the discovery of the termination of the Niger was the main purpose of both expeditions is obvious from the instructions issued to their leaders.[4] Peddie was told that 'the main objective of the

[1] C.O. 267/38, MacCarthy to Bathurst, 17 May 1814.
[2] H. Nicolson, *The Congress of Vienna* (London, 1942), p. 98; C. Petrie, *Lord Liverpool and his Times* (London, 1954), p. 219.
[3] C.O. 264/40, MacCarthy to Bathurst, 16 March 1815; C.O. 267/41, Mac-Carthy to Gordon, 1 June 1815; C.O. 268/19, Bathurst to MacCarthy, 15 May 1816.
[4] C.O. 268/19, Instruction to Peddie, 23 Aug. 1815; C.O. 267/43, Memorandum of an Instruction to Captain Tuckey, enclosed in Barrow to Goulburn, 8 Feb. 1816, printed in J. K. Tuckey, *Narrative of an expedition to explore the River Zaire, usually called the Congo, in South Africa, in 1816* (London, 1818), pp. xxxi-xlii.

expedition (and that to which your attention will be so far exclusively directed as to consider every other as of secondary importance), is the discovery of the mouth of the Niger, and course of that river from the point at which it was visited by Mr. Park to that at which it may be found to terminate'. Tuckey also was informed that the expedition which he was to undertake for the exploration of the course of the Congo or the Zaire 'was originally grounded on a suggestion of its being identical with the Niger'. Consequently he was to give prior attention to exploring to its source the branch that flowed from the north. If he found penetration up the Congo blocked by unforeseen and invincible obstacles, he was to proceed to the Bight of Benin to ascertain whether the Rio de Rey and Rio Formosa were separate rivers or two branches of the same river.

If the objects of the Peddie and Tuckey expeditions were the same, the motives of their patrons show slight but significant differences. The Colonial Office was concerned for 'the extension of British commerce in that quarter'. The Admiralty's aims, on the other hand, were primarily scientific. Tuckey was told:

that a river of such magnitude as the Zair, and offering so many peculiarities should not be known with any degree of certainty beyond, if so far as, 200 miles from its mouth, is incompatible with the present advanced state of geographical science, and little creditable to those Europeans, who, for three centuries nearly, have occupied various parts of the coast near to which it empties itself into the sea.

Similarly Tuckey was to investigate the rivers which were said to flow into the Bight of Benin, because 'on the supposition of the union of these two great streams (the Rio del Rey and the Rio Formosa) the continental geographers have raised an hypothesis that the Niger, after reaching Wangarra takes first a direction towards the south, and then bending to the south-west, discharges itself into the Gulf of Guinea'.

The essentially scientific nature of Tuckey's expedition is even more evident from its personnel. While Peddie's party included no naturalist,[1] Tuckey's was accompanied by a team of three distinguished scientists. They were Dr. Chretien Smith, Professor of Botany at the University of Christiania in Norway, who was then on a tour of Britain to collect species for the new botanical

---

[1] It was not until his arrival in Senegal that Peddie on his own initiative employed a German naturalist named Krummer whom he met there.

garden at his University, Mr. Tudor, a comparative anatomist, and Mr. Cranch, a collector of objects of natural history who was then employed at Kew.[1] The instructions to these gentlemen are illuminating. Professor Smith was instructed to collect specimens of plants growing on the banks of the Congo. Being a geologist as well, he was also to collect specimens of stones and minerals. Tudor was to concentrate on land animals, whose habits he was to study, while Cranch was to operate on the river and collect specimens of unknown fishes, crustacea, amphibians, and other aquatic animals.

It is obvious then that while Peddie's expedition followed the pattern of Park's second mission—his military escort, for example, was to be 100 strong—Tuckey's expedition was reminiscent of earlier expeditions launched by the Association. The marked scientific character of Tuckey's was not owing to the Admiralty, which sent it out, but to the person in that department who planned it. And he was John Barrow. As he was to remain for the greater part of the period of this study a passionate promoter of African exploration, and as his work in this connexion is hardly known, he deserves some consideration here.

Barrow assumed the responsibility for arranging this expedition by virtue of his post as Second Secretary to the Admiralty from 1804 to 1845. But before he confined himself to the sedentary work at the Admiralty he had, like his intimate friend Banks, rambled among the mountains of Cumberland and Westmorland, served on a mission to China (1792-5), and worked as a civil servant in South Africa (1799-1803).[2] He travelled very extensively in China and Africa and published his discoveries and observations on their peoples and institutions in his *Travels in China* (1804) and *Travels in South Africa* (1814). His interest in travel and exploration did not end with his return from South Africa to England. Like Beaufoy, he was convinced that ignorance of any part of the world was a stigma on the scientific spirit of the age which had to be removed. He therefore organized the British expeditions sent during the first three decades of the nineteenth century to explore the Arctic regions and to solve the other thorny problem of the North-West passage.[3] In the introduction to the journal of the Tuckey expedition, Barrow expatiated

[1] Tuckey, op. cit., pp. lxiii–lxxviii, 'Memorandum of an Instruction'.

[2] John Barrow, *An Autobiographical Memoir* (London, 1847), pp. iv, 137–41; *D.N.B.*, i, 1225–7.

[3] *Journal of the R.G.S.*, vol. 50; Barrow, op. cit., p. 33.

upon the urgency of exploring the north-western coast of Australia, of obtaining accurate information about the great archipelagoes of islands and reefs in the Pacific and Indian Oceans, and of ascertaining the velocity and direction of the Gulf Stream. It is quite clear then that, unlike Banks, Barrow was passionately interested in geography and geographical exploration. Indeed he was one of the founders of the Royal Geographical Society and one of its first four vice-presidents.[1]

Barrow was also a keen student of natural history. When he stayed in London before his departure for South Africa (1795–7), he spent three days a week at Kew studying botany, and this interest greatly occupied his attention in South Africa. He was particularly elated when, soon after his arrival there, he was asked to go on a mission to the interior, because he felt as if the lessons he 'had so recently received in the Botanical Gardens of Kew had been taken on purpose to qualify me for exploring the rich forests of Erica and Protea and the plentiful harvest of these and other beautiful plants that I knew would be met with in South Africa. . . .'[2]

With these interests, Barrow was quick to seize the opportunity when the end of the Napoleonic wars turned the attention of the Government again to African exploration and the now urgent need of new markets. As he wrote:

To what purpose indeed could a portion of our naval force be at any time, but more especially in a time of profound peace, more honourably or more usefully employed, than in completing those *minutiae* and details of geographical and hydrographical science, of which the grand outlines have been boldly and broadly sketched by Cook, Vancouver, Flinders, and others of our own countrymen . . . in ascertaining with greater precision the position of particular points in various parts of the globe—on the shores of Asia Minor—of northern Africa, and of the numerous islands in the Mediterranean—the coasts, harbours, and rivers of Newfoundland, Labrador, Hudson's Bay, and that reproach to the present state of European navigation, the existence or non-existence of Baffin Bay, and the north-west passage from the Atlantic to the Eastern Ocean . . .[3]

Thus when Peddie's expedition left England on 26 September 1815, and Tuckey's followed on 16 July 1816—a delay due to nothing more than the difficulty of constructing an appropriate vessel to go up the

[1] Barrow, op. cit., p. 484; *Journal of the R.G.S.*, vol. 30, pp. 15–21.
[2] Barrow, op. cit., p. 142.
[3] Tuckey, op. cit., pp. ii–iii.

Congo[1]—it was with the greatest enthusiasm that the Colonial Office as well as Barrow and the scientific world waved them good-bye. However, both expeditions proved as tragic as Park's second journey. Tuckey's party had travelled only 150 miles up the Congo when eighteen of the forty-nine men died, mostly of fever. Among the victims were the leader and all the scientists. The rest were therefore obliged to return to England only three months after they had set out.[2]

Though the Peddie expedition entered the Senegal in September 1816 and remained in Africa until 1821, a fact which is hardly known, it returned to England in 1822 without having penetrated beyond Segu. Its failure was owing to the climate of the western coast, the opposition of some of the chiefs of the interior, and finally, the political unrest in the region of the Senegambia. Peddie, his assistant, Campbell, and Cowdry, the surgeon to the expedition, and many of the 100 soldiers and civilians fell victims to the climate within two years of the expedition's arrival in Africa. The war between Futa and Bambara in 1816 forced the mission to abandon the Senegal and try to push into the interior via the Rio Nunez (Republic of Guinea) in 1817. But when they had advanced 200 miles along the banks of that river, the opposition of the King of Futa Jallon checked further progress in that direction.[3] Thwarted on both the Senegal and the Rio Nunez, the mission, now under the command of Major Gray and Staff-Surgeon Dochard, turned to the Gambia in January 1818. Six months later it had advanced as far as Bulibani in Bondu. Unfortunately the party was delayed in that town by the King of Bondu, for one frivolous excuse after another, for eighteen months. The real cause of the delay was the fear of European occupation of the country generated throughout the whole of Senegambia by the

[1] On the very strong advice of Banks, and after prolonged arguments, it was decided that a steamboat should be constructed for the exploration of the Congo. When this was completed and christened the *Congo* it was found to be unsuitable for the purpose. The engine was therefore removed and the *Congo* was converted into an ordinary boat with oars and sails. (For details see Tuckey, op. cit., pp. xxiii–xxv.)

[2] Tuckey, op. cit., p. xliii. In spite of their short stay on the river, such was the minuteness of the observations of Tuckey and the team of scientists that the narrative of their accounts ran into 390 quarto pages, to which is added an appendix of 108 pages on the objects of Natural History collected by them. As the Congo region is outside my field, this expedition will not be treated in any further detail.

[3] Gray, William, and Staff-Surgeon Dochard, *Travels in West Africa* (1825), pp. 3–4, 24–25, 34–35; C.O. 267/45, Campbell to MacCarthy, 25 Apr. 1817.

resumption of French activities in Galam and the re-establishment of their old factory at Bakel in 1818.[1]

While they were detained in Bulibani, Gray sent Dochard to the King of Segu to ask for freedom of passage through his kingdom in the event of the mission being permitted to leave Bondu. Dochard left in July, and, following more or less the steps of Park, he set eyes on the Niger in November 1818—the second European to accomplish this—at a point about 75 miles south-west of Segu. Although he remained in Bambara for almost two years, he had to return to Bondu without the required permission. He was not even allowed to enter Segu, because of the intrigues of the Moorish traders who filled the Court with tales of the dangerous consequences 'which might follow his admitting Europeans to his presence'.[2] Despite these intrigues, the King of Segu remained very hospitable and friendly to Dochard throughout his long stay. The decisive factor in the failure of this diplomatic mission, therefore, was not so much the machinations of the Moors as the political situation at the time of Dochard's visit. Led by Shehu Ahmadu,[3] the Fulani of Masina had conquered Jenne and had advanced to within two days' march of Segu when Dochard arrived on the Niger. Dochard remained so long in Bambara because of his conviction that 'the war with them [the Fulani] alone keeps him [the King of Segu] from coming to a decision'.[4] This war, unfortunately, went on longer than Dochard had expected, and indeed continued intermittently until 1860. He was therefore obliged to return to Bondu in June 1820.

Detained in Bondu, frustrated in Bambara, and alarmed by the impending rainy season, Gray and Dochard reluctantly decided to abandon the attempt. In October 1821, therefore, the party returned to the coast, from which they left for England in January 1822. If the Tuckey expedition was thwarted mainly by the fevers of the west coast, that of Peddie was wrecked primarily by the opposition of the African kings and the political conditions of the day—factors often ignored by writers on African exploration.

The failure of this expedition marks the end of the Government's

[1] Gray, op. cit., pp. 120, 173, 263, 353; C.O. 267/49, Gray to MacCarthy, 11 Aug. 1819.

[2] C.O. 267/49, MacCarthy to Bathurst, 18 Nov. 1819 and encl., Dochard to Gray, 28 Apr. 1819.

[3] See Appendix IV, p. 244.

[4] C.O. 267/49, Dochard to Gray, 21 Feb. 1820, encl. in MacCarthy to Bathurst, 15 Sept. 1820.

attempts to establish commercial relations with the Niger and to explore the interior via the Senegambia and the Guinea coast. It should be clear from the circumstances leading to the dispatch of the expeditions between 1805 and 1816 and, in particular, from the instructions issued to the leaders, that the Government did not assume responsibility for African exploration in 1805 for anti-slavery or humanitarian reasons. Nor did it continue to shoulder this responsibility in order, as Plumb puts it, 'to keep the abolitionists happy'.[1] The Government was not, in other words, responding to the pressure exerted by the abolitionists when it entered the field of African exploration. Indeed, it is obvious from the annual reports and the balance sheet of the African Institution[2]—the society formed by the abolitionists in 1807, immediately after the abolition of the slave trade, to repay 'the wrongs which the natives of Africa have suffered in their intercourse with Europe by adopting such measures as are best calculated to promote their civilization and happiness'— that the attention of the society was focused on Europe and not on Africa, and that the pressure it exerted was not to get the Government to promote African exploration but rather to negotiate for the abolition of the slave trade by the other European powers.[3] The Government was acting on rosy hopes of lucrative trade with the

[1] Plumb, 'The Niger Quest'.

[2] African Institution, Annual reports of the Committee, 1801-16; Special report of the African Institution and appendixes, 1815. D. R. Thorpe, 'A letter to William Wilberforce', Quarterly Review, vol. 13, pp. 119-20. The gross income of the Society between 1807 and 1815 was £9,850. Of this only a total of £1,695. 8s. 10d. (17 per cent.) was spent on items which can be specifically described as aimed at promoting the civilization of Africa, such as educating three Africans in Britain, paying the salary of two European teachers sent out to Africa (£728. 4s. 10d.), and procuring and sending seeds and plants to Sierra Leone (£499. 16s. 7d.). The rest was spent on propaganda and in sending petitions to Parliament.

[3] The abolitionists concentrated their efforts on Europe because of their belief that unless the slave trade was first abolished by all the European powers, no attempts to educate Africans or promote legitimate trade would succeed. In their report in 1811 the Directors noted: 'The civilization and improvement of Africa are indeed the great ends which the African Institution proposed to pursue. But what rational expectations can be formed of any material progress in the attainments of those ends while the slave trade continues to flourish?' Three years later they repeated the same view with even greater conviction, 'Persuaded as they always have been and, if possible, now more and more convinced that the continuance of this inhuman traffic must greatly impede, if not absolutely frustrate, all the great objects of the Institution, the Directors have in this as in former years, applied their main efforts towards its total abolition.' It is interesting to note that this view was reversed by the abolitionists of the 1830's led by Buxton. See below, pp. 72-73, 98-99.

Niger regions through the Senegambia, hopes which the French were by 1800 seriously threatening to thwart. Though all three expeditions failed, the hopes entertained about the interior were as strong in 1820 as they had been in 1805, and they continued to be so as long as Timbuctu and Katsina remained enigmas and the mouth of the Niger a mystery. These hopes alone made probable the continuation of Government efforts. When the scientific interests of Barrow were added to these commercial considerations, this continuation was a certainty.

After the failure of the attempts made from 1805 to 1820, the problem was not the practicability or utility of penetrating into the interior but the direction in which the penetration should be made. The main lesson of the three fatal expeditions of the period was that without a climate more suitable to Europeans, without the genuine co-operation of the African chiefs, and without more stable political conditions no headway could be made. All these requirements ruled out the Senegambia and the Guinea coast as gateways into the interior. Just at this time, however, and indeed before the fate of the Peddie–Gray mission had become known in 1821, a more reliable route had been opened in North Africa.

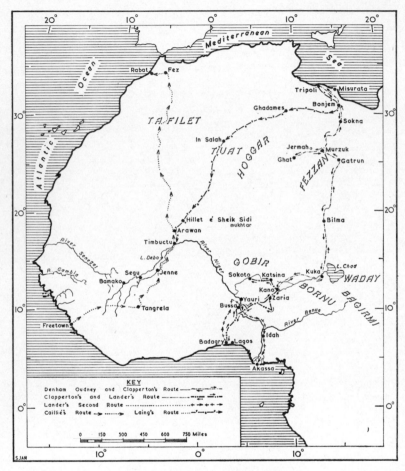

KEY

Denham Oudney and Clapperton's Route	-----
Clapperton's and Lander's Route	-----
Lander's Second Route	+++++
Caillié's Route	-----	Laing's Route	-----

0 150 300 450 600 750 Miles

Map 2. African Exploration 1821–30

CHAPTER III

The Northern Gateway, 1818-25

A NUMBER of factors combined to make the Regency of Tripoli an ideal gateway to the interior of Africa during the first three decades of the nineteenth century. The first of these was geographical. Tripoli stands at one of the narrowest crossings of the Sahara. It therefore affords a shorter bridge between the Mediterranean and the Sudan than any of the other Barbary states.

The second and the more important factor was political. After having murdered his eldest brother in the presence of his mother, exiled the second in succession, and deposed their father, Yusuf Karamanli established himself on the throne of Tripoli in 1795 and continued to rule unchallenged and with despotic efficiency till 1830.[1] Not only did he consolidate his position on the throne, but after a series of ruthless and bloody campaigns he also established a very effective hold on the recalcitrant Arab tribes who occupied the hinterland of the Regency and controlled the caravan trade routes.[2] In 1811 he also conquered Fezzan, and Muhammad al-Makani, whom he appointed governor in place of the hereditary monarch, soon established law and order throughout the oasis.[3] Thus by 1818 nearly half the entire route from Tripoli to Bornu was under the control of the Pasha of Tripoli. Furthermore, the Pasha was by then on very intimate terms with Muhammad al-Kānami, the Sheikh of Bornu, and with Muhammad Bello, the Sultan of the Sokoto Empire. Bornu had a military alliance with Tripoli and relied on this particularly for guns and ammunition for her war against Bagirmi, a kingdom to the south-east.[4] In the light of all these conditions it may be concluded that the Pasha was not overstating the case in 1817

---

[1] Richard Tully, *Ten years' residence at the court of Tripoli* (2nd edition, 1957), pp. 167–8, 179–80, 284, 290, 335; F.O. 76/16, Warrington to Bathurst, 5 July 1822.

[2] Tully, op. cit., pp. 108, 134, 147, 198; F.O. 76/5, McDonough to Pelham, 12 Dec. 1802; G. F. Lyon, *A narrative of the travels in Northern Africa, 1818–1820* (1821), pp. 21, 54–55.

[3] C.O. 2/8, Ritchie to Bathurst (undated); Lyon, op. cit., pp. 3–4.

[4] F.O. 8/8, Ritchie to Bathurst, 28 Oct. 1818; F.O. 76/15, Warrington to Bathurst, 22 Oct. 1821.

when he told Captain Smyth, who had been sent out by the British
Admiralty to survey the coast of North Africa, that the road to
Bornu was as beaten as that to Benghazi, a port east of the town of
Tripoli. And the Pasha's offer to guarantee the safety of any traveller
who wanted to go to Bornu was not an empty boast.[1]

Nonetheless, however conducive these geographical and political
conditions were to the penetration of the interior, Tripoli could not
have become such an ideal gateway without the diplomatic support
of the Pasha. Largely as a result of the work of the British Consul-
General from 1814 to 1846, Colonel Hanmer Warrington, relations
between the Pasha and the British remained cordial for the best part
of Yusuf Karamanli's reign.

The record of British consuls in Tripoli from 1780 had been far
from enviable. Richard Tully, whose consulship is best known and
remembered, was deep in the bog of bankruptcy when he was recalled
in 1790.[2] Lucas, the explorer, who succeeded to this post from 1793–
1801, did much to raise British prestige. But his successor, W. W.
Langford, had to be recalled in 1812 after he had been placed under
house arrest and declared *persona non grata* by the Pasha.[3] It was
thus an unenviable legacy of strained relations between the British
Consulate and the Pasha that Warrington, Langford's successor,
inherited in 1814.

No sooner had the new Consul-General arrived at Tripoli than he
set himself the task of re-establishing Anglo-Tripolitanian relations
on a firm and friendly footing. He took a personal interest in the
progress and welfare of the Regency and its people. Thus he introduced vaccination into Tripoli in 1816, suggested ways and means of
increasing the agricultural output of the state, proposed as early as
August 1817 that a British vice-consular post should be established
at Murzuk, the capital of the oasis of Fezzan, to improve the commercial links with the interior, and vigorously advocated the development of direct trade between Britain and Tripoli.[4] Moreover, when
the Pasha asked for a loan of 200,000 Spanish dollars (£40,000) to

[1] C.O. 2/9, Smyth to Penrose, 26 Nov. 1817, encl. in Barrow to Goulburn,
2 Feb. 1818.
[2] Tully, op. cit. Tully left a debt of £3,607, over £800 of which was borrowed
from the Pasha. F.O. 76/4, Lucas to Napean, 12 Nov. 1798; F.O. 76/4, Lucas to
Dundas, 5 Feb. 1794.
[3] F.O. 76/7, Langford to Liverpool, 15 July 1801.
[4] F.O. 76/9, Warrington to Bathurst, 11 Sept. 1815; F.O. 76/10, Warrington
to Melville, 5 Aug. 1816; F.O. 76/14, Warrington to Bathurst, 7 Feb. 1820;
F.O. 76/11, Warrington to Bathurst, 24 Aug. 1817.

meet his urgent financial needs, Warrington strongly urged the Colonial Office to grant it.[1]

By such acts and by a display of genuine sympathy with the problems of the Pasha, Warrington very soon won his absolute confidence. He was more and more consulted by the Pasha on many problems, both domestic and foreign, and so strong had his influence at the Court become by the 1820's that those European countries which had no diplomatic relations with Tripoli entrusted the British Consul with their affairs. Thus by 1825 Warrington was acting as Consul for Austria, Hanover, the Netherlands, Portugal, the two Sicilies, and Tuscany.[2] Between 1815 and 1827 he used his good offices to settle differences between Tripoli and Denmark, Sardinia, Tuscany, and Sweden.[3] Indeed, in the decade 1815 to 1825 Warrington became, to all intents and purposes, the Pasha's Foreign Secretary.

Warrington's influence was neither confined to the Court nor exercised only on behalf of European powers. He also very often interceded with the Pasha on behalf of the ordinary people of the Regency. Ritchie and Lyon were overwhelmed by the friendliness of the Arab tribes of the Gharian Mountains during their visit there in February 1819. On inquiring into this they were told that it was out of their affection for the British Consul, who had once persuaded the Pasha not to increase their tribute as he had intended.[4] The British consulate became an asylum for the Pasha's oppressed subjects and slaves throughout Warrington's term of office. Through his timely intervention many a life was saved and many a slave liberated.[5] These benevolent services of the British Consul generated among the people of the Regency a very high respect for the British in particular and for Christians in general. British officials and explorers who visited Tripoli during this period—Smyth, Ritchie, Denham, and

[1] F.O. 76/18, Warrington to Horton, 30 June 1824. The affairs of Barbary were not transferred to the Foreign Office until 1835.

[2] F.O. 76/16, Warrington to Horton, 21 July 1822; F.O. 76/21, Warrington to Huskisson, 26 Dec. 1827.

[3] F.O. 76/9, Warrington to Bathurst, 20 Nov. 1815; F.O. 76/19, Warrington to Horton, 22 Apr. 1825; F.O. 76/19, Warrington to Bathurst, 2 Oct. 1825; F.O. 76/21, Warrington to Bathurst, 1 May 1827.

[4] Lyon, op. cit., p. 29.

[5] D. Denham and H. Clapperton, *Narrative of Travels and Discoveries in Northern and Central Africa in the years 1882, 1823 and 1824* (London, 1826), p. xii. F.O. 76/9, Warrington to Maitland, 28 July 1815. Within six months of his arrival about a hundred Christian slaves were liberated.

Oudney—unanimously noted the very warm reception accorded them wherever they went, the extreme popularity of the British flag in that state, and the tolerance shown to Christians.[1]

It is thus obvious that in the second and third decades of the nineteenth century the Regency of Tripoli, with its political stability, the very friendly disposition of its people, and above all the readiness or rather the anxiety of the Pasha to co-operate with the British Government, afforded the best gateway to the interior. These conditions were, in the words of Barrow, 'a golden opportunity' which should be seized forthwith.[2]

This friendly and co-operative attitude of the Pasha towards Britain was clearly demonstrated in 1817, when he readily granted permission to Captain Smyth not only to remove any objects of antiquarian interest that he might find anywhere in the Regency, but also to travel farther inland to increase his collections.[3] It was the successful execution of this trip to the interior of Tripoli that encouraged Smyth and Warrington to broach the question of exploring the course of the Niger through that Regency. At this interview the Pasha informed Smyth and Warrington of his friendly relations with Bornu and obligingly promised to send an escort to conduct any travellers to that kingdom. This offer was immediately conveyed through Admiral Penrose, the Commander-in-Chief in the Mediterranean, to the Admiralty.[4]

Greatly disappointed but by no means discouraged by the failure of the Tuckey expedition, Barrow immediately forwarded this offer to the Colonial Office. In reply, Goulburn, the Colonial Under-Secretary, expressed Lord Bathurst's readiness to authorize the purchase of any presents for the Pasha, and wrote to Barrow: 'concert with Sir Joseph Banks and I will be at your service to execute what you may decide'. Barrow sent a copy of this letter to Banks with the urgent request that he should look round for some person either in England or on the continent who knew a little

[1] Smyth, who was there in 1817, only three years after Warrington's arrival, reported that 'Mohametan intolerance has greatly subsided in this Regency', and at Sockna, over 200 miles south, Oudney and Clapperton found crowds lining the street and shouting with unaffected glee 'Inglesi, Inglesi'. F.O. 76/11, Smyth to Penrose, 24 Feb. 1817, encl. in Admiralty to Goulburn, 8 May 1817.

[2] D.T.C. 20/50, Barrow to Banks, 8 Oct. 1817.

[3] F.O. 76/11, Smyth to Penrose, 24 Feb. 1817, encl. in Barrow to Goulburn, 8 May 1817; Quarterly Review, vol. 18, p. 370.

[4] F.O. 76/11, Penrose to Admiralty, 25 Jan. 1817, encl. in Barrow to Goulburn, 6 June 1817.

Arabic, 'for we shall not be able to find another Lord Bathurst at home or another Pasha at Tripoli so favourable for the undertaking.'[1] These letters show beyond any doubt that the persons behind African exploration were still the veteran Banks, now within three years of his grave, and his friend Barrow.

On the recommendation of Banks, Joseph Ritchie, a young man of twenty-nine, who was then private secretary to Sir Charles Stuart, the British Ambassador in Paris, was selected to undertake the mission.[2] Born in Yorkshire in 1788, Ritchie was trained for the medical profession and in 1813 became a surgeon at the Lock Hospital in London. He did not, however, confine his interest to medicine but extended it to other fields of science, especially natural history, and to literature. He was an intimate friend of John Keats, a copy of whose poem 'Endymion' he took with him to Africa, and was himself the author of a number of poems.[3] Lyon, his companion, described him as 'a gentleman of great science'.[4]

The preparations which Ritchie made for his mission show that he was far more interested in natural history than in geographical discovery. For instance, he pleaded that as the natural productions of the interior of Africa had not been fully examined, a person who was competent 'to execute the laborious details of collecting and preserving' should be added to the mission.[5] Secondly, among the goods left on his death were one camel load of corks for preserving insects, two loads of brown paper for preparing plants, five hundred-weight of books, and two chests of instruments. This scientific equipment alone occupied eight of the twenty two camels hired for the mission.[6] It was undoubtedly because of his interest in natural history that he became known to Banks.

The duties with which Ritchie was charged were outlined in his instructions. In the first place he was to proceed in the capacity of His Majesty's Vice-Consul to Fezzan.[7] Having established himself there, he was to collect information of every kind respecting the interior of northern Africa and forward it to England through

[1] D.T.C. 20/50, Goulburn to Barrow, 23 Sept. 1817, encl. in Barrow to Banks, 8 Oct. 1817.
[2] D.T.C. 20/50, Barrow to Banks, 8 Oct. 1817.
[3] *D.N.B.*, vol. 48, pp. 323–4.
[4] *Quarterly Review*, vol. 18, p. 375; Lyon, op. cit., p. 1.
[5] C.O. 2/9, Ritchie to Barrow, 11 June 1818.
[6] Lyon, op. cit., p. 196; F.O. 76/15, Warrington to Bathurst, 16 July 1821.
[7] F.O. 8/7, Bathurst to Ritchie, 1 Feb. 1818.

Tripoli. He was also to make collections of 'insects, plants and minerals', taking care not to excite the jealousy of the people. But the 'grand object' of the appointment, he was told, was his eventual advance under proper protection to Timbuctu, Katsina, or any other city which conditions would allow him to visit. Later he was enjoined to proceed first to Bornu, and was given six packages containing presents which were to be distributed to the Sultan and the other rulers of the interior.[1] To facilitate his mission, he was advised to learn the language of the people and investigate the usual modes of communication between Fezzan and the Sudan. On his eventual arrival at Timbuctu, he was to collect all possible information as to the course of the Niger and the probability of his being able to trace it to its termination. These instructions, it might be noted, were drawn up by Barrow.[2] This accounts for their general scientific nature and the omission of all reference to commerce.

With these instructions and credentials to the Pasha of Tripoli, Ritchie finally left England on 3 March 1818, when Peddie and his party were pushing into the interior from Bathurst. After five months' stay in Paris, Ritchie set off for Malta, where he enlisted the services of Captain Lyon of the Royal Navy, and John Belford, a shipwright from the dockyard.[3] He finally arrived at Tripoli in October 1818. After a delay of six months, he departed with full vice-consular powers and successfully established himself and his party in Murzuk in May 1819.[4] Murzuk, unfortunately, proved to be the farthest point that Ritchie reached. He died there six months after his arrival.[5] After a further three months' stay Captain Lyon and Belford abandoned the mission. Thus, while Gray was still waiting in Bondu for the return of Dochard and for fresh supplies, Lyon and his partner commenced their homeward journey and arrived in England in August 1820.

Why did this mission which set off under such propitious conditions come to such an inglorious end? Ritchie's biographer in the *Dictionary of National Biography* was correct when he observed that the failure of the mission was due to mismanagement, but wrong

[1] F.O. 76/11, C.O. to Ritchie, 1 Apr. 1818.
[2] C.O. 2/9, Barrow to Goulburn, 29 Jan. 1819.
[3] Lyon, op. cit., p. 2.
[4] C.O. 2/9, Warrington to Penrose, 24 Oct. 1818, encl. in Croker to Goulburn, 16 Nov. 1818.
[5] C.O. 2/9, Lyon to Goulburn, 23 Nov. 1819.

when he put the responsibility for this on 'the home authorities who supplied them with inadequate funds, and burdened them with ill-selected merchandise which proved unsaleable'.

In the first place it is not true that the mission was provided with inadequate funds. A generous salary of £600 per annum was voted for Ritchie.[1] On his arrival in Paris, however, he wrote back to reject this arrangement. His reasons were that no provisions were made for the salaries of his assistants and that it would be difficult to obtain his own when he got to Bornu. He therefore asked for a lump sum to be voted for the mission.[2] The Colonial Office agreed to this and managed to persuade the Treasury to place the handsome amount of £2,000 at Ritchie's disposal.[3] This sum was to cover all expenses of the mission for the first two years in Africa. It is important to note that Ritchie expressed his 'entire satisfaction' with these new arrangements.[4] But he did not handle the money with any circumspection. He spent £400 on instruments of astronomy and natural history, and about £1,000 of the remainder was spent in Paris on other equipment and merchandise for the mission.[5] According to Lyon, the mission left Tripoli with a total sum of only 300 dollars (£60), though Ritchie himself puts the amount at £225.[6] But even if Ritchie was correct, that amount could certainly not have maintained the entire mission for two years as it was meant to do. Ritchie realized the gravity of the situation and not only informed Warrington and Admiral Penrose of it, but also wrote to the Colonial Office, on the eve of his departure for Fezzan, for a further grant of £1,000. Penrose and Warrington also appealed for an increase. Here again the Colonial Office persuaded the Treasury to vote the required £1,000 for the mission.[7] As ill luck would have it, the letter which contained the news of this increase arrived an hour after the burial of Ritchie.[8] Destitute and emaciated, Lyon and Belford could not but give up the attempt. Had Ritchie accepted the Treasury's arrangements for the annual grant of £600 and later negotiated similar

[1] C.O. 2/8, Harrison to Goulburn, 16 Dec. 1817.

[2] C.O. 2/9, Ritchie to Goulburn, 18 Apr. 1818.

[3] C.O. 2/9, Goulburn to Ritchie, 8 May 1818.

[4] C.O. 2/8, Ritchie to Bathurst, 11 May 1818.

[5] C.O. 2/9, Ritchie to Goulburn, 24 March 1819. He claimed to have spent £300 on transport expenses from Paris to Tripoli.

[6] Lyon, op. cit., p. 56.

[7] F.O. 8/11, Goulburn to Harrison, 20 Jan. 1819; F.O. 8/7, Goulburn to Ritchie, 11 June 1819.

[8] C.O. 2/9, Lyon to Bathurst, 22 Nov. 1819; Lyon, op. cit., p. 193.

annual allowances for his assistants, all these difficulties could have been avoided.

In the second place, it is not true that the merchandise was unsaleable, as it contained such stock-in-trade of caravan traffic as penknives, scissors, looking-glasses, pins, needles, and paper. Indeed, soon after Ritchie's death, Lyon succeeded in selling 'many trifles'. The proceeds from this enabled him to pay off all the debts which the mission had incurred and to save 150 dollars (£30).[1] Admittedly, the mission did not sell anything before Ritchie's death, but this was certainly not because of the opposition of the Governor of Fezzan, as Lyon alleged, or because the articles were unsaleable, but because Ritchie persistently refused to allow Lyon to trade. After three months of progressive debilitation owing to malnutrition, Lyon recorded, 'Mr. Ritchie being again attacked by illness, I much wished him to allow of my selling some of our powder to procure him a few comforts, but to this he would not consent'.[2] Ritchie had two reasons for refusing to allow Lyon to trade. First, he believed that trading would lower him and his colleagues in the eyes of the natives. Secondly, as he was certain of his recovery from his illness and of their eventual advance into the interior, he was reluctant to dissipate their means in Fezzan.[3] Both reasons are as stupid as they are illogical. Such a sale would have enabled them to afford the basic nourishment which, most probably, would have saved Ritchie's life and made further progress into the interior possible. Quite clearly, nobody should be blamed for the failure of this mission but Ritchie himself.

Lyon's letter to the Colonial Office informing them of Ritchie's death, as well as Warrington's optimism, influenced official reaction in England to the failure of this mission. Lyon pointed out that the road to Bornu was 'perfectly safe', that the Sheikh and Sultan of Bornu had assured them of a good reception, and that, granted permission, he would continue the mission.[4] Any further official misgivings were dispelled by Warrington, who expressed the Pasha's readiness to assist any subsequent attempts and his own conviction that 'the great object' could most assuredly be accomplished via Tripoli and Fezzan.[5] That the Government was convinced by these

[1] Lyon, op. cit., p. 194.
[2] Ibid., pp. 118, 189.
[3] Ibid., p. 118; C.O. 2/9, Warrington to Goulburn, 5 Sept. 1820. This letter contains a list of the merchandise which the mission left at Tripoli.
[4] C.O. 2/9, Lyon to Bathurst, 22 Nov. 1819.
[5] F.O. 76/13, Warrington to Bathurst, 28 Dec. 1819.

arguments is borne out by Bathurst's reply to Warrington and Lyon. After having expressed his concurrence with the Consul-General's view that it was 'highly inexpedient to lose the favourable opportunity which at present exists of penetrating into the interior with the assistance, or at least the acquiescence of the native authorities', he appointed Lyon to succeed Ritchie as 'British vice-consul at Fezzan'.[1] He even empowered Lyon to proceed ultimately to Bornu in full consular capacity. Credentials and presents to be given to the Sultan of Bornu were accordingly sent out. A copy of Ritchie's instructions was also forwarded to Lyon.

These new orders arrived in Tripoli towards the end of June. But they were too late, as Lyon had left for England about the middle of May. Though on his arrival in England Lyon had again expressed his eagerness to return to Africa, he wrote two days later declining to go back.[2] His reason for this *volte-face* was the Government's refusal to promote him to the rank of Commander. His only motive for accompanying Ritchie, he stated quite frankly, 'was from a natural wish to rise in my profession'.[3] The bewilderment and utter helplessness of the Colonial Office are evident from Goulburn's minute on Lyon's letter, which he forwarded to Barrow. 'Dear Barrow,' he asked, 'what should under these circumstances be done as to our African mission?' Shortly after learning of Lyon's decision, the Government, ironically enough, received an offer from the Pasha to pass any travellers to Bornu and guarantee their return upon payment of £5,000. This offer was approved by the Treasury on condition that a qualified person was obtained.[4] Undoubtedly these two events intensified the Government's search for new travellers.

Through James Robinson Scott, a former lecturer in Botany at Edinburgh University, Barrow learned of Walter Oudney of the Royal Navy. Scott described Oudney as being a surgeon who was also a very clever botanist. He strongly suggested that the Government should furnish the natural history department of the expedition to Bornu with instruments for collecting plants and animals for the

---

[1] F.O. 8/7, Bathurst to Warrington, 24 Apr. 1820.

[2] C.O. 2/9, Lyon to Goulburn, 23 Aug. 1820.

[3] C.O. 2/9, Lyon to Goulburn, 25 Aug. 1820. It is interesting to note that Captain Marryat, who was originally selected by the Colonial Office to accompany Ritchie, declined the offer for the same reason. (C.O. 2/9, Marryat to Goulburn, 4 May 1818.)

[4] F.O. 8/11, Goulburn to Harrison, 11 Oct. 1820; F.O. 8/7, Bathurst to Warrington, 30 Aug. 1821; C.O. 2/14, Treasury to Goulburn, 4 Jan. 1821.

British Museum. In offering his services for the mission, Oudney expressed the pleasure he would feel 'in having such a favourable opportunity of exploring the natural history of a country so imperfectly known'.[1] Nine months later Oudney was informed that he had been selected to lead the mission and that his request for Lieutenant Hugh Clapperton to accompany him as his assistant had been granted.[2]

While Barrow was eagerly searching for explorers, the Colonial Office received an application from Lieutenant Dixon Denham of the 64th Regiment asking to be sent to Africa. His plan, drawn up after consultation with Lyon, was to proceed via Ghadames (south-west of Tripoli) and Ghat to Katsina, and from there to Bagirmi, Waday, and the Nile.[3] The Colonial Office accepted this application and arranged for Denham to meet Oudney and Clapperton at Barrow's office in August 1821.[4] It was at this meeting that the three travellers saw each other for the first time.

What, then, were they sent out to do? Oudney's instructions are particularly revealing, since they were adapted by the Colonial Office from the instructions issued to Ritchie.[5] In the first place, Oudney, like Ritchie, was to proceed in a vice-consular capacity; but while Ritchie's post was only temporary, Oudney's was to be permanent. Secondly, the reason for Ritchie's appointment was given simply as 'the successful prosecution of the discoveries now attempting in the interior of Africa'. Oudney's instructions significantly added 'and the extension of our commerce in the interior of that continent'. In fact Oudney was furnished with specimens of British manufactures such as light clothes, knives, razors, files, saws of different sizes, hammers, tea-trays, fish hooks, drugs, and blotting paper.[6] He was told to exhibit these specimens to 'such merchants as may visit Bornu, acquainting them with the prices at which they may be supplied in any quantity'. This, the Colonial Office explained to the Treasury, would enable Oudney to ascertain how far it might be possible 'to create in the interior of Africa a demand for these articles'.[7] Having

[1] F.O. 76/14, Oudney to Byron, 11 Nov. 1820; James Robinson to Byron (extract), encl. in Barrow to Goulburn, 15 Nov. 1820.
[2] C.O. 2/14, Oudney to Barrow, 8 Aug. 1821.
[3] C.O. 2/13, Denham to Bathurst, 17 March 1821.
[4] F.O. 8/11, Goulburn to Denham, 24 Aug. 1821.
[5] F.O. 8/7, Bathurst to Ritchie, 1 Feb. 1818, and amendments.
[6] F.O. 8/11, Goulburn to Warrington, 5 Oct. 1821.
[7] F.O. 8/11, Goulburn to Harrison, 31 Aug. 1821.

arrived in Bornu, he was, like Ritchie, to send to England all the information he could collect about the interior. To facilitate this he was to learn the language of the people. Again like Ritchie, and with the usual caution, he was to collect objects of natural history. The 'grand object' of Oudney's appointment, however, was not merely to gain information about the real state of the interior of northern Africa; he was also to familiarize the natives with the British name and character. To accomplish these two objectives, he was to remain for some time near the residence of the Sultan of Bornu.

Denham's and Clapperton's assignments were simply to make geographical discoveries and observe the nature of the country and its peoples. They were to explore particularly the area to the south and east of Bornu, 'principally with a view of tracing the course of the Niger and ascertaining its *embouchure*'. Denham was empowered to recruit in Malta a carpenter who could construct a boat for the navigation of the river if necessary. He was, however, asked to endeavour to acquaint himself with the manners and the language as well as the mode of travelling of the Bornu people before moving southward.

When news of the successful establishment of the mission in Bornu arrived in England in October 1823, the Colonial Office wrote to congratulate its leaders on their achievement, and drew their attention to their respective primary objectives. Oudney was asked again not to leave Kuka too soon:

for although the main object of your mission is discovery, yet it is not less an object of the highest national interest that you should, by cultivating the friendship of the Sultan of Bornu and of the Sheikh of Kalmi, endeavour to establish some permanent relations between them and this country.[1]

Before proceeding eastward as he had planned to do, Oudney was asked to explore the Chad and ascertain whether there was any outlet on its eastern or south-western shores. Similarly Denham was peremptorily ordered not to go to Egypt through Darfur but through the area south of Bornu in order to trace 'to the termination that river which runs to the eastward and south of Bornu'.[2]

It is quite obvious both from the original instructions given to Oudney and from the additions of October 1823 that the Govern-

[1] F.O. 8/8, Bathurst to Oudney, 6 Oct. 1823, encl. in Bathurst to Warrington, 6 Oct. 1823.
[2] F.O. 8/8, Bathurst to Oudney, 6 Oct. 1823, encl. in Bathurst to Warrington, 6 Oct. 1823.

ment did not consider this expedition simply as one for geographical discovery and the collection of objects of natural history. Indeed Bathurst summed up the purpose of the Oudney–Denham mission as 'principally that of establishing a permanent British resident at the Court of Bornou, and that of conducting from there an expedition into the interior of Northern Africa for the purpose of ascertaining the geography of that interesting though yet unknown continent'.[1] To facilitate communication between Bornu and Tripoli, the Colonial Office even adopted Warrington's suggestion of establishing a permanent vice-consul in Fezzan at a salary of £150 per annum, since this offered greater possibilities 'than any other course of promoting knowledge of the interior of Africa, and of advancing *British interests* in that Quarter'.[2] The Treasury, however, rejected the proposal on the ground that the advantage to be derived from the appointment was not likely to be sufficiently important to justify the salary suggested for it.[3] The point that should be noted here is not that the recommendation was turned down, but that the Colonial Office should have made it at this time and talked of 'British interests' in the Sahara.

Oudney and Clapperton left England in September 1821, and Denham followed a month later. All three assembled in Tripoli and set off for the interior in January 1822. Having stayed in the interior for three years, the expedition returned to Tripoli in January 1825 and to England four months later. Judged by its casualty rate as well as by its discoveries, it was the most successful of the expeditions yet sent to Africa. Of the three leaders only Oudney died of illness in January 1824. And the volume of information in its journal concerning the ethnographical, political, and commercial conditions in the Sahara, Bornu, and Hausaland was unprecedented and spectacular.[4] But in two particular fields the results of the mission were far from satisfactory. Geographically, it failed to explore the regions south of Bornu or solve the problem of the Niger's termination. This failure was mainly due to the wars that were raging between Bornu and Bagirmi in the east, and between the

[1] F.O. 8/7, Bathurst to Warrington, 30 Aug. 1821.
[2] F.O. 8/11, C.O. to Treasury, 8 Nov. 1821.
[3] F.O. 76/16, Treasury to Horton, 17 Jan. 1822.
[4] Denham and Clapperton, op. cit. This journal was jointly edited by Denham and Barrow. For a discussion of the state of commerce and the trans-Saharan trade as well as of the ethnographical and political conditions revealed by these and subsequent explorers, see Chapters V and VIII, and Appendixes IV and V.

Fulani and the Nupe and Hausa in the west, which prevented
Denham from pushing into the region south of Bornu and compelled
Bello to debar Clapperton from proceeding to the Niger from
Sokoto.[1] Nevertheless the expedition did succeed in exploring and
charting for the first time the northern, western, and southern shores
of the Chad and its two rivers, the Shari and the Yobe (Yeou of
Denham). Secondly, the whole area of the Central Sahara, Bornu,
and the Sudan was also correctly mapped and the boundaries of the
desert, the savanna, and the forest belts delineated. The oasis of
Ghat, one of the important nerve centres of the caravan traffic, was
also explored for the first time.[2]

In the field of natural history, too, the accomplishments of the
expedition fell far below expectations. This, however, could not have
been avoided in the circumstances. Oudney, who was charged
with that responsibility, remained in such a chronic state of illness
that he was unable to make any collections. Moreover, the means
they had for collecting and preserving specimens were quite inadequate. For example, their only instrument for cutting was a
penknife. In spite of these two serious handicaps, they managed to
bring home 100 specimens of zoological objects and a herbarium of
300 species. One of the five of these species which were hitherto
unknown was quite appropriately named after Oudney.[3]

Taking all these discoveries and the information furnished about
the interior together, it can be said that if the success of the mission
was not complete and decisive, it was certainly impressive. It was a
fitting tribute to the explorers' endeavours that they were presented
to King George IV, given promotions, and favourably mentioned in
contemporary periodicals and journals. For example, the *Edinburgh
Review* commented on their journal:

The appearance of this work forms an era in modern discovery. We
scarcely know, since the time of Marco Polo, with the exception of perhaps
Park, any instance in which so much new ground has been gone over by a
single mission. Regions have been surveyed, the very existence of which

[1] Denham and Clapperton, op. cit., pp. 134–6, 240–1; C.O. 2/13, Denham to
Horton, 1 June 1825; F.O. 76/17, Toole to Warrington, 24 Sept. 1823, encl. in
Warrington to Horton, 17 Oct. 1823.
[2] Denham and Clapperton, op. cit., pp. xxxviii–xxix, 14, 31–32; C.O. 2/13,
Oudney to Bathurst, 16 Aug. 1822; Denham and Clapperton, op. cit., pp.
xlii–xlvii.
[3] For details of the analysis of these objects, see Appendix xxi and xxii of
Denham and Clapperton, op. cit.

was before unknown and others, of which only a faint rumour had reached across the immense deserts by which they were enclosed.[1]

Park's first mission marked the first milestone in the exploration of the interior of Africa; Denham and Clapperton's mission determined the second.

A number of questions are naturally posed by this first successful venture in the exploration of the interior of Africa in the nineteenth century. Why was it so successful, and what were the main effects of its discoveries and activities in England and Africa?

Its striking success was due to a number of factors, the first of which was the very efficient way in which it was organized. The credit for this should go partly to the Colonial Office and the Treasury, but mainly to Warrington. The acceptance by the Government of the arrangements made by Warrington with the Pasha to conduct the travellers to and from Bornu for the payment of £5,000 made it possible for the mission to be escorted to Bornu by an impressive battalion of 100 cavalry and 100 infantry.[2] Secondly, to avoid the fate of Ritchie, salaries of £600, £300, and £150 per annum were fixed for Oudney, Denham, and Clapperton. Moreover, Warrington was empowered to honour any bill drawn on him by the travellers.[3] Thus the lump-sum allocation which partly accounted for the failure of Ritchie's mission was avoided. In addition to these provisions, very generous presents were placed at the disposal of the travellers for distribution among the potentates in the interior, and specific requests from any of these chiefs were also promptly complied with. For example, watches, pistols, a dagger, and rockets asked for by the Sheikh of Bornu were given to John Tyrwhitt when he was sent out in February 1824 to strengthen the staff of the mission.[4] Indeed, the Colonial Office was convinced, as they explained to the Treasury, that 'the opportunity now offered of exploring even yet further than Bornu the interior of Africa is not to be lost'.[5]

[1] *Edinburgh Review*, vol. 44, p. 173. The *Quarterly Review* paid a similar tribute. (Vol. 33, pp. 518–19.) C.O. 392/1, Horton to Denham, 28 June 1825.

[2] F.O. 76/16, Warrington to Wilmot, 21 July 1822; Denham and Clapperton op. cit., pp. xxxv–xxxvii; F.O. 8/7, Bathurst to Warrington, 30 Aug. 1821.

[3] Instructions to Oudney and Denham.

[4] F.O. 76/17, Denham to Warrington, 4 Apr. 1823, Oudney to Warrington, 1 Apr. 1823, encl. in Warrington to Horton 17 July 1823; F.O. 8/8, Bathurst to Oudney, 6 Oct. 1823, encl. in Bathurst to Warrington, 6 Oct. 1823; Denham and Clapperton, op. cit., p. 254.

[5] F.O. 8/11, Goulburn to Harrison, 31 Aug. 1821; F.O. 8/7, Bathurst to Warrington, 30 Aug. 1821. By June 1822, even before the mission had left Fezzan for Bornu, the total cost had reached £10,930, including the £5,000 given to the Pasha.

These financial arrangements and the liberal disposition of the Government towards the mission could hardly have proved effective but for the presence of Warrington in Tripoli. For instance, the seven months' delay of the party at Murzuk caused by the failure of the Pasha, for financial reasons, to provide the escort, would probably have lasted longer but for the persistent pressure brought to bear on him by Warrington.[1] Again, when the mission reached Bornu, the leader of the military escort declined to go beyond Bornu or even to allow the travellers to do so.[2] If this opposition had been sustained, it would have limited lamentably the scope of the travellers' activities. But as the result of an interview which Warrington had with the Pasha, an order was dispatched to Boo Khaloum, the leader of the escort, to allow the travellers absolute freedom of movement in any direction.[3] Thus Clapperton was enabled to proceed to Hausaland.

Warrington's contribution to the success of the mission did not end here. Fully convinced that the failure of Ritchie's mission was due not only to financial mismanagement, but also to the fact that they were disguised as Muslims in Arab dress, he insisted again and again, and ultimately won his point, that Denham and his party should wear plain English clothes.[4] The question whether the travellers would have been less successful if they had proceeded as Muslims is answered by themselves. Clapperton wrote:

Had we not adopted your advice by appearing always in our true and un-disguised characters, we should not have accomplished what we have done. . . . It was as Christians, as Englishmen, and as servants of His Majesty we were freely received, highly respected and kindly treated everywhere . . . as such and such alone I owe the friendly and liberal reception which I experienced from Bello.[5]

Though Denham expressed exactly the same view, it was nonetheless

[1] F.O. 76/16, Warrington to Bathurst, 1 May 1822; Warrington to Horton, 11 June 1822; 15 June 1822; 20 July 1822; C.O. 2/13, Denham to Bathurst, 15 June 1822; Denham to Bathurst, 26 Aug. 1822.

[2] F.O. 76/12, Oudney to Warrington, 1 Apr. 1823, encl. in Warrington to Horton, 17 July 1823.

[3] F.O. 76/17, H.H. the Pasha of Tripoli to Boo Khaloum, encl. in Warrington to Horton, 10 July 1823.

[4] F.O. 76/13, Warrington to Goulburn, 28 Dec. 1819; F.O. 76/14, Warrington to Bathurst, 1 July 1820; F.O. 76/15, Warrington to Bathurst, 21 Sept. and 21 Oct. 1821.

[5] F.O. 76/19, Clapperton to Warrington, 10 Feb. 1825, encl. in Warrington to Bathurst, 9 Feb. 1825; F.O. 76/16, Denham to Warrington to Horton, 22 Apr. 1822; C.O. 2/13, Denham to Horton, 1 June 1825.

an over-simplification. As we shall see presently, other factors—such as the attitude of the Sheikh of Bornu—were even more decisive. No one can dispute the fact, however, that had the travellers disguised themselves, they would not have enjoyed the freedom of movement and conversation which were so essential to their investigations.

Warrington was also mainly responsible for fitting out the expedition before its departure for Bornu. Having referred to the fate of Ritchie, he advised Oudney not to pay too much attention to economy and thereby sacrifice 'the necessary comforts which you have been in the habit of enjoying in your own country and which will be of infinite service in case of sickness'.[1] He went on to prepare a list of articles which he deemed indispensable and recommended that they should have in reserve a sum of at least 2,500 dollars (£500). Oudney and his friends very wisely accepted all these important suggestions and drew a bill for £1,000 to implement them. Fortunately this was approved by the Government.[2] The advantageous position of this mission as compared with the last is clearly shown in the optimism with which Oudney looked forward to their stay in Murzuk. He wrote with confidence:

We must necessarily be exposed to the same climate but under different circumstances. . . . Ritchie and his party suffered severely from poverty and deficiency of proper nourishment, we are tolerably rich in money and abundantly provided with good provisions and comforts in case of sickness attacking us. They had large quantities of goods for exchange but [they were] not suited for the market . . . what we possess can always be bartered to great advantage.[3]

Oudney and his colleagues did remain in Murzuk from April to November 1822 without any casualty—a tribute to Warrington's foresight, Oudney's wisdom, and the British Government's generosity.

But the effects of these careful arrangements would have been nullified if the mission had encountered any strong opposition from the powers in the interior. In this respect the explorers were exceedingly fortunate in gaining the absolute confidence and benevolent co-operation of the two most powerful rulers of the day, namely, Muhammad al-Kānami, the Sheikh of Bornu, and Muhammad

---

[1] F.O. 76/15, Warrington to Oudney, 24 Oct. 1821, encl. in Warrington to Bathurst, 26 Oct. 1821.
[2] C.O. 2/13, Oudney to Bathurst, 25 Oct. 1821 and 21 Jan. 1822.
[3] C.O. 2/13, Oudney to Goulburn, 24 Jan. 1822.

Bello, the Sultan of the Fulani Empire. The Sheikh was particularly accommodating. The reception which he gave the travellers and their military escort reminds one, in pomp and splendour, of the triumphs accorded to victorious generals in the heyday of the Roman Empire. Oudney informed Warrington:

Our reception was exceedingly flattering, an amazing number of the Sheikh's horsemen (they say 5,000) came out to receive [us] about two miles from Kuka. They had a fine appearance, many had armour, and many steel chain jackets, they all rode down to pay their respects . . . When we entered the town and arrived near the entrance to the Sheikh's house, the sides of the streets were lined with these men in armour and the door filled with foot guards. . . .[1]

The friendly attitude displayed in this grand welcome persisted. Indeed, during their long stay in Bornu the Sheikh treated them like his children. Five months after their arrival Oudney reported that the Sheikh conducted himself 'as a father to us', and that 'to his kindness our reception and comfort are principally due'. The same sentiments were repeated in subsequent dispatches.[2] He advanced them loans whenever they needed money, frequently gave them presents, and paid them regular visits during which various topics, including religion and British activities in India, were discussed. He allowed them to accompany his military expeditions or provided them with guides and escorts when they travelled on their own. It was through such expeditions that Denham had the opportunity of exploring Mandara, Loggun, and the south-eastern shores of the Chad.[3] The Sheikh also gave Oudney and Clapperton letters of introduction to the governors of Kano and Katagum, to Hat Sallah, his own 'man of business' in Kano, and to Sultan Bello when they left for Hausaland. Clapperton subsequently received hospitable treatment on the way from Bornu to Kano merely because he was the 'friend of the Sheikh'.[4]

[1] F.O. 76/17, Oudney to Warrington, 1 Apr. 1823, encl. in Warrington to Horton, 17 July 1823. Denham describes the scene in even greater detail and mentions the music and dancing that accompanied the martial display. (Denham, op. cit., pp. 62–65.)

[2] C.O. 2/13, Oudney to Horton, 14 July 1823; F.O. 76/18, Denham to Warrington, 12 Oct. 1823, encl. in Warrington to Horton, 2 Feb. 1824; F.O. 76/18, Oudney to Warrington, 12 Sept. 1823, encl. in Warrington to Horton, 12 March 1824; F.O. 76/18, Clapperton to Warrington, 10 Dec. 1823, encl. in Warrington to Horton, 18 Aug. 1824.

[3] Denham, op. cit., pp. 99–104, 223–5, 259–60.

[4] F.O. 76/18, Clapperton to Warrington, 10 Dec. 1823, encl. in Warrington to Horton, 18 Aug. 1824; Clapperton, op. cit., pp. 6, 21,′40–41, 44.

In Hausa, Bello was no less friendly and accommodating. A military escort was sent out to conduct Clapperton from Kano to Sokoto, and the leader was instructed to supply him 'with everything necessary for the journey'.[1] During Clapperton's stay in Sokoto, Bello visited him regularly and discussed a diversity of topics with him. The Sultan showed his very friendly disposition beyond any doubt when at the first interview he returned to Clapperton all the books and papers which were taken from Denham by the Fulani on the ill-fated expedition to Mandara.[2]

This attitude of the two rulers calls for some explanation. In the first place, both Al-Kānami and Bello were very highly educated and enlightened men who welcomed the opportunity for exchange of ideas afforded by contact with Europeans. Their conversations ranged over astronomy, philosophy, and theology.[3] There were also some more material considerations. As far as Al-Kānami was concerned, one of the reasons for his attitude was certainly his relations with the Pasha of Tripoli. The war with Bagirmi was still undecided, and the Sheikh could therefore not afford, even were he so inclined, to maltreat the Pasha's august guests. Indeed the triumphant welcome given to the mission was less in their honour than in that of the Pasha's escort. In addition, both he and Bello were convinced of the very rich dividends which strong contacts with such a powerful country as Britain would yield. For instance, Al-Kānami attributed his easy victory during the campaign against the Bagirmi in April 1824 to the guns presented to him by the British Government.[4] The list of fourteen articles which the Sheikh asked from his 'friend' the King of England is also significant. It included a machine for minting money, 300 hand grenades, two small brass guns (two pounders), and a small supply of powder and ball. He also asked for one or two shipwrights and a blacksmith to be sent down with their families.[5] It is equally significant that he insisted on one of the explorers being

[1] Clapperton, op. cit., p. 64.
[2] Denham had accompanied this expedition in the hope of exploring those regions. But in the battle in which the Bornu forces were defeated and routed, Denham was captured and his papers were seized. Indeed it was only a quarrel among his captors over his clothes, which they stripped off him, that enabled him to escape death or captivity. (Clapperton, op. cit., p. 83; Denham, op. cit., pp. 134–6.)
[3] Clapperton, op. cit., p. 85.
[4] These were manipulated by Hillman during the war. Denham, op. cit., pp. 208, 210, 249–50.
[5] C.O. 2/13, Denham to Horton, 28 June 1825.

left there permanently as a consul.[1] Bello also asked for ammunition as well as physicians. With their acumen and foresight, both were quick to realize that any kind treatment of the travellers would not go unrewarded. Consequently they did everything in their power to ingratiate themselves with the travellers and the British Government.

The last but by no means the least of the reasons for the success of the mission was the conduct of its members. The behaviour of Denham and Clapperton to the African rulers was a model of patience, tact, and prudence. While they conciliated the potentates and men of influence by timely presents, they tried to win the ordinary people by medical attention. Again, fearing that his Jewish servant's touchiness about religion would impede his progress in Sokoto, Clapperton tactfully left him in Kano.[2] Similarly, in spite of his extreme anxiety to visit Nupe, Clapperton obediently gave up the idea when Bello withheld his permission.

What, then, were the main effects of this mission's discoveries and activities in Africa and England? The first obvious effect was to prove the security of the route between Tripoli and Bornu. Denham, attended by a single Arab, travelled from Fezzan to Tripoli in May 1822. Lieutenant Toole, who was sent out to join the mission in August 1823 and was loaded with money and valuable presents, crossed with only two camel drivers and four other Arabs. Commenting on his feeling of security, he said, 'these peoples have seen enough of Englishmen to know they gain immensely by them'.[3] Secondly, the very fact that the travellers succeeded, although they moved about as Christians in English dress, buried the myth that the Muslim had an instinctive hatred for the Christian and that a 'cruel death' awaited any person who went beyond Fezzan undisguised.[4] It is true that religious discussions came up wherever they went and at times resulted in bitter dissension, but many a time, too, these discussions ended amicably. In fact, respect for the travellers was very often heightened when the Muslims learnt to their utter surprise that the English believed at least that there was one God and that they even knew how to pray. Oudney observed on this point:

All classes of people have been amazingly kind and not viewed us with that horror which Mohametans in some places view Christians; we have had,

[1] C.O. 2/13, Denham to Tyrwhitt, 30 July 1824, encl. in Tyrwhitt to Horton, 7 Aug. 1824.
[2] Clapperton, op. cit., p. 66.
[3] Denham, op. cit., pp. 108–10, 113, 124–5; Clapperton, op. cit., pp. 48–49, 94.
[4] Lyon, op. cit., p. 200.

indeed, a toleration shown us much greater than is to be found among a great many of our sectarians.[1]

The mission thus demonstrated that once the protection of the African chiefs was ensured, religious differences need not prove an insuperable obstacle.

Thirdly, if by 1818 the British name and influence had percolated as far as Fezzan, this mission extended it across the Sahara to Bornu and the Sudan. By 1825 there was a house in Murzuk known as the 'English house' in which Ritchie and Lyon, Denham and his group, and Toole and Tyrwhitt had all been accommodated.[2] The long stay of the mission in Bornu from February 1823 to August 1824 and Clapperton's seven months' tour of the Sudan went a long way towards familiarizing some of the people of those regions with the name of the English as well as the person of an Englishman. Clapperton and his friends moved very freely among the people and had various discussions with them. Through such personal contacts and conversations a great many of the fantastic ideas entertained on both sides were discarded. For example, the son of the Governor of Kano refused at first to take a cup of tea which Clapperton offered him because he said he had been told that the English had the power of changing people into rats, dogs, and monkeys. But when one of Clapperton's servants drank the tea and remained normal, the Governor's son apologized for his conduct and accepted a fresh cup.[3] Similarly, a nephew of Bello's confessed that before he met Clapperton he considered a Christian as little more than a monster.[4] On the other hand, Clapperton was astounded by the learning of Bello, who knew all the signs of the Zodiac and many of the stars by their Arabic names, and was familiar with the names of some of the ancient sects such as the Nestorians and the Socinians.[5]

Largely as a result of the activities of Ritchie and Lyon in Fezzan, the fame of the medical skill of British travellers had long preceded Oudney and his colleagues. This is borne out by the fact that wherever they passed they found people lined up to consult them on all

[1] C.O. 2/13, Oudney to Horton, 14 July 1823; C.O. 2/13, Denham to Horton, 1 June 1825; Clapperton, op. cit., p. 49.
[2] F.O. 76/17, Toole to Warrington, 8 Oct. 1823, encl. in Warrington to Horton, 7 Nov. 1823.
[3] Clapperton, op. cit., p. 55.
[4] Ibid., p. 47.
[5] Ibid., p. 85.

sorts of ailments. On their way from Fezzan to Ghat, for instance, Oudney and Clapperton found their tent surrounded by many sick people, 'the female part forming the majority'.[1] Two months after their arrival in Bornu, Oudney reported that he had patients from all quarters as long as he was able to attend to them.[2] In Sokoto, Bello expressed his disappointment on hearing of the death of Oudney, for he was particularly anxious to see 'an English physician who might instruct his people in the healing art'.[3]

Other technical skills and activities of the travellers also enhanced their prestige. For instance, Belford had made a carriage for the Governor of Fezzan. As usual, news of this spread into the interior, and soon after their arrival the Sheikh of Bornu asked his visitors to make a similar one for him. Hillman was ready to oblige and he constructed for the Sheikh not only a carriage but also some chairs, to his unspeakable delight.[4] But the people of the interior were impressed most of all by the firework displays and the effectiveness of the travellers' guns. The mission had a good supply of rockets, and first let off some in Fezzan. The effect was to throw the whole town into confusion. The Premier rushed into the house of the travellers, exclaiming that 'death was come upon Fezzan for the stars were falling . . .'.[5] In Bornu it became the favourite pastime of the Sheikh to fire rockets before his most recalcitrant subjects to show them 'the effect of these terrible fire-engines'. The fame of the rockets spread throughout the Sudan, and both the Governor of Katagum and Bello himself asked Clapperton about those he had given the Sheikh.[6]

Similarly, the presents liberally lavished on the chiefs impressed them with the material benefits they would derive from connexion with the British. For instance, a very handsome sword was sent to Hateeta, a Tuareg chief of Ghat, in appreciation of his kind attentions to Lyon.[7] This chief felt so highly honoured and so proud that he remained ever after a supporter of the British. He escorted Oudney and Clapperton from Fezzan to Ghat, and later received Laing with

[1] Denham, op. cit., pp. liv–lv; Clapperton, op. cit., p. 23.
[2] F.O. 76/17, Oudney to Warrington, 1 Apr. 1823, encl. in Warrington to Horton, 17 July 1823.
[3] Clapperton, op. cit., p. 84.
[4] Denham, op. cit., pp. 81–82, 201.
[5] C.O. 2/13, Denham to Bathurst, 4 May 1822.
[6] Clapperton, op. cit., pp. 30, 93.
[7] Lyon, op. cit., p. 293; C.O., Denham to Bathurst, 1 Apr. 1822.

every hospitality in Ghadames and conducted him to Tuat. As a consequence, he became known in Ghat as 'the friend of the English' a title which he bore even as late as 1850, when Richardson and Barth visited that town.[1] Again, when Tyrwhitt arrived at Kuka with the rockets, pistols, and watches which the travellers had promised the Sheikh, he commented:

There are no friends like these; they are all truth; and I see, by the Book, that if the Prophet had lived only a short time longer, they would have been all Moslem.[2]

Ridiculous as this is, it nevertheless provides evidence of how high the reputation of the English for honesty was at the court of the Sheikh. This impression was not confined to Bornu. In Kano the Arab merchants were ready to accept Clapperton's bill on the consul in Tripoli for any supply of goods or money.[3] In southern Fezzan, a Tibu trader who was returning to his own country readily offered to sell some dates to Denham and asked him to leave the money with the Caid (judge) at Murzuk. 'I know who the English are,' he told Denham, who was much surprised, 'are they not almost Moslem and people of one word?'

It is clear that the main effect of the mission's activities in Africa was to make the name and prestige of England known to some extent in the Sahara and the Sudan. It is not surprising that the travellers brought back letters from the rulers of Bornu and Sokoto expressing their anxiety to establish firm contacts with the English.[4] In addition to his letter, the Sheikh also sent the King of England a handsome horse, four parrots, two ostrich bones, and some specimens of dresses and manufactures of Bornu.[5]

No less noticeable was the impact of the mission's discoveries on the people of England. Readers of the accounts of the mission must have become convinced that far from being in a state of nudity, savagery, and barbarism, most of the peoples of Bornu and Hausaland were decently clothed and generally expert in the arts of weaving and dyeing, and that some of them were well versed in history and Islamic law and theology. The report of horsemen in coats of mail

[1] Henry Barth, *Travels and Discoveries in North and Central Africa* (1857), vol. i, pp. 194-5. See below, p. 187.
[2] Denham, op. cit., p. 254.
[3] Clapperton, p. 44.
[4] The letters are printed in Clapperton, pp. 139-41.
[5] C.O. 2/13, Denham to Horton, 1 June 1825; Clapperton, op. cit., p. 54.

and iron helmets manufactured in the Sudan must have shaken to their foundations the notions entertained by thousands of European readers concerning the military ability and technical skill of some of the Sudanese peoples.

Though Oudney did not live long enough to submit a report on the commercial side of the mission, the information provided by the other travellers also convinced the commercially minded that the natives were already familiar with European goods. In Kano, Clapperton bought an English cotton umbrella, 'an article he little expected to meet with, yet by no means uncommon'.[1] He also saw in the markets of Sokoto and Kano copper and pewter dishes with English stamps, pieces of linen bearing American stamps, coarse muslin, and some painted Manchester cottons. These goods were believed to have been brought from the Atlantic coast.[2] The great demand in the interior for arms of all kinds was also emphasized. In return for these, English traders could obtain any quantity of ostrich feathers, ivory, gum arabic, raw hides, and indigo.[3] Both Clapperton and Denham also emphasized the facility with which Bornu and Sudan could be reached from the Guinea coast and the strategic importance of Bello's dominions. The Fulani Empire, according to Clapperton, possessed 'advantages over every other part of the interior of Africa for carrying on trade with Great Britain not by the long and tedious route over the deserts of Northern Africa, but by the short route from the Bight of Benin which is only ten days' journey to Raca, one day to Nyffi (Nupe) and twelve days farther to Socatoo (Sokoto)'.[4] The long-cherished hopes of exploiting the commercial potentialities of the interior were thus once again strengthened.

But while the discoveries of the expedition generated feelings of profound optimism in the commercial world, they only confounded the geographical world over the Niger issue, since each traveller came to a different conclusion. After the exploration of the Shari and the Yobe, both of which terminated in the Chad, Oudney became convinced that the Niger could terminate only 'in the lakes at Nyffe'. Indeed, it was with a view to visiting Nupe that he went on

[1] Clapperton, op. cit., pp. 54–55.
[2] C.O. 2/13, Clapperton to Horton, 6 June 1825.
[3] C.O. 2/13, Denham to Horton, 1 June 1825.
[4] C.O. 2/13, Clapperton to Horton, 6 June 1825. Raca was about thirty miles above Raba and was destroyed during the Fulani–Nupe wars between 1825 and 1830.

the journey to the Fulani Empire.[1] Having persuaded himself that the Chad could have no outlet eastwards, Denham came to the negative conclusion that 'no river could be found to run across the continent from west to east, at least not north of the equator'.[2] From oral evidence he collected from the natives, however, he seemed to have been inclined to the Niger–Nile theory, though he supposed that the Niger passed farther south of Bagirmi. Warrington, who subscribed to this view, suggested Latitude 10° N. as the possible line along which the Niger flowed to join the Nile.[3] From the information collected in Kano and Sokoto, in particular from Bello and the Arabs, Clapperton associated himself with the Niger–Benin theory advanced by Reichard, the German geographer, in 1808 and re-iterated by James McQueen, a West Indian planter and arm-chair geographer, in 1821.[4] The *Edinburgh Review* supported Oudney's theory, while the *Quarterly Review* and Barrow accepted Denham's.[5] The result of these conflicting views was to bring the Niger question once more into the limelight.

If the discoveries of the mission stimulated merchants and con-founded geographers, they also agitated the Colonial Office and the humanitarians about the slave trade and its abolition, which had been mentioned for the first time in the correspondence between Ritchie and Lyon and the Colonial Office. The arrival of these explorers in Tripoli in 1818 had coincided with the return of the Governor of Fezzan from his first *razzia* (slave raiding expedition) into the interior. Ritchie became convinced that their six months' delay in Tripoli was owing to the Pasha's fear of the wave of hostility and vindictiveness set in motion in the interior by the *razzia*. He therefore suggested that, to open the road into the interior, Britain should become a mediator between the Pasha and the persecuted people of the Sudan. Not only would this end the slave trade, he argued, but the travellers could advance under the safe shield of such a title into the very centre of the country. He pointed out, however, that the Pasha would expect some compensation, as that traffic constituted

[1] C.O. 2/13, Oudney to Horton, 14 July 1823; F.O. 76/17, Oudney to Warrington, 15 May 1823, encl. in Warrington to Horton, 2 Aug. 1823.

[2] C.O. 2/13, Denham to Clapperton, 15 May 1823.

[3] Denham, op. cit., pp. 145, 179–80; F.O. 76/17, Warrington to Oudney, 1 Aug. 1823, encl. in Warrington to Horton, 2 Aug. 1823.

[4] Clapperton, op. cit., pp. 42, 76–77, 87, 89, 96; J. McQueen, *A Geographical and Commercial View of Northern Central Africa* (1821), pp. 2, 54, 92.

[5] *Edinburgh Review*, vol. 44, pp. 211–13; *Quarterly Review*, vol. 33, pp. 469–71; C.O. 2/13, Barrow to Horton, 11 Nov. 1823.

his main source of income.[1] Ritchie was a scientist, not a humanitarian, and his interest in abolition arose from his conviction that as
long as the raids for slaves continued, no exploration could be done
in Africa along the line of Tripoli and the Sahara. He informed
Warrington that 'if peace and good harmony would be kept up, the
road to the Guinea will be as clear as the road from London to
Edinburgh', whereas if slave raiding continued, 'the door to the interior would be shut to Europeans forever'.[2] Warrington had already
drawn the attention of the Colonial Office to the same point himself,[3]
and he therefore warmly supported Ritchie. He pleaded that the
Pasha should be prevailed upon, if not to abolish the trade entirely,
at least to suspend it for five years.[4]

The Colonial Office's reaction to this was immediate and encouraging. The suggestion of financial compensation was welcomed.
Bathurst informed Ritchie that

The abolition of the slave trade in the northern part of Africa is an object
which His Majesty's Government have so much at heart, that if its continuance in any case depends upon its being looked to as a source of
revenue, you may consider yourself at liberty, if other proposals should
fail of effect, to offer on the part of the Prince Regent a pecuniary compensation to a limited extent, as the price of its utter and effectual abolition.[5]

This compensation was to be paid by annual instalments over a
period of eight or ten years. It is evident from this that the Government was beginning to evince some interest in the trans-Saharan
traffic in slaves, which had hitherto been entirely neglected. In fact
Ritchie was asked to ascertain what the attitude of the ruling powers
in the interior would be to the idea of Britain becoming a mediator
between them and Tripoli, and to collect information about the
extent of that traffic. This interest was, however, a mere momentary
whim, for though Warrington succeeded in persuading the Pasha to
discontinue the trade for the annual payment of £2,000, the Colonial
Office did not even comment on this arrangement. The minute which
this very important letter received was simply 'Put by'.[6]

[1] C.O. 2/9, Ritchie to Bathurst, 29 Nov. 1818; Ritchie to Goulburn, 10 May
1819.
[2] C.O. 2/8, Ritchie to Warrington, 20 Oct. 1819.
[3] F.O. 76/12, Warrington to Bathurst, 9 Oct. 1818.
[4] F.O. 76/13, Warrington to Bathurst, 28 Dec. 1819.
[5] C.O. 2/8, Bathurst to Ritchie, 10 Aug. 1819.
[6] F.O. 76/14, Warrington to Bathurst, 30 May 1820. For Warrington's later
role in the attack on the trans-Saharan slave trade, see Chapters VI and VII.

After the death of Ritchie, Lyon revived the question. In a long dispatch after his return from Fezzan to Tripoli, he emphasized the evil effects of the raids and mentioned the intention of the Governor of Fezzan to conquer Bornu. He very strongly pleaded that the campaign be stopped through the Pasha. Once the Governor was established in the interior, he argued, 'Sudan would be lost forever to the promoter of freedom'. He continued rather passionately:

The whole of the negro country is open to any peaceful man or men. The produce of Sudan is sufficient to enrich its inhabitants if they were stimulated to industry by finding the sale of their slaves was put a stop to in Barbary. Gold, elephant teeth, senna, fine cloths and excellently prepared leathers were very cheap. . . . Sudan is considered as a healthy country and even should it prove otherwise, a death there, in the cause of suffering humanity is enviable. I am a young man, my Lord, and perhaps presumptuous in thus forcing myself on your Lordship's notice—but I have seen so much of this detestable traffic in slaves now carried on that I will (should I be permitted) devote the remainder of my days to the cause of freedom. . . .[1]

These were indeed inspiring and noble sentiments. But what were their effects? Though Lyon was permitted—in fact solicited—to go back to Africa, yet, as we have seen, he refused for the simple reason that his application for promotion had been turned down. His humanitarian ardour would seem to have evaporated in the hot climate of the Mediterranean. And there is no evidence that the Colonial Office was moved. The passionate letter was put into cold storage and in the instructions drafted for Lyon no mention was made of the slave trade. Even more significant was the fact that the problem was not mentioned in the very elaborate instructions given to Denham and Oudney. It is true that the slave question was raised in the correspondence between these travellers and the Colonial Office. But in the five years that the mission stayed in Africa the Colonial Office referred to it in only two dispatches—in April 1822 and October 1823. On both occasions Oudney and his group were instructed merely to abstain 'most cautiously from any act which might bear the remotest construction of your approbation of the proceedings so revolting to humanity'.[2] The Colonial Office had certainly not seen any connexion between the exploration of Africa and the abolition of the slave trade.

[1] C.O. 2/9, Lyon to Bathurst, 25 Mar. 1820.
[2] F.O. 8/8, Horton to Oudney, 22 Apr. 1822; F.O. 8/8, Horton to Denham, 9 Oct. 1823.

Nevertheless, Denham and his colleagues did not shut their eyes to the problem. By coming into contact with the grim facts of the traffic, which will be discussed later,[1] and by becoming convinced that no commerce could thrive there without its suppression, they (like Lyon) became converts to the cause of abolition. It is therefore not surprising to find them submitting both accounts of the traffic and recommendations for its suppression.

Their eighteen months' stay in Bornu, the greatest source for slaves sent across the Sahara, enabled the travellers to make a detailed study of the traffic. Denham informed the Colonial Office of the disgust with which the Sheikh and people of Bornu carried on that particular trade. But it could not be abandoned, because the Moorish traders would not accept any mode of payment for their goods except slaves. According to Denham, the Sheikh admitted the inhumanity of the trade and even pointed out that it was against the tenets of Islam. 'But what are we to do?' the Sheikh is reported to have asked helplessly: 'the Arabs who come here will have nothing else but slaves. Why don't you send us your merchants? You know us now, and let them bring their women with them and live amongst us, and teach us what you talk to me about so often, to make boats, build houses and make rockets also.'[2] Denham also commented on the richness of the country in ivory, ostrich feathers, and indigo, which could be easily exchanged for any goods exported to Bornu.

In Sokoto Clapperton also discussed this very question on several occasions with Sultan Bello. When the Sultan asked him at one of their interviews what he could give in return for the presents sent him by the British Government, Clapperton replied that the most acceptable service would be to co-operate with the British in ending the slave trade. Impressed by Clapperton's arguments of the benefits he would derive from a strong commercial and political link with Britain, Bello promised to abolish the trade in his dominions.[3] Clapperton entertained no doubts at all about Bello's sincerity. He reported on his arrival in England:

I am thoroughly convinced that he is sincere in his wishes for a friendly footing with England. Indeed, I cannot speak too highly of this excellent man, whom, should he live, and the Government here feel disposed to cherish a friendly relation with him, would be able, with very little assis-

[1] See pp. 120–2, 128–9.
[2] C.O. 2/13, Denham to Horton, 1 June 1825.
[3] Clapperton, op. cit., pp. 84–90, 105–6.

tance from us, to put an end to that detestable traffic in slaves, by opening to him a free and uninterrupted passage to the sea-coast, from which he is now no more than ten days.[1]

It is clear, then, that both Denham and Clapperton independently hit on the same remedy. It was only by the establishment of commercial contacts with the people of the interior and by supplying their needs in exchange for their indigo, ivory, gum, and ostrich feathers that the traffic in slaves could be extirpated.

The idea of developing legitimate commerce in Africa was nothing new. The 'Saints', and in particular Clarkson and Wilberforce, had always advocated it. The African Institution had it as its cardinal aim. However, neither the 'Saints' nor the Institution saw the promotion of legitimate commerce as a means of overthrowing the slave trade. To them, this, as well as the spread of Christianity and the promotion of civilization, were meant to atone for the sins which had been committed against Africa. Indeed, until the 1820's, naval patrols and treaties granting right of search were the remedy for the slave trade generally accepted by the Government and the abolitionists. This is quite conclusively proved by the fact that the African Institution concentrated on the parliaments of Europe rather than on the farms of Africa.

The person who appears first to have seen the development of legitimate commerce as the only effective means of overthrowing slavery and the slave trade was James McQueen. In the three memoranda which he submitted to the Government in July 1820 and elaborated and published in the following year,[2] McQueen did not only express his view that the Niger flowed into the Bight of Benin. He also dwelt on the density of the population and the fertility of the regions up the Niger, the volume and value of the commerce carried on between those regions and Barbary via Kano, Timbuctu, and the Sahara, and the ease with which this could be diverted to the west coast. Furthermore, he contended that naval patrols and equipment treaties were all 'a waste of time and means' and that the only effective way of abolishing the slave trade was to teach the African chiefs and slave traders that they might be rich without selling men and that 'it is in the labour and industry of the population and in the cultivation of the soil that true wealth exists'. He then suggested the formation of

[1] C.O. 2/13, Clapperton to Horton, 6 Jan. 1825.
[2] C.O. 267/52, Memoranda to H.M.'s Ministers by James McQueen, 31 July 1820. McQueen, op. cit.

a joint-stock company which would monopolize the trade up the Niger, and the establishment of military posts which would protect the company's agents.

McQueen's theory of the termination of the Niger was ridiculed by scholars of the day and his plans were rejected by the British Government.[1] So firmly was the Government's policy of abolishing the slave trade geared to abolition treaties and naval squadrons that although such treaties were concluded between 1808 and 1825 with Holland, Sweden, France, and Spain, and although the number of ships in the squadron was increased,[2] no mention was made of the abolition of the slave trade in the instructions issued to explorers sent into the interior of Africa.

Denham and Clapperton's suggestions, however, did not suffer the same fate as those of Warrington, Ritchie, and McQueen. On the eve of his second expedition, Clapperton was asked, *inter alia*,[3] to impress on Bello's mind 'the great advantages he will derive by putting a total stop to the sale of slaves to Christian merchants through native slave dealers on or near the coast, and by preventing other African powers from marching caravans of slaves through his dominions . . . the happy results of his co-operation will cause him to be ranked among the benefactors of mankind'. Clapperton was to emphasize that English merchants would bring all the articles of merchandise that the Sultan and his people would require in exchange for such as they produced. Clapperton was also specifically ordered to ascertain in what manner and from what parts of the country slaves were obtained. Finally he was to consider and report 'what measures may appear most advisable for putting a stop or at least materially checking this inhuman traffic, not only in those districts under the control of the Sultan, but also in those parts from which the trade is chiefly supplied with victims'.

This was the first time that the attention of a European explorer of the African interior was so clearly drawn to the burning question of the slave trade and its abolition. If previously this had not been among the motives underlying the drive into the interior, from now on it became one of the most important of them. From the second Clapperton expedition, African exploration was undertaken not merely to satisfy scientific, geographical, and commercial curiosity,

---

[1] C.O. 267/52, McQueen to Bathurst, 14 Aug. 1820.
[2] C. Lloyd, *The Navy and the Slave Trade* (London, 1949), pp. 44–45.
[3] See Chapter IV, pp. 76–77.

but also to prevent the inhuman traffic in slaves. It is clear, therefore, that the application of the theory of legitimate commerce in the
interior was certainly not the cause but rather the effect of the exploration of Africa begun in 1788. In this sense, the Oudney–Denham–
Clapperton expedition of 1821–5 was an important turning point in
the history of British penetration into the interior. It marks the end
of the phase when scientific and commercial interests were the sole
considerations and heralds the era when they become inextricably
mixed with humanitarian questions.

In the history of the exploration of the African hinterland, the
period 1818 to 1825 was particularly productive. It is true that the old
problem of the Niger was still as tantalizing and as much of a chal-
lenge as it was in the days of Ptolemy or Al-Idrisi. Nevertheless this
should not tarnish much the brilliance of the success attained. Large
areas of the Sahara and the Sudan were explored for the first time by
Europeans. A number of traditional myths such as those about the
instinctive hatred of the Muslim in the interior for the Christian
visitor were exploded. The security of the routes, wherever the co-
operation and protection of the ruler were obtained, was amply
demonstrated. For the first time in the nineteenth century Europeans
lived and moved freely among the people of the Sahara and the
Sudan. Letters from potentates in these areas arrived at the Court of
St. James's. Impressed by the skill, the medical attention, the display
of guns and fireworks, and the exotic presents of these travellers, the
Africans had become alive to the value of establishing links with the
British. It is significant that requests for envoys, doctors, merchants,
shipbuilders, and carpenters were made. On the solicitation of the
Sheikh of Bornu, and pending the approval of the British Government, Tyrwhitt was in fact left as the vice-consul at the Court of
Kukawa. On the whole the activities of the travellers laid a very firm
foundation for the establishment of permanent relations with some
of the empires of the western Sudan. But would the British Government sanction Tyrwhitt's post? Were the requests of the rulers going
to be met? In short, was an edifice of lasting relations to be built on
the foundations laid by Denham, Oudney, and Clapperton? For the
answers to these questions we must turn to the next chapter.

CHAPTER IV

Sokoto, Timbuctu, and the Niger, 1825-41

THE achievements of the expedition of 1821–5 were soon followed by measures calculated to strengthen the links already forged with the rulers in the interior and extend British sphere of influence even further. The first of these measures was the immediate confirmation of Tyrwhitt's appointment as vice-consul in Bornu, a post to which a salary of £300 was attached. The vice-consul's main task was to cultivate the friendship of the Sheikh and to increase British prestige and influence.[1] Moreover, two months after the return of the mission, Warrington was given specific instructions about his relations with the African merchants and others who might come from Bornu and Hausaland to Tripoli:

You will on the arrival of such merchants show them such civilities as may induce them to form a favourable opinion of the British character, pointing out to them at the same time the advantages which are likely to accrue to their country and themselves between England and the kingdoms in the interior of Africa.[2]

In the same spirit, Denham was asked by the Government in October 1825 to defer till the spring the repatriation of the Mandara boy whom he had brought with him to England, so that he might still further improve his education and increase his acquaintance with England.[3] Finally, the Government actually dispatched two expeditions to the interior, one led by Commander Clapperton, the other by Major Gordon Laing.

A week after his return to England, Clapperton had informed the Colonial Office of Bello's promise to send messengers down to the Guinea coast in July 1825 to conduct him to Sokoto. He therefore asked to be sent back as soon as possible to conclude anti-slave-trade

[1] C.O. 392/3, Horton to Tyrwhitt, 3 May 1825, encl. in Horton to Warrington, 4 May 1825.
[2] C.O. 2/19, Hay to Warrington, 22 July 1825.
[3] C.O. 2/13, Denham to Colonial Office, 5 Oct. 1825, and minute. The boy was retained in England till October 1826, but what happened to him after that date could not be traced.

and commercial treaties with Bello and to promote further geographical explorations.[1] The Colonial Office responded favourably to
this request and got the Treasury to sanction an allocation for it
immediately. To meet the requests of the Sheikh of Bornu and Sultan
Bello, Clapperton was also supplied with 2 light field pieces, 4 barrels
of gunpowder, 24 muskets, 4 fowling pieces, 4 pairs of pistols, 2
double-barrelled guns, 3 swords of African pattern, 100 yards each
of scarlet cotton, silk, blue cloth, coarse muslin, and satin silk, 12
large scarves or shawls of various colours, 3 large umbrellas, candles,
and medicines.[2]

On 30 July 1825 Clapperton was given his instructions.[3] The first,
and indeed the most important, task assigned to him was to conclude
a treaty with Sultan Bello to overthrow the slave trade by the development of legitimate commerce. His second task was geographical. His
attention was to be particularly concentrated on the Niger, which he
was to follow to its termination. He was also to make inquiries about,
and if possible ascertain the sources of, the numerous rivers that
emptied into the Bights of Benin and Biafra, their navigability, and
the type of vessels required. Objects of natural history as well as
specimens of economic metals, manufactures, and other products
were also to be collected.

In addition to these instructions, Clapperton was given letters
addressed to the Sultan of Sokoto and the Sheikh of Bornu.[4] In the
letter to Bello, the British Government emphasized their anxiety to
put an end to the traffic in slaves. They described his promise to co-
operate in this task as 'the fore-runner of peace and happiness to the
inhabitants of Africa', and pointed out the ease with which the commodities obtained from the Arabs in exchange for human beings
could be supplied by British merchants in return for the many
articles which his people produced. In the letter to the Sheikh of
Bornu, the Government's gratitude for his kind treatment of Denham
and his group was expressed. The Sheikh was further informed that
as a proof of 'His Majesty's desire of evincing his great regard and of
continuing that friendly intercourse so happily established', an
officer was being sent to inquire after his health and welfare and to
present him with 'a few articles as specimens of arts and manufactures

[1] C.O. 2/13, Clapperton to Horton, 7 June 1825.
[2] C.O. 2/13, Hay to Tyrwhitt, 21 July 1825.
[3] C.O. 2/13, Instructions to Clapperton, Bathurst to Clapperton, 30 July 1825.
[4] C.O. 392/3, His Majesty to Sheikh Ben Muhammad al-Kānami; another to
Sultan Bello, both dated 30 July 1825.

of [His Majesty's] kingdom, with which and many others of various kinds the merchants of his country would always be ready to supply those of Bornu, in return for its articles of produce, provided a safe road could be opened with the sea coast.'

The mission was to consist of Clapperton, the leader; Captain Pearce, R.N., his next-in-command; Dr. Dickson and Dr. Morrison, surgeons and naturalists; Richard Lander, Clapperton's personal attendant; and Columbus, a West Indian who attended on Denham in Bornu.[1] On their arrival in the interior, Captain Pearce, Dr. Morrison, and Columbus were to continue to Bornu with the letter and presents for the Sheikh, and later to explore the eastern shores of the Chad and the regions south of Bornu. Tyrwhitt, the vice-consul in Bornu, was told to acquaint the Sheikh with the impending visit of the expedition and to assist Pearce and his colleagues in every way.[2] On the eventual withdrawal of the mission, Pearce and Dickson were to be left behind at Sokoto as consul and surgeon to the Sultan. The consul was subsequently to concert with the agents of the Sultan such measures as might put a stop to 'the passage of slaves from Houssa and other provinces of the Felatah nation to the sea coast'.

The British Government's increased diplomatic and commercial penetration of the African interior was even extended westwards from Bornu and Hausaland to Timbuctu, as signified by the dispatch of Laing to that mysterious city. Though Warrington suggested as early as March 1822 that the British Government should take advantage of the good disposition of the Pasha to send out a mission to explore 'the whole country in the south-west direction',[3] nothing was done until news of the successful establishment of the Oudney–Denham expedition in Bornu reached England. Referring to the smallness of the expenses incurred by the expedition during its journey into Bornu, Barrow urged Lord Bathurst to 'allow Captain Laing to go with the caravan to Tombuctoo then turn easterly and make for Burnou, as a point d'appui.'[4]

Laing was not a stranger to that continent, and the desire to go to Timbuctu had been haunting him since 1821. In that year, while he was serving in Sierra Leone as a Lieutenant in the West Indian Regiment, he had applied to the then Acting Governor of Sierra Leone to

[1] Instructions to Clapperton. Richard Lander, *Records of Captain Clapperton's last expedition to Africa* (1830), vol. 1, pp. 15–16.

[2] C.O. 2/13, Hay to Tyrwhitt, 21 July 1825.

[3] C.O. 76/16, Warrington to Bathurst, 14 Mar. 1822.

[4] C.O. 2/14, Barrow to Horton, 11 Nov. 1823.

be allowed to 'penetrate into the interior of Africa as far as Tombuctoo [Timbuctu] by way of Teembo'.¹ This application was forwarded
to the Colonial Office. It was, however, turned down on the grounds
that Gray was already employed in 'a similar service' and Oudney
had already been selected to push into the interior via the northern
coast.² In November 1822 Laing was sent by MacCarthy, then
Governor of Sierra Leone, on a diplomatic mission into the interior
'to spread a knowledge of this Colony among the natives and to
promote commerce and peace and union among all the tribes'.³ He
successfully accomplished this mission, pushed as far north as
Falaba (Lat. 10° N.), and explored the sources of the Niger. This
exploration only raised to its maximum pitch his desire to go to
Timbuctu and to follow the river to its termination. MacCarthy encouraged Laing and strongly recommended him to the Colonial
Office.⁴ However, the attack on the Fantis by the Ashantis in 1823
drew both MacCarthy and Laing to the Gold Coast. Laing was
stationed at Anomabu, which he successfully defended against the
invading forces.⁵ After the war, in which MacCarthy met his death,
Laing returned to England. Barrow's suggestion shows quite conclusively that soon after his arrival Laing approached the Government again about a trip to the interior.

The offer of Hateeta, the Tuareg chief, to conduct any British
explorers through Ghadames to Tuat and to answer 'with his head'
for their safety⁶ won over Bathurst, the Colonial Secretary. After
expressing his reliance on the assurances which Warrington had conveyed of Hateeta's fidelity, the Colonial Secretary asked the Consul-
General to induce Hateeta to remain in Tripoli until the arrival of 'an
experienced officer whom I intend shortly to dispatch to Africa for
the purpose of proceeding direct to Timbuctoo'.⁷ Immediate measures
were taken to send off Laing. To give him respect and dignity com-

---

¹ C.O. 267/53, Laing to Grant, 5 Mar. 1821, encl. in Grant to Bathurst, 4 Apr.
1821.
² C.O. 268/19, Bathurst to Grant, 20 Aug. 1821.
³ C.O. 267/56, MacCarthy to Bathurst, 8 Nov. 1822.
⁴ C.O. 267/58, MacCarthy to Bathurst, 12 Apr. 1823. Laing published the
account of his mission in 1825 under the title, *Travels in the Temanee, Kooranko
and Soolemana countries of West Africa.*
⁵ C.O. 267/58, Laing to MacCarthy, 11 Apr. 1823, encl. in MacCarthy to
Bathurst, Cape Coast, 12 Apr. 1823. Undoubtedly it was while he was serving at
Anomabu that he heard of the Volta, and this ultimately led him to his hypothesis
of the identity of the Volta and the Niger.
⁶ F.O. 76/18, Warrington to Horton, 12 Aug. 1824.
⁷ C.O. 8/8, Bathurst to Warrington, 6 Dec. 1824.

mensurate with the importance of the mission which he was about to undertake, Laing was promoted from lieutenant to major on 13 January 1825. A week later his instructions were drawn up.

As these instructions were prepared five months before the return of Denham and Clapperton, they reveal the same old scientific and commercial motives. His first and most important target was of course Timbuctu, where he was to stay and gather as much information as possible respecting the manners, customs, resources, and trade of its inhabitants. He was to find out 'particularly whether there appears to be any channel afforded for the extension of our commerce from any part of the coast'.[1] Having accomplished this, he was to advance eastwards to Sokoto to meet Denham's party. If he failed to fall in with them, he was to push on into Bornu, explore the Shari, and return to England via the Nile and Egypt. With these instructions Laing left England in February 1825.

It is clear from the confirmation of Tyrwhitt's post, the instructions to Warrington about the treatment of the people from Bornu and Sudan, and the sending out of Laing and Clapperton, that the Government did promptly follow up the progress made by Denham and Clapperton. Five months after Laing's departure for Tripoli, Clapperton and his associates began their advance from Badagry on the west coast, and it was confidently hoped that both parties would meet at the Court of the Sultan of Sokoto.[2] Certainly a vice-consul in Bornu, a consul and a surgeon in Sokoto, an agent in Timbuctu, and a free and regular intercourse with these regions by means of the Niger, would have brought much benefit, commercial and humanitarian, and might even have fundamentally altered the course of history in these areas. However these hopes were never fulfilled. For, in spite of the well-meaning efforts of the Government, no English envoy set foot in Bornu or Sokoto from 1827 till 1851, nor were any consuls, doctors, or merchants seen in these regions until after 1860. The reasons for the failure of this very vigorous drive into the interior were the death of Tyrwhitt, the disappointing outcome of both Clapperton's and Laing's missions, and finally the unsuccessful attempts made to use the Niger as a commercial highway after the discovery of its mouth.

Had the British vice-consular post in Bornu continued to exist,

---

[1] F.O. 392/3, Instructions to Laing, 20 Jan. 1825.
[2] F.O. 76/19, Warrington to Bathurst, 22 June 1825; Royal Society (R.S.) 374 (La)/87, Warrington to Laing, 27 July 1825.

contacts with Bornu would undoubtedly have been maintained. Unfortunately Tyrwhitt died of fever in November 1824, three months after the departure of Denham and Clapperton.[1] Rumours of his death reached Tripoli in June 1825 and were confirmed by a letter from Al-Kānami two months later. As the news arrived in Britain three months after the departure of Clapperton's second mission, it was hoped that either Dr. Morrison or Columbus could fill the vacant post.

Here again the course of events frustrated expectations. Of Clapperton's party of six, only Clapperton himself and his personal assistant, Lander, survived the march from Badagry to Kano. Columbus died in Badagry, and Pearce and Morrison succumbed to fever on the same day—27 December 1825—a month after the mission had left Badagry.[2] As all members of the Bornu branch of the mission had perished, Clapperton planned to go first to Sokoto and Timbuctu and then recross Hausaland to Bornu and Adamawa.[3] But he got only as far as Sokoto, where he died of fever on 31 April 1827 without having concluded any treaty with Bello or having been allowed to proceed to Bornu. Lander left Sokoto a month after his master's death and managed to arrive at Badagry in November 1827 and at Portsmouth in April 1828. Though Lander twice crossed the Niger, its termination remained as enigmatic as before.

For the failure of this mission and for Clapperton's death, modern historians have blamed Bello. It has been repeatedly asserted by Brown, Bovill, Simmons, and Plumb that it was the cold reception given to Clapperton, coupled with Bello's refusal to honour his own promise to sign the anti-slave-trade treaty, that dispirited Clapperton and rendered him an easy victim to the fever by which he was attacked.[4] Bello is thus made to appear as a scoundrel or a barbarian who did not know the meaning of a promise. This assessment of Bello's character is not borne out by the available evidence.

In the first place, there is no evidence to support either Bovill's view that Clapperton was given a 'cold reception' or Plumb's conten-

[1] F.O. 76/19, Warrington to Horton, 20 Aug. 1825.
[2] Lander, op. cit., vol. 1, pp. 78–80; C.O. 2/15, Clapperton to Hay, 28 Dec. 1825.
[3] C.O. 2/15, Clapperton to Hay, 29 Feb. 1826.
[4] R. Brown, *The Story of Africa and its Explorers* (London, 1892–5), vol. 1, p. 250; Jack Simmons, *African Discovery* (London, 1948), p. 26; C. Howard and J. H. Plumb, *West African Explorers* (1951), p. 16; E. W. Bovill, *The Golden Trade of the Moors* (1958), p. 214.

tion that Clapperton found at Sokoto 'hostility instead of friendship'. On the contrary, in the first letter he wrote to Lander, whom he had left at Kano, Clapperton informed him that the Sultan 'appeared glad to see me and welcomed me to his country with the utmost cordiality'.[1]

Secondly, Bello's failure to sign the treaty was due neither to the intrigues of the Arab merchants, as Lander contended and some modern historians have too readily accepted,[2] nor to sheer caprice. It is true that the Arabs intrigued against the explorers. But Clapperton informed Lander that Bello did not 'altogether relish their counsel and . . . judges correctly of the falsehood practised to serve their own ends'.[3] The Sultan's change of front was caused partly by Sokoto–Bornu relations and partly by the conduct of Clapperton. Though relations between Sokoto and Bornu were exceedingly friendly during Clapperton's first mission, they had deteriorated by the time of his second. Indeed the Sheikh of Bornu had begun an invasion of the Sokoto Empire and had inflicted a severe defeat on the forces of Katagum and Bauchi when Clapperton entered Kano for the second time.[4] A few days after the departure of the explorers for Sokoto, the Bornu army besieged Kano. Unfortunately, in examining the presents for the Sheikh, Bello discovered, among other things, guns and pistols. With news of the invasion and siege of Kano still trickling in, the surprising fact is not that Bello should have confiscated the presents and forbidden the travellers from going to Bornu, but that for the greater part of their stay in Sokoto he should have been so friendly, and so helpful to Lander after Clapperton's death. It is interesting to note that Clapperton himself realized that the Bornu invasion was the main impediment to his progress. 'This cursed Bornu war,' he informed Lander, 'has overturned all my plans and intentions, and set the minds of the people generally against me, as it is pretty well understood by both rich and poor that I have presents for their enemy the Sheikh. I wish, with all my heart, it was ended; no matter whether the Felatah or Bornuese be victorious, so I could pursue my journey.'[5]

But although Clapperton appreciated the trying nature of the

[1] The letter was dated 26 Oct. 1826 and is printed in Lander, op. cit., vol. i, p. 222.
[2] Lander, op. cit., vol. ii, p. 23; Howard and Plumb, op. cit., p. 16.
[3] Ibid., vol. i, p. 225.
[4] Ibid., vol. i, p. 198, vol. ii, p. 63.
[5] Ibid., vol. i, pp. 251–2.

times, he failed to show Bello the sympathy and understanding that he definitely deserved. For instance, when the Sultan sent an officer to demand the presents for the Sheikh, together with—naturally enough—'all arms and ammunition which we should want ourselves', Clapperton completely lost his temper. In spite of the caution of the official and even of the entreaties of Lander himself, Clapperton repeatedly accused Bello and his people of being 'a nation of scoundrels and robbers'.[1] Though these highly insulting words were reported to Bello, he nevertheless sent another messenger to Clapperton to inform him of his intention to write to 'his friend the King of England' to explain his conduct. Clapperton's reply to this was as insolent as ever. He told Bello that his sovereign would not 'even look at the superscription of a letter from Bello after being made acquainted with the dastardly action by which he had so disgraced himself'.[2] There was surely nothing roguish or treacherous about Bello's conduct. No prince would allow ammunition to be conveyed to his enemy. In the unsettled and difficult political conditions with which Bello was confronted, only tact, shrewd diplomacy, and a genuine appreciation of his personal difficulties would have won him over. Probably owing to his ill health and exhaustion, which were apparent even before he left Kano for Sokoto, Clapperton lost the tact and patience which had characterized his conduct during his first visit. In view of the crude and disdainful manner in which he handled the situation, it is not surprising that Bello's warm welcome froze into cold indifference and neglect during the latter part of Clapperton's stay. That tact and diplomacy could have succeeded and that Bello was still well-disposed to the English was shown by the ease with which Lander won him over with the help of a mallam and persuaded him to provide guides to Kano.[3]

Aliyu, the successor of Bello, spoke nothing but the truth when he told Barth twenty years after Clapperton's death that 'the then state of war between Bello and the Sheikh Al-Kānami, the ruler of Bornu, had disturbed their amicable relations with that eminent officer, whom in such a conjuncture they had not felt justified in allowing to proceed on his errand to their enemy'.[4] Yet, in spite of the letter which Bello wrote to the British Government to explain his conduct,

[1] C.O. 2/16, Lander to Bathurst, 27 May 1827; Lander, op. cit., vol. i, pp. 258-9.
[2] Lander, op. cit., vol. i, p. 259.
[3] Ibid., vol. ii, pp. 86-88.
[4] Barth, *Travels*, vol. iv, pp. 134-5; F.O. 101/36, Barth to Clarendon, 3 May 1853.

and Barrow's justifiable conclusion that 'circumstanced as Bello then was, he could not well have acted otherwise than he did',[1] the Government at the time, like many modern historians, attributed the failure of the mission and the death of Clapperton to the Sultan's so called *volte-face*. The result was that all the high esteem in which Bello was held in England vanished overnight, and with it all prospect of an immediate re-establishment of relations with his Court.

This strong though by no means justifiable belief in the unreliability of African rulers seems to have been further confirmed by the fate of Major Laing. Accompanied by Babani, the Governor of Ghadames, whom he had hired on the recommendation of both Warrington and the Pasha as his guide and protector to and from Timbuctu, and with four servants, Laing left Tripoli in July 1825. He reached Ghadames, an important caravan centre 290 miles southwest of Tripoli, in September. Here his party was joined by Hateeta, 'the friend of the English', who conducted them to In Salah, the capital of the fertile oasis of Tuat. The reception which was given to Laing at these two important trading centres provides further evidence of the popularity of the British in the Sahara. The people of Ghadames, according to Laing, 'vied with each other in the continued performance of kind and hospitable acts'.[2] As Laing pointed out, this hospitable and friendly attitude of the people emanated from 'the exalted opinion they had formed of the august sovereign whom I have the honour to serve, and the character of the country to which I have the happiness to belong'.[3] Equally warm was Laing's reception at In Salah. Over a thousand people came out to meet him about a mile from the town. He was asked numerous questions about his rifle and the rockets, 'the fame of which had preceded me'.[4]

Laing had planned to remain at In Salah for only five or six days, but, for reasons to be discussed later, he was forced to stay there for five weeks. Hateeta returned to Ghat, since Laing could not afford to retain him any longer. On 10 January 1826 Laing resumed his south-

[1] C.O. 2/18, Barrow to Hay, 19 Oct. 1829.
[2] C.O. 2/20, Laing to Warrington, 13 Sept. 1825. The continuous flow of presents into their house prompted Jack, one of the servants, to remark that 'this is a fit day to sing Psalms and pray', a remark which inspired Laing to write:
Scarce in Gadamis am I seated,
Sir Jack my prayer book brings:
And says a Christian when well treated
Te Deum always sings.
[3] C.O. 2/15, Notes on Ghadames, encl. in Laing to Horton, 26 Oct. 1825.
[4] R.S. 374/1a/104, Laing to Warrington, 3 Dec. 1825.

ward march. Sixteen days later, two of his servants were killed in an
attack on his caravan, and he himself received about twenty-four
sabre cuts, 'eighteen of which were severe'.[1] He was conveyed on
horseback to the village of the famous learned sheikh and *marabout*
(priest) Sidi Muhammad, the father of Al-Baka'i, who was to be the
saviour of Barth.[2] Though Babani died here shortly after their arrival,
Laing rather miraculously recovered from his severe wounds. On the
eve of his departure in July 1826, however, an epidemic of yellow
fever broke out in the village, and among the large number of
victims were Sidi Muhammad and Laing's remaining servants. Since
the Sheikh had taken considerable interest in Laing's situation and
had promised to forward him to Timbuctu,[3] his death was particularly unfortunate for the mission. Sidi Muhammad was succeeded by
his younger brother, Siki Mukhtar, who kindly allowed Laing to
continue his journey to Timbuctu. Having by now lost all the original
members of his party, Laing took his leave after a long halt of five
months. On 18 August 1826, the very month in which Clapperton
reached Sokoto, Laing entered the mysterious and romantic city of
Timbuctu.[4]

His description of the city was disappointingly brief. He gave only
its size, which he estimated at four miles in circumference, and mentioned the abundance of records in it. The general impression that
the city made on him, however, was favourable, for he informed
Warrington that in every respect except in size, 'it has completely met
my expectation'. This statement, as vague and mysterious as the city
itself, whetted rather than satisfied the curiosity of Laing's contemporaries. The *Edinburgh Review*, for instance, commented that 'this
mention of records suggests a source of information never heard of
before in central Africa'.[5]

Laing did not write to Tripoli or England during the first four
weeks of his stay in Timbuctu. But there was a good reason for this.
He had originally hoped to remain there for at least six months, dur-

[1] F.O. 76/23, Laing to Warrington, 5 Oct. 1826, encl. in Warrington to Murray,
2 Sept. 1828.
[2] See below, pp. 193–5.
[3] F.O. 76/20, Laing to Warrington, 1 July 1826, encl. in Warrington to Bathurst, 4 Nov. 1826.
[4] That Laing accomplished this cannot be doubted, for there is still extant in
the Public Records Office the only letter which he wrote from that city. C.O.
2/20, Laing to Warrington, 21 Sept. 1826. This letter did not reach Tripoli until
August 1828 or England until 2 Oct. 1828.
[5] *Edinburgh Review*, vol. 49, p. 148.

ing which he would explore all the regions to the south and south-west before embarking on the Niger.[1] There was therefore no need to send home incomplete observations. In fact, he stayed there for only four and a half weeks. From the letter which he wrote the day before his departure it is clear that he was compelled to leave the town rather abruptly. Three days later his party was suddenly attacked near Arawan, a caravan trading centre, and he and one of his two servants were killed. The remaining servant managed to escape to Timbuctu, whence he reached Tripoli two years later.[2]

The murder of Laing posed two questions which haunted his con-temporaries and have baffled historians ever since, namely, who was responsible for the attack and ultimately for the murder of Laing, and what happened to his papers? The answer given to the former ques-tion by Warrington in Tripoli and accepted in Britain both by the Government and by the *Quarterly Review* was that the attack on Laing in the desert and his subsequent murder near Timbuctu were planned by the Pasha of Tripoli and his foreign minister, Hassuna D'Ghies.[3] His papers, according to this version, were safely brought to Tripoli but were given to Hassuna D'Ghies, who sold them to the then French consul at Tripoli, Baron Rousseau, 'for a deduction of 40% on a large claim he had, say 60,000 francs, against Hassuna'.[4] By a remarkable coincidence, the French traveller René Caillié re-turned from Timbuctu at the very time when investigations about Laing were going on, and it was generally believed in Tripoli and England that Caillié never set foot in Timbuctu and that the journal that was published under his name was compiled by Rousseau from Laing's papers. That respectable and learned journal the *Quarterly Review* described Caillié's description of Timbuctu as 'so obvious an imposture' and all his observations as 'unworthy of notice'.[5] On the strength of these allegations, the British Government made very strong representations to both the French and Tripolitanian Govern-ments. In the good old fashion of 'gun-boat' diplomacy, the letter to the Pasha was sent on a ship-of-war and Warrington was instructed

[1] R.S. 374 (La)/112, Laing to Sabine, 1 Jan. 1826.

[2] F.O. 76/23, Warrington to Murray, 2 Sept. 1828.

[3] F.O. 76/22, Warrington to Bathurst, 31 Mar. 1827; F.O. 76/23, Warrington to Murray, 2 Sept. 1828; *Quarterly Review*, vol. 42, pp. 450-75.

[4] F.O. 76/26, Warrington to Hay, 10 Aug. 1829.

[5] F.O. 76/26, Warrington to Hay, 3 Dec. 1829; C.O. 2/20, Cox (The American consul in Tripoli) to Warrington, 20 Nov. 1829; *Quarterly Review*, vol. 42, pp. 460, 463.

'to strike his flag' unless the Pasha promised in writing to take proper steps to ascertain the fate of the travellers.[1] These representations led in France to the institution of a commission of inquiry into the charges against Baron Rousseau. Shocked by the accusation, the Pasha wrote a very lengthy reply professing his ignorance and promising to send messengers into the interior to inquire about the fate of Laing.[2] But neither the findings of the French commission, which completely exonerated Rousseau, nor the Pasha's reply satisfied the British Government and public. In 1829 the Colonial Office sent Major James Fraser of the Royal Navy to Tripoli to investigate the allegations. Accepting the submissions of Warrington and his associates as gospel truth, Fraser naturally decided against the Tripolitanian Government and Rousseau.[3]

All the explorers who visited Timbuctu subsequently—Barth in 1854, Oscar Lentz in 1880, Felix Dubois in 1894, and Bonnel de Mézières in 1911—also made exhaustive inquiries into the fate of Laing. All of them concluded that the Pasha and Hassuna d'Ghies had nothing to do with Laing's murder, and that the explorer's papers never got to Timbuctu or Tripoli.[4] From oral and documentary evidence, all these explorers were convinced that Laing was murdered by Ahmed Lameida, the fanatical chief of the Arab Berabish tribe. According to Barth and Dubois, Laing's papers were not destroyed but were in the possession of the descendants of Lameida, but de Mézières concluded that the papers were burnt on the spot by the murderers. In spite of all this, some modern British writers still cling to Warrington's and Fraser's version of the episode. For instance, in a recently published work, *The Slaves of Timbuctu*, Robin Maugham, relying heavily on an unpublished manuscript by a Miss M. Moseley, came to the conclusion that Laing's murder was organized by the Pasha and his Foreign Minister, Hassuna D'Ghies, and that his papers were brought to Tripoli and sold to Baron Rousseau, whom he calls 'an adroit plagiarist'.[5]

[1] F.O. 76/42, Hay to Backhouse, 9 Aug. 1829; F.O. 76/23, Huskisson to Pasha of Tripoli, 31 Jan. 1828; F.O. 76/23, C.O. to Warrington, 31 Jan. 1828.

[2] F.O. 76/23, Pasha to Huskisson, 25 Apr. 1828, encl. Warrington to Huskisson, 23 Apr. 1828.

[3] F.O. 76/27, Fraser's Report, 11 Dec. 1830.

[4] C.O. 101/44, Barth to Hammond, 4 Jan. 1858; Barth, op. cit., vol. iv, pp. 453–5; Oscar Lentz, *Timbuctoo* (Paris, 1886), pp. 96–98; Felix Dubois, *Timbuctoo the Mysterious* (English translation, London, 1896), pp. 325–30; Bonnel de Mézières, *Le Major A. Gordon Laing* (Paris, 1912), pp. 20–21.

[5] Robin Maugham, *The Slaves of Timbuctu* (London, 1961), pp. 130–57.

From the records it is clear that the Pasha of Tripoli and Hassuna D'Ghies were in no way responsible either for the attack on Laing or for his murder, as Warrington alleged and Miss Moseley and Maugham dutifully accept. If the purpose of the plot of the Pasha and his Foreign Minister was to collect Laing's papers and sell them to the French, surely the alleged first attempt to kill the explorer would have been made on his return from rather than on his way to Timbuctu.

It is, however, true that Laing himself described the first attack as a tale 'of base treachery and woe' and promised to write from Timbuctu how he was 'betrayed and nearly murdered'.[1] Unfortunately, he did not tell us who the traitor was. Warrington, followed rather blindly by the British Government, and more recently by Maugham, of course jumped to the conclusion that it was Babani, 'the secret agent of the Bashaw [Pasha]'.[2] But this conclusion is absolutely unjustifiable. Although Laing did mention Babani's name in the letter reporting the attack, all that he said about him was that 'some imputation is attachable to the old Sheikh'. In the postscript to this letter, however, Laing enumerated his charges against Babani. These were the Sheikh's refusal to repay an amount of 400 dollars (£80) which his guide had borrowed from him, his refusal to bear any expenses *en route*, and lastly the fact that he had stolen Laing's gun while he was convalescing. Surely if Laing had believed that Babani was responsible for the attack he would have said so. But he did not. Indeed, it seems that the three charges constitute the 'imputation' which Laing attached to Babani.

It should be obvious to any unprejudiced student of Laing's letters that it was not Babani but rather the Hoggar Tuareg, the inhabitants of the area south-west of Tuat, who were responsible for the first attack on Laing. When Laing arrived at Tuat, he saw merchants who had been waiting there for six to ten months on account of the insecurity of the route to Timbuctu caused by the wars between the Hoggar Tuareg and the Arab tribe the Awlad D'leim. For these wars Laing blamed the latter tribe, whom he described as 'an extensive Arab Tribe whose life is devoted to hunting, rapine and war and [who] from their constant vigilance are the terror of travellers'.[3] It was these

[1] F.O. 76/23, Laing to Warrington, 10 May 1826, encl. in Warrington to Murray, 2 Sept. 1828.

[2] F.O. 76/23, Warrington to Murray, 2 Apr. 1828; Maugham, op. cit., pp. 140-1.

[3] C.O. 2/15, Laing to Horton, 25 Dec. 1825.

wars which kept Laing in Tuat for so long, and not Babani, as
Warrington and Miss Moseley contend, and it was the arrival of news
of the victory of the Hoggar over the Arabs that enabled him and the
merchants to resume their march. Two days before the attack, Laing
wrote to R. W. Horton of the Colonial Office that his party had been
joined by two soldiers of the victorious Tuareg army. He added opti-
mistically that 'since meeting with the Tuareg, Timbuctu began to
appear within our reach' and that his 'prospects are bright and my expectations sanguine'.[1] He noted, however, that they were compelled
to await the arrival of the victors and mentioned the Ghadamase merchants' fears of the exorbitant demands that the Tuareg victors would
make. As the victors were reported to be thirty miles away, it is obvious
that they joined Laing's party two days later, the very day when the
attack took place. Instead of escorting them as Laing had expected,
the Tuareg victors rather attacked and nearly murdered them. Considering the high note of optimism struck in his letter two days earlier,
the confidence with which he expected the arrival of these people, and
the assurances given by the first two arrivals, who were in fact no
other than spies, it is not surprising that Laing should have described
the whole episode as one of base treachery.

There is also no justification for the view that Laing's murder after
his departure from Timbuctu was planned by the Tripolitanian
Government. That Laing was suddenly sent out of the city because of
the hostility of the Fulani of Masina cannot be challenged, because
Laing himself said so in the single letter which he wrote from that
city. As the Fulani of Masina conquered the city only a month before
Laing's arrival, the Tripolitanian Government could not have heard
of it. There could therefore have been no collusion between them and
the new overlords of Timbuctu to bring about the explorer's abrupt
departure from that city. Dubois was obviously misinformed about
the attitude of the Governor of Timbuctu, who at the time was not a
Fulani but a Tuareg, for Laing himself described him as 'an excellent
man . . . who trembles for my safety and has strongly urged my
immediate departure'.[2] From the inquiries of all the subsequent
explorers, as well as from the deposition of the only servant who
managed to escape, it is clear that it was the Arab chief appointed by
the Governor to guide Laing who was responsible for the murder.
But whether that chief acted on his own initiative, and if so whether

[1] C.O. 2/15, Laing to Horton, 24 Jan. 1826.
[2] C.O. 2/20, Laing to Warrington, 21 Sept. 1826.

his motives were mercenary or religious, or whether he acted on the instructions of the Fulani of Masina, it is impossible to say. One thing can be positively asserted, and that is that the Tripolitanian Government had no hand at all in the murder.

As for Laing's papers, although Warrington managed to produce a witness who claimed to have handed these papers to Hassuna D'Ghies, and although Miss Moseley and Maugham in their un-flinching devotion to Warrington admit this, these papers do not appear to have reached even Timbuctu. Only one person could have saved them and brought them to Timbuctu, namely Laing's servant. But when he was examined he confessed that he was so stunned by the blow he had received that he never thought of the papers.[1] If he did not secure them, then it is extremely unlikely that Laing's assassins would have brought them to Timbuctu, let alone to Tripoli. On the other hand, de Mézières states that it was recorded in two separate chronicles that these papers, together with all Laing's other effects, were burned.[2] In view of this documentary evidence, and considering the fact that the French envoys sent out during the visit of Dubois and de Mézières failed to find the papers, I am on the whole inclined to de Mézières's view that the papers were burned where the brave traveller fell.

For Laing's mission to be a success, a strong military escort should have been provided and the protection and assistance of a powerful and influential person in the interior secured. Experienced as he was, Warrington tried to arrange for both. He concluded an agreement with the Pasha under which the latter was to conduct Laing to and from Timbuctu with a military escort for a payment of 10,000 dollars (£2,000).[3] To treat the explorer in case of sickness and take his place if he died, Warrington also suggested that a surgeon should be added to the party. Without even waiting for the approval of the Colonial Office, he advanced the Pasha 2,000 dollars and applied to the Governor of Malta for a surgeon. The result of these arrangements was that Laing left Tripoli accompanied by what was described as 'a handsome escort of 150 cavalry'.[4] Warrington also succeeded in

[1] F.O. 762/3, Deposition of Laing's servant, 1 Sept. 1828, encl. in Warrington to Murray, 2 Sept. 1828.
[2] Mézières in fact succeeded in finding where Laing was buried and exhumed the body. For details, see de Mézières, op. cit.
[3] C.O. 2/15, Warrington to Laing, 24 May 1825, encl. in Warrington to Bathurst, 24 May 1825.
[4] F.O. 76/19, Laing to Bathurst, 18 July 1825.

obtaining letters of introduction to traders in Timbuctu and, above all, to the famous *marabout* Sidi Muhammad.

But the Colonial Office ordered Warrington to cancel forthwith his arrangements with the Pasha and also reprimanded him for applying to the Governor of Malta for a surgeon without first awaiting instructions from London.[1] The outcome of this parsimonious conduct on the part of the British Government was that Laing left Ghadames without the military escort and Tuat without Hateeta. To worsen the situation, Sidi Muhammad, who so carefully nursed Laing and would willingly have shielded him with his powerful influence, died even before he set foot in Timbuctu. Without an escort or a protector, only a miracle could have saved Laing. As ill luck would have it, this miracle never happened.

The Pasha told Laing and Warrington with admirable frankness at one of their palavers that 'if you wish to go that road, you must open the door with a silver key'.[2] With his many years of experience of conditions of travel in the Sahara, and with the example of the Denham–Clapperton mission in mind, Warrington accepted this dictum and acted accordingly. On grounds of economy the British Government rejected the Consul-General's arrangements and thus jeopardised the success of Laing's mission. If Laing had been accompanied by an assistant and a military escort, it is very probable that his life might have been saved, or at least that his papers would have been rescued. The parsimony of the British Government, more than anything else, caused the death of Laing and the failure of the mission. But Warrington was too emotionally involved—Laing had married one of his daughters shortly before his departure for the interior—to view the whole episode with the objectivity and detachment it deserved. Swayed by his own prejudices against the Arabs, and overwhelmed by his paternal affection for his bereaved daughter, he misled the British Government and public by falsely accusing the Tripolitanian Government of treachery and robbery. As the fate of Clapperton was still fresh in people's minds, this unfounded story was only too readily believed. Indeed the British Government stuck so firmly to Warrington's version of the incident that they paid no heed to the special ambassador dispatched by the Pasha to London in 1830 to give the true version and re-establish the old friendly relations between the two countries. Warrington was asked to inform the

[1] F.O. 76/40, Bathurst to Warrington, 5 July 1825.
[2] C.O. 2/20, Laing to Warrington, 17 Oct. 1825.

Pasha that the British Government 'will never rest satisfied until the papers themselves are produced, or a satisfactory account is given of the manner in which they have been disposed of'.[1]

The strain between Tripoli and England caused by the fatal outcome of the Laing mission and the consequent withdrawal of the British Government's support for the Pasha helped to unleash a series of revolutions which ended in a fundamental change in the political *status quo* in Tripoli and also affected the British drive into the interior from the north. The first of these revolutions was led by Abd al-Jalīl, the powerful Sheikh of the Awlad Sulayman. Seeing the isolation and helplessness of the Pasha as a good opportunity to revenge the atrocity Yusuf had perpetrated against the tribe in 1817, Abd al-Jalīl raised the standard of revolt in 1831.[2] This was followed a year later by the second revolution led by Sidi Ahmed, the son of the exiled brother of Yusuf. He was declared Pasha by his followers and joined forces with Abd al-Jalīl, on whom he conferred the governorship of Fezzan and Bani Walid. Warrington supported Ahmed and the Sheikh because of his belief that their success 'would establish British influence for the next half century'; while the French Consul and the D'Ghies family backed Yusuf Karamanli and his sons.[3] Taking advantage of this division, the Sultan of Turkey sent a squadron under Mustafa Najib to strengthen his hitherto nominal hold on the Regency. Najib landed in May 1835, arrested the entire Karamanli family, declared that dynasty abolished, and proclaimed himself Governor of the Regency.[4] Though by 1837 the Turks had completely mastered the coastal districts, all attempts to subdue Abd al-Jalīl and his followers had failed. In 1838, therefore, the Governor appealed to Warrington to mediate between him and the Sheikh. But while these negotiations were going on two Arab chiefs, bribed by the Governor, enticed the Sheikh in May 1842 to a meeting at which they murdered him and all his entourage.[5] The eldest son of

[1] F.O. 76/28, Rais Omar to Murray, 4 Nov. 1830; F.O. 76/40, Goderich to Warrington, 30 Apr. 1831.
[2] F.O. 76/29, Warrington to Hay, 30 Sept. 1831; Abd al-Jalīl to Warrington, 27 July 1831, encl. in Warrington to Goderich, 4 Aug. 1831; F.O. 76/40, Hay to Warrington, 9 Nov. 1831.
[3] F.O. 76/32, Warrington to Goderich, 1 Aug. 1832; F.O. 76/32, Warrington to Hay, 23 Aug. 1832; 11 Aug. 1834.
[4] F.O. 76/38, Proclamation of Mustafa Najib, 1 June 1835, encl. in Warrington to Aberdeen, 6 June 1835.
[5] F.O. 84/427, Warrington to Aberdeen, 1 June 1842; Richardson, *Travels*, vol. ii, p. 353.

the Sheikh and the rest of the Awlad Sulyman retreated from Fezzan
to the northern regions of the Chad, where they have remained ever
since.

The death of Abd al-Jalīl and the effective occupation of Fezzan
by the army of the Sultan of Turkey brought to an end the series of
events triggered off by the breach between the Governments of
Britain and Tripoli over the death of Laing and the loss of his papers.
Certainly the failure of the Laing expedition had far-reaching consequences. It strained Anglo-Tripolitanian relations, contributed to
the abolition of the Karamanli dynasty, and firmly shut the northern
gateway into the interior for over a decade.

Far from quenching enthusiasm for going into the interior of
Africa, the prominence given to the fatal result of the Clapperton
and Laing missions in British journals and newspapers had the
opposite effect. Indeed, from November 1828, when Richard Lander
returned to England, to January 1830, no less than fifteen applications were received by the Colonial Office from people asking to be
sent on missions of exploration to Africa. As all but one of these
applications asked for financial assistance, the Government turned
them down. The single exception was from a Mr. C. H. Coulthurst,
who volunteered to go at his own expense to ascertain the mouth of
the Niger, and only asked for letters of introduction to the Sultans of
Sokoto and Bornu.[1] Barrow supported Coulthurst's application and
suggested that since the two rulers were at war with each other,
Coulthurst should be accredited to only one of them, namely, the
Sultan of Bornu. In this same letter Barrow also suggested that
Lander, who had been 'pressing to go again', should be sent out to
complete the exploration of the Niger and the area between Bornu
and the Nile.[2] As always, the views of this great promoter of African
exploration were accepted. Not only was a letter of introduction
given to Coulthurst but the Colonial Office also extended an invitation to Lander to continue his work in Africa.[3] Richard Lander
readily accepted this invitation and requested that his brother John
should be allowed to accompany him. Probably realizing their folly
over the Laing mission, the Colonial Office granted this request.

[1] C.O. 2/18, Coulthurst to Aberdeen, 10 Sept. 1829.
[2] C.O. 2/18, Barrow to Hay, 19 Sept. 1829.
[3] C.O. 2/18, Lander to Barrow, 16 Oct. 1829. Coulthurst did not leave England
until late in 1831. He reached the Bight of Biafra and began the ascent of the
Cross river, but had not travelled far up the Cross when he was turned back by
the inhabitants. He died in July 1832 on his way from Calabar to Fernando Po.

The Landers' task was twofold. First they were to make for the Niger at the point where Richard had crossed it and from there follow it to its termination 'wherever that may be'. Secondly, they were to conduct exhaustive inquiries about Park's papers, which were believed to be still in existence in Bussa or Yauri.[1] On 9 January 1830 the brothers left Portsmouth in the brig *Albert*.

Unlike most of the expeditions to Africa, this was an absolute success. The Landers hit on the Niger at Bussa in June 1830. After inquiring in vain at that place for Park's papers, they rowed up the river to Yauri. Investigations into the fate of the papers here too proved unrewarding. After several interviews with the Sultan and his elders, the Landers concluded that 'the long-sought papers are at present nowhere in existence'.[2] They therefore began their homeward journey by boat down the Niger on 22 August 1830. After a series of delays and accidents, they finally entered the Bight of Benin through the Nun, one of the many outlets of the Niger, and landed at Clarence in Fernando Po in December 1830.[3] From here Richard sent home the long-awaited solution to the problem which had haunted scholars since the time of Herodotus. He wrote with pride and authority that 'the rivers of Benin, Formosa, Bonny, New Calabar, Nun—all collectively called the "Oil Rivers"—communicate and are fed by the Niger, so that the opinion of Reichard respecting them is clearly authenticated'.[4] He also confirmed McQueen's view of the numerous and populous villages and towns that flanked the river on both sides and the facility with which a lucrative commercial intercourse could be established there.

The news of the solution of the Niger problem spread throughout Europe and even penetrated into the United States of America. That it was considered a feat worthy of national acclaim and recognition is amply demonstrated by the fact that the Landers were received by the King and Richard was given an annuity of £100.[5]

The reaction in British learned, humanitarian, and mercantile circles was even more interesting. The *Edinburgh Review* expressed

[1] C.O. 392/1, Instructions to Lander, 31 Dec. 1829.

[2] Richard and John Lander, *Journal of an expedition to explore the course and termination of the Niger*, 3 vols. (1832), vol. ii, pp. 35–44.

[3] The island was then occupied by the British and was being used as the base for their anti-slavery patrols; it was abandoned in 1834.

[4] C.O. 2/18, Lander to Hay, 7 Jan. 1831.

[5] C.O. 2/18, Treasury to Hay, 14 July 1831.

the sentiments of British geographers when it described the Landers'
journal of the expedition as recording 'perhaps the most important
geographical discovery of the present age'.[1] If the fatal outcome of
the Clapperton and Laing missions blocked the overland routes into
the interior, water communication seemed to open to the humanitarians an easier and less dangerous means of arriving at the courts
of Sokoto and Bornu. The Colonial Office was in fact soon inundated
with applications from such people. One of the most interesting of
these was from Miss Holliday, a thirty-one-year-old schoolmistress.
She volunteered to go to the Court of Bornu to teach the children of
the principal people. Her aim in life was, she stated, 'to lessen as far
as individual influence could extend, the civil and religious darkness
of any part of that unfortunate but highly interesting continent'.[2]

Commercially minded people were no less enthusiastic about the
Landers' discoveries. MacGregor Laird, a member of a family of
Birkenhead shipbuilders, expressed their hopes in these significant
terms:

The long sought-for highway into Central Africa was at length found, as
open by the Niger as that by the Rhine, the Danube, the Mississippi, or
the Orinooko [Orinoco], is into their respective countries. To the merchant
it offered a boundless field for enterprise, to the manufacturer, an extensive
market for his goods; and to the energy and ardour of youth, it presented
the irresistible charms of novelty, danger, and adventure.[3]

Indeed, taking for granted the profitable nature of any commercial
intercourse with the populous regions of the interior, British business-
men concerned themselves with the nature of British manufactures
to be sent out, the commodities to be procured in exchange, and
above all the mode in which trade was to be conducted. One of them,
Paul Read, suggested that the Government should send an expedition
to take possession of one or two of the islands that dotted the Niger.
On each of these a fort should be erected where a few troops under
the command of an officer who would also be the governor could be
stationed. A number of convicts should be sent to these stations to
cultivate the soil and raise food for the troops. Private traders should
be allowed to establish factories on these islands and be protected in

---

[1] *Edinburgh Review*, vol. 55, p. 397.
[2] C.O. 2/19, Miss A. Holliday to Goderich, 31 Mar. 1832. This, of course, was
rejected by the Government.
[3] M. Laird and R. A. K. Oldfield, *Expedition Into the Interior of Africa* (London,
1837), vol i, pp. 2–3.

their commercial transactions. The cost of each establishment, he hoped, could be met from dues collected from traders. By way of driving his appeal home, Read concluded that 'in the present depressed state of our manufacture and commerce, such an undertaking would serve to render the Government deservedly popular'.[1]

Left to the British Government alone, such plans would never have been implemented. In conformity with the prevalent theory of *laissez-faire*, it was argued in official circles that once the commercial highway had been discovered, it was up to individual merchants and traders to exploit it.[2] Luckily there were private individuals who were only too ready to embark on these ventures. Indeed, no sooner had the journal of the Landers emerged from the printing press than 'several highly respectable merchants of Liverpool' joined together under the designation of 'The African Inland Commercial Company'.[3] The person most responsible for the formation of the Company was MacGregor Laird, and his family owned about a quarter of the total shares. The Company's aim was to open direct communication with the interior of Africa and establish a permanent settlement at the junction of the Benue and the Niger 'for the purpose of collecting the various products of the country'. The abolitionists seem to have associated themselves with the merchants, for it was said of the Company that 'by introducing legitimate commerce with all its attendant blessings into the centre of the country, they knew that they were striking a mortal blow at that debasing and demoralising traffic which has for centuries cursed that unhappy land'.[4] The Company built one sailing and two steam vessels; the steam vessels were to go upstream and bring down the commodities to the sailing vessel, which was to remain at the mouth of the river. Under the command of Richard Lander and with a crew of forty-eight, including William Allen, who was sent by the Admiralty to survey the river, the vessels left Liverpool on 19 July 1832.

The attempt at a practical exploitation of the discoveries of the Landers was not, it is interesting to note, made only by British merchants. Five months after the arrival of their vessels on the Niger, an American trading fleet of three vessels, a brig and two

[1] C.O. 2/19, Read to Goderich, 7 May 1832. The *Edinburgh Review* also suggested that steam vessels should be used and a station set up on the Niger. (*Edinburgh Review*, vol. 55, pp. 418–19.)
[2] Laird and Oldfield, op. cit., vol. ii, pp. 389–90.
[3] C.O. 2/19, Forsyth to Hay, 7 Apr. 1832.
[4] Laird and Oldfield, op. cit., vol. i, pp. 3–4.

schooners, sent out by a company of a few enterprising merchants of Rhode Island, entered the River Nun.[1]

Had success crowned these private efforts, and had an establishment been formed at the confluence, there is no doubt that contacts would have been made sooner or later with Nupe, Sokoto, and Bornu, as indeed the activities of the Royal Niger Company were to demonstrate later in the century.[2] Unhappily, as a humanitarian and commercial venture, the Liverpool expedition was a disastrous failure. Of the total crew of forty-eight that went up the Niger, only eight survived the short period of two years that they remained up-river. Even more discouraging was the fact that only two of the unfortunate victims—one of whom was Lander—died as a result of an attack by the natives. All the others succumbed to the fever of the Niger regions. And the expedition did not even succeed in collecting enough ivory and other commodities to defray its cost.[3]

The American expedition was no less disastrous. Lander's friend King Boy, who had ransomed him from imprisonment on his first expedition, did not allow the Americans to proceed up the Nun. They therefore turned to the Brass river, where they also encountered strong opposition from the King. Though their supercargo was alleged to have been accidentally shot, Laird believed that he was intentionally killed by Brassmen. The climate also took a heavy toll of their crew. In less than six weeks the number was reduced from sixteen to five. Among the victims was the captain himself. The mate therefore abandoned the attempt and returned to Rhode Island.[4]

Though gravely disappointed by the fatal outcome of these initial efforts, some of those who served on the Liverpool expedition were not discouraged. While admitting that the immediate cause of the failure was the climate, Allen, Oldfield, the surgeon, and Lander himself before his death, were confident that the difficulty could be easily surmounted.[5] The first real stumbling block in the way of development of trade up the Niger, they all agreed, was not the

[1] C.O. 2/19, Lander to Hay, 9 May 1833; Laird and Oldfield, op. cit., vol. i, p. 344.

[2] J. E. Flint, *Sir George Goldie and the Making of Nigeria* (London, 1960), pp. 37–40, 89–91, 114–17, 170–2.

[3] Laird and Oldfield, op. cit., vol. i, p. 239.

[4] C.O. 2/19, Lander to Hay, 9 May 1833; Laird and Oldfield, op. cit., vol. i, pp. 345–8.

[5] C.O. 2/19, Lander to Hay, 9 May 1833; Laird and Oldfield, op. cit., vol. ii, pp. 181–2, 407–8.

climate but rather the political instability in the region of the confluence. The second was the pioneering nature of the venture which
made immediate profits clearly impossible and the British Government's support correspondingly indispensable. In a very long letter
to the Admiralty, an extract from which was forwarded by Barrow
to the Colonial Office, Allen vigorously developed these points and
appealed to the Government to assume responsibility for opening up
trade on the Niger and to establish a colony which would serve a
dual purpose as a centre of civilization and a depot for British
traders.[1] Although the Colonial Office admitted the validity of the
explorers' arguments, they nevertheless expressed their regret that
Allen's project could not 'at the present moment be entertained'.[2]

By 1834, then, the northern gateway was firmly shut, thanks to
the fatal outcome of the Laing mission and the consequent diplomatic
breach between the Tripolitanian and British Governments. The
southern gateway remained open, but owing to lack of official patron-
age it could not be effectively utilized. The African Inland Commercial Company was itself wound up shortly after the return of the
expedition to Liverpool in November 1834. Intrepid individual
traders such as Jamieson and his employee Beecroft attempted to use
the Niger. These attempts were, however, confined to the Oil Rivers,
and only in 1836 and 1840 did Beecroft go beyond the delta.[3] It
appeared as if the recent discoveries made by Denham, Clapperton,
and the Landers were doomed to neglect or oblivion. This, however,
did not happen. For in August 1841 a fleet of three ships sent out
by the British Government appeared on the Niger and ascended as far
as its confluence with the Benue.[4] What brought about this change

[1] C.O. 2/19, Allen to Barrow, 6 Oct. 1834, encl. Barrow to Hay, 14 Oct. 1834.
[2] C.O. 392/2 C.O., to Barrow, 30 Oct. 1834.
[3] K. O. Dike, 'John Beecroft, 1790–1854', *Journal of the Historical Society of
Nigeria*, vol. i, p. 11.
[4] As this expedition is outside my field, it will not be exhaustively dealt with
here. For a detailed study see Gallagher, 'Fowell Buxton and the New African
Policy, 1838–42', *Cambridge Historical Review*, vol. 10, no. 1; W. L. Mathieson,
Great Britain and the Slave Trade, 1839–65 (1929), pp. 28–57; C. C. Ifemesia,
'British Enterprise on the Niger, 1830–69' (unpublished Ph.D. thesis, London,
1959); R. Coupland, *The British Anti-Slavery Movement* (1933), pp. 173–5;
A. F. Madden, 'The Attitude of the Evangelicals to the Empire and Imperial
Problems, 1820–50', pp. 537–44 (unpublished D.Phil. thesis, Oxford, 1950).
Among the crew, it may be pointed out, was a team of scientists. They were Dr.
F. R. Vogel, botanist; Dr. William Stanger, geologist and explorer; Mr. C. G.
Roscher, miner and mineralogist; Mr. Lewis Fraser, from the London Zoological
Society, and Mr. John Ansell, collector of plants.

in the British Government's attitude to the drive up the Niger, and
what effect did the circumstances that led to the dispatch of this
expedition have on the subsequent British penetration into the
Sahara and the Sudan?

The tremendous increase in the volume of the transatlantic slave
traffic in the 1820's and 1830's, despite the abolition acts, treaties
with European powers against the trade, and the naval squadron,
showed the inadequacy of these measures. A new approach to the
problem of the abolition or suppression of the slave trade became
necessary. In 1837 Buxton claimed to have discovered this new
solution, and it was its adoption and implementation by the Government which led to the dispatch of the 1841 expedition. This new
approach was based on Buxton's principle of 'the deliverance of
Africa by calling forth her own resources'. To put this principle into
practice, the slave traffic was to be impeded by increasing and con-
centrating the squadrons on the west coast and by signing treaties
with African chiefs. Secondly, legitimate trade, or as it was constantly
referred to in the instructions to the leaders of the 1841 expedition,
'innocent trade', was to be established and encouraged by setting up
trading establishments in the interior. Thirdly, cultivation of the
soil was to be encouraged and taught by the formation of an agricultural company which would acquire land and set up model farms.
Lastly, the indigenous people were to be educated and civilized by an
association 'on the plan of the African Institution'.[1]

Although Buxton appeared to have hit on the principle and the
plan for its execution quite originally in the summer of 1837,[2]
neither of them was new. As we have seen, McQueen in 1820
advanced the same principle and proposed methods for its implementation which were even more ambitious than those of Buxton.
For instance, he did not simply advocate acquisition of a small piece
of territory for experimental purposes, but the entire colonization of
the whole length of the Niger region from the delta to the sources of
the Senegal and the Gambia. 'We have done this in India, and why
cannot we do it in Africa?' he asked the British public and Government in 1820.[3] The second Clapperton mission of 1825 and that of
the African Inland Company in 1832, it may be recalled, were both
based on the same principle. It is indeed significant that the Govern-

[1] T. F. Buxton, *The Remedy* (1838), pp. 121-2.
[2] Charles Buxton, *Memoirs of Sir Thomas Fowell Buxton* (1848), p. 429.
[3] McQueen, op. cit., pp. 191-2.

ment not only invited McQueen to submit his views on the impending mission but also asked him to serve on it as one of the commissioners. Although McQueen declined to serve, he sent a long memorandum in which he restated his old ideas and even proposed terms for the treaty to be signed with the African chiefs.[1] There was nothing revolutionary about the adoption of this policy in 1839-41, as Gallagher would have us believe.[2] For if McQueen's plan was rejected, Denham's and Clapperton's were accepted and indeed implemented. Pruned of their verbiage of humanitarianism and sentimentality, the instructions issued to the commissioners of the 1841 expedition and the draft letter to African chiefs were the same as those given to Clapperton in 1825. Both missions were to conclude treaties against the slave trade, persuade native rulers to encourage legitimate trade, and establish consuls at the African courts.

The real importance of the campaign of Buxton and his associates lies not so much in propounding new ideas as in popularizing a principle preached since the 1820's and compelling the Government to readopt it. Indeed, so vividly did the principle and ideas of Buxton catch the imagination of the British public in the late 1830's that, although the Government were not fully convinced of some of the details—for example, the acquisition of territory and the establishment of model farms—they could only have rejected any part of the plan at the great risk of being defeated at the impending elections.[3]

Even though the expedition failed, the British Government and people did not lose faith in the theory of legitimate commerce. At the very first meeting of the African Civilization Society after the return of the expedition was known, Lord John Russell, then Secretary of State for the Colonies, boldly asserted the soundness of the principle.[4] It is also clear from the evidence given before the Select Committees of 1842, 1848, and 1849 that many people still considered the development of legitimate commerce the most effective means of overthrowing the slave trade. Asked by the Committee of 1848 for his views on the subject, Palmerston himself answered, 'in proportion as legitimate commerce increased, you will find the disposition to slave trade to diminish, especially if the legitimate

[1] C.O. 2/22 No. 69, Slave Trade, Buxton to Colonial Office, 12 Jan. 1839.

[2] J. Gallagher, 'Fowell Buxton and the New African Policy, 1838-42', *Cambridge Historical Review*, vol. 10, no. 1.

[3] Gallagher, op. cit., pp. 46-47.

[4] C. Buxton, *Memoirs*, p. 557.

commerce is protected.'[1] Indeed the ease with which Livingstone won
over the British public in the 1850's was partly owing to the fact that
he was preaching a crusade with which they were already in sympathy.
The immediate effect in England of the failure of the 1841 expedition
was not to discredit the principle of legitimate commerce but rather,
as Dr. Madden has pointed out, to minimize drastically the great
influence which the humanitarians had been exerting on the Government since the 1800's.[2] The pressure which they had so successfully
exercised both in the lobbies of the Houses of Parliament and in the
corridors of the Colonial Office now lost its thrust. Moreover, the
failure brought home once more the unsuitability of the climate of
the lower regions of the Niger for Europeans. Of the total com-
plement of 145 Europeans, forty-nine died (forty-three from fever)
in two months. It was the incredibly high rate of mortality which led
to the abandonment of the attempt. It became clear, therefore, that
if the theory was to be implemented it could only be done in a more
hospitable region. Moreover, such Buxtonian additions as experimental farms, which involved the employment of Europeans, had to
be reconsidered. Thwarted in the south, it was obvious that the
British Government would once again turn their attention to the
north as they did after 1818. With the effective occupation of the
Regency of Tripoli by the Turks by 1840, the northern gateway was
once more open.

The other important point about Buxton's campaign, which has so
far never been mentioned by any historian but which was a very
important by-product, was that it drew the attention of the British
public for the first time to the existence of the trans-Saharan slave
trade, and thereby intensified the urge to turn northward.[3] To win
converts to his cause, Buxton set himself the task of proving that all
wars in the interior of Africa were fought to obtain slaves for sale,
and of showing the brutalities and the high rate of mortality involved
in bringing slaves from the interior to the north and west coasts of

[1] Report of Select Committee on Slave Trade, 1848 P.P. Slavery 38, Q. 161.
See also the evidence of Matson, Carr, Joseph Smith, Bandinel, and Laird before
the same Committee.
[2] Madden, op. cit., pp. 623–6.
[3] Though the question of the Barbary States and the slave trade had been
raised at the World Congresses at Vienna, London, Aix-la-Chapelle, and Verona
between 1815 and 1820, it was the trade in Europeans that was discussed and the
one in Negroes across the Sahara was never raised. See K. Mackenzie, 'Great
Britain and the Abolition of the Slave Trade, 1812–22', unpublished B.Litt.
thesis (Oxford, 1952), pp. 100–1.

Africa and to the Americas. He collected together for the first time accounts by African explorers of the wars that were raging in the interior and the raids carried out for the capture of slaves. He also assembled descriptions of the brutalities and loss of life caused by the raids and by the march across the Sahara to the north coast.[1] He informed his readers, for instance, that 'the Mohammedan towns of Jenne, Timbuctoo, Kano, Sackatoo [Sokoto] in Houssa, Kouka and Angornu in Bornou, Wawa or Wara [Wao] the capital of Darfur are so many large warehouses where the stores of human merchandise are kept for the supply of the Arab carriers or traders who convey them in caravans across the desert'.[2] The whole section on what he called 'The March' was devoted exclusively to the march of slaves across the Sahara. Here he compiled telling passages descriptive of this march from the journals of Park, Burkhardt, Gray, Lyon, Caillié, Denham, and Clapperton. He estimated the death rate of the Saharan crossing at approximately 42 per cent. and the total number of slaves carried annually to Barbary and Egypt at 20,000, as compared with 30,000 to the east coast and Arabia and 120,000 to the west coast and the Americas.[3] That Buxton succeeded in bringing the trans-Saharan slave trade into the limelight is borne out by the fact that the British and Foreign Anti-Slavery Society sent out a mission to the Barbary States shortly after the publication of his account, and its conventions of 1840 and 1843 sent petitions to the Barbary rulers and the Sultan of Turkey calling on them to abolish the trans-Saharan slave trade.[4] Bandinel, an official in the Foreign Office, also mentioned the trans-Saharan traffic in his book on the slave trade.[5] Thus from 1839 onwards, thanks mainly to Buxton, the British public, or at least the Government and the British and Foreign Anti-Slavery Society, turned their attention to this hitherto neglected branch of the traffic.

It was not until thirteen years after the 1841 expedition that another Government mission went up the Niger. However, the popularity given to the principle of legitimate commerce, the revival of interest

[1] Buxton, *The African Slave Trade* (1839), pp. 37-49.

[2] Ibid., pp. 41-42.

[3] Ibid., pp. 74-87, 165, 170.

[4] Br. Emp. MSS. 522/9114, General Anti-Slavery Conventions, 1840 and 1843; Second Annual Report of the British Anti-Slavery Society, 1842, pp. 299-302; for the mission see below, pp. 174-89.

[5] James Bandinel, *Some Account of the Trade in Slaves from Africa* (1842), pp. 299-302.

in the Sudan and the Niger regions, and, above all, the focusing of attention on the trans-Saharan slave trade, of whose existence people in Europe and England were hardly aware, made subsequent attempts to drive into the interior almost inevitable. But before examining the attempts which were made from the north, let us first take a look at the traffic across the Sahara, with particular reference to the slave trade on which the Government and other humanitarian bodies from now on concentrated.

CHAPTER V

The Caravan Trade in the Nineteenth Century

THE trans-Saharan traffic to which the attention of the British people was so dramatically turned in the thirties was of very remote antiquity. Mauny and Lhote have convincingly shown that as early as 1000 B.C., chariots were being drawn across the Sahara along two main routes: a western route from Morocco through Zemmour and Adrar to the banks of the Senegal and the Niger, and a central route from Tripoli through Ghadames, Ghat, and Hoggar to Gao on the Niger.[1] By the fifth century B.C., the desert traffic—mainly in animals such as monkeys, lions, panthers, and elephants, in carbuncles, emeralds and chalcedony and other precious stones, and in slaves— had become so important that 'the Carthaginians began their great Sahara expeditions in an effort to cut out all intermediaries and to get into direct contact with the source of the riches in which they traded'.[2] Three centuries later the Saharan trade was centred on the Tripoli–Fezzan–Bornu route (the Garamantian route) and constituted one of the main sources of the riches of Carthage. The phenomenal development of this desert traffic did not take place, however, until the introduction of the camel into Tripolitania by the Romans, probably in the first century A.D.[3] The rapid spread of the camel through Barbary and into the Sahara and beyond was begun by the Arabs and the Berbers. The process seems to have gathered

[1] R. Mauny, 'Notes on the Protohistoric period in West Africa', *Journal of the West African Science Association*, vol. 2, 1 Aug. 1952, no. 2; R. Mauny, 'Une route préhistorique a travers le Sahara occidental', *Bull. de l'FAN*, 1950, pp. 341– 60; H. Lhote, *The Search for the Tassili Frescoes* (English translation, London, 1959), pp. 124–8.

[2] Gilbert and Colette Charles-Picard, *Daily Life in Carthage at the time of Hannibal* (English translation, London, 1961), p. 219.

[3] For the fascinating literary battle on the subject of the introduction of the camel into Barbary, see V. Monteil, *Essai sur le chameau au Sahara occidental* (*1952*); Sir Mortimer Wheeler, *Rome Beyond the Imperial Frontiers* (London, 1954), p. 121; O. Brogan, 'The Camel in Roman Tripolitania', *Papers of the British School at Rome XX* (*1954*); E. E. Bovill, *The Golden Trade of the Moors* (London, 1958), pp. 41–42.

momentum and reached its climax during the Hilalian invasions in the middle of the eleventh century. As a consequence of the use of this singularly endowed beast of burden, a complicated network of caravan routes had come into existence by the end of the eleventh century, by means of which commercial, religious, and cultural contacts were established and maintained between the Mediterranean world and the Sudan. Traffic along these routes reached its peak in the period 1490–1590, when the Songhay Empire under the Askias and the Bornu Empire under the Sefuwas dominated the Sahara and the Sudan and maintained such political stability and order as have probably not been known in these areas since that time.

From the end of the sixteenth century, however, the traffic began to decline, and by the nineteenth century it had become concentrated on four main routes. These were the Morocco–Taodeni–Timbuctu route, with its important branch the Mabruk–Tuat route in the west, the Ghadames–Air–Kano and the Tripoli–Fezzan–Bornu routes in the centre, and the Cyrenaica–Kufra–Waday route in the east. According to Bovill, the greatest of these routes was the Taghaza–Timbuctu route, 'pre-eminent in the gold trade and still more important as a cultural highway'.[1] This may well have been so in the period up to the end of the sixteenth century. The available evidence for the nineteenth century hardly justifies Bovill's view.

The ebb and flow of traffic on these routes were determined by two factors, namely the political conditions in the Sudan and the security of the routes in the Sahara. In both respects the odds were heavily against the western route. Bovill himself describes, with remarkable scholarship, the anarchy that followed the overthrow of the Songhay Empire in the early 1590's by the armies of Al-Mansur, the Sultan of Morocco, and the failure of the Moroccans to establish any effective administrative machinery in their newly conquered domain.[2] The seventeenth and eighteenth centuries saw rivalry among the Tuareg, the Fulani, and the Bambara for the overlordship of the 'regions of Timbuctu'. In 1660 the Bambara defeated the Moorish soldiers and seized Timbuctu, only to lose it to the Tuareg in the middle of the eighteenth century. The Tuareg themselves were thrown out of the town by the Fulani of Masina in 1826, shortly before Laing's arrival.

[1] Bovill, op. cit., p. 235.
[2] Bovill, op. cit., pp. 165–90; see also Felix Dubois, *Timbuctu the Mysterious* (English translation, London, 1897), pp. 238–49.

By the time of Barth's visit in 1853, conditions were still unstable[1] and continued so until the end of the century. Surely these three centuries of continuous instability and wars in the Jenne–Timbuctu–Gao regions could not but unfavourably affect the caravan traffic.

The confusion and insecurity in the regions of the Niger bend extended into the desert. The sway and order of the Askias had stretched as far north as the ancient salt mines of Taghaza. With their overthrow, and the failure of the Sultans of Morocco to establish their hold on these regions, a political vacuum was created which the Tuareg tribes, such as the Hoggar, the Aulimmiden, and the Tadmekket, and the Arab tribes like the Berabish and the Awlad D'leim tried to fill. The wars, raids, and counter-raids among the Tuareg and the Arab tribes continued throughout the eighteenth and nineteenth centuries. These inevitably made the crossing from Timbuctu to Tuat and Morocco a very precarious and often impossible venture. Laing, it may be recalled, learned on his arrival at In Salah that intercourse between Tuat and Timbuctu had been suspended for a whole year owing to the wars between the Hoggar and the D'leim. The annual caravan from Morocco did not arrive while Barth was at Timbuctu in 1853 because of the civil war among the Tajakant Tuareg 'who almost exclusively kept up the communication with Morocco'.[2] In spite of his overwhelming influence over the Tuareg and Arab tribes of the western Sahara, Al-Baka'i was so convinced of the insecurity of the Timbuctu–Tenduf route that he refused to allow Barth to return to England that way.[3]

As a result of the chronic anarchy and the wars between the Fulani and the Tuareg in the south, and the raids and counter-raids among the Tuareg and the Arabs in the Sahara, the western route became so unsafe that the traffic along the Taghaza–Timbuctu route in the nineteenth century was virtually limited to the single large annual caravans to and from Timbuctu. Indeed, far from being the greatest, the western route was the least active and least important of the four principal routes of the nineteenth century. The best evidence of the nature of the traffic and political conditions along the western route is provided by the state of its once famous termini, Timbuctu and Gao, by the nineteenth century. Timbuctu, the great commercial and educational

---

[1] See below, pp. 193–5.
[2] Barth, op. cit., vol. iv, pp. 468, 489.
[3] Barth, op. cit., vol. v, p. 32.

metropolis which Leo Africanus described in such glowing terms at
the beginning of the sixteenth century, had by the 1820's been
reduced to a town of a circumference of only 3–4 miles. Caillié, who
was there in 1827, could not conceal his disappointment. He noted
that he found it 'neither so large nor so populous' as he had expected.
In 1854, Barth found Gao, the famous capital of the Songhay Empire
and the main market for the gold of Wangara, 'the desolate abode
of a small and miserable population'.[1] Bovill quotes an English
merchant who reported in 1638 that 'the golden trade of Gao hath
long since been intermitted'. This decline affected not only the gold
trade but even the traffic in slaves. For in 1788 James Matra reported
that 'the caravans to the south have decreased very considerably for
many years; their decay originated from a great diminution in the
number of slaves imported'.[2] The traffic along the western route
certainly never recovered its former greatness but continued to
decline as the anarchy let loose by the Moroccan conquest increased
in intensity. Dubois, who traversed the area from Senegal to Timbuctu in 1894, was quite correct when he wrote:

The Moors were the first cause of the work of disintegration which steadily
increased during the two centuries of their reign, to reach its maximum in
the present day. . . . During all this time, agriculture was interrupted and
commerce destroyed. The river was deserted of its canoes, and the traffic
of the caravan became impossible.[3]

By overthrowing the peace and order of the Askias, the Moroccans
killed the goose that literally laid the golden eggs.

The other route which steadily lost its importance in the course
of the nineteenth century was the Tripoli–Fezzan–Bornu route. With
the fall of the Songhay Empire and the consequent chaos, the
political centre of gravity shifted from the upper Niger to the Chad,
from Timbuctu and Gao to Birni-Ngazargamo, the then capital of
the Bornu Empire. This empire remained in the ascendant throughout the seventeenth and eighteenth centuries and successfully maintained its sway over the region of the Sahara as far as the southern
border of Fezzan.[4] Though the Jihad of 1804 and the subsequent
wars shook Bornu to its foundations, the close alliance which

---

[1] Caillié, op. cit., vol. ii, pp. 50–51; Barth, vol. v, p. 216. Laing estimated the
circumference of Timbuctu at 4, Caillié at 3 and Barth at 2½–3 miles.
[2] Bovill, op. cit., p. 190; F.O. 582/8, Matra to Sydney, 17 Nov. 1788.
[3] F. Dubois, op. cit., p. 141.
[4] Barth, op. cit., vol. ii, pp. 650–8; Y. Urvoy, *Historie de l'Empire du Bornou*
(1949), pp. 75–84.

Al-Kānami, the Sheikh of Bornu, established with the Pasha of Tripoli in the first three decades of the nineteenth century kept the Tripoli–Fezzan–Bornu route wide open. In describing the Morocco–Timbuctu and Fezzan–Bornu routes in 1825, Laing stated that 'the latter is a regular trading route under the power of the Bashaw [Pasha], along which a child might travel, but in this there are many conflicting interests and the Bashaw's influence ends at Ghadames'.[1] Indeed, it seems that from about the beginning of the seventeenth century until the 1820's the Fezzan–Bornu route was the most active of all. This is evident from the prosperous state in which Denham and Clapperton found Kuka (or Kukawa), the recently built capital of Bornu, and Ngornu, the main emporium of the empire.[2]

After the death of Al-Kānami in 1837, however, the wars among Bornu, Waday, and Bagirmi, in which Ngornu was entirely destroyed, greatly disturbed the stability of the Chad region. The unrest in the south coupled with the radical political changes in Tripoli had disastrous effects on the traffic along the old route. In the first place, the political revolutions in Tripoli between 1830 and 1842 brought traffic along the route to a complete standstill,[3] and a substantial part of it was therefore diverted into the Waday–Benghazi and the Sudan routes. Secondly, the substitution of the feeble Turkish administration, whose influence did not even fully reach the southern provinces of Fezzan, for the oppressive though relatively powerful and influential Karamanli government, enabled the Tuareg and the Tibu, the two great peoples of the Sahara, to revive their traditional raids and plundering expeditions against each other. As a result of the wars between the Tuareg and Tibu, for instance, the road from Murzuk to Bornu was completely blocked between April 1851 and June 1852.[4] As late as 1906, Hans Vischer, who travelled from Tripoli to Bornu, reported that the raids were still going on. These internecine wars and raids were further intensified by the activities

[1] C.O. 2/20, Laing to Warrington, 13 Sept. 1825.

[2] Denham, op. cit., pp. 79–81.

[3] F.O. 101/3, Wood to Warrington, 10 Apr. 1840; Benghazi, 1 Aug. 1839, encl. Warrington to Bidwell, 21 Aug. 1839; F.O. 101/4, Warrington to Palmerston, 10 Apr. 1840; F.O. 101/4, Warrington to Bidwell, 31 Dec. 1840.

[4] F.O. 101/34, Crowe to Palmerston, 9 Mar. 1852; F.O. 101/34, Herman to Malmesbury, 20 July 1852 and encl., Gagliuffi to Herman, 3 July 1852; F.O. 101/34, Barth to Herman, 25 Feb. 1852, encl. in Herman to Malmesbury, 2 Nov. 1852; H. Vischer, *Across the Sahara* (1910), pp. 65–66, 257, 265.

of the Awlād Sulayman, who settled in the northern regions of the Chad in the 1840's and earned their living solely by plundering and raiding all and sundry. In 1861, Fremaux, the former British Vice-Consul at Murzuk, reported that while peace and security prevailed on the Ghat–Kano route, the highroad to Bornu from Fezzan was 'still infested by marauding parties of the Ouled Soliman [Awlād Sulayman] tribe'.[1] The activities of the Tuareg and the Tibu rendered this route so insecure and so disturbed that although traffic along it revived in the forties, it became, as on the western route, essentially an annual affair.

Commercially, it was the Ghadames–Air–Kano route which was the most important in the nineteenth century. After the Jihad and the successful establishment of the twin Fulani Empires of Sokoto and Gwandu, the political centre of gravity shifted once again from Bornu to Hausaland, from Kuka to Sokoto and Kano, where it has remained ever since. If the western half of the Sokoto Empire—the Gwandu Empire—was far from stable, the Sokoto Empire itself remained from the forties onwards relatively peaceful and quiet.[2] Equally peaceful and relatively stable was the Saharan sector of the route from Kano through Air and Ghat. By the beginning of the last century, that portion of the Sahara was under the exclusive domination of two of the most powerful of the Tuareg tribes, the Azger controlling the oasis of Ghat and the Kel Owi that of Air, or Aheer.[3] As both depended mainly on the caravan trade for their livelihood, they did everything to ensure the security of the routes. Richardson, Barth, and Duveyrier, who travelled through these parts of the Sahara in 1845–6, 1850, and 1860 respectively, emphasized the relative security of the Sudan route and the honesty of the Kel Owi and Azger Tuareg. Richardson described the Tuareg of Air and Ghat as bearing an excellent character as traders and travelling companions, and mentioned their devotion to 'the peaceful pursuits of commerce'. Barth also reported that the Sudan route was more favourable 'than the route to Bornu because on the former the Tuareg were always ready to furnish any number of camels to carry merchandise and to guarantee their safety, while the road to Bornu is in such a precarious state that the merchant who selects it must

---

[1] F.O. 84/1144, Fremaux to Herman, 21 June 1861, encl. Herman to Russell, 26 July 1861; Barth, op. cit., vol. iii, pp. 7–8, 37–40, 67–100.

[2] See below, pp. 242–3.

[3] F. R. Rodd, *People of the Veil* (1926), pp. 388–93.

convey his merchandise on his own camels and at his own risk'.[1] As a result of the wholesome state of affairs along the Sudan route, and of the relative stability in the area east of Katsina, traffic was not limited to annual large caravans; small caravans were to be seen on it almost all the year round. The full flood of opulence and prosperity in which both Clapperton in 1824 and Barth in 1854 found Kano, the main terminus of the route, bears ample testimony to the relative strength and richness of the commercial current that flowed along it.

While the Sudan route was commercially the most important up to the late fifties, the Cyrenaica–Kufra–Waday road became, especially during the latter half of the nineteenth century, the most active, certainly culturally, and probably commercially as well. This route seems to have been as ancient as the old Garamantian route, for it passes through the area where, according to Herodotus, the Garamantians in their four-horse chariots chased and enslaved the Troglodytes. Moreover, some historians, including Bates, Bovill, and Rodd, have identified Agysimba, which Septimus Flaccus is believed to have reached during his famous four months' campaign in A.D. 100, with Tibesti.[2] But if the route was known in ancient times, it seems to have been rarely used in medieval and modern times until the beginning of the nineteenth century. The reopening of this eastern route was due to the rise of the Waday, with the accession of Abd al-Karim to the throne in 1805. When after ten years of victorious wars he had turned his little state into a powerful kingdom, it became, according to Barth, 'the chief object of his exertions to establish a direct communication with the ports on the coast of the Mediterranean, in order to supply himself with those manufactures which, before the spoil of Bagirmi, had been almost unknown to the people of Waday'.[3] The efforts of Abd al-Karim and his successors were rewarded, for by 1840 the Waday–Kufra–Benghazi route had become a well-known thoroughfare, mainly for slaves.

[1] Richardson, *Travels*, vol. ii, p. 141; F.O. 84/598, Richardson to Warrington, 24 Sept. 1845, encl. in Warrington to Aberdeen, 15 Oct. 1845; F.O. 101/30, Barth to Bunsen, 5 June 1850; F.O. 101/30, Barth to Palmerston, 24 May 1851. H. Duveyrier, *Exploration du Sahara: Les Touareg du Nord* (1864), pp. 259–60.

[2] O. Bates, *The Eastern Libyans* (London, 1914), p. 103; Rodd, op. cit., pp. 324–6; Bovill, op. cit., pp. 40–41. Other historians have identified Agysimba with Air or Chad. (See A. Kwapong, 'Africa Antiqua' in *Transactions of the Gold Coast and Togoland Historical Society*, vol. ii, Part I, 1956, p. 8.)

[3] Barth, op. cit., vol. ii, p. 664; vol. iii, pp. 530–1.

However, the raids of the Awlad Sulayman and the wars with Bornu in the forties and fifties rendered the southern end of the route exceedingly insecure. The northern section of the route to the coast was even more disturbed and dangerous as a result of the conflicts between the Bedouin tribes of southern Cyrenaica, especially the Zuwaya of the oases of Aujila and Kufra and the Tibu of Tibesti and Ennedi.[1] These wars and disturbances rendered the route so unsafe during the first half of the century that traffic along it, as on the other two routes, was restricted to single annual caravans.

But the introduction of the puritanic Islamic order of the Sanusi into Cyrenaica by its founder, Sayyid Muhammed 'Ali al-Sanusi, in 1843, brought about revolutionary changes in conditions on the route during the second half of the nineteenth century. The order spread rapidly into the Sahara and western Sudan and the number of its branches increased from 22 in 1853, three years before the death of Al-Sanusi, to 143 at the death of his son and successor, Sayyid Muhammed Al-Mahdi, in 1900. Five of these were in Morocco, 25 in Fezzan, 45 in Cyrenaica, and 15 of the remainder were in Waday, Kanem, Zinder, and Timbuctu.[2] Not only did this spread give a great fillip to Islam in the Sahara and the western Sudan; it also in a number of ways affected traffic on the eastern route, along which most of the branches were concentrated. Al-Sanusi and his son were able to win over most of the Bedouin tribes of Cyrenaica, the Zuwaya of Kufra, the Tibu of Tibesti, and the Awlad Sulayman of Kanem, and to establish and maintain peace and friendship among them. The result was that during the latter half of the nineteenth century the eastern route became remarkably safe. Hassanein Bey, the Egyptian Oxford graduate who travelled along the route in 1923, met some Bedouins who told him that in the days of Al-Mahdi a woman could walk from Barca in Cyrenaica to Waday unmolested. At the end of his trip he himself concluded that

there can be no doubt that the influence of the Senussi brotherhood upon the lives of the people of that religion is good. The *Ikwhan* (or teachers) of the Senussi are not only the teachers of the people, both in the field of religion and of general knowledge, but judges and intermediaries both between man and man and between tribe and tribe . . . The importance of

---

[1] A. M. Hassanein Bey, *The Lost Oases* (1925), pp. 62–65; E. E. Pritchard, *The Sanusi of Cyrenaica* (1949), pp. 11–13; *Encyclopedia of Islam*, vol. iv, pp. 154–5.
[2] Pritchard, op. cit., pp. 24–25; *Encyclopaedia of Islam*, vol. iv, pp. 154–5; H. Duveyrier, *La Confrérie musulman de Sidi Mohammed ben Ali as Senoussie* (Paris, 1884), pp. 28–38.

these aspects of the Senussi rule in maintaining the tranquility and well-being of the people of the Libyan desert can scarcely be overestimated.[1]

The *Zawiyas* (lodges or headquarters) of the branches of the brother-hood, which were usually built along the route, served as hotels for pilgrims as well as traders; and, as each of these lodges had to maintain itself from alms, tolls, and its own commercial activities, their governors often became great caravan traders themselves and gave every stimulus to the trade. Al-Mahdi himself is said to have dug wells between Kufra and Waday to facilitate the flow of the caravan traffic. Even Duveyrier, the bitter critic of the order, admitted—and this was confirmed by Hassanein Bey—that Al-Mahdi did manage 'to establish the ancient commercial relations between Waday and the Mediterranean'.[2]

If the Benghazi–Kufra–Waday was the least important of the routes at the beginning of the nineteenth century, it is quite evident that with the establishment of the Sanusi Brotherhood it became culturally and commercially the most important. Indeed, by the first decade of the present century it was the only route along which the old large annual caravans continued to move. When Hans Vischer visited Murzuk in 1906, he discovered that all the financiers and important caravan traders had left that town long ago and were continuing their trade on the one remaining trans-Saharan trade route from Waday and Darfur through eastern Borgu and Tibesti to Kufra and the Libyan desert to Benghazi. The great French travellers and scholars Gautier and Chudeau also found that whereas by 1905 the route from Bornu to Fezzan was hardly ever used and all traffic along the Morocco–Timbuctu route had been diverted to Senegal, large caravans were still leaving Benghazi for Waday carrying mainly guns and ammunition to be bartered for slaves.[3] Though Bovill does not say when the last of the caravans left the Sudan, it is obvious that it was during the second decade of our own century, and it was along the eastern rather than the western route. What finally disrupted the last of the ancient links between the Sudan and Barbary was the French occupation of Waday, Tibesti, and Borgu between 1906 and 1914 and the Italian occupation of Cyrenaica in 1911–12.

Each of these routes had in the nineteenth century as in medieval

[1] Hassanein Bey, op. cit., p. 67.

[2] Duveyrier, *La Confrerie*, op. cit., pp. 15–16; Hassanein Bey, op. cit., p. 64.

[3] Vischer, op. cit., p. 148; E. F. Gautier and R. Chudeau, *Missions au Sahara* (1909), vol. ii, pp. 294–5.

times four main points. These were the northern termini, the rendez-vous or *points de depart au sud*, the refreshment centres, and the southern termini. Mogador remained, as it had been through the centuries, the main terminus for the western route. Algiers, Constantine, and Tunis were the termini for the branch route through Tuat. However, the French occupation of Algeria in 1830, the ordinance of 1843 which abolished the importation of products from Sudan and the Sahara into Algeria, and the abolition of the slave traffic in Tunis in 1840–2 reduced the traffic from Tuat northward to a spasmodic trickle until the 1850's.[1] As is obvious from the map, Tripoli was until the late fifties the terminus of the Sudan and Fezzan routes as well as the branch route from Tuat. It was this which made that Regency such an important gateway into the interior. The terminus for the eastern route was Benghazi. The rise of its population from 5,000 in 1817 to 16,500 in 1911 and the fact that the greatest increase took place in the last decades of the Turkish rule clearly bears out the increasing importance of the traffic along the eastern route.

All the caravans usually assembled at one point before they set out for the Sudan. These centres had certain things in common. They were places where provisions could be obtained, where beasts of burden, camel drivers, and guides could be hired, and where bankers or their representatives resided. The traditional rendezvous for the western route had been Sijilmasa, the capital of the oases of Tafilet. Both Ibn Battuta and Leo Africanus started their journey into the Sudan from there. The one described it as 'a very fine town with quantities of excellent dates', and the other recorded that the inhabitants were rich and 'had traffic into the land of the negroes'.[2] Towards the end of the eighteenth century, however, Sijilmasa was razed to the ground during the civil war in Morocco. When Walter Harris visited that oasis in 1893, he found nothing of the once famous town 'but acres, almost miles of shapeless ruins'. By the nineteenth century, the oasis of El Haha and its capital Tenduf had inherited the role played by Tafilet and Sijilmasa. Harris observed that 'only a very small amount of the Sudan trade comes into Morocco by this route [via Tafilet to Morocco], the greater proportion being taken

[1] A. Bernard and N. Lacroix, *La Penetration Saharienne* (1830–1906) (Alger, 1906), p. 23; below, pp. 222–5.

[2] Ibn Battuta, *Travels in Asia and Africa*, translated by H. A. R. Gibb (1929), p. 317; Leo Africanus, *History and Description of Africa*, Hakluyt Society (1896), p. 784.

via Tenduf and the Sus to Mogador'. Merchants from Tafilet and El Harib in the north, from the districts of Wadnoun and the Draa in the west, assembled at Tenduf.[1] From this centre the caravan often divided into two; one branch went directly south to Taodeni and Arawan, the other eastward to Tuat and then southward, to meet the first branch again at Arawan. From here they advanced together on Timbuctu. (See Map 3—The Caravan Routes.)

Another *point de depart*—and probably the most important one until the late fifties—was Ghadames. It was there that caravans from the Regency of Tripoli and southern Tunis and Algeria assembled. Some then travelled westward through Tuat to Timbuctu, others went directly south to Ghat and Kano, while a third branch pushed southwestward through Murzuk to Bornu. The city retained in the nineteenth century the position which it enjoyed even in the days of Leo Africanus as the home of most of the bankers and wholesalers and the headquarters of most of the trading firms operating in the interior. Richardson found at least four principal firms there in 1845. Five years later Barth described Ghadames as the residence of wealthy merchants who embarked all their capital on commercial enterprises and brought home their own merchandise, and said that 'all the money with which the inhabitants of Tawat [Tuat] trade belongs to the people of Ghadames'.[2] In all the important southern termini, such as Jenne, Timbuctu, and Kano, there were resident agents of the Ghadames capitalists and firms. Most of the men of that town were also traders themselves and were known all over the Sudan for fair dealing. Laing, Richardson, and Duveyrier, who visited Ghadames in 1825, 1845, and 1860 respectively, commented on the business acumen of the people of Ghadames. Laing found to his amazement that 'they calculate with profound nicety the expense of carriage to distant countries, duties, customs, risk, trouble, the percentage that their goods will bear, and even do business by means of Bills and unwritten agreements or promises'.[3]

For the eastern route the main rendezvous was Djalo, in the oasis

---

[1] W. B. Harris, *Tafilet* (1895), pp. 264, 305; O. Lentz, *Timbuctou* (1886), vol. ii, p. 37; D. Mackenzie, *The Flooding of the Sahara* (1877), pp. 154–5.

[2] Barth, op. cit., vol. i, pp. 169, 397; F.O. 101/16, Richardson to Warrington, 13 Nov. 1845.

[3] C.O. 2/5, Notes on Ghadames, Laing to Horton, 26 Oct. 1825; F.O. 101/16, An account of the oasis and city of Ghadames, Richardson to Warrington, 13 Nov. 1845; Ibn Battuta, op. cit., p. 335; Barth, op. cit., vol. i, p. 461; Rodd, op. cit., p. 369.

of Aujila. The oasis had been a very important centre in the period, before the sixteenth century, when there was a brisk direct trade in gold between Gao, Agades, and Cairo. The overthrow of the Songhay Empire and the decline of Gao and Agades brought this traffic to a complete stop. Still Aujila retained its position as a resting place for the pilgrim caravans. It did not regain its commercial importance until the reopening of the Benghazi–Waday route and the establishment of the *pax Sanusi*. When Henderson, the British Vice-Consul at Benghazi, visited the oasis in October 1875, he found Djalo 'the main starting point of the numerous caravans to and from Wadai and Bornu', the centre of a large and valuable trade, whose inhabitants were 'all well to do and many of them very wealthy'.[1]

After these rendezvous, the next important points on the routes were the refreshment centres. These centres may appropriately be compared to the coaling stations in maritime navigation. They were usually situated in fertile oases where food and fresh water could be obtained and camels and guides exchanged. As the caravans remained at these centres for long periods, a fact which differentiated them from the resting places where caravans halted at the end of a day's march, they were often great trading centres, and traders from the Sudan as well as from the northern coast often disposed of their merchandise there and returned. These centres thus served as points where the batons of the trans-Saharan traffic commercial relay were changed. Tuat and Arawan were the main such centres on the western route. In the market of Arawan, for example, exchange usually took place between the 'gold' caravans from the south and the caravans from Ghadames, Tuat, and Tenduf.[2]

On the Sudan route, Ghat and Iferuan (in Air) were the main 'coaling stations'. Ghat was particularly famous for its water, which Oudney and Clapperton described as 'clear, well-tasted and in abundance'. It was also the busiest market centre in the Sahara, especially from the forties onwards, and the terminus for most of the smaller northern and southern caravans. Its markets were held twice a year, in winter (December–January) and summer (June–July). The winter one, which was the greater of the two, was attended by caravans from nearly all parts of the Sahara and the Sudan. Richardson, who attended the winter *souk* of Ghat in 1845, gives the following vivid account of it:

[1] F.O. 84/1412, Henderson to Derby, 24 Dec. 1875.
[2] Caillié, op. cit., vol. iii, pp. 97–103; Barth, op. cit., vol. v, pp. 22, 26, 460–1.

Caravans from Soudan, including all the large cities, but especially from Kanou, from Bornou, from the Tibboo [Tibu] country, from Touat, from Fezzan, from Souf, from Ghadames, and from Tripoli, Tunis and the north coast, visited the Ghat Souk [market] of this winter. The number of merchants, traders and camel-drivers was about 500, the slaves imported from Soudan to Bornou about 1000, the camels employed in the caravans about 1050. . . . The main commerce of these caravans consisted of the staple exports of slaves, elephants' teeth and senna, the limited value of which, at the market this year, was estimated at £60,000, which value would be doubled on arriving at the European markets.[1]

Both Barth in 1850 and Duveyrier in 1860 found it still an important and thriving commercial centre.[2] Agades, which was the other refreshment centre on the Sudan route until the sixteenth century, Barth found in ruins. By about the beginning of the nineteenth century, Iferuan had taken the place of Agades. The new centre owed its importance to its excellent water supply and its situation at the junction of the old *hajj* route from Timbuctu and the routes from Tuat to Air and from Ghat to Kano.[3]

On the old Garamantian route, Murzuk continued to be, as it had been from very early times until the eighteen-forties, the main refreshment centre for caravans from Ghadames, Tripoli, and Cyrenaica to Hausaland and Bornu, as well as the chief slave market of the Sahara. But even by 1845 it was in decline, on account, as Richardson correctly pointed out, 'of the rival Touarick city of Ghat and especially from the disturbed state of the Bornu route during the last few years'.[4] Though the market did not regain its former importance, the slave caravans continued to arrive there from Bornu and Ghat until the mid-fifties, when the increasing diplomatic attack on the trade and the other factors already discussed completely diverted the slave caravans to Ghat and Kufra. By 1860 the decadence of Murzuk and Fezzan had reached an advanced stage. When Duveyrier went there in 1861 he found that many people had migrated either to the coast or to the Sudan.[5] At that time El Giof in the oasis of Kufra was to the eastern route what Ghat and Murzuk were to the central routes. Its effective use as a refreshment centre

---

[1] Richardson, *Travels*, vol. ii, pp. 115–16, 195; F.O. 101/16, The Souk of Ghat in Winter 1845, Richardson to Warrington, 1 May 1846.

[2] Barth, op. cit., vol. i, pp. 237–68.

[3] Rodd, op. cit., pp. 115, 318–19

[4] Richardson, *Travels*, vol. ii, p. 346.

[5] H. Duveyrier, *Exploration*, pp. 283–4.

dates from the mid-fifties, when the first lodge of the Sanusi was established there and the Zuwaya gave up their predatory habits. The growing importance of Kufra was accentuated in 1894 by the establishment of the headquarters of the order there. This has been appropriately described by Hassanein Bey as marking an important era 'in the development of trade between the Sudân and the Mediterranean coast by way of Kufra'.[1] Instead of a centre of brigandage, Kufra and its capital, El Giof, became from the fifties onwards the peaceful abode of convinced Muslims and a safe resort for traders and pilgrims.

The fourth and final important points on the caravan routes were the southern termini: Timbuctu for the western route, Kano for the Sudan, Kukawa for the Garamantian, and Wara and Abeche for the eastern route. All these had one thing in common, and that is that the caravans from the north hardly ever went beyond them. At these centres the merchandise from Barbary was off-loaded and the Sudanese commodities were loaded for the return trip. The disposal of the merchandise from the north, however, varied from centre to centre. At some very little actual retail trading was done. The imports from the north were quickly transported in bulk to other points farther south, where they were sold. These were, in fact, no more than entrepôts. Other termini were not merely entrepôts but also market centres where most of the goods were retailed. The termini were thus the end of the traffic from the north and the beginning of that to the south. They therefore formed very important joints in the commercial and cultural chains which bound together Barbary and the more thickly populated forest regions farther south.

Timbuctu was the most typical of the entrepôts. In view of the chronic anarchy and the rivalry between the Fulani and the Tuareg for the mastery of the town, it is obvious that very little retail trading could be done there. Indeed, the fanatical Fulani, according to Barth, drove away the pagan Mandingo and Bambara traders 'who carry on almost the whole commerce with the countries to the south of the Niger'. Caillié described the market of Timbuctu as 'a desert' in comparison with that of Jenne. Dubois found it in the nineties attended only by 'women with little baskets, little calabashes and little mats selling insignificant little things, red, green, white, drab and black spices and vegetables for infinitely little sums of cowries, just as in any, no matter what, little market in no matter what little

[1] Hassanein Bey, op. cit., p. 64.

town of the Sudan'.[1] But if the wars and the fanaticism of the Fulani drove away the retail traders, they did not deprive the town of its strategic situation as the most accessible point to both camels from Barbary and canoes on the Niger. Some of the houses whose exteriors shocked Dubois by their dilapidated and desolate appearance were, as he discovered when he entered some of them, more or less warehouses filled with goods awaiting transportation southward or northward.[2] The goods from the north were conveyed from these warehouses in Timbuctu first to its port, Kabara, five miles south, and thence in boats up-river to Jenne, Segu, Sansanding, Bamako, and Bure, or southeastward to Dore, the capital of Libtako. (See Map 3.) It was at these centres that some of the goods were retailed. The rest were conveyed farther south and west to such places as Tangrela, Kong, Bobo-Dioulasso, and to Begho and Dormaa in the Brong–Ahafo region of modern Ghana. In the markets south and west of Jenne it was not unusual, especially before the mid-fifties, to find such commodities as salt and calico from Barbary and the Sahara competing with similar or identical goods brought via the Senegal and the west coast.[3]

A classic example of the combined market and entrepôt type of terminus was Kano. Until the end of the eighteenth century Katsina was the main terminus of the Sudan route and an even more important market centre than Kano. But the Jihad of 1804, followed by the guerilla warfare between the Goberawa and the Fulani, which went on intermittently throughout the century, drove all the foreign

[1] Caillié, op. cit., vol. ii, p. 51; Dubois, op. cit., p. 211. Barth's description of Timbuctu, and especially of its commerce (vol. v, pp. 17–37) should be received with some reservation. For although he remained there for eight months, he was kept more or less as a prisoner and never had a single opportunity to walk round the town himself or visit any of its markets. With his characteristic sense of honesty, he stated himself that his sketch of the commercial life of Timbuctu could not 'make the slightest pretension to completeness, as I did not enter into such free intercourse with the natives as would have enabled me to combine a sufficient number of facts into a graphic view of the commercial life of the city. The people with whom I had most intercourse could offer little or no information on the subject. My situation in Kano had been very different.' (Vol. v, p. 17.) In fact, the picture he painted of the commercial life of the city contrasts sharply with that of Caillié in 1826 or of Dubois in 1894 and seems to be more true of the sixteenth than of the nineteenth century.

[2] Dubois, op. cit., pp. 259–65.

[3] Park, *Travels*, pp. 305–6; Caillié, op. cit., vol. i, p. 453; Dubois, op. cit., pp. 163–9, 176; Barth, op. cit., vol. v, pp. 26–27, 36; I. Wilks, 'A Medieval Trade Route from the Niger to the Gulf of Guinea', *Journal of African History*, III, 2, 1962.

merchants to Kano.[1] The growth of Kano was rapid, for already by
the time of Clapperton's visit in 1824 it was enjoying the position as
the emporium of Hausaland which it had when Barth visited it in
1851.[2] A comparison of Clapperton's and Barth's descriptions of its
market shows that the fortune of that town took a course diametric-
ally opposite to that of Timbuctu and Katsina. While the story of
Kano was one of continuous progress and activity, that of the others
was one of gradual decline and desolation. Clapperton estimated the
population of Kano at between 30,000 and 40,000; Barth estimated
it at 30,000, but added that this doubled itself during the caravan
season, that is, between January and April every year.[3] A comparison
of this with the population of Timbuctu, which Barth generously
estimated at 10,000, shows how important Kano was. In its market,
which was described as 'crowded from sunrise to sunset every day',
both Clapperton and Barth saw traders from towns as far apart as
Tripoli to the north and Salaga in modern Ghana to the south, and
from In Salah in Tuat to the northwest and Masena, the capital of
Bagirmi, to the southwest. Clapperton also noticed to his astonishment that 'the merchants understand the benefits of monopoly as
well as any people in the world; they take good care never to over-
stock the market, and if anything falls in price it is immediately
withdrawn for a few days'.[4] In addition to being a great commercial
centre, Kano was also an important entrepôt from which trade
routes radiated westward through Gwandu and Fada N'Gurma to
Wagadugu, southwestward through Bussa and Nikki to Salaga in
modern Ghana, southward via Zaria, Raba, Ilorin, Oyo, Ibadan,
and Abeokuta to Badagry in modern Dahomey, and eastward
through Katagum to Bornu, Bagirmi, and Adamawa on the Benue.

But what distinguished Kano even more from the other termini
was the fact that it was, besides a market and an entrepôt, a great
industrial centre. Its chief manufacture was cotton cloth, which was
woven on narrow looms from native-grown cotton and usually dyed
blue in colour.[5] This was made up in different forms: robes or shirts,
turkedi or oblong pieces of dark blue material worn by women,
zenne or plaids, of which there were a great variety, and *rawani*, or
black veils. These various types of dress were distributed all over

   [1] Barth, vol. ii, pp. 79–81; Bovill, op. cit., p. 238.
   [2] See below, pp. 281–2.
   [3] Barth, op. cit., vol. ii, p. 124.
   [4] Clapperton, op. cit., p. 53.
   [5] Barth, op. cit., vol. ii, pp. 125–7, vol. iv, p. 26; Clapperton, op. cit., p. 53.

Africa. Cloth manufactured in Kano was worn in Murzuk, Ghat, Tripoli, and Morocco to the north, Timbuctu, Sansanding and even Arguin to the west, throughout Bornu and Adamawa, and in Nupe and even Lagos in the south. According to Barth, about 300 camel-loads of Kano cloth were conveyed annually to Timbuctu, and the trade in salt in Timbuctu and Arawan was 'entirely carried on by means of the *turkedi*'. Indeed, these Kano textile manufactures were in such great demand in Timbuctu that when the direct route between the two towns was blocked during the second half of the nineteenth century by the political disturbances in the intervening regions, they were conveyed by the very circuitous route northward through Ghat, then westward to Tuat, and finally southward to Timbuctu.[1] Barth estimated the value of the cloth exported annually from Kano at 300 million Kurdi (£25,000). Though this seems inconsiderable by modern standards, yet if we consider that in Barth's day fifty to sixty thousand cowries (or £4–£5) could support a Kano family for a year, the income from the cloth industry was by Hausa standards certainly substantial. The other main industries were tanning of hides and making of leather-wear such as sandals, shoes, and bags. In view of the triple role played by Kano, Barth's informers were justified in calling it the 'African London, Birmingham and Manchester'.[2]

The traditional terminus of the Fezzan–Bornu route was Ngornu (Denham's 'Angornu'), a few miles southeast of modern Kukawa. By the time of Denham it was the largest and most populous town in Bornu and its market, according to Oudney, was attended at times by as many as 'eighty or a hundred thousand persons'.[5] But after this expedition the wars between Bagirmi and Bornu forced traders to emigrate to Kuka (or Kukawa), the new capital of Bornu built by Al-Kānami in 1814. By the time of Barth, the new capital had superseded Ngornu as the terminus of the reduced caravan traffic from the north. Like Kano, it was both a market town and an entrepôt, though in both roles it was less important. Thus while the market of Kano was held daily and attended by over 30,000 people during the caravan season, that of Kukawa was held only on Mondays, and between 12,000–15,000 people attended. As an entrepôt, it supplied via Bauchi the towns of Abinsi, Ibi, Muri, Wukari,

---

[1] Richardson, *Travels*, vol. ii, p. 117; Barth, op. cit., vol. ii, pp. 126–7; vol. iv, p. 515; vol. v, pp. 26–27.

[2] Barth, vol. ii, p. 92.

[3] C.O. 2/13, Oudney to Horton, 28 Mar. 1823; Denham, op. cit., pp. 79–80.

and Yola on the Benue to the southwest, as well as the regions of Bagirmi to the southeast, with goods from the Mediterranean. It also monopolized the exceedingly lucrative trade with the western Sudan in the exclusive Bornu product of natron. Kukawa continued to play its commercial roles, thanks to its links with Kano, until the nineties, when the whole of Bornu was devastated by the fanatical adventurer Rabeh.

On the eastern route, Wara retained its commercial importance, though the political capital of Waday was shifted from Wara to Abeche in 1850. This was largely because it was near the residence of the great traders, the Jellaba, who were believed to have immigrated to Waday from the valley of the Nile about the middle of the eighteenth century. The Jellaba hardly ever went to the northern coast themselves, but conveyed southward the goods brought from the north. They were divided into several groups, each of which controlled a particular route southward or eastward. Thus one group monopolized the trade between Waday and the celebrated copper-producing centre of Hofra al-Nahas on one of the tributaries of the White Nile, while other groups frequented the markets of Bagirmi, Bornu, and Kano.

While the flow and ebb of the traffic, as well as the prosperity of the caravan centres, fluctuated according to the vagaries of Sudanese and Saharan politics, certain features of this traffic remained as they had been since the days of Ibn Battuta and Leo Africanus. These included the time for the departure of the caravans southward, the difficulties encountered *en route*, the merchandise involved, and the system of exchange and transportation. As a rule the caravans left the Barbary states between September and October, when the winter season in the desert begins, and started the return journey from the Sudan at the beginning of the tropical rainy season in April or May. Barring accidents and undue delays, the journey lasted from seventy to ninety days, depending on the size of the caravan and the weight of each camel load.[1] Nothing illustrates the dangers and ravages of the trans-Saharan traffic more vividly than the hundreds of skeletons that littered the routes. James F. Church, one of the explorers of the

[1] There were two main types of caravans, the large annual ones which could consist of between 500 and 2,000 camels, and the small casual ones which could have anything from 5 to 100 camels. As a rule, the smaller the number of camels the greater the speed of the caravan. The average rate was 15–16 miles a day of 8 hours for a heavily laden caravan, 17–18 miles for a moderately laden one, and 20–22 a day of 10 hours for a lightly laden one.

1850's, recorded that so strewn with skeletons of human beings and camels was the route from Teggery in Fezzan to Kukawa that 'an explorer unacquainted with the track across the desert might almost without guide trace his way by their aid'.[1] Most of these were undoubtedly the remains of poor negro slaves. Writers such as Buxton and Richardson tended to assume too readily that the mortality was caused only by the inhuman treatment of slaves by the caravan drivers. There were, however, many natural causes which made the crossing of the desert one of the most hazardous enterprises in the world. The first cause of mortality was undoubtedly thirst, due mainly to the filling up of wells either as a result of sandstorms or even by robbers.[2] Though in most cases the sand was cleared, yet very often this operation took so long—at times a whole day, as both Denham and later Barth themselves experienced—that many people who arrived there on the verge of exhaustion perished before water was obtained. This explains why most of the skeletons were concentrated near or around wells. At times the water was found to have dried up entirely, and this might result in the death of the whole caravan, beasts, masters, and slaves. According to Jackson a caravan of 200 men and 1,800 camels perished for this reason on the route from Timbuctu to Tafilet in 1805.

The second cause of hardship and death was the weather.[3] The sharp variation in temperature—from as high as 110° F. by day to as low as 20° F. at night—often proved fatal to the naked slaves. The Vice-Consul at Benghazi reported in 1857 that 810 of the Waday caravan died near Aujila 'from no want of either the means of subsistence or transport but from the intense cold which from the great radiation of heat after sunset prevails in the desert'.[4]

A third scourge of trans-Saharan travellers was sandstorms. These were caused by strong winds filling the whole air with sand, and could last from a few hours to six or seven days. The whirling particles of sand could penetrate everywhere, inflaming the eyes,

[1] Br. Emp. MSS. S22/922, Church to Chamorouzou. See also Denham, op. cit., pp. 7, 9–10, 11–13; Vischer, op. cit., pp. 171, 238.

[2] Caillié, op. cit., vol. ii, pp. 117–18; Denham, op. cit., pp. 13, 15, 205; Lyon, op. cit., p. 331; C.O. 2/13, Oudney to Horton, 28 Mar. 1823; F.O. 84/774, Gagliuffi to Reade, 4 Aug. 1849, encl. in Reade to Palmerston, 20 Jan. 1849; F.O. 84/815, Crowe to Palmerston, 20 Jan. 1850; Barth, op. cit., vol. v, p. 417.

[3] Lyon, op. cit., pp. 256–7, 332; Caillié, op. cit., vol. ii, p. 95; Denham, op. cit., p. 280; Richardson, Travels, vol. ii, p. 4; Barth, op. cit., vol. i, pp. 573–4, vol. ii, p. 296, vol. v, p. 436.

[4] F.O. 101/29, Herman to Palmerston, 12 Oct. 1857 and enclosures.

smiting the face, and cracking the skin. As one later traveller succinctly put it, 'one feels it [the sand], breathes it, eats it, drinks it—
and hates it'.[1] If the storm raged for a long time and was strong
enough to blow along large pillars of sand, a whole caravan could be
buried alive. Besides filling up wells, the winds could cause evaporation of water from the goat-skin bags and thus aggravate the delicate
water problem.

In addition to the difficulties caused by these geographical or
natural factors were those caused by the activities of robbers and
marauding bands. Laing, it may be recalled, was nearly killed during
an attack by such people. It was to prevent such attacks that large
numbers of traders travelled together. The fear of attack also led to
the practice of hiring guards, a practice well established even by the
time of Leo Africanus.[2] These guards were either the rulers of the
territory which the caravan was traversing or people appointed by
the rulers. No caravan from Timbuctu to Azawad could be free from
attack unless it was escorted by 'some well-known person belonging
to the tribe of Tadmekket'.[3]

Because of the duration of the journey and a means of transportation which necessitated loading and unloading almost daily, the
goods transported had to be both non-perishable and light. This in
fact is what the list of merchandise[4] reveals. Exports into Sudan
were made up of goods from Europe, Barbary, and the Sahara.
Those from Europe, it is interesting to note, came from most of the
countries of western Europe, and consisted largely of cloth, the most
important items being bleached and unbleached calicoes and cotton
prints of various colours, mostly from England, and silks (used for
embroidery), muslins, and linen manufactured in France. The next

---

[1] Caillié, op. cit., vol. ii, pp. 114–15; Lyon, op. cit., p. 70; Denham, op. cit.,
pp. xix, 15, 28, 294; Hassanein Bey, op. cit., p. 85.

[2] Leo Africanus, op. cit., p. 829.

[3] Caillié, op. cit., vol. ii, p. 148; Barth, op. cit., vol. i, pp. 181–2, 360, vol. v,
p. 482.

[4] Proceedings (1790), op. cit., pp. 181–91; F.O. 76/12, Warrington to Bathurst,
17 Apr. 1818; F.O. 101/3, Wood to Warrington, 1 Aug. 1839, encl. in Warrington
to Bidwell, 21 Aug. 1839; F.O. 101/9, Gagliuffi to Warrington, 20 May 1843,
encl. Warrington to Bidwell, 9 June 1843; F.O. 101/18, Commercial Report of
Tripoli, Crowe to Palmerston, 26 May 1847; F.O. 101/16, Richardson to
Warrington, An Account of the oasis and city of Ghadames, 13 Nov. 1845;
idem, The Souk of Ghat in winter, 1 May 1846; Barth, op. cit., vol. ii, pp. 126–
40; vol. v, pp. 34–36; Wyon, op. cit., pp. 152–9; Clapperton, op. cit., pp. 42, 53,
121–2; Gautier and Chudeau, op. cit., vol. ii, pp. 292–4; Dubois, op. cit., pp. 178–
9, 252–60.

export was common writing paper, mainly from Italy. In view of the large number of arabic manuscripts that have been already discovered in Northern Nigeria alone, this item must have been of very great importance.[1] Beads of different sizes, shapes, and colours brought mainly from Italy, especially Venice, and sword blades made in Germany and England were next in importance. These broad, straight, and long blades were mounted and sheathed in Kano and Bornu and re-exported to all parts of the Sudan and the Sahara. As these swords were one of the main weapons of the Tuareg and Fulani, there was always a great demand for them. Looking-glasses of different sizes, and needles, mainly from Germany and France, were the other major items. Other miscellaneous articles were files, chisels, snuff-boxes, razors, scissors, Dutch knives, brass, and trinkets. Guns, pistols, and ammunition were not exported from the north until the last decade or two of the nineteenth century, when, according to Gautier and Chudeau, they formed the principal European merchandise conveyed from Benghazi to Waday.[2] The articles manufactured in Barbary and Egypt and exported to the Sudan included shawls and burnouses from Morocco, red caps, red sashes, and trousers from Tunis and Egypt, and long striped carpets and coarse silk from Tripoli. According to Barth, the silk from Tripoli was highly valued in the Sudan, where it was used for ornamenting robes, shawls, and sandals. Korans and other books illuminated with gold and crimson were also exported mainly from Morocco. Other interesting miscellaneous items from Barbary were horses, spices, perfumes, and above all cowries, which were the currency of western Sudan.

Having left the northern termini with these articles, the caravans then collected the exports of the Sahara. These consisted mainly of narcotics and provisions, such as tobacco from Wadi Draa and Tuat and dates from Fezzan. The most important and traditional export of the Sahara was, and still is of course, salt from Taodeni and Bilma on the western and Fezzan–Bornu routes. Until the last three or four decades of the last century this commodity found its way from these two places into the whole of the Sudan and as far south as the forest regions of the western coast of Africa. The salt from

---

[1] My thanks are due to Mr. H. F. C. Smith of Ahmadu Bello University, Zaria, for drawing my attention to this.

[2] Lyon, op. cit., p. 152; Barth, op. cit., vol. ii, p. 139; Gautier and Chudeau, op. cit., vol. ii, p. 294.

Taodeni is quite different from that obtained in Bilma; it is rock salt dug out in large lumps by slaves and trimmed down into blocks of different sizes. That of Bilma is obtained from the crystallization of water strongly impregnated with salt which collects in pits dug for the purpose. These crusts are collected and made into conical loaves of different heights and diameters. Salt from the Sahara was not conveyed into the Sudan by caravans from Barbary alone. Large annual caravans from the Sudan, especially from Walata, Timbuctu, and Air came to the salt mines to convey this precious and indispensable commodity. During Barth's stay in Agades in 1850, a caravan of 10,000 camels left there for Bilma; even as late as 1914, when the salt trade was in decline, the caravan of that year from Air to Bilma consisted of 500 camels.[1]

Another commodity which was added to those of the north, particularly on the two central routes just before they reached the southern terminus, was natron (Denham's trona), which was produced mainly in the basin of Lake Chad and in the natron lake in the district of Muniyo in western Bornu.[2] It is carbonate of soda left behind in crusts after the evaporation of the pools and collected particularly on the southeast coast of the Chad during the rainy season. These crusts were hewn out in large slabs and conveyed first to Kukawa and other natron markets in Bornu, and then to Kano and other parts of the Sudan. Natron was used in several ways. It was used as medicine by all the people. Hans Vischer always took natron with his meals while he was in Bornu and he testifies to 'its good effects even in cases of fever'.[3] In areas where salt was scarce natron was used instead. It was also beaten to powder and mixed with snuff, to which it imparted a high degree of pungency; it was also given to horses and cattle as food. Finally it was used in dyeing leather and cloth.

Some of the commodities enumerated did not end their journey in the southern termini but continued southward, generally in new hands and by different means of transport. These included cloth, salt, natron, caps, beads, and the unwrought silk of Tripoli. Between Badagry and the Niger, the Landers met several caravans from Kano bound for Gonja with natron, rock salt, and Kano cloth. In

[1] Barth, op. cit., vol. ii, p. 428; Rodd, op. cit., p. 218; Gautier and Chudeau, op. cit., p. 297. The Taodeni salt mines are still being operated.

[2] Barth, op. cit., vol. ii, pp. 66–75.

[3] Vischer, op. cit., pp. 301–2; Barth, op. cit., vol. i, p. 389, vol. iii, p. 53, vol. iv, pp. 66–67; John and Richard Lander, op. cit., vol. i, p. 228.

the market of Kulfu in Nupe, described as 'the principal town of trade in Nyffe [Nupe] at present, and at all times a central point of trade in this part of the interior' where caravans assembled from Yoruba regions, Yauri, Borgu, Hausaland, and Bornu, Clapperton saw horses, natron, unwrought silk, beads, silk cords, robes, and turbans, all brought from Bornu and Kano.[1] In the other great Nupe market centres of Raba and Egga, both on the Niger, the Landers and later Oldfield saw Arabs dealing in horses, red caps, natron, red cloth, raw silk, beads, and turbans brought from the north.[2] The most important of these articles which went south were beads, salt, silk from Tripoli, which was used in the great and famous Nupe cloth industry, and natron. Barth estimated the quantity of natron re-exported annually from Kano to Nupe at 20,000 ass loads 'at the very least'. Natron, beads, and silk from Tripoli were distributed not only throughout Nupe, Yorubaland, and the regions of Benue but also as far south as Calabar, Lagos, and Badagry.[3]

It is interesting to note that these articles passed mainly into the hands of the Hausas at Kano and the Mandingo at Jenne and Segu, and that the beasts of burden used for the southern traffic were different from those of the north. Throughout the Sudan, as far north as Air, the beasts of burden were asses and bullocks. Caillié often fell in with caravans of asses and bullocks while crossing from northern Sierra Leone to Timbuctu. On their way from Kano to Bornu, both Clapperton and Barth met caravans 'of the ass and the bullock going peaceably side by side as is always the case in negroland'. All the beasts of burden of the caravans which the Landers came across during their journey from Badagry to Kano were asses.[4] The regions south of the southern termini were too wet and too infested with tsetse flies for the camel.

In return, traditional merchandise was brought from the Sudan: cloth, hides, and leather goods—saddles, water skins, and sandals—

[1] H. Clapperton, *Journal of a second expedition into the interior of Africa* (London, 1829), pp. 135–8.

[2] Richard and John Lander, op. cit., vol. i, pp. 135, 152, vol. ii, p. 290, vol. iii, p. 43; Laird and Oldfield, op. cit., vol. ii, pp. 89–91; Richard Lander, *Records*, vol. i, p. 182, vol. ii, p. 47.

[3] C.O. 84/857, Barth to Crowe, 15 March 1851, encl. in Crowe to Palmerston, 7 Nov. 1851; Barth, op. cit., vol. ii, pp. 132, 135; Lyon, op. cit., p. 153; Vischer, op. cit., p. 301.

[4] C.O. 2/13, Oudney to Horton, 28 Mar. 1823; Caillié, op. cit., vol. i, pp. 32, 40, 395; Clapperton, op. cit., p. 39; Barth, op. cit., vol. i, p. 361, vol. ii, pp. 5, 7, 56.

ostrich feathers, ivory, gum, wax, civet,[1] gold dust, kola nuts, and slaves. By the late 1850's, however, most of these commodities were obtained in very small quantities. A typical example was gold dust. Until about the middle of the seventeenth century, this was the most valuable of the Sudan exports. It was because of this that Ghana, Timbuctu, and Gao became so famous in Europe. But, as we have seen, the traffic in this began to decline in the seventeenth century, and by the middle of the nineteenth century the quantity of gold exported to Barbary was insignificant. It was not found at all along the eastern, Fezzan, or Sudan routes. Denham and Clapperton reported that 'gold is neither found in this country [Bornu] nor is it brought into it'.[2] Richardson saw only a very small quantity in the winter market of Ghat, and that was brought from Tuat. He noted that though gold would pay extremely well if it could be obtained in large quantities, yet there 'was a very small quantity purchaseable and often none at all'. Barth also described the annual quantity of gold from Timbuctu to the north as very small and estimated it at not more than £20,000 per annum.[3] But with the successful drive of the French up the Senegal into the gold-producing regions of Bambuk, Bore, and Lobi from the forties, and with the increasing British trading activities at the Niger–Benue confluence from the sixties, the flow not only of gold, but also of ivory, ostrich feathers, and gum began to be diverted westward and southward, while the markets of Jenne and Timbuctu were by the eighties and nineties being supplied with European goods from the Senegal region.

Indeed at the beginning of and throughout the nineteenth century the mainstays of the Sudan export trade were Kano cloth, kola nuts (*cola nitida*), and slaves. The first was exported in considerable quantities into the Sahara. Kola nuts were, in bulk at least, the largest export. These precious nuts were obtained mainly from Ashanti in Ghana.[4] From here they were and still are conveyed northwestward

---

[1] This is a kind of strong musty perfume obtained from the secretion of civet cats kept in cages.

[2] Denham, op. cit., p. 325; Clapperton, op. cit., p. 17.

[3] F.O. 101/16, The Souk of Ghat in winter, 1 May 1846; Richardson, *Travels*, vol. i, p. 133, vol. ii, p. 118; Barth, op. cit., vol. v, p. 22.

[4] There are two principal varieties of Kola: *cola acuminata*, which has more than two cotyledons and *cola nitida*, which has only two. *Cola nitida* was and still is preferred; it occurs naturally only in Ashanti, Ivory Coast, and Eastern Liberia. In the twentieth century it was introduced into Nigeria, where previously only *cola acuminata* grew. See J. M. Dalziel, *The Useful Plants of Western Tropical Africa* (London, 1937), pp. 100–7.

to Sansanding, Segu, and Jenne, then up the Niger to Timbuctu and northeastward across the Niger to Kano and Bornu.[1] Large quantities were consumed in the Sudan, but a substantial quantity was re-exported from these Sudanese markets into the Sahara and Barbary. The kola nut is of an oval or bean-like shape about the size of a walnut. It has two main uses. It is chewed and eaten as food, and its bitter-sweet liquid acts not only as a stimulant but also as an anti-dote, to some extent, against thirst. It was this latter property which made the nut so invaluable to caravan traders and inhabitants of the Sahara. Indeed, it was called by explorers the coffee of the negroes, and Barth quite correctly described it as being as necessary to the negroes as 'tea or coffee to us'. Secondly, it is used among many negro peoples for several social functions. For instance, the most traditional way of welcoming a guest among the Yorubas and the Ibos of Nigeria is to present him with a bowl of kola nuts. The kola nut is to this day as valuable as it was in the days of Leo, and thousands of bags are still exported from Ashanti in Ghana to the north. The only difference is that the nuts are now conveyed by motor vehicles instead of by asses.

By and large, however, slaves were the main Sudan export in the nineteenth century, as they had been from time immemorial. On this all the explorers and the consular agents agreed. Slaves were the main if not the only merchandise along the Bornu–Fezzan and Waday–Benghazi routes. Richardson was not exaggerating when he reported in 1846 that 'slaves were the grand staple commerce of the Sudan and Bornu caravans and without slaves their commerce would hardly exist'. In 1858 the Consul-General in Tripoli also observed that the slave trade constituted 'more than two-thirds of the value of all the caravan trade'.[2] Some of the slaves were prisoners of war, but most of them were obtained through raids or razzies conducted for the purpose.[3] From the various figures supplied by the explorers as well as by the consular agents in the Sahara and Barbary states, the number of slaves exported annually along the four main

[1] Caillié, op. cit., vol. i, p. 331; Barth, op. cit., vol. ii, p. 131, vol. v, pp. 25–30; John and Richard Lander, op. cit., vol. ii, p. 191.

[2] C.O. 2/13, Denham to Horton, 1 June 1825; F.O. 84/373, Warrington to Palmerston, 20 July 1841; F.O. 97/430, Report on the Slave Trade of the Great Desert, Richardson to the Anti-Slavery Society, 12 June 1846; F.O. 84/1062, Herman to Clarendon, 10 Mar. 1858.

[3] Lyon, op. cit., pp. 245–50, 262–3; Denham, op. cit., pp. 116, 131; Barth, op. cit., vol. iii, pp. 118, 225, 232–3, 284; C.O. 2/13, Oudney to Bathurst, 20 May 1822; F.O. 47/430, Report on the Slave Trade.

routes may be estimated at about 10,000 rather than 20,000 as Buxton thought.[1] Of these, until about 1860, 5,000 were exported to the Regency of Tripoli, about 2,500 to Morocco, and the rest smuggled into Algeria and Tunis. About 2,500 of the slaves exported to Tripoli were re-exported annually to Constantinople, Mytilene, and Izmir in Turkey, to Scio and Rhodes in the Dardanelles, to Cyprus, and even as far north as Prevesa and Aulona in Albania.[2]

It is evident that as compared with the volume of slave traffic across the Atlantic from the west coast, which has been estimated at 70,000 per annum at least by the beginning of the nineteenth century, the trans-Saharan traffic was only a trickle. In spite of this, it had certain unique features which made it probably even more hideous than the trans-Atlantic traffic. First, about 60 per cent. of the slaves were young women and 10 per cent. of the rest were children under the age of ten. The reason for this was simply that slaves were used in Barbary and the Levant mainly as domestic servants. A second and an even more hideous feature was that a good number of the men were eunuchs employed in all Sudan, Barbary, and the Levant as keepers of harems, reliable courtiers, and generals of the rulers. These eunuchs were obtained by gelding. From this operation only one out of every ten, according to Barth, survived. However, as Bovill has pointed out, this repulsive practice of gelding was not confined to Africa but was long practised in Christian Europe. In the Middle Ages large establishments of eunuchs were maintained in France, and even as late as the end of the nineteenth century, the Soprani of the Sistine Chapel of the papal choir were all eunuchs.[3] The third dreadful feature was the hardship and privation suffered by the slaves during the march across the Sahara.

In addition to the difficulties already discussed, which were suffered alike by both slaves and their captors, by animals as well as human

---

[1] Buxton, *The Slave Trade*, p. 45. About 2,000, 4,500, 1,500, and 2,000 slaves were annually exported along the western, Sudan, old Garamantian, and eastern routes respectively.

[2] F.O. 84/867, Saunders to Palmerston, Prevesa, 3 Feb. 1857; F.O. 84/974, Campbell to Clarendon, Rhodes, 30 June 1851; F.O. 84/1000, Ongley to Canning, Candia (in Crete), 10 Apr. 1856; F.O. 841/857, Crowe to Palmerston, 17 Jan. 1857; F.O. 84/885, Crowe to Palmerston, 31 Jan. 1852; F.O. 84/974, Herman to Clarendon, 22 Jan. 1855. The number of slaves exported from Tripoli is based on figures compiled from the books of the Customs Dept. These returns are quite full and give the names of vessels, the number of slaves each vessel carried, and their destination.

[3] Barth, op. cit., vol. ii, p. 220; Bovill, op. cit., p. 245.

beings, there were others experienced only by the unfortunate slaves. First, while all the free men were mounted on camels and horses, the slaves went always on foot. As they generally walked barefoot, they often developed blisters and sores, caused either by the heated sand or by the rugged path. Thus incapacitated for walking, they were heartlessly abandoned to perish. Secondly, it was natural that they should become exhausted and thirsty before those who were mounted. But their cries for food and water or for a short rest were often only responded to with 'whips which were in constant use'. Caillié and Richardson, who both travelled with slave caravans, described the scenes in very moving terms. The former wrote:

Nobody suffered more intensely from thirst than the poor little slaves, who were crying for water. Exhausted by their sufferings and their lamentations, these unhappy creatures fell on the ground, and seemed to have no power to rise, but the Moors did not suffer them to continue there long when travelling. Insensible to the suffering which childhood is so little fitted to support, these barbarians dragged them along with violence, beating them incessantly till they had overtaken the camels, which were already at a distance.[1]

It is obvious which members of the caravan would be sacrificed first if there was a shortage of food or water. To worsen the plight of the slaves, they were not allowed freedom of movement. Two or more male slaves were often chained together round the neck and at the same time made to carry loads on their heads. One result of these sufferings was that some of the slaves succumbed on the way. It is difficult to determine the rate of mortality with any precision. Buxton estimated it at 42 per cent. and Church at 90 per cent. These figures are obviously exaggerated. The Vice-Consuls fixed it at from 5–30 per cent. under normal circumstances. Probably it may not be too wide of the mark to put the figure at 20 per cent. But even those who survived the trip arrived at the northern rendezvous as mere 'living skeletons'. The British Vice-Consul at Benghazi, who visited Djalo in 1875, saw slaves from Waday who 'were emaciated to mere skeletons, their long, thin legs and arms and the unnatural size and prominence of their knees and elbows, hands and feet, giving them a most repulsive and shocking appearance'.[2] Indeed, the slaves always had to be fattened before they were sent to the markets

---

[1] Caillié, op. cit., vol. ii, p. 114; F.O. 97/430, Richardson, Report on the Slave Trade; F.O. 101/16, Richardson to Warrington, 1 May 1846.
[2] Lyon, op. cit., p. 120; F.O. 84/1412, Henderson to Derby, 24 Dec. 1875.

of Barbary for sale. It may be pointed out, however, that once these slaves were sold, they were treated with every leniency and humanity in the Sudan, Barbary, and the Levant. They were, in fact, considered as human beings—indeed as members of the family—rather than as chattels as they were in the Americas, and often rose to become courtiers, ministers, or even governors of provinces.

The medium of exchange in which the caravan trade was carried on varied from place to place. While the silent trade mentioned by Herodotus had long ceased, barter was still very widely used in commercial transactions. In Arawan and Timbuctu gold was exchanged for a fixed weight of salt, a certain piece of Kano or European cloth, or a number of kola nuts.[1] In addition to barter, various types of currency were in circulation. Throughout the Sahara and in some of the markets in the Sudan, such as Kano, Timbuctu, and Kukawa, the currencies were French francs and the Spanish and Austrian or Maria Theresa dollars. The two last were minted in Vienna and imported mainly from Morocco. The Maria Theresa dollars were a particular favourite among the Sudanese women because of the head of the Queen that appeared on them.[2] The most widespread currency, however, was cowries or *Kurdi* (*cypraea moneta*). These were obtained from the Indian Ocean and imported into the Sudan from both the north and west coasts. They were the ordinary medium of exchange throughout all areas from the western boundaries of Bornu to the mouth of the Gambia and Senegal, and from the oasis of Air and Timbuctu in the north to the west coast. Large numbers of them were used in any transaction, since as many as 3,000 in Timbuctu and 2,500 in Kano were equivalent to a single Spanish or Austrian dollar, and 12,000 to £1. The counting of these cowries, as the explorers experienced, was 'the most tedious of all commercial transactions in these countries'. However, as Clapperton pointed out, there was a compensating advantage in that 'no forgery can imitate'.[3] In Bornu, Waday, and Bagirmi cowries were not accepted as legal tender. The medium of exchange consisted of strips of cotton of different sizes; but these were used only in small bargains; all the large ones involving slaves, ivory, and horses were done by barter.[4]

¹ Park, *Travels*, p. 305; Barth, op. cit., vol. iii, pp. 381–2, vol. v, p. 26.
² Barth, op. cit., vol. ii, p. 142; Richardson, *Travels*, vol. ii, p. 118; C. H. Robinson, *Hausaland* (London, 1896), p. 62.
³ Clapperton, op. cit., p. 51; Caillié, op. cit., vol. i, p. 373; Barth, op. cit., vol. ii, pp. 28–29, 142–3.
⁴ Barth, op. cit., vol. iii, pp. 75 ,381–2, 558–9; Denham, op. cit., p. 70.

To sum up, the caravan trade in the nineteenth century was but a fraction of its former volume. The imports into Sudan consisted mainly of cloth and salt, while the main exports were slaves, Kano cloth, kola nuts, and ivory. Gold, which used to be the most valuable commodity in the days of Ibn Battuta and Leo Africanus and continued so until the middle of the seventeenth century, was by the nineteenth century almost negligible. It seems that the total value of the exports from and the imports into the Sudan via the Sahara did not exceed one eighth of a million pounds sterling. But so hard does tradition die that despite the accounts of explorers, it was generally believed by Europeans in Barbary and Europe until about the last two decades of the last century that the trans-Saharan traffic was very valuable. Indeed, the African Association valued it at £1 million in 1793, and Donald Mackenzie, a British trader in Morocco, estimated it at £4 million in 1871. So widespread was this belief in England that as late as 1879 Mackenzie succeeded in forming the North West African Company to exploit that traffic.[1] By the nineteenth century, the caravan trade had dwindled until it was almost entirely a traffic in slaves.

[1] F. V. Parsons, 'The North-West African Company', *The Historical Journal*, vol. ii, 1958, pp. 136–53; D. Mackenzie, *The Flooding of the Sahara* (1871), pp. vii–xi. The Company went bankrupt only four years later.

CHAPTER VI

The Diplomatic Attack on the Trans-Saharan Slave Trade

WARRINGTON first brought the trans-Saharan branch of the African slave trade to the notice of the British Government in October 1818. Even before the arrival of Ritchie and Lyon, he had urged Lord Bathurst, the Colonial Secretary, to launch an attack 'on the successful and increasing traffic in human flesh, particularly as that infernal trade not only causes continued hostility [between] different kingdoms in the interior but . . . can be the only cause likely to obstruct the researches from this quarter to the very heart of Africa'.[1] As we have seen, the Government did show some interest, but this evaporated as quickly as it had been generated.[2] But Warrington, daily confronted with the inhumanities of the trade, could neither forget nor ignore it. Besides, he was among those who sincerely believed that a very lucrative trade with the interior could be developed across the Sahara if only the traffic in slaves with its concomitant raids and insecurity were abolished. Undeterred, therefore, by the Government's indifference, Warrington let no favourable opportunity slip without taking up the question of abolition with the Tripolitanian authorities.

In 1823, for instance, exploiting his very great influence at the Court, he persuaded the Pasha to suspend the trade in slaves for a certain number of years 'at a moderate annual payment'. He hoped that this limited agreement might lead to a complete cessation of the trade, since during the interlude the dealers would be compelled to turn to legitimate commerce; and it was in a mood of profound optimism that he forwarded the agreement to the Colonial Office.[3] Unfortunately, no heed whatsoever was paid to it. Still undaunted, Warrington brought up the question again three years later. In 1826,

[1] F.O. 76/12, Warrington to Bathurst, 9 Oct. 1818.
[2] See above, pp. 68–70.
[3] F.O. 76/17, Warrington to Horton, 30 Apr. 1823.

Hassuna D'Ghies, whom Warrington then described as 'an honourable man full of humane feelings' but whom he alienated a year later by falsely accusing him of having plotted Laing's death, succeeded his father as Foreign Minister of Tripoli. Deeply concerned about the slave trade himself, D'Ghies readily agreed to co-operate with Warrington in drawing up ten proposals for its abolition. The Pasha was to promise not to send any army on slave-raiding expeditions, to prohibit the importation or exportation of slaves by land or sea, and to abolish slavery. He was also to use his influence to persuade the rulers of the interior to adopt similar measures and to receive a certain number of British agents. In return for all this, the British Government was to give the Pasha a compensation of 30,000 dollars (£6,000) per year for ten years, to allow him to raise the duty on imports and exports from 3 to 6 per cent., and to induce all the European powers to accept the new duty. If these measures were to involve the Pasha in any trouble the British Government was to come to his assistance. Hassuna gave every assurance that the Pasha would accept these terms if the British Government would do so too, and Warrington therefore forwarded the proposals in a private and confidential letter to Lord Bathurst. He added in a postscript that the annual payment might be reduced to 20,000 dollars and 'indeed, the whole altered to your Lordship's wishes'.[1]

The Colonial Office very promptly rejected the proposals. First, they stated that the principle of compensation was not to be applied 'until all other proposals for effecting that object had failed'. Secondly, they expressed doubts as to the Pasha's ability to win the co-operation of the rulers of the interior, without which the trade would only be diverted into different channels. But what they considered 'infinitely more objectionable than any other part of the arrangement' was the clause about doubling the import duty. An official wrote:

To obstruct the existing trade of His Majesty's subjects with Tripoli by a system of high duties is a measure which would at all times be considered of the most questionable policy: but as it never could be consented to under any circumstances, unless upon the conditions of imposing corresponding duties upon the trade of other Powers with Tripoli, it is evident that in order to render such an arrangement effective, we must be prepared to go to war with every power which should think proper to resent the violations of treaties to which that arrangement would necessarily give rise.[2]

[1] F.O. 76/20, Warrington to Bathurst, 27 Feb. 1826.
[2] F.O. 76/40, Hay to Warrington, 30 Apr. 1826.

Assuming that these objections were all valid, the rejection of the whole arrangement can hardly be justified. Undoubtedly the Pasha could not have obtained the co-operation of the rulers in the interior, and, as will be seen later, the traffic would have been diverted into other channels. But surely, with the sincere co-operation of the authorities, at least the exportation of slaves from Tripoli could have been stopped. And since Tripoli was then the only exporter of slaves from Barbary to the Levant, this would have been a great blow to the traffic. Again, at a time when the British Government were paying compensation in one form or another to Spain and Portugal for their measures against the transatlantic slave traffic, it is incomprehensible that they refused to do the same thing in Tripoli except as a last resort. Finally, it is clear from Warrington's postscript that the proposals were by no means final and that the Colonial Office could have amended them to meet their objections. But, strangely enough, not a single amendment was suggested. Warrington was simply informed that 'it would tend to no useful result to enter at present into any further discussion of the arrangements which that overture had in view'. Why the British officials were so pessimistic and what other time they had in mind, the Consul-General was not told. In short, the real cause for the rejection of the proposals was not that they were impracticable, but that the British Government were still indifferent to the trans-Saharan and Mediterranean slave trade. Hence this good opportunity was allowed to go begging and the attack on this branch of the trade was indefinitely postponed.

The subsequent controversy over Laing's mission, followed by the political disturbances in Tripoli, compelled Warrington to shelve the question until 1837, when the Sheikh Abd al-Jalīl offered to meet any wishes of the British Government if he were recognized as the Bey of Fezzan by the Sultan of Turkey. From that year until the Sheikh's death, therefore, Warrington appealed several times to Lord Ponsonby, the British Ambassador at Constantinople, to persuade the Sultan to recognize the Sheikh as the Bey of Fezzan.[1] While Warrington was pulling these wires in Constantinople, he at the same time impressed on London that the time was opportune for another attack on the slave trade. He suggested two lines of approach. One was that negotiations should be opened with the Arab Sheikhs, and

[1] F.O. 101/4, Warrington to Ponsonby, 8 Apr. 1840, encl. in Warrington to Palmerston, 10 Apr. 1840; Warrington to Ponsonby, 31 Dec. 1840, encl. in Warrington to Bidwell, 31 Dec. 1840.

the other, to be discussed in the next chapter, was that a British vice-consular post should be established in Fezzan.[1]

This time Warrington's suggestions met with success. The Foreign Secretary, Lord Palmerston, asked Warrington 'to take such steps as you think will be most likely to induce the Moorish Chiefs to give up themselves, and prevent other persons from continuing the practice of procuring slaves for exportation from Tripoli to the Levant'.[2] The British consuls in the Barbary States and in Turkey were also asked to negotiate for the abolition of the trade, and in the following year (1841) were instructed to forward to London copies of any laws passed for the purpose of regulating, restricting, or preventing the traffic in slaves.[3] This favourable response and the prompt measures adopted by the Government positively indicate the abandonment of the attitude of indifference and non-co-operation which they had displayed for two decades towards Warrington's abolition proposals.

The reasons for this reversal of policy are not far to seek. By 1839 the Foreign Office, presided over by Palmerston, the avowed god-father of abolition, had assumed responsibility for British policy towards the Barbary States. Furthermore, Warrington's voice had hitherto been the only one raised in Britain against the slave trade across the Sahara. But by 1839 he had two allies, besides Palmerston. They were Fowell Buxton and the British and Foreign Anti-Slavery Society. As a result of the active propaganda of Buxton, the trans-Saharan slave traffic was brought into the limelight. Two months after Warrington's suggestion of a new diplomatic approach to the Arab chiefs, Buxton himself pointed out to the Foreign Office the opportunity which the Eastern crisis of 1840–1 afforded for obtaining a treaty for the suppression of the slave trade both in Egypt and the Ottoman Empire.[4] The British and Foreign Anti-Slavery Society, which was formed in 1839 for the peaceful extinction of the slave trade and universal abolition of slavery,[5] also paid particular atten-

[1] F.O. 84/333, Warrington to Bidwell, 1 Aug. 1840; F.O. 101/4, Warrington to Bidwell, 18 May 1840.

[2] F.O. 84/333, Palmerston to Warrington, 22 Oct. 1840; F.O. 101/4, Bidwell to Warrington, 5 July 1840.

[3] F.O. 84/333, Palmerston to Ponsonby, 22 Aug. 1840; Palmerston to Ponsonby, 9 Nov. 1840; F.O. 84/33, Circular, 27 Dec. 1841.

[4] F.O. 84/305, Buxton to Palmerston, 20 Oct. 1840.

[5] The British and Foreign Anti-Slavery Society, *60 Years Against Slavery* (1900), p. 1; *Report of the British and Foreign Anti-Slavery Society* (1840). The Society exists to this day under the name of the Anti-Slavery Society.

tion to the trans-Saharan and Mediterranean slave trade. Soon after its inauguration the Society sent out to Malta James Richardson, an agent whose remarkable role in the campaign will be discussed later.[1] In the very month that Warrington advanced his suggestions, the Society also submitted to Palmerston the first of a long series of addresses calling on him to press for the abolition of the slave trade and slavery in the Ottoman Empire. The Foreign Secretary immediately forwarded this address to the British Ambassador in Turkey for necessary action.[2] By 1840 then, the abolition of the northern branch of the African slave traffic had become a national concern and could no longer be treated in a cavalier manner. Thus, as a result of the perseverance of Warrington and pressure from Buxton and the humanitarians, the attack on the oldest branch of the African slave trade belatedly began, and from 1840 onwards was carried on simultaneously in Tripoli, Morocco, and Turkey.

On the strength of the instructions from the Foreign Office, which were reiterated in May 1841, Warrington invited Abd al-Jalīl, who was then in Murzuk, to a meeting somewhere in the district around the Gulf of Syrte.[3] Nothing was heard from the Sheikh until January 1842, when he wrote to apologize for his long silence and agreed to meet Warrington at the appointed place.[4] Three months later the long-expected meeting took place. This palaver came off successfully. In a letter to the Colonial Office, the Sheikh agreed to abolish the slave trade and slavery, promote legitimate commerce, and persuade the rulers of the interior to do the same. But in return he demanded free access to the coast, and especially to the port of Benghazi, and his recognition by the Porte as the Bey of Fezzan. On the advice of Warrington, the Sheikh also wrote a letter to the Sultan of Turkey in which he professed his allegiance and asked him to appoint a commission to investigate the anarchy prevalent in Tripoli. The Consul-General forwarded all these letters to the Foreign Office with the recommendation that they should be transmitted to the British ambassador at Constantinople for prompt action.[5]

[1] See below, pp. 142–3, 145, 147, 174–89.
[2] F.O. 84/333, Palmerston to Ponsonby, 22 Aug. 1840.
[3] F.O. 84/373, Palmerston to Warrington, 18 May 1841; F.O. 84/373, Warrington to Palmerston, 1 July 1841.
[4] F.O. 84/427, Abd al-Jalīl to Warrington, 29 Jan. 1842, and Warrington to Bidwell, 15 Mar. 1848.
[5] F.O. 84/427, Abd al-Jalīl to Aberdeen, 22 Apr. 1842; Abd al-Jalīl to Sultan Abd al-Megid, encl. in Warrington to Aberdeen, 26 Apr. 1842.

Warrington felt highly elated about this palaver, and justifiably so. As Abd al-Jalīl controlled Fezzan and was then widely known in Bornu (he married the sister of the Sultan of Bornu in 1835), his services would have been invaluable in the enforcement of regulations against the slave trade and the development of legitimate traffic. With the overwhelming influence of the British Government over the Porte at the time, it seemed that the Sheikh's demands could be easily granted. Indeed, in May 1842 Sir Stratford Canning, then British ambassador in Constantinople, informed Warrington not only that he had obtained the recall of Askar Ali, the Turkish Governor of Tripoli—a step which the Consul-General had been pressing for since 1840—but also that the Sheikh's petition declaring his allegiance and asking for peace had been favourably received by the Turkish ministers and that the new Governor being posted to Tripoli would be accordingly instructed.[1] Unfortunately, even before reports of the interview reached England, and before news of the removal of Askar Ali arrived in Tripoli, the benevolent Sheikh was, as we have seen, murdered, in May 1842.[2] Askar Ali was a great slave trader himself, and Warrington's view that Ali redoubled his efforts to vanquish the Sheikh on hearing of the latter's promise to abolish the slave trade might well be true.[3] Considering the favourable view that the Porte was reported to have taken of the Sheikh's petition, no event could have been more unfortunate for the abolition of slavery and the opening up of the routes into the interior than Abd al-Jalīl's death. With the effective occupation of Fezzan by the Turks, any further efforts for the abolition of the trans-Saharan slave traffic through Fezzan and Tripoli had to be made in Constantinople.

While Warrington was frantically exerting himself in Tripoli, Sir Thomas Reade, the British Consul in Tunis, was negotiating with the Bey for the abolition of the hideous traffic. Here the campaign was, diplomatically, an immediate and resounding success. From his very first interview with the Bey on the subject in April 1841, Reade came out with a copy of an order prohibiting the export of slaves from the Regency. This was accompanied by a firm promise by the Bey to do everything in his power to abolish the slave trade and the institution of slavery itself as soon as possible. This order would probably not

---

[1] F.O. 101/8, Canning to Warrington, 18 May 1842; Richardson, *Travels*, vol. ii, p. 353.

[2] See above, p. 91.

[3] F.O. 84/427, Warrington to Aberdeen, 1 June 1842.

have been taken seriously had the Bey not followed it up with the liberation of all his slaves.[1]

Incredible and inexplicable as Reade's achievement is when it is viewed in isolation, this and the subsequent measures become less mysterious when viewed against the background of the political situation in Tunis. In 1837 the French had occupied the province of Constantine on the western frontier of Tunis and had begun to cast envious glances eastward. East of Tunis, the Sultan of Turkey had by that date made good his occupation of the coastal districts of Tripoli, and people in Turkey were openly speaking of repeating in Tunis the successful operation in Tripoli.[2] Flanked on both sides by these ambitious powers, the Bey perceived that it would stand him in good stead to obtain the support of another great power. The obvious choice was Britain. With her eyes on the trade routes to India and the markets of Greece, Turkey, and the Levant, Britain herself was as interested to prevent the Mediterranean from becoming a French lake as were the Sultan of Turkey, the Bey of Tunis, and the Sultan of Morocco.[3] There was also another side to the coin. After the vacillations of the 1810's and 1820's, British foreign policy towards the Ottoman Empire had by the late thirties crystallized into one of maintaining its integrity. While Czar Nicholas was speaking of the Sultan of Turkey as the 'sick man of Europe', Palmerston described as 'pure and unadulterated nonsense' all talk about the decay of the Turkish Empire. His aim was not merely to maintain its integrity, but 'by reforming it to make it more capable of resisting its enemies and able to play its part in the balance of power in Eastern Europe'.[4] As Tunis was always regarded in theory as an integral part of the Ottoman Empire, Britain would not see the Regency appropriated by the French or even recognized as a completely sovereign state. Either development, it was feared, would have been taken as the signal for the death of the 'sick man' and would have encouraged Russia or Egypt to nibble at that Empire. On the other hand, if the Sultan were allowed effectively to occupy Tunis, France would have demanded

[1] F.O. 84/373, Reade to Palmerston, 30 Apr. 1841, and encl., Bey to Reade, 29 Apr. 1841.
[2] A. Raymond, 'British policy towards Tunis, 1830–1884' (unpublished Oxford D.Phil. thesis, 1954), p. 55.
[3] E. R. Flournoy, *British policy towards Morocco* (1935), pp. 31–32; R. Robinson and J. Gallagher, *Africa and the Victorians* (London, 1961), p. 77.
[4] C. K. Webster, *The Foreign Policy of Palmerston* (1951), vol. i, pp. 82–88, vol. ii, p. 540.

some compensation or probably declared war on Turkey. The obvious answer to the diplomatic situation was the maintenance of the *status quo*, and precisely this became the object of British foreign policy towards the Barbary States and the Ottoman Empire until the seventies.[1]

Thus, when in 1837 the Bey became alarmed by French expansion eastward, Palmerston promptly allayed his fears. He assured him of Britain's full support and assistance so long as he remained true to the Sultan, 'according to the relations now subsisting between him and the Porte', and promised to take steps in Paris to protect the Regency from any unprovoked aggression from France. Granville, the British ambassador in Paris, was accordingly instructed to inform the French Government that 'Great Britain could not see with indifference any attempt of France so to encroach upon the territory of Tunis as to alter the political relations which now connect the Bey of that Regency with the Porte'.[2] On the other hand, when in 1841 the Sultan of Turkey attempted to reduce Tunis to a mere province by demanding payment of annual tribute and control of her finances as well as her foreign policy, Reade supported the Bey in his appeal to the Foreign Office. Palmerston acted with dispatch in this case also. Ponsonby was asked to warn the Porte not to attempt to make any change 'in the relations which had hitherto subsisted between the Bey of Tunis and the Sultan'.[3] Thus from 1837 onwards the position of the Bey depended largely on Britain's policy of maintaining the *status quo*. Consequently, until that policy was abandoned in 1878, it became the aim of the Beys of Tunis to win the goodwill and friendship of Britain, and sometimes to buy it at any price. In the light of all this, it is hardly surprising that the Bey should have acted so promptly when Reade informed him that nothing would be more 'gratifying not only to the British Government itself, but to the British nation generally', than the abolition of the traffic in slaves and slavery itself.

The reaction of the Foreign Office to the first anti-slavery measure introduced by the Bey was such as to spur him on. Reade was instructed to express to him the appreciation of the British people and to assure him that 'nothing could tend to interest the English

[1] Raymond, op. cit., pp. 35, 60–62; Flournoy, op. cit., pp. 54–55, 256–63; Robinson and Gallagher, op. cit., pp. 76–79.
[2] Raymond, op. cit., p. 74; Flournoy, op. cit., p. 56.
[3] Quoted by Raymond, pp. 109–10.

nation in his favour so strongly as a continuance in this course and
as the complete abolition of slavery in the Regency of Tunis'. The
Bey was also asked to rely upon the friendship and good offices of
Britain 'to dispose the Sultan in his favour as long as he pursues the
wise and prudent course which he has hitherto followed'.[1] So inspirited
was the Bey by the British Government's remarks that only the fear
of precipitating an internal revolution compelled him and Reade to
take the politic decision to proceed by stages. Five months later the
Bey issued another proclamation abolishing slave markets and prohibiting the public sale of slaves.[2] This again was followed by immediate practical steps. The public slave markets in Tunis and other
towns were razed to the ground.

This measure was given an even warmer reception in Britain than
the first. The British and Foreign Anti-Slavery Society sent an
address of congratulation to the Bey. Its agent in Malta, James
Richardson, presented him with 'a testimonial of gratitude' on behalf
of British residents in Malta, Gibraltar, Leghorn, Florence, Naples,
and Tripoli,[3] who expressed their ardent admiration of his action
and the hope that it would incite other Muhammedan and Christian
sovereigns to follow his example.

Feeling highly flattered, and anxious to ingratiate himself even
more with the British Government and public, the Bey only waited
for an opportune moment to strike another blow at the traffic. This
seems to have arrived eight months later, after the storm of protests
raised by the first two measures had settled down. In April 1842 the
third order was issued, which completely abolished the importation of
slaves into Tunis by land or sea. It also ordered that any slave who
set foot on Tunisian soil after 27 April automatically became free.
After another eight months' delay, the Bey issued a new order declaring free all children born of slaves after 8 September.[4] Only the
lack of funds for the payment of compensation to slave owners prevented him from abolishing slavery outright. But that inevitable step
was taken four years later. In January 1846 a proclamation was issued
liberating every slave in the Regency and declaring the institution of
slavery illegal. In his letter informing Reade of this final step, the Bey
stated significantly that he took it because 'we know it is also an

[1] F.O. 84/373, F.O. to Reade, 22 June 1841.
[2] F.O. 84/373, Reade to Palmerston, 7 Sept. 1841.
[3] British and Foreign Anti-Slavery Society, *Third Annual Report*, 1842, p. 34;
Br. Emp. MSS. S18/C21/30, Richardson to Scoble, 16 Jan. 1842.
[4] F.O. 84/427, Reade to Aberdeen, 10 Dec. 1842.

object of attention to the great and illustrious British Government, and we pray the most High that our opinions be always in unison with their own on every point'.[1] This final act was naturally received 'with great satisfaction' by the British Government, and as a demonstration of their gratitude, they presented to the Bey a carriage with harness for six horses and seven British carpets of various sizes.[2]

The proclamation of January 1846 brought to a victorious conclusion the diplomatic campaign against the slave traffic in Tunis. The various measures were enforced with every sincerity. Commissioners were sent out even to the remote provinces of the Regency to issue *tiskeras* or papers of freedom to every slave who presented himself. Indeed, a missionary who toured the Regency in March 1846 concluded that 'it may now be safely declared that slavery is abolished in the Regency of Tunis'.[3] It is true that slaves were smuggled into the Regency, especially in the fifties and sixties, but all those who were detected were promptly liberated by the Bey.[4] The ease with which this victory was accomplished was certainly owing to political conditions in Tunis as well as to the skilful diplomacy of Reade and his great interest in abolition. Though the exigencies of British foreign policy and fear of French occupation of Tunis would have compelled Britain to interest herself in the fate of the Bey, there is no doubt that these bold and humane measures raised his prestige in the eyes of the Government and people of Britain and won him their ungrudging support.

Meanwhile the attack on the slave trade was being waged in Morocco also. Hay, the British Consul-General there, did not move until he received the circular of December 1841 asking for copies of the laws passed in connexion with the slave trade. This circular was communicated to the Sultan. In reply, the Sultan stated that he was not aware that the traffic in slaves had been prohibited 'by the laws of any sect', and that it was a matter on which 'all sects and nations have agreed from the time of the sons of Adam . . . up to this day'. This reply touched off a lively exchange between the Consul-General and the Sultan, in which Hay tried to persuade the Sultan to abolish

[1] F.O. 84/648, Mushir Ahmed Bey to Reade, 22 Jan. 1846, encl. in Reade to Palmerston, 24 Jan. 1846.
[2] F.O. 84/648, Aberdeen to Reade, 24 June 1846; F.O. 84/693, Palmerston to Reade, 16 Sept. 1847.
[3] F.O. 84/648, Reade to Aberdeen, 31 Mar. 1846 and encl.
[4] F.O. 84/1204, Wood to Russell, 1 Jan. 1863.

the slave trade.[1] In his long dispatch, Hay first of all proved to the Sultan that he was wrong in his view that no sect or nation had abolished that traffic by reviewing the progress that had been made in that direction during the preceding thirty-four years. He mentioned the lead taken by Britain, the countries that had followed her example in Europe, and the fact that even 'rulers of several Moslem states' such as Muscat, Tunis, and Egypt, were also issuing orders against the traffic. He then concluded with a passionate appeal for his co-operation.

Hay's brilliant dissertation elicited only a more positive refusal from the Sultan. He pointed out that as the 'making of slaves and trading therewith' were sanctioned by the Koran, which 'admits not either of addition or diminution', to abolish the trade or in any way impede it was completely out of the question. The Consul-General became so convinced of the hopelessness of the attempt to convince the Sultan that he abandoned it. But he salved his own conscience and that of the Foreign Office by pointing out that slaves in Morocco were not numerous, that they were exceedingly well treated, and that for the past thirteen years not a single slave had been exported from that country.[2]

Though Hay's observations about the slave traffic in Morocco were true, they were not enough to cause in British humanitarian circles the same feeling of complacency as in the British consulate in Morocco and in the Foreign Office. Hence, a year after these official exchanges, the Anti-Slavery Society sent Richardson from Malta on a mission to the Sultan. In an address to be presented by Richardson, the Anti-Slavery Society appealed to the Sultan to abolish the slave trade and slavery on the ground that as God had made all men equal, it was sinful to enslave fellow human beings.[3] Richardson arrived in Tangier in December 1843.

For reasons to be dealt with presently,[4] Hay was instructed by the Foreign Office to assist Richardson 'unofficially'.[5] On Richardson's departure for Mogador, however, Hay gave him a letter of introduction to Willshire, the British Vice-Consul there, asking him to request

---

[1] F.O. 84/427, Hay to Aberdeen, 12 Mar. 1842 and encl., Hay to Sultan, 4 Feb. 1842; Hay to Sultan, 26 Feb. 1842; Sultan to Hay, Mar. 1842.

[2] F.O. 84/427, Hay to Aberdeen, 12 Mar. 1842.

[3] *Anti-Slavery Reporter*, 15 Nov. 1843; Br. Emp. MSS. S20/E/20/20, Hinton to Aberdeen, 11 Dec. 1843; F.O. 84/486, Hay to Aberdeen, 11 Dec. 1843.

[4] See below, pp. 144–5.

[5] F.O. 84/486, F.O. to Hay, 16 Dec. 1843.

permission from the Governor there for Richardson to proceed to the Sultan's Court.[1] Willshire had already gone to Morocco when Richardson reached Mogador. When the Vice-Consul returned he brought the rather disheartening news that the Sultan had already got wind of Richardson's mission, and had not only refused to receive him, but had ordered him to leave the kingdom immediately. This was too bitter a pill for Richardson to swallow. He informed Willshire that the Anti-Slavery Society would not consider that he had discharged his duty until he had left no stone unturned for the accomplishment of his mission.[2] With the co-operation of the Vice-Consul, Richardson obtained an audience with the Governor of Mogador. At this interview he pleaded that the address of the Anti-Slavery Society should be received by the Sultan. But in reply the Governor merely repeated the Sultan's former view that the demand for abolition was against the Muslim religion, and refused even to touch the address.[3] Like Hay in 1842, Richardson had to admit defeat. He left Morocco in April 1844.

Though these attacks failed, the question of abolition disappeared completely from the correspondence between the British consuls in Morocco and the Foreign Office until 1857. In that year the Consul-General was suddenly asked for information about the traffic and the attempts which had been made to abolish it. He replied quite frankly that after the correspondence that took place 'in the time of my predecessor' (i.e. 1842), he did not think that any beneficial results would be obtained as long as the same Sultan continued to reign in Morocco. Like his predecessor, he also tried to minimize the gravity of this failure by pointing out the paucity of slaves in Morocco, and the leniency with which they were treated.[4] Though the Consul-General ended his note with a promise not to lose any favourable opportunity that might present itself to bring up the question, it seems this opportunity never arose. Indeed the next attack on the Moroccan slave trade was not made until 1885, when the Anti-Slavery Society sent out its Secretary and Treasurer on a mission to

[1] F.O. 84/540, Hay to Willshire, 16 Jan. 1844, encl. in Hay to Aberdeen, 17 Jan. 1844.
[2] F.O. 84/540, Willshire to Richardson, 5 Mar. 1844; Richardson to Willshire, 7 Mar. 1844, encl. in Hay to Aberdeen, 28 Mar. 1844.
[3] F.O. 84/540, Address by Richardson to the Governor of Mogador and its reply, encl. in Willshire to Hay, 21 Mar. 1844; Br. Emp. MSS. S22/G38, Richardson to Beaumont, 22 Mar. 1844.
[4] F.O. 84/1029, Hay to Clarendon, 14 Oct. 1857.

Morocco.[1] But although the Society continued to send petitions and addresses to the British Government, it was not until the French occupation of Morocco in 1912 that the hideous traffic and the institution of slavery were abolished.[2]

It is obvious then that while the campaign in Tunis was a glorious success, that in Morocco was a deplorable failure. As in Tunis, this failure and the reluctance of the British Government and Consuls to raise the question with any frequency were due primarily to the diplomatic situation in the Mediterranean in general, and to British relations with the Sultan in particular. Though from the thirties onwards British policy in Tunis and Morocco was precisely the same one of maintaining the *status quo*, the rulers' reaction to it was different. While the Bey of Tunis felt himself absolutely helpless in the face of Turkish and French expansion and therefore ready to buy British support at any price, the Sultan of Morocco, on the other hand, felt powerful enough even to treat the European powers with impunity, especially in the thirties and forties. In 1836 and 1841, for instance, in spite of the warnings of Palmerston, the Sultan fitted out vessels of war to capture ships of 'those states whose Governments had no treaties with Morocco'. One of these vessels actually captured a Spanish provision boat in 1841.[3] Moreover, the Sultan openly and defiantly supported Abd al-Qadir, the leader of the Arab resistance to French occupation in Algeria, thereby constantly inviting a French invasion of Morocco.[4] Britain could not, of course, see Morocco occupied by France or Spain, and the only way to avoid this was by persuading the Sultan not to give France or Spain 'any just pretences for hostilities' against him. That the Moroccan authorities knew of Britain's vital interest in the maintenance of the integrity of their kingdom is evident from a conversation which the Governor of Tangier, who acted as the Moroccan Foreign Minister, had with Hay. The Governor told Hay that his Government trusted that Britain would defend Morocco in any attack by France

as surely as the British will not for their own sake—allow the French to insult us and become masters of the streight! [*sic*][5]

[1] Br. Emp. MSS. S22/G28, Report of the Deputation of the Anti-Slavery Society to Morocco in November 1885.
[2] Br. Emp. MSS. S22/G28, Anti-Slavery Society to le Baron, 6 Nov. 1912.
[3] Flournoy, op. cit., p. 52.
[4] Ibid., pp. 59–61.
[5] Quoted by Flournoy, p. 63.

Obviously then, as far as Morocco was concerned, it was the British Government which had to angle for the Sultan's friendship and co-operation and not vice versa as in Tunis. It became absolutely necessary therefore for British representatives in Morocco to avoid any subjects which would have exasperated the Sultan and his advisers. And nothing could have done this more than an insistence on, or even repeated pleas for, the abolition of the slave trade and slavery. It was for fear of offending the Moroccan authorities so soon after the discussion of abolition that Hay was asked to give only unofficial assistance to Richardson. Indeed, Hay violently reprimanded Willshire for merely arranging the audience which Richardson had with the Governor of Mogador, on the ground that the subject of the interview was 'unnecessarily offensive to the declared sentiment of the Moorish Government or to the distinctly pronounced religious tenets of the people'.[1] The stronger bargaining power of the Sultan of Morocco rather than his having deeper religious convictions than the Bey tilted the balance in his favour and brought about the failure of the campaign against the slave trade in Morocco in the nineteenth century.

In Turkey, the abolition campaign was neither a complete failure nor an immediate success. Even before the death of Abd al-Jalīl in 1842, some 'skirmishes' had already taken place in Turkey. As early as December 1839, Richardson had warned the Anti-Slavery Society and the British Government that 'unless we are prepared for a double crusade, not against Europe and America only, but against Africa and Asia as well, it will be in vain to contend against that traffic'.[2] The Society took this up and, as we have seen, sent its first address to the Government in August 1840. In the face of pressure from the Society as well as from Buxton and his group, the Government could not but take up the question with the Porte; but the reluctance and caution with which they did so is evident from their communication with Lord Ponsonby. In the draft letter to the Ambassador, a very long lecture was delivered to the Porte on the inhumanity and ungodly nature of the trade in slaves and on the abolition campaign since 1807, and a demand for a complete abolition of the slave trade and slavery throughout the Ottoman Empire was made. Palmerston's minute on this draft is very noteworthy:

[1] F.O. 84/540, Hay to Willshire, 5 Apr. 1844, encl. in Hay to Aberdeen, 5 Apr. 1844.
[2] The *Harlequin* (later the *Malta Times*), 14 Dec. 1839.

This is all nonsense, [he wrote] slavery is so ingrained in the social habits of Mohammedans that no ambassador could with a grave face act upon the draft. It would have been much shorter to tell Lord Ponsonby to ask the Sultan to become a Christian.[1]

He therefore cancelled the whole draft and substituted a brief one in which he simply forwarded the address of the Anti-Slavery Society to Lord Ponsonby and asked him to take such measures as might appear to be likely in any degree 'to mitigate the evils of the slavery in the Turkish dominions or to be effectual in diminishing the extent to which the practice of making slaves is carried on'.

The reason for this cautious tone, which was to ring in subsequent correspondence with the Porte on the subject, was the dilemma in which the British Government found themselves. As we have seen, British policy had been committed from the thirties to maintaining the integrity and promoting the survival of the tottering Ottoman Empire. And it was very widely believed in British official circles that slavery was such an important prop to the political, social, and economic institutions of the Empire that its sudden abolition would precipitate a collapse. Ponsonby's reply to the note from the British Foreign Office further strengthened this belief. He reported that the Ottoman imperial race was perpetuated by mothers who were slaves and that most admirals, generals, and ministers of state had originally been slaves. 'To carry what your Lordship desires into execution,' he wrote, 'it will be necessary to limit the law of succession to the Crown, and alter the policy that has so long guided the Sultans in that respect and also to change fundamentally the political and civil institutions and laws and the domestic arrangement of the people.'[2] In his view, nothing but universal confusion would be the consequence of such violent changes and probably those persons intended to be most benefited by them would be the greatest sufferers. Thus, though in the thirties and forties Britain's diplomatic advantage in Turkey was as strong as it was in Tunis, she could not exploit it.

On the other hand, British public opinion was especially critical of the Turkish slave trade because it involved not only Negroes but also white men, most of them Christians from Georgia and Circassia. The only way the British Government could appease the public and at the same time avoid worsening the plight of the 'sick man of Europe' was to approach the question with great caution and modera-

[1] F.O. 84/333, Palmerston to Ponsonby, draft and minute, 22 Aug. 1840.
[2] F.O. 84/333, Ponsonby to Palmerston, 27 Dec. 1840.

tion. Hence on the receipt of Ponsonby's reply of December 1840, the Foreign Office tactfully shelved the question.

In spite of the pressure of the Anti-Slavery Society, it was not until 1846 that the attack on the Turkish slave trade was resumed. It was sparked off by two factors. During his travels in the Sahara from 1845-6,[1] Richardson sent very copious and often highly coloured reports about the volume and mortality involved in the traffic, reports which were given very wide publicity in England by the Anti-Slavery Society. He also suggested remedies, one of which was the closing down of the slave markets in Tripoli and Constantinople. On his return to England in August 1846 he urged this on the Foreign Office. Richardson's campaign produced an effect similar to that of Buxton's in the thirties. The Government could no longer maintain its diplomatic silence on the subject.

The second factor which reopened the issue even more effectively than the first was the outcome of the campaign against the East African slave trade—which had been going on since the first decade of the nineteenth century. In 1845 Seyyid Said, the Imam of Muscat, signed a treaty with the British Government in which he agreed to abolish the export to Arabia of slaves from any part of his dominions in Africa. He also empowered the British navy and ships of the East India Company to enforce the treaty in the Red Sea and the Persian Gulf.[2] This treaty was to come into force on 1 January 1847. But before then the East India Company's representative in the Persian Gulf suggested that unless Persia and Turkey, the other two major powers in the Gulf, also issued firmans prohibiting the trade in their respective ports and authorized the British Government to enforce them, the treaty with Said would be difficult to put into effect.

In August 1846, therefore, the British ambassadors in Constantinople and Teheran were informed of the suggestion of the Company's representative and instructed to negotiate for the requisite firmans.[3] Wellesley, who had replaced Ponsonby, was also asked to demand the suppression of the slave markets in Constantinople. The reaction of the rulers to these requests is particularly noteworthy. While the Sultan of Turkey promptly complied (he closed the markets in January 1847 and issued the firman a month later), the Shah of

[1] See below, pp. 174-9.

[2] See text of treaty in R. Coupland, *East Africa and its invaders* (Oxford, 1938), p. 515.

[3] F.O. 84/647, Palmerston to Wellesley, 31 Aug. 1846; Palmerston to Sheil, 31 Aug. 1846.

Persia, on the same old religious grounds, refused. Indeed, he had to be threatened before he complied with the request in June 1848.[1] But even then he persistently refused until August 1851 to grant the British navy the right of search. The readiness with which the Sultan of Turkey and the Bey of Tunis granted the British Government's urgent requests, and the refusal of the Shah of Persia and the Sultan of Morocco, show quite clearly that the determining factor in these negotiations was not a ruler's religious convictions, but rather his political and bargaining power *vis-à-vis* the British Government.

These concessions of January and February 1847 were the first victory scored by the British Government in the diplomatic battle against the slave trade in the Ottoman empire. Though the firman was limited only to the Ottoman slave trade to the Persian Gulf, it was nevertheless a very important victory in principle. By showing that it was in fact not 'unmuslim' to abolish the traffic in slaves, it struck at the very foundation of the main argument hitherto advanced by the Porte and even by Ponsonby.

If the campaign against the East African slave trade and Richardson's reports from the Sahara sparked off the second attack on the Turkish slave trade, the next one was precipitated by another report sent by F. H. Gilbert, the British Vice-Consul at Benghazi, about the very high mortality suffered by a recent caravan from Waday. He pointed out that in a journey of 8 days, 32 slaves died or were abandoned to their fate because of 'the swelling of their feet in traversing the hot sands'.[2] Palmerston was profoundly moved by this report. 'Is there no mode of preventing this?' he asked Addington, the Under-Secretary. Addington answered realistically:

None, unless we get the consent of the Turkish Government. We might, however, with some chance of success, press the matter on the Turkish Government. They have already, by agreeing to our proposition to prohibit the importation of slaves from Africa into the Persian Gulf, admitted the principle, (without however in any way interfering with the system of slavery existing in the Turkish Dominions) that the suffering endured by African slaves between the time when they are first made captives and the time when they arrive at their destination in Turkey are so great and so

[1] F.O. 84/691, Wellesley to Palmerston, 18 Jan. 1847; F.O. 84/647, Wellesley to Palmerston, 1 Feb. 1847; Sheil to Palmerston, Teheran and encl., 30 Nov. 1846; F.O. 84/774, Palmerston to Sheil, 31 Dec. 1849; F.O. 84/857, Palmerston to Sheil, 4 Apr. 1851; Sheil to Palmerston, 4 Aug. 1851.
[2] F.O. 84/693, Crowe to Palmerston, 27 Sept. 1847.

disproportional to any advantage derived by Turkey from the use of such slaves that the practice of introducing them from Africa ought to be abolished. The trade in slaves through Tripoli and other ports in the Mediterranean to Constantinople and the Levant is open to every objection which existed to the trade from the East coast of Africa to the Persian Gulf.[1]

Unfortunately, what seems obvious and straightforward to detached civil servants does not often appear in the same light to calculating politicians and diplomats. Such a clear demand for abolition even of the slave trade, let alone slavery, would, it was feared by the politicians, have precipitated the collapse of the Ottoman Empire. Addington's sane suggestions were therefore set aside. In the instructions to the British Ambassador no demand was made for the abolition of the slave traffic. Instead, copies of Crowe's and Gilbert's reports were sent to Lord Cowley to be communicated to the Turkish Government 'for their consideration and as an instance of the sufferings endured by the African slaves who are introduced into the Turkish dominions through the Ports of the Mediterranean'.[2]

Taking this as a request for nothing more than an order prohibiting the atrocities caused by the traffic, the Sultan immediately issued the first of the many vizirial letters to the Governor of Tripoli in November 1847. In it he ordered the Governor in very strong terms to see that none of the atrocities reported by Gilbert occurred again.[3] This order was bound to remain a dead letter, especially as its implementation was left to the slave dealers themselves. In spite of its obvious inadequacy, however, Palmerston was so persuaded by the sheer force of the language as to minute that warm thanks should be given to the Turkish Government 'for the most excellent instruction which does high honour to the human and generous feelings of the Sultan'.

Palmerston's complacency was soon ruffled by another report from Tripoli. Just when the vizirial order was being drafted, the Consul-General reported that the Pasha and other officials of Tripoli were carrying on the trade. He pointed out the great facilities that their official positions gave them and concluded that there could be little hope of the cessation of the trade as long as those deeply involved

[1] F.O. 84/693, Minutes by Palmerston and Addington on Crowe to Palmerston, 27 Sept. 1847.
[2] F.O. 84/691, Palmerston to Cowley, 20 Nov. 1847.
[3] F.O. 84/691, Cowley to Palmerston, 17 Nov. 1847, encl. vizirial letter to Pasha of Tripoli, Nov. 1847, and minute by Palmerston.

were appointed to high posts.[1] Palmerston promptly forwarded this
letter to the British Ambassador in Turkey with the specific demand
that the Porte should instruct the Pasha of Tripoli as well as persons
employed in official situations not to engage in a trade 'which inflicts
great misery on the African race'.[2] Here again, the very limited nature
of Palmerston's demand should be noted. Always anxious to meet
the wishes of the British Government, the Sultan issued two orders
to the Pasha of Tripoli, in February and August 1848, forbidding him
and all officers of the Regency in the service of the Porte to trade in
slaves. These two vizirial orders were rigidly enforced.[3]

Once the exclusion of Turkish officials from the slave trade had
been accomplished, one would have expected that the British Government would automatically and immediately demand an order preventing Turkish Government vessels from conveying slaves from
Barbary. It was, however, not until two years later that any such
demand was made. In May 1850 the Turkish steam vessel *Esseri
Djedid* was reported to have conveyed 444 slaves from Tripoli to
Constantinople. Nothing would have been done about this but for
the fact that the chief engineer of the vessel was an Englishman. 'Sir
S. Canning', Palmerston minuted, 'should remonstrate with the
Turkish Government against the employment of vessels in which
British subjects are serving for purposes which render those British
subjects liable to penalties under the law of England.'[4] This was clearly
a technical point which the Porte could neither refute nor feel
offended by. As usual, as soon as the Porte received this remon-
strance, it gave a 'distinct assurance' that orders would be issued to
prevent further embarkation of slaves in Turkish steam vessels.
Surely if the trans-Mediterranean slave trade was to be abolished, the
order had to be made applicable to all Turkish vessels, a fact which
was obvious to the civil servants. But here again the politicians saw
things differently, for in the draft reply to Canning's letter Palmerston
crossed out the section asking for the extension of this order to cover
all Turkish vessels.[5] Clearly, as late as 1850 Palmerston had not

[1] F.O. 84/693, Crowe to Palmerston, 9 Nov. 1847.
[2] F.O. 86/693, Palmerston to Cowley, 29 Dec. 1847.
[3] F.O. 84/737, Cowley to Palmerston, 3 Feb. 1848; Canning to Palmerston,
15 Oct. 1848, and encl., vizirial order to the Pasha of Tripoli, 28 Aug. 1848;
F.O. 84/774, Crowe to Palmerston, 2 Mar. 1849.
[4] F.O. 84/815, Crowe to Canning, 20 May 1850, encl. in Cumberbatch to
Palmerston, 9 July 1850, and minute by Palmerston.
[5] F.O. 84/815, Canning to Palmerston, 19 Aug. 1850; Palmerston to Canning,
24 Sept. 1850.

abandoned his cautious approach to the question. Hence, when the vizirial order was eventually issued in November 1850, the prohibition was limited to Turkish steam vessels.[1]

The British Government were finally compelled to abandon this cautious approach and make more positive demands for abolition by the reports that kept pouring in of the increase in atrocities and in the volume of the trade in both white and black men. The first report, which shocked and disgusted the Foreign Office, was sent by the British Vice-Consul in Murzuk in August 1849. He stated that a Bornu caravan of 1,600 slaves had perished from thirst after killing a large number of camels 'in order to drink their blood and the water in their stomachs'.[2] Palmerston, whose patience was now wearing thin, asked Canning to bring the report to the notice of the Turkish Government, and

to urge them to consider whether at the moment when they are receiving generous support from the Governments and universal people of England and France because the Porte is nobly facing danger rather than perform an act of inhumanity, it would not be proper and becoming to take effectual steps for preventing such barbarous and inhuman cruelties as these from being inflicted on multitudes of innocent persons by men who are impelled to such crimes solely by the sordid hope of pecuniary profit.[3]

Five months later Gagliuffi again informed the Government that 795 out of 1,770 slaves from Bornu had perished 'in agonies of thirst'. Enclosed in the letter bearing this information was another report, from the Vice-Consul at Benghazi, that 1,200 slaves had arrived from Waday after 400 had perished in the desert. To crown all this, Crowe sent the return of slaves exported from Tripoli to the Levant in 1849 and 1850, which showed that the number had increased from 1,474 to 2,733.[4] A copy of each of these reports was forwarded to the British Ambassador at Constantinople with the request that the facts should be brought before the Porte and steps taken to prevent such occurrences in future.

The report which finally led to a definite demand for abolition

[1] F.O. 84/815, Order to Captain Pasha by the Grand Vizir, 13 Nov. 1850, encl. in Canning to Palmerston, 16 Nov. 1850.

[2] F.O. 84/774, Gagliuffi to Reade, 4 Aug. 1849, encl. in Reade to Palmerston, 24 Aug. 1849.

[3] F.O. 84/774, Gagliuffi to Reade, 4 Aug. 1849, encl. in Reade to Palmerston, 24 Aug. 1849, and Palmerston's minute; Palmerston to Canning, 17 Oct. 1849.

[4] F.O. 84/815, Crowe to Palmerston, and encl. 20 Jan. 1850; Palmerston to Canning, 15 Sept. 1850; F.O. 84/857, Palmerston to Canning, 21 Mar. 1851.

came from Turkey in the course of the Crimean War. In September 1854 Canning informed the British Government that the Turks had taken advantage of the invasion of the eastern shore of the Black Sea by British and French soldiers to revive the trade in whites. The trade, he added, had been carried on clandestinely before the war in defiance of Russian prohibitions, but the Turks were now openly conveying white Christians for sale in Constantinople and other places. The indignation generated in London by this report is evident from the reply of Clarendon, then Foreign Secretary, to Canning:

It is unnecessary [Clarendon wrote] to say that Her Majesty's Government have learned with indignation that the services which the Allies have rendered to the Sultan should have aggravated a state of things so atrocious and disgusting. The honour of England no less than the interests of humanity require that no effort should be spared at this moment for the suppression of slavery in the Ottoman dominions, and if the necessary measures for that purpose are not taken by the Turkish Government, you will make a more formal application to the Porte.[1]

Two things should be particularly noted about this dispatch. The first is the force of the language, which contrasts markedly with the previous cautiously worded sentimental appeals. The second is that, for the first time, the British Government mentioned the 'suppression of slavery in the Ottoman dominions'. Disgusted by repeated reports of the misery and mortality caused by the trade, and infuriated by the thought of Muslims enslaving Christians, especially at a time when Christian armies were defending Muslim Turks, Clarendon left the ambassador in no doubt about the feelings of the British Government on the slave question.

Even without waiting for instructions from London, Canning and the French Chargé d'Affaires made strong representations to the Porte and demanded the abolition of the slave trade from Georgia and the eastern regions of the Black Sea. Of course at a time when the very existence of the Ottoman Empire depended in large measure on the goodwill of England and France, such a joint demand could not but be immediately met,[2] and the Porte issued the required firman on 1 October 1854, before the instructions from the Foreign Office had reached Constantinople. The Sultan's consent to the demand for the abolition of the trade in whites, in September 1854, is the second

[1] F.O. 84/949, Canning to Clarendon, 9 Sept. 1854; F.O. 84/949, Clarendon to Canning, 27 Sept. 1854.
[2] F.O. 84/945, Canning to Clarendon, 25 Sept. 1854.

important landmark in the campaign against the Turkish slave trade. It once more endorsed the principle established by the abolition of the trade in the Persian Gulf. With the slave trade in the Gulf and in the Black Sea abolished, attention could now be focused on the only remaining branch, that from Barbary to the Levant. And this victory provided the British Government with a thin end of a wedge, which they used at the first opportunity.

In February 1855, on receiving reports from the British Consul in Crete about a considerable trade in slaves between that island and Barbary, Clarendon instructed Canning 'to urge the Porte to extend the benevolent intentions which they have shown as regards the suppression of the Circassian slave trade in slaves and to put a stop to the trade in African slaves between the coast of Barbary and Candia [Crete]'.[1] This was the first clear request for the abolition of part of the trade from the Barbary coast. But it was a very limited request. The draft of the dispatch had asked for the entire abolition of the 'importation of African slaves into the Turkish dominions'. But in his amendment Clarendon reduced this to the traffic 'between the coast of Barbary and Candia'. Obviously the Government was still reluctant to force the issue. Once again, on the application of Canning to the Porte the request was immediately granted. In March 1855 a vizirial order was sent to the Pasha of Tripoli informing him of the prohibition of the slave traffic between Barbary and Candia and asking him to take measures for its enforcement.[2]

That this order would be ineffective should have been apparent to anybody with any knowledge of the geography of the Mediterranean and the role played by the island of Crete and its chief port, Candia, in the slave traffic. Candia itself was not an importer of slaves, but primarily a coaling station for ships plying between Barbary and the Levant. Yet according to this order only ships exporting slaves to that port could be arrested. Therefore, although from January to April 1856 no less than fourteen ships from Tripoli, Derna, and Benghazi carrying a total of 994 slaves called at Candia on their way to Albania, Rhodes, Mytilene, Constantinople, and Cyprus,[3] not one of the slave dealers was arrested because their vessels were in transit.

[1] F.O. 84/974, Clarendon to Canning, 21 Feb. 1855.
[2] F.O. 84/974, Canning to Clarendon, 19 Mar. 1855, and encl., vizirial order to Ali Pasha, 18 Mar. 1855.
[3] F.O. 84/1000, Ongley to Canning, Candia, 10 Apr. 1856, encl. in Ongley to Clarendon, 10 Apr. 1856.

Besides these reports from Candia, even more alarming ones began to pour into the Foreign Office from Rhodes and Mytilene. The Vice-Consul at Mytilene reported in June 1855 that between 15 April and 2 June 283 'negresses and young negroes' were disembarked at that port.[1] Reports of this kind were exasperating to the Foreign Office and forced the officials at last to attempt to grasp the nettle. In August 1855, after referring to the reports from Candia, Rhodes, and Mytilene, Clarendon asked Canning to inform the Porte that:

Her Majesty's Government observe with extreme regret the increase of this nefarious traffick in Ottoman vessels, evidently protected by Ottoman authorities. No means for preventing these proceedings appear to be taken by the Porte, and Her Majesty's Government, however reluctant they may be to bring discredit upon the Turkish flag, will be compelled to send cruizers to the Mediterranean for the purpose of checking and chastising the traders.[2]

But since this letter arrived in the heat of the Crimean War, Canning did not bring it to the notice of the Sultan.

The end of the war and the impending peace talks in Paris created a good opportunity for an onslaught on the African slave traffic. In a lengthy address on slavery in Turkey in March 1856, the Anti-Slavery Society urged the Government to take advantage of this opportunity to stipulate in any treaty about to be entered into with Turkey for the abolition not only of the slave trade, but also of slavery itself in the Turkish dominions.[3] Clarendon passed this address on to Canning asking him to tell the Turkish Government that

at this moment when Peace is about to be concluded, the Porte could do nothing more acceptable to Her Majesty's Government and to the British nation than to adopt measures which should be really effectual for putting an end to the Slave Trade.[4]

[2] F.O. 84/974, Newton to Campbell, Mytilene, 22 June 1855, encl. in Campbell to Clarendon, Rhodes, 30 June 1855.

[2] F.O. 84/974; for reports from Rhodes, see Campbell to Clarendon, 7 July 1855; idem, 17 July 1855; F.O. 84/974, Clarendon to Canning, 9 Aug. 1855; F.O. 84/974, Canning to Clarendon, 20 Aug. 1855.

[3] F.O. 84/1004, 'Few observations on the subject of slavery in Turkey', the Committee of the Anti-Slavery Society to Palmerston, Mar. 1856. This was published also in the Anti-Slavery Reporter, 1 Apr. 1856, pp. 81–85.

[4] F.O. 84/1000, Clarendon to Canning, 13 Mar. 1856.

The political conditions of the day made the outcome of this request a foregone conclusion. No sooner had the Sultan received it in April 1856 than he issued a firman abolishing the trade in slaves by land or sea between Tripoli and Turkey, and instructed the Pasha of Tripoli to see to its immediate enforcement.[1]

The vizirial order of April 1856 was certainly a considerable improvement on that of March 1855, but it had some obvious flaws: though the import and export of slaves were forbidden, their sale in the Regency was still permitted; no penalties were laid down for the infringement of the order, and the pashas of the other provinces of the Ottoman Empire were not informed of it. The attention of the British Government was drawn to these flaws by the consular reports which continued to come in from the Mediterranean ports regarding the great increase in the volume of the traffic and the refusal of the Turkish authorities to take any action, on the ground that they had not been officially informed of the order.[2] Each of these reports was, as usual, forwarded to Canning with instructions that he should urge the Porte to adopt 'stringent measures' to carry into effect its various orders.[3]

It was in response to these requests that a firman was issued in January 1857 which declared (laying down penalties) the 'final abolition of the negro slave trade with a view to the extinction of slavery itself throughout the Sultans' dominions'.[4] Slave traders in Tripoli were to be granted a period of eight weeks to bring in and dispose of their slaves. After that period, any black slaves that arrived in Tripoli were to be liberated 'on the spot', and the slave trader was to be imprisoned for a year for the first offence and an additional year for any subsequent offence. After a period of six weeks from the date of the order any vessel seen in the Mediterranean with slaves on board was to be seized, her captain imprisoned, and the slaves liberated. In Turkey and other provinces of the Empire,

[1] F.O. 84/1000, Grand-Vizir to Ali Pasha, 19 Apr. 1856, encl. in Canning to Clarendon, 24 Apr. 1856; Herman to Clarendon, 28 Apr. 1856.

[2] F.O. 84/1000, Bilotti to Campbell, Scio, 4 June 1856, encl. in Campbell to Clarendon, 9 June 1856; Brant to Clarendon, Smyrna, 12 July 1856; Calvert (Consul for Dardanelles) to Clarendon, 11 Sept. 1856; Calvert to Clarendon, 20 Sept. 1856; Ongley to Clarendon, Candia, 23 Dec. 1856; Herman to Clarendon, 12 Dec. 1856.

[3] F.O. 84/1000, Clarendon to Canning, 28 July 1856; idem, 9 Oct. 1856, 26 Dec. 1856.

[4] F.O. 84/1028, Canning to Clarendon, 31 Jan. 1857, and encls, The Sublime Porte to Canning, 29 Jan. 1857, and Firman prohibiting the slave trade.

except the 'holy' province of Hejaz, the firman was to be enforced
after a period of three months. While slaves already owned could still
be kept, their sale and purchase were forbidden. Copies of this firman,
with covering vizirial letters, were sent to the governors of all the
provinces of the Ottoman Empire except Hejaz. In these letters the
Governors were asked to proclaim the firman 'in due form' and to
prevent the departure of negro slaves 'after the date of the proclamation from any place situated within the province and to assure entire
enforcement of the firman'.

This firman brought to a successful conclusion the attack on the
slave trade from Tripoli to the Ottoman Empire. It was certainly a
very comprehensive document and, as the British Foreign Secretary
commented, 'the regulations which [it contains], if carried out in
good faith, are sufficient for the purpose for which they are required'.[1]
But, would the regulations be carried out 'in good faith'? There was
the rub. As long as the institution of slavery was given legal recognition, it should have been obvious to the British Government that the
Turkish authorities would not and could never effectively enforce
this firman themselves. As the Anti-Slavery Society pointed out and
the Consul-General in Tripoli reiterated six years after the passing
of the law,[2] the surest way of achieving the abolition of the slave
trade was the abolition, as at Tunis, of the institution of slavery.
However, still sticking to their conviction that such a measure would
have been disastrous to the Empire, the British Government persistently refused to demand this

An alternative move—and indeed an easier one—would have been
for Britain to enforce this firman herself. Some of the consuls in the
Mediterranean, as well as Canning, the British Ambassador in
Constantinople, urged the British Government to conclude a treaty
with the Porte granting British vessels the right to search Turkish
vessels in the Mediterranean and the Red Sea.[3] Clarendon welcomed
this suggestion and minuted that a draft convention should be prepared. This was done and after some amendments was approved by
Palmerston himself.[4] From the enclosed nature of the Mediterranean

[1] F.O. 84/1028, Clarendon to Canning, 9 Apr. 1857.
[2] F.O. 84/1204, Herman to Russell, 30 Apr. 1863.
[3] F.O. 84/1000, Biliotti to Campbell, 4 June 1856, encl. in Campbell to
Clarendon, 4 June 1856; F.O. 84/1028, Canning to Clarendon, 31 Jan. 1857, and
minute by Clarendon.
[4] F.O. 84/1500, Draft Treaty between Her Majesty and the Sultan of Turkey
for the abolition of the traffic in slaves, Feb. 1857.

and the short coastline of the Regency of Tripoli, a British naval squadron of only three or four vessels could have easily stopped any contraband in slaves. But this draft was never forwarded to Constantinople. The Government suddenly dropped the idea in 1857, perhaps for the same reason as was given by William H. Wylde, the Head of the Slave Trade Department of the Foreign Office, for the rejection of an identical suggestion twelve years later. On that occasion Wylde argued:

The steamers that carry the slaves carry also passengers of all denominations, pilgrims of all shades of colour, free blacks who are domestic servants of some of the passengers, and free blacks travelling on their own account. How could the Commander of a cruiser discriminate between the slaves and the free blacks when, as I hear is the case, the former are dressed up the same as their free countrymen? And suppose a mistake did take place, and one of our cruisers were either to detain a vessel or take out of her an individual who might turn out to be the servant of some French subject or an individual under French protection, what correspondence we should probably have with the French Government on the subject. I would have long since proposed that we should endeavour to negotiate with Turkey a treaty for the suppression of the slave trade, had I not foreseen great difficulties in carrying out to any practical end any engagements we might make with Turkey giving us the right to act *in the Mediterranean*.[1]

He concluded by expressing his firm opinion that there would be great objections to giving British cruisers the right to search or detain Turkish vessels in the Mediterranean, while any convention which gave the consular officers more power than they then exercised for the prevention of the slave traffic would 'be objectionable on other grounds'. In short, Wylde was for the maintenance of the *status quo*. Another official at the Foreign Office[2] was, however, not convinced. While admitting Wylde's argument of the possibility of making mistakes in the enforcement of such a convention, he felt that the object to be attained was of such importance that it was 'worthy of the difficulty and risk to be incurred'. In the face of such clear division of opinion between the officials, the onus of decision fell on the Secretary of State himself. And as Clarendon accepted Wylde's view in 1869, he may have done so in 1857.

With the refusal of the British Government to assume responsibility for enforcing the firman, that task devolved on the Porte and the

---

[1] F.O. 84/1305, Minute by Wylde on Elliot to Clarendon, 20 July 1869.
[2] The name of this official could not be deciphered.

Ottoman provincial authorities. The responsibility was in some cases discharged, depending on the vigilance of the British consular agent on the spot and the nature of the pressure which he brought to bear on the authorities. But without the genuine willingness of the authorities themselves, the orders could not be and were not completely enforced. As early as July 1858 the acting Consul-General in Tripoli described the firman as 'a mere fiction', and five years later the substantive Consul-General called it 'a solemn mockery'.[1] Throughout the remainder of the century reports continued to flow in from Tripoli, Crete, and Constantinople of flagrant infringements of the firmans and vizirial orders. As usual the British Government forwarded these reports to Constantinople and asked for strong measures to be adopted. These requests, in turn, produced more vizirial orders to the provincial authorities, which were ignored. Slavery was eventually abolished in Turkey in 1889; yet reports came in from the agents of the British and Italian Anti-Slavery Societies as late as 1907–10 that slaves were being shipped from Benghazi to the Levant.[2] The nefarious traffic did not completely stop until the Italian occupation of Tripoli in 1911.

The firman of January 1857 brought the diplomatic attack on the Saharan and Mediterranean slave trade to a successful conclusion. By that date the slave trade had been abolished on paper at least throughout all of Barbary except Morocco, and throughout the Ottoman Empire except in Hejaz. It is apparent that, faced with a clash between humanitarian and political interests, the British government readily sacrificed the former to the latter. In Morocco, where the agitation of the question would have had adverse political repercussions for Britain, it was conveniently forgotten. In Tunis, where it could be pressed without any ruinous political consequences, the campaign was over in a year. In Turkey, similar fears of serious political effects prevented the British Government from demanding abolition of the trade until thirteen years after the first attack. For the same reason the British Government persistently refused to negotiate a treaty which would have ensured the enforcement of the vizirial orders promulgated against the trade. But for the pressure of the Anti-Slavery Society, and the fact that white Christians were

---

[1] F.O. 84/1062, Reade to Malmesbury, 20 July 58; F.O. 84/1204, Herman to Russell, 12 Nov. 1863.
[2] Br. Emp. MSS. S22/G283, Slave Trade in Tripoli; Report on Slave Trade in Tripoli by Madame Terrier.

involved in the Turkish slave traffic, the abolition campaign might even have been called off in Turkey, as it was in Morocco, after the skirmishes of the early forties.

While these diplomatic battles were raging at the various courts of Barbary and the Levant, another campaign was being waged on the same branch of the African slave trade in the Sahara itself. It is to this that we must now turn.

CHAPTER VII

The Vice-Consulates of the Sahara

SINCE the attack on the trans-Saharan and Mediterranean slave traffic began after the theory of legitimate commerce had been generally accepted as the remedy for that evil it was natural that attempts should be made to apply the theory in the Sahara too. This was especially so because the spearhead of the attack on this branch of the traffic, Colonel Warrington, was himself one of the earliest advocates of legitimate trade. When he resumed the campaign for abolition in 1840, he suggested not only a diplomatic approach to the Arab chiefs but also his old plan of promoting legitimate commerce by the establishment of a British vice-consulate at Murzuk in Fezzan,[1] which he thought would be more efficacious. He told James Richardson, the agent of the Anti-Slavery Society in Malta, that if something could be done to promote commerce with the interior 'there would be more done in two years to abolish slavery than all the acts of Parliament, all the Foreign Treaties and all the Anti-Slavery Societies have as yet done'.[2]

Partly because of the Government's belief in 'the great advantages to be derived to the British Commerce' and partly for reasons already discussed,[3] Warrington's oft-repeated suggestion of a vice-consular post in Fezzan was at last approved, and he was asked to recommend a suitable person.[4] His choice fell on Gagliuffi, an Italian trader who had lived in Tripoli for fourteen years and who was at the time the agent and personal friend of Abd al-Jalīl. This nomination was approved, and Warrington was empowered to furnish Gagliuffi with 'a letter of authority constituting and appointing him British Vice-Consul and with instructions for the guidance of his official conduct founded on the instructions which have been

---

[1] F.O. 101/4, Warrington to Bidwell, 18 May 1850.
[2] Br. Emp. MSS. S22/928, Warrington to Richardson, 5 Mar. 1843, encl. in Richardson to Scobie, 29 May 1843.
[3] See above, pp. 135–6.
[4] F.O. 84/333, Bidwell to Warrington, 5 July 1840.

addressed to yourself'.[1] A firman recognizing Gagliuffi as the British
Vice-Consul at Murzuk was obtained from the Porte through Ponsonby. Owing to the state of war between the Turks and Abd al-Jalīl
however, and to the determined opposition of the Pasha, Askar Ali,
the Vice-Consul's departure was delayed for three years. The recall
of Askar Ali in May 1842 and the subsequent Turkish occupation of
Fezzan cleared the way for Gagliuffi.

The instructions which Warrington gave to the Vice-Consul on the
eve of his departure dealt mainly with the slave trade.[2] He was asked
to direct his 'zeal and exertion' primarily to the abolition of the
horrid traffic. He was to do all in his power to discourage the trade
and see to the better treatment of slaves. In all his commercial
transactions he was to have nothing to do with that traffic directly or
indirectly. He was to send regular reports about politics, and do
everything to establish trade and improve the conditions of the
people of Fezzan. With these instructions and a letter of introduction
to the Commander-in-Chief of Fezzan, Gagliuffi left Tripoli at the
head of a small caravan of twenty-three camels on 25 January 1843.
He entered Murzuk two months later. On 29 March, at 9 a.m., the
first British vice-consulate in the Sahara was formally and cere-
moniously established with the hoisting of 'the glorious standard of
Her Britannic Majesty' accompanied by 'the usual salute of twenty-
one guns'.[3]

It is important to note that initially the British Government did not
attach much importance to this post, nor did they have any intention
of establishing another vice-consulate in the Sahara. When the
nomination of Gagliuffi was approved in October 1840, Warrington
was categorically informed that 'no salary will be assigned to him
and . . . the post will not give him any claim upon Her Majesty's
Government either at the present time or when it shall cease'.[4]
When Warrington suggested five years later that a second post
should be established at Ghadames, the Government turned it
down.[5] But they gradually came round to Warrington's way of

[1] F.O. 101/4, Warrington to Bidwell, 1 Sept. 1840; Backhouse to Warrington,
9 Oct. 1840.
[2] F.O. 84/486, Warrington to Gagliuffi, 24 Jan. 1843, encl. in Warrington to
Aberdeen, 5 Feb. 1843.
[3] F.O. 101/9, Gagliuffi to Warrington, 30 Mar. 1843, encl. in Warrington to
Bidwell, 22 Apr. 1843.
[4] F.O. 101/4, Backhouse to Warrington, 9 Oct. 1840.
[5] F.O. 101/12, Warrington to Aberdeen, 4 June 1845.

thinking and not only gave increasing support to the Murzuk post, but even established a second one. Twice in 1843 Gagliuffi applied for some financial assistance. Instead of demanding the abolition of the post, the Government rather unexpectedly agreed to grant Gagliuffi a gratuity, though not a salary, of £150 for 1843.[1] Again in 1846, in response to repeated requests for further financial assistance, the Government granted the same amount for that year and also for the two previous years. In November 1846 Gagliuffi once more asked for a salary. This was granted, and a figure of £200 a year was fixed, and at the same time the Government approved the establishment of a second vice-consular post at Ghadames.[2] For the latter post Palmerston recommended Richardson, and in the consular estimates of 1847 and 1848 the surprisingly large sum of £500 was voted as his yearly salary.[3] These two concessions indicate the evolution of a definite British policy in the Sahara. What were the reasons for this change and the canons of this policy?

Lord Palmerston's dispatch of February 1847, in which he granted Gagliuffi's request, provides clues for the answer to these questions. Crowe, who was then British Consul-General in Tripoli,[4] was informed:

Upon mature consideration of the difficulties which have been overcome by the patience and perseverance of M. Gagliuffi and the ultimate advantages which may be expected to result from continuing to maintain a British Consular Agent on the verge of the desert, compared with the probability that France would hasten to occupy the post if the British Consular Officer were withdrawn, I am of opinion that it is advisable to maintain M. Gagliuffi at Mourzouk with a fixed salary exclusive of a small allowance for presents and medicines.[5]

It is clear from this dispatch that it was in the hope of some 'ultimate advantages' and in fear that the French might occupy the post if it were abandoned that the Government decided rather belatedly to

[1] F.O. 101/9, Gagliuffi to Warrington, 13 May 1843, encl. in Warrington to Bidwell, 2 June 1843; Gagliuffi to Warrington, 17 Dec. 1843; F.O. 101/10, Canning to Warrington, 6 Apr. 1844.

[2] F.O. 101/15, Palmerston to Crowe, 15 Feb. 1847.

[3] F.O. 101/20, Minute by Addington on Crowe to Palmerston; Addington to Treasury, 30 Jan. 1849.

[4] Warrington was forced by the Foreign Office to retire in July 1846 owing to his quarrel with the Consul of Naples in Tripoli. This disciplinary act, as he confessed, filled him 'with sorrow and surprise' and indeed sent him to his grave only a year later.

[5] F.O. 101/18, Palmerston to Crowe, 27 Feb. 1847.

grant Gagliuffi's request. It is evident, too, from the dispatches from Tripoli on which the Government based its decision that the advantages which it had in view were the development of British commerce in and across the Sahara and the extinction of the slave trade through this and through the rigid enforcement of the anti-slave-trade orders issued by the Governments of Tunis and Turkey. All those who advocated this forward policy—Gagliuffi, Warrington, Richardson, and Dickson, who was ultimately appointed to the post at Ghadames—were unanimous in their view of the feasibility of developing a very lucrative commerce in the Sahara and the western Sudan via the desert. In his letter of December 1843 Gagliuffi pointed out that if he were given the necessary assistance and support, 'in a short time a profitable and extensive trade may be opened with the interior of Africa'. Five years later Dickson also reasserted the importance of the traffic carried on between Tripoli and the western Sudan and the ease with which British manufactures and colonial produce could be introduced in large quantities into the interior. He also drew attention to the commercial importance of Ghadames, 'the main depot for the transit of trade into Ghat, Touat, Timbuctoo, Kashna, Sukkatoo, and Kanou'; and warned the Government that 'owing to the exertions of the French in Algeria, and the proximity of Touat to the frontiers of their colony, the valuable trade at Timbuctoo may eventually be diverted into the channels of Algeria to the exclusion of that of Ghadames and to the detriment of British trade'.[1]

If these people were certain about the development of British commerce in and across the Sahara, they were even more so about the decisive role of the consular posts in the campaign against the trans-Saharan slave trade. They all pointed out that the consuls would be able to see that the orders issued by the Turkish and Barbary authorities against the trade were rigidly enforced, and that they could encourage the development of legitimate commerce by drawing the attention of the people to the commercial value of their natural products and teaching them how to exploit them.[2] Both Richardson and Dickson cited the successful attempt made by Gagliuffi to promote the collection of gum and bees-wax in Fezzan,

[1] F.O. 101/20, Dickson to Crowe, 25 Aug. 1848, encl. in Crowe to Palmerston, 1 Sept. 1848.
[2] F.O. 101/15, Gagliuffi to Crowe, 24 Nov. 1846; F.O. 101/16, Report on the oasis of Ghat, Richardson to Warrington, 11 May 1846; Richardson, *Travels*, vol. ii, pp. 361–2; F.O. 101/20, Dickson to Bidwell, London, 17 Nov. 1848.

and mentioned how indigo, 'as yet a nascent commodity' in Bornu and Tuat, could be obtained in large quantities 'were the natives of those regions only instructed as to the proper mode of preparing this dye'.[1] Indeed, like Warrington and Buxton earlier, Richardson deemed this a much more effective and less expensive way of combating the slave trade than most of the measures hitherto adopted. He expressed the opinion that

'a little more money spent in promoting individual enterprise or the establishment of British vice-consuls throughout the remote and vast provinces of Central Africa would do the British Government infinitely more honour and the people of Africa more good than granting exorbitant pensions to public servants and fitting out costly and armed expeditions for the suppression of the slave traffic in one coast whilst another coast is left entirely open for the triumphant development of this infamous commerce'.[2]

None of the arguments here advanced were new, since they were those which, as we have seen, led to the sending out of the 1841 expedition.[3] The tragic failure of that expedition, as has been pointed out, merely showed that the theory of legitimate commerce could be applied only in areas where the climate was more suitable to Europeans. Richardson expressed the opinion current in abolitionist circles when he informed Palmerston that 'the failure of the Niger expedition [of 1841] has begun to recommend this scheme [establishing vice-consular posts in the Sahara] to the public mind'.[4] The early expeditions across the Sahara, and in particular the survival of Gagliuffi in Fezzan, demonstrated that the Sahara was probably more conducive to European health than the Guinea coast. This explains why after the failure of the expedition in 1841 the British Government took more and more interest in the posts in the Sahara.

It is, however, also clear from Palmerston's letter of February 1847 that it was not only the hope of developing British commerce and of abolishing the slave trade that influenced the British Government. The fear of French expansion inland was just as strong and perhaps even stronger. This fear was generated by reports from the Barbary States. As soon as Palmerston returned to the Foreign Office for the

---

[1] F.O. 101/20, Dickson to Crowe, 25 Aug. 1848; F.O. 101/16, Richardson to Warrington, 11 May 1846.

[2] F.O. 97/430, Richardson to the Committee of the Anti-Slavery Society, 12 June 1846.

[3] See above, pp. 97–99.

[4] F.O. 101/23, Richardson to Palmerston, 5 Oct. 1848.

third time in July 1846, he was presented with a series of alarming reports from Morocco, Tunis, and Tripoli of increasing French expansionist activities in northern Africa. It was reported from Morocco in 1846 and 1847 that the French were exerting themselves to gain ascendancy.[1] In Tripoli a French official was said to be gleaning information from the merchants who traded to the interior about the state of commerce and the condition of the Africans.[2] At the same time Gagliuffi also drew the attention of the Foreign Office to the French drive into the interior. Indeed, his second reason for the retention of the post at Murzuk—a reason which he believed would 'hasten decision'—was that as soon as the British withdrew the French would move in and establish communication with the interior, to the detriment of British commerce. He warned the Government that 'the French were insinuating themselves little by little'. In forwarding this letter to the Foreign Office, Crowe endorsed Gagliuffi's view. He stated that though commercially the post was of no avail, 'it may yet be thought inexpedient to suppress it having been once established, more especially as there is every probability that France would hasten to occupy the abandoned post'.[3] Two years later Dickson also laboured this point. In applying for the post of Vice-Consul at Ghadames, he emphasized the need to forestall the designs of the French on Tuat and the interior. 'It would be desirable,' he wrote, 'that a British agent be placed at Ghadames to co-operate with the British Vice-Consul at Murzuk, in as much as by creating a trade in the place, we would facilitate the intercourse with the interior and repress the ambitious designs of France.'[4]

These reports of the activities of the French in northern Africa in the forties were by no means unfounded. As a result of the successful opposition of the Arab tribes in the interior under the militant leadership of Abd al-Qadir in the thirties, the French had been compelled to concentrate their efforts on the area north of the Atlas. By the early forties the occupation of Oran in the west and Constantine in the east had completed the conquest of the coastal areas. The French therefore began to look farther afield—eastward to Tunis and southward into the Sahara and the Sudan. They began their expansion into

[1] Flournoy, op. cit., pp. 113, 116.
[2] F.O. 101/13, Warrington to Aberdeen, 3 Mar. 1846; F.O. 101/13, Warrington to Aberdeen, 23 Mar. 1846.
[3] F.O. 101/15, Crowe to Palmerston, 24 Nov. 1846, and encl., Gagliuffi to Crowe, 24 Nov. 1846.
[4] F.O. 101/20, Dickson to Bidwell, 17 Nov. 1848.

the Sahara with the occupation of Biskra and Laghouat in 1844, and similar progress was made in the region south of Oran.[1] Further advance was checked by the increasing opposition of al-Qadir and his followers, and it was not resumed until after the revolution of 1848.

Now although Palmerston had accepted the French occupation of Algeria as a *fait accompli*, he was not prepared to see the boundaries extended in any direction. Thus in 1840 he refused to assist the French in their war against al-Qadir. The reasons which Palmerston gave for his refusal were typical of him:

It is certainly not for our interest [he wrote] that Abd el Kader should be extinguished or that he should become a protected dependent of France, though at no distant time France will probably succeed in establishing her political ascendancy over the whole of Algeria and in making that province a considerable element of power to France. There seems to be no invincible difficulty to prevent France from making that large and important portion of North Africa stand in the same relation to France in which India does to England.'[2]

The numerous reports of the mid-forties seemed to justify Palmerston's predictions and, as Gagliuffi foresaw, prompted immediate counter-measures. In Morocco, for instance, the rank of the British representative was raised to that of Chargé d'Affaires to correspond to that of the French and Spanish representatives.[3] It was obvious from its situation that no town could have been more suitable than Ghadames for the establishment of a post for checking French expansion from Algeria into the Sahara. It is therefore not surprising that Palmerston should have approved the establishment of the second vice-consular post in that town.

From 1847 onwards, then, the posts in the Sahara were of political and strategic as well as commercial and humanitarian importance. While diplomatic negotiations against the slave trade were going on in Barbary and Turkey, the vice-consuls in the Sahara were simultaneously attacking the traffic at its source, developing British trade, and keeping the French out of the Sahara. Every attention was therefore paid to these posts in the late forties and throughout the fifties. Thus in January 1849 the Foreign Office cheerfully approved Gagliuffi's application for naturalization as a British subject on the

---

[1] A. Bernard and N. Lacrois, *La Pénètration saharienne 1830–1906* (Paris, 1906), pp. 8–12; Flournoy, op. cit., p. 115.

[2] Palmerston to Russell, 18 Nov. 1840, in the *Broadlands Papers*.

[3] Flournoy, op. cit., p. 121.

grounds that 'his becoming British would give him more weight in his office of British Vice-Consul of Murzuk'.[1] Not until its abolition was the Murzuk post ever vacant. When Gagliuffi went on leave in March 1855, after a continuous residence of twelve years, the post was filled for nearly a year by W. F. Warrington, the son of the late Colonel Warrington; and from 1855 to 1860 it was held by Gaetano de Fremaux, a native of Malta. As a result of Crowe's persistent opposition to the appointment of Richardson because of his indiscretion, prejudice, and intemperance, the Ghadames post was not established in 1847.[2] But when in September 1848 Crowe warmly recommended C. H. Dickson, Palmerston readily appointed him.[3] Owing to delays in London and Tripoli, however, it was not until New Year's Day of 1850 that Dickson hoisted the Union Jack in Ghadames 'amidst repeated volleys of musketry'.[4] The flag continued to fly there as in Murzuk until 1860.

How, and with what success, did the Vice-Consuls discharge their duties? As one might expect, the problem which first occupied their attention was the slave trade and its abolition. They sent frequent reports about the traffic, checked the practice of sending out *razzias*, and saw that the firmans and vizirial orders were enforced. Their reports described the size of the slave caravans that arrived, the treatment of the slaves *en route* and the rate of mortality. From 1844 onwards there exist, especially for Murzuk, annual returns giving the number of slaves, where they came from, and their destination. We have already seen the disgust which some of these reports and returns caused in London, and the stimulus which they gave to the diplomatic campaign in Constantinople. Richardson, who stayed in Murzuk from 22 February to 6 March 1846, reported that 'the traffic in slaves is well watched on this route and reported upon'.[5] The fact that the main stream of the traffic had been diverted from Murzuk to Ghat in the west and Kufra in the east by the late fifties[6] provides evidence of the pressure which the British consular agents brought on the reluctant Turkish officials to enforce the various

[1] F.O. 101/22, Addington to C.O., 2 Jan. 1849; F.O. 101/20, Grey to Palmerston, 26 Dec. 1848, and encl., application by Gagliuffi, 15 Nov. 1848.

[2] F.O. 101/18, Crowe to Bidwell, 18 Mar. 1847; F.O. 101/20, Crowe to Palmerston, 8 July 1847.

[3] F.O. 101/20, Dickson to Crowe, 25 Aug. 1848; F.O. 101/20, Crowe to Palmerston, 1 Sept. 1848; F.O. 101/21, F.O. to Crowe, 31 Jan. 1849.

[4] F.O. 101/24, Dickson to Crowe, 2 Jan. 1850, encl., Crowe to F.O., 22 Jan. 1850.

[5] Richardson, *Travels*, op. cit., vol. ii, p. 360. [6] See pp. 221–5.

abolition laws. Indeed it was largely for this reason that the Murzuk post was retained until May 1861.

The Vice-Consuls also succeeded in stopping the official slave-raiding expeditions from Tripoli and Fezzan to the Sudan. Gagliuffi began the attack on this practice even before his arrival at Murzuk. On his way to Fezzan he met a sheikh bearing letters to the Pasha of Tripoli from the Bey of Fezzan, who was proposing 'an expedition to the black country'. Arguing that such *razzias* would alienate the people of the interior to the detriment of commerce, Gagliuffi asked Warrington to see that the proposal was rejected and the practice 'for ever abolished'.[1] Warrington won the consent of the new Pasha to the request, and from that time no more cases of official *razzias* were reported. Though the cessation of *razzias* did not radically reduce the volume of the traffic, it was still a worthwhile achievement, since they often endangered peaceful activities and rendered the routes insecure by causing a great deal of fear and ill-feeling among the people of the interior.

As humanitarian agents, the Vice-Consuls tried to promote the general welfare of the people. The British Government regularly supplied Gagliuffi with medicines which enabled him to set up a sort of dispensary where medical treatment was administered free of charge to the people. This dispensary contained such medicines as worm emetic, purgative pills, fever powders, sulphate and quinine pills, eye powders, and a strong solution of nitrate of silver for ophthalmia. But the quantity of these medicines was very limited. At first his allowance for medicines was only £10 per annum,[2] though in 1847 this was nearly doubled by Palmerston. Yet there is no doubt that he did some useful work. He claimed to have 'saved many persons from death, who are now praying continually for the prosperity of our Gracious Sovereign Lady'.[3] Moreover, his example was followed by the Bey, with whom he was on the best of terms. In 1846 Richardson saw at Murzuk a large house appropriated as a hospital for the poor and directed by a Greek doctor.[4] The Vice-Consul also

---

[1] F.O. 84/486, Gagliuffi to Warrington, Sockna, 26 Feb. 1843, encl. in Warrington to Aberdeen, 14 Mar. 1843.

[2] F.O. 101/4, Warrington to Buckhouse, 10 Dec. 1840; F.O. 101/5, Bidwell to Warrington, 19 Jan. 1841.

[3] F.O. 101/10, Gagliuffi to Warrington, 27 July 1841, encl. in Warrington to Aberdeen, 19 Aug. 1844.

[4] Richardson, *Travels*, vol. ii, p. 346; idem, *A Mission to Central Africa* (1853), vol. i, p. 85; Barth, op. cit., vol. i, p. 171.

helped in embellishing Murzuk and giving it the air and character of a Turkish city on the coast. For instance, on his suggestion a new colonnade was built in the main street in front of the shops to afford shelter from the fiery rays of the sun, and new barracks were erected for the troops.[1] These services undoubtedly made Gagliuffi's name and also that of the British exceedingly well-known and popular in Fezzan in particular and in the Sahara in general.

In their role as political agents, the Vice-Consuls did all they could to establish contacts with the chiefs of the Sahara and the Sudan and to win their friendship and co-operation. One of the first things that Gagliuffi did on his arrival at Murzuk was to collect the names and titles of the various chiefs of the Tuareg and the Tibu. As he quite correctly pointed out:

It is indispensable to enter into relation with all of them for the general views [sic]. When those Sheikhs are known, one may be sure that the caravans arrive safe at their destination; it is also favourable to those who are agents to find protection and to be enabled to trade freely.[2]

The positions of Ghadames and Murzuk as centres for both the *hajj* (pilgrim) and trade caravans enabled the Vice-Consuls to gather these data. They readily gave hospitality to important personages and merchants of distinction and influence on their way to and from Mecca or Barbary. In addition to guaranteeing the security of traders and their agents, these people also carried the name of Britain with them into their countries. During his stay with Gagliuffi, Richardson noted how most strangers dealt with the consul in preference to the Ottoman authorities or the people of Murzuk. He also mentioned a famous *marabout* (priest) from Morocco who, while in Murzuk on his way from Mecca, deposited all his money with the Vice-Consul.[3] Some of these contacts proved very lasting and valuable. A classic example was the relationship which Gagliuffi established with Al-Hajj Bashīr, the Grand Vizir or Prime Minister of Bornu.

This important official arrived at Murzuk from Mecca in January 1844. Gagliuffi accommodated him in his house and had discussions with him on ways and means of opening up trade with the interior. He also impressed on him the advantages which his master, the

---

[1] Richardson, *Mission*, vol. i, p. 85.
[2] F.O. 101/9, Gagliuffi to Warrington, encl. in Warrington to Bidwell, 9 June 1843.
[3] Richardson, *Travels*, vol. ii, p. 361.

Sheikh of Bornu, might obtain if, instead of depopulating the country and selling the captives as slaves, he made them cultivate indigo, cotton, and other crops. Bashīr, a very intelligent and well-educated man, expressed his concurrence with the views of the Vice-Consul and his readiness to trade with the British. He asked for drums, fifes, and trumpets for the troops, cotton-gins, and a machine for minting money. These he promised to pay for with ivory, wax, and ostrich feathers.[1] The friendship which developed between the two men continued when the Vizir returned to Bornu. They maintained a regular correspondence and became commercial agents for each other. Gagliuffi was also made the Vizir's trustee for the house which he bought in Murzuk, and anyone going to Bornu derived great advantage from the Vice-Consul's letter of recommendation.[2] It was Al-Hajj Bashīr who later received Barth so warmly and contributed so much to the success of his exploration. Barth himself testified to the honesty and strength of the friendship between Gagliuffi and the Vizir.[3]

Gagliuffi also established contacts with the Tibu of Bilma and the Tuareg of Ghat and acted as an intermediary between the Tibu and the Turkish authorities. There is extant a copy of a letter which the Sultan of the Tibu addressed to Gagliuffi declaring his allegiance to the Porte.[4] The correspondence between Gagliuffi and the sheikhs of Ghat testifies to the smooth relations he had with them also. The Vice-Consul informed the sheikhs of Ghat of the expedition of Richardson and Barth and asked for a pledge for the safety of the explorers—a request which was readily granted.[5] Moreover, to strengthen their relations with the Tuareg and to keep the routes open, the Vice-Consuls more than once thwarted an invasion of Ghat by the Bey of Fezzan. In 1846 Gagliuffi and Richardson successfully appealed to Warrington to ask the Pasha to stop the invasion of Ghat which the Bey was preparing.[6] In 1852 Gagliuffi and Dickson reported independently the 'alarm and confusion' produced among the people of Ghat by the military preparations of the Lieutenant-

[1] F.O. 84/540, Gagliuffi to Warrington, 27 Jan. 1844, encl. in Warrington to Aberdeen, 28 Feb. 1844.
[2] Richardson, *Travels*, vol. ii, pp. 314, 361.
[3] F.O. 101/45, Barth to Wodehouse, 11 Dec. 1858.
[4] F.O. 101/26, Richardson to Palmerston, and encls., Murzuk, 9 May 1850.
[5] F.O. 101/26, The Chiefs of Ghat to Gagliuffi, encl. in Richardson to Palmerston, 8 May 1850.
[6] F.O. 101/16, Richardson to Warrington, 1 May 1846.

Governor of Fezzan. Consequently Crowe appealed to the Pasha of Tripoli to stop the impending invasion. At the same time he sent the Vice-Consuls' reports to the Foreign Office and suggested that nothing but the removal of Hassan Pasha from the Government of Fezzan could calm the excited desert people, allay the fear of aggression, and restore public confidence and security. The Foreign Office, with equal haste, referred these letters to the British Ambassador at Constantinople and instructed him to ask the Sultan whether he had sanctioned the invasion of Ghat by the Governor of Fezzan. The Sultan expressed his ignorance of the development and ordered the Pasha to stop it.[1] Incidentally, the concern which the British agents in Tripoli, as well as the Foreign Office, showed in this matter reveals how keen at the time was British interest in the Sahara. By such prompt measures and by correspondence with the Tibu, the Tuareg, and Bornu, the Vice-Consuls contributed immensely to the revival and strengthening of the fame of Britain in the Sahara, to the disadvantage of Turkey and France.

The commercial activities of the Vice-Consuls were, however, not very successful. It is true that Gagliuffi established some legitimate trade in Fezzan and Bornu. In fact he claimed that two-thirds of the capital of the Arab merchants was employed in legitimate commerce by the early fifties.[2] But since there was no decrease but rather an increase in the volume of the slave traffic in the fifties,[3] the success achieved in the establishment of legitimate trade was obviously not as great as Gagliuffi would have us believe. The Vice-Consuls themselves also attempted to trade. They had agents in Tuat, Ghat, Kukawa, Kano, Zinder, Sokoto, and Gummel, to whom they consigned goods mainly of British manufacture with the strict advice that they should be bartered only for ivory, gum, wax, senna, and gold dust.[4] When Barth was in Timbuctu, a merchant arrived there from Tuat with bales of calico belonging to the Vice-Consul at Ghadames. He noted that as a result of Dickson's commercial transactions the market of

[1] F.O. 101/30, Crowe to Malmesbury, 29 Mar. 1852, and encls.; Gagliuffi to Crowe, 6 Mar. 1852; Dickson to Crowe, 16 Jan. 1852; Crowe to Izzet Ahmed Pasha, 10 Mar. 1852; F.O. 101/33, F.O. to Herman, 18 Aug. 1853.

[2] F.O. 101/45, Gagliuffi to Clarendon, 13 Oct. 1855.

[3] 1,200 slaves were exported from Tripoli in 1846 and 2,000 in 1847, 3,194 in 1855, and 2,087 in 1856.

[4] F.O. 101/15, Gagliuffi to Crowe, 24 Nov. 1846, encl. in Crowe to Palmerston, 24 Dec. 1846; F.O. 101/20, Crowe to Bidwell, 20 Nov. 1848; F.O. 101/36, Gagliuffi to Clarendon, 13 Oct. 1855; F.O. 101/45, Herman to Clarendon, 19 Apr. 1856.

Timbuctu had been glutted with calicoes, to the detriment of the Moroccan and other traders, and ascribed the traders' opposition to his presence in Timbuctu partly to this dumping.[1] But the Vice-Consuls did not grow rich from these ventures. The fact that Gagliuffi repeatedly appealed to the British Government for financial help indicates that he could not maintain himself on his own trading speculations alone. Indeed, without the annual salary neither he nor any of his successors could have stayed at Murzuk. By 1846 Gagliuffi had even piled up huge debts—one, amounting to about £900, to a Turkish subject on whose behalf the Porte had to apply to the British Government.[2] Dickson's business was no more lucrative. He gave up his post after four years and volunteered for the Crimean war. And at the end of hostilities he refused to return to Ghadames.[3]

The failure of these attempts to develop legitimate commerce in and across the Sahara was due partly to lack of capital and partly to conditions in the area. Warrington appreciated the need for capital and tried to provide it. In October 1842 he drew up the prospectus for a company to be named 'The African Society'.[4] It was to consist of a maximum of thirty and a minimum of fifteen shares of 1,000 dollars (£200) each. It was to be under a full-time director with the Vice-Consul at Murzuk as one of its principal agents. Its field of operation was to include the interior of Africa and the sea-ports of the Regency of Tripoli, 'as well as such markets abroad as the said Directors should deem fit to make advantageous speculation with'. Though the Pasha of Tripoli bought five shares, Warrington failed to sell the rest either in Tripoli or in England. Nothing therefore came of the project, and Gagliuffi had to rely on his own capital, which was by no means adequate. Only three months after his arrival, he complained of this and appealed to both the Government and the Anti-Slavery Society to provide him with more capital. He pointed out that many of the people who traded to the interior were convinced of the inhumanity of the traffic in slaves and would readily give it up if they were given some merchandise on credit to be exchanged for produce. He gave every assurance that money thus invested would never be lost. He wrote to Warrington:

---

[1] Bath, op. cit., vol. v, p. 5.
[2] F.O. 101/15, Crowe to Palmerston, 24 Dec. 1846.
[3] F.O. 101/35, Dickson to Clarendon, 25 Apr. 1854.
[4] F.O. 101/7, Warrington to Aberdeen, 1 Oct. 1842, and encls.

If you think that by advice and writing you will attain this object, you are deceived, facts and money are required; this has great power and using it with policy and caution a good result may be hoped for.[1]

This appeal fell on deaf ears. Neither the Government nor the Anti-Slavery Society raised a penny to meet the request, the former because the idea was inconsistent with its policy of *laissez-faire*, and the latter for the simple reason that it had not the means. Like Warrington, Dickson realized the need for the backing of a Company and drew up plans for one whose capital was to be £20,000. Richardson was shown a copy of the prospectus of this company on his second visit to Murzuk and forwarded it to Palmerston with the suggestion that it might be brought to the notice of the Board of Trade and the Council of Merchants of Liverpool and Manchester. 'The field is now open,' he pleaded, 'and any English Company disposed to embark on legitimate commerce in this portion of Africa may do so tomorrow and without any great risk.'[2] But in spite of Richardson's plea, and a trip to London by Dickson himself, this project suffered the same fate as Warrington's eight years earlier. Without adequate capital the Vice-Consuls failed to embark on any large-scale commercial operations.

But even if they had had the necessary financial backing, it is still doubtful whether they could have made much better headway in the conditions prevailing in the Sahara. In the first place, while their diplomatic activities improved conditions along the routes from Tripoli to Fezzan, Ghadames, and Ghat, they did not affect those on the Fezzan–Bornu and Tuat–Timbuctu routes. Though Mohammed, the son of Abd al-Jalīl, and his followers regarded Gagliuffi and Warrington as friends and communicated for some time with them, yet the consular agents failed to persuade them to give up their predatory practices. Consequently the caravan route to Bornu was more insecure than ever from the early forties onward.

Furthermore, because of the number of days spent by a caravan from the Sudan to the coast, the innumerable dangers involved in the crossing, and above all the fact that the caravan traffic in the nineteenth century was predominantly in slaves, it was extremely improbable that any lucrative British trade could have been developed

[1] F.O. 84/486, Gagliuffi to Warrington, 13 May 1843, encl. in Warrington to Aberdeen, 2 June 1843; F.O. 84/486, Gagliuffi to Warrington, 20 May 1843, encl. in Warrington to Aberdeen, 9 June 1843.

[2] F.O. 101/26, Richardson to Palmerston, 25 May 1850; F.O. 101/20, Dickson to Crowe, 25 Aug. 1848, encl. in Crowe to Palmerston, 1 Sept. 1848.

in and across the Sahara. But it was not until the late fifties that this was realized both in Tripoli and in London, with consequences to be described later.[1]

The Anti-Slavery Society as well as the British Government and their agents advocated legitimate commerce as a remedy for the slave trade. But to begin with the Society wanted to obtain first-hand information about the traffic in the region and the best way to apply the remedy, and it was for this purpose that they employed James Richardson. After the failure of his efforts in Morocco[2] he had paid a brief visit to England and returned to Tunis at the beginning of 1845 to continue his mission.[3] By 1845 the Bey had almost brought his revolutionary and laudable measures against the hideous traffic to their completion. Richardson's aim here was to collect information which would enable him to give publicity to the Bey's action. 'Sufficient attention,' he said, 'has not been given to these extraordinary measures of the Bey, his noble courageous conduct has not excited that admiration in the breast of British philanthropists and abolitionists which it ought to have done.'[4] Moreover, he argued, since the attack on the slave traffic would affect the Bey's popularity as well as his pocket, a new orientation in British policy towards him was called for. Accordingly, at the end of his visit he wrote a book entitled *The Regency of Tunis* which he forwarded to Palmerston for publication.[5] In this work he traced the history of Tunis from the tenth century, gave an account of her population and commerce, and discussed her foreign relations. The greater part of the book was, of course, devoted to the slave traffic and the recent measures introduced for its abolition. Richardson advocated the policy of preserving the *status quo* in the Regency, protecting the ruling dynasty against the designs of the Porte and the aggression of France, aiding the Bey to develop the natural resources of the country, and persuading him to adopt a more liberal system of commerce. With a characteristic lack of originality, Richardson did no more than restate what had been the British Government's policy towards the Regency since the thirties.

Richardson left Tunis early in May 1845 and arrived at Tripoli two weeks later. In concert with his old friend, Warrington, he began

---

[1] See below, pp. 221–2.   [2] See above, pp. 142–3.
[3] This was Richardson's second visit to Tunis, the first being in 1842.
[4] F.O. 102/29, Richardson to Palmerston, 29 Mar. 1847.
[5] F.O. 102/29, Richardson to Palmerston, 29 Mar. 1847 and encl., *The Regency of Tunis*. This work still remains unpublished.

preparations for his journey into the interior. Warrington obtained a passport for him from the Pasha. To enable him to promote the health of the people in the Sahara as 'an act of humanity as well as sound policy', Warrington also supplied his friend with a box of medicines for free distribution.[1] This first Richardson mission to the interior was to be one of reconnaissance. He wrote to Warrington:

I will here take the liberty of stating to you that my objects in going to Ghadames are mainly two. First to obtain statistical knowledge of the commerce of Ghadames and the interior of Africa. . . . Second—to obtain statistics as to the traffic in slaves, and to ascertain how the negroes are procured whether in war or kidnapped, or otherwise unlawfully and in-humanly furnished to the slave dealers, as well as to obtain information on the moral and social condition of the inhabitants of Soudan and how it may be successfully ameliorated and a better and lawful system of com-merce introduced.[2]

Richardson left Tripoli on 2 August 1845. *En route* he was sur-prised, though delighted, to find that news of himself had percolated into the desert and that he was hailed at every turn as 'Consul of Ghadames'.[3] It was more or less in that capacity that he was accorded a rousing welcome by the Governor and people of the town. During his two months' stay in that town, he conducted searching investiga-tions into the commerce of Ghadames with special reference to the slave traffic, natural resources, and the occupations of the inhabi-tants. He was particularly impressed by the strategic position of the city and the routes which radiated from it to Bornu, Air, and Timbuctu. He took a keen interest in the inhabitants of the town. He found ophthalmia and diarrhoea especially rampant and spent the greater part of his time administering medicine to all comers, from the Turkish Governor down to the poorest person.[4] He expressed his conviction, however, that the people were victims more of the extortions of the Turkish officials than of disease. So heavy, he con-tended, were the taxes levied on the people that, if nothing was

[1] F.O. 84/598, Warrington to Aberdeen, 2 Aug. 1845; Richardson, *Travels*, vol. i, pp. 18–24.

[2] F.O. 84/598, Richardson to Warrington, 30 July 1845, encl. in Warrington to Aberdeen, 3 Aug. 1845.

[3] Richardson, *Travels*, vol. i, pp. 23, 30. When Warrington suggested that a second vice-consular post should be established at Ghadames, he strongly recommended Richardson for the post. As may be recalled, the suggestion was firmly turned down by the British Government. See above, pp. 162, 167.

[4] Ibid., vol. i, pp. 110–11, 115, 123, 126; F.O. 101/16, Richardson to Warring-ton, 27 Aug. 1845.

done about it, Ghadames would be reduced in a few years to a mere 'watering place for miserable and straggling caravans'. During his stay, therefore, he posed as a champion of the people and wrote dispatches to Warrington and the Foreign Office appealing for the intervention of the British Government. He informed Warrington that it was 'just possible that the hand of foreign diplomacy may be stretched out to save from ruin a city which has flourished for 1,000 years'.[1] It was this meddling with the internal affairs of the town which led to his rejection by Crowe as a suitable person for the vice-consular post at Ghadames. Indeed, Richardson's interference was also reported to the Porte, which instantly requested his recall.[2] But Richardson was not at Ghadames when the order to that effect arrived.

With respect to the slave traffic, Richardson became convinced from his inquiries that, for a true and complete account, he must plunge deeper into the interior. 'One thing is certain,' he wrote, 'unless I go to the first-hand traffickers in human flesh—to the heart of Africa itself, I can never get the information which I require.'[3] So, before the Government's decision about the second vice-consular post at Ghadames was known, Richardson had outlined to the Foreign Office a plan for a mission to the Sudan. He was to go through Ghat to Kano and return to England either by going down the Niger or by proceeding upstream and westward to Timbuctu.[4] As this would imply a considerable extension of his original assignment, he asked for financial support. He was, however, so impatient that without waiting for news about the vice-consular post or his new project he left Ghadames in November for Ghat, where he arrived fifty days later.

At Ghat, as at Ghadames, Richardson's inquiries ranged from the origins, history, occupations, and system of government of the people to their trade in goods and men. He found that Ghat was of even greater strategic importance for the crusade against the slave trade than Ghadames. One of his primary concerns here, however, was to win the friendship and confidence of the Azger Tuareg of Ghat, whom he correctly described as holding 'the keys to the Great desert',

[1] F.O. 84/598, Richardson to Warrington, 25 Sept. 1845; F.O. 101/16, Richardson to Warrington, 24 Oct. 1845.
[2] F.O. 101/18, Crowe to Bidwell, 31 March 1847; F.O. 101/19, Richardson to Bidwell, 1 Feb. 1847.
[3] Richardson, *Travels*, vol. i, p. 153.
[4] F.O. 101/16, Richardson to Aberdeen, 13 Sept. 1845.

and without whose consent there could be no intercourse between north and central Africa.[1] Richardson invited the sheikhs and other important persons to tea and discussed the question of abolition. He also distributed free medicines to the sick. In this work he was greatly assisted by Hatecta, on whom he called immediately he arrived at Ghat and who, he found, was still known as 'the friend or consul of the English'.[2] He obtained from Hateeta and other Tuareg chiefs a guarantee for the security of any British subject who might visit their country. In fact one of them, Shafou, whom Richardson wrongly described as the 'Sultan of the Tuareg of Ghat', sent a letter accompanied by presents to the Queen. In his letter,[3] he declared the Ghat people's friendship with Britain. And in answer to Richardson's request for the abolition of the slave trade (which he described as their sole profession), he asked Her Majesty to show them in what manner they could do away with it. 'If we find you are right,' he wrote, 'we shall follow your advice, but if you are wrong, your order shall not be executed.' The presents which he sent consisted of a knife, a spear, a shield made of bullock skin, and a leather cushion. From this letter as well as from the attitude of the other sheikhs of Ghat it would seem that Richardson did succeed in intensifying the regard which the people of Ghat had for the British.

Though he had originally thought of Ghat as only his first stop on the journey to Kano, Richardson was compelled by circumstances entirely beyond his control to return to Tripoli.[4] The physical exertion of riding tediously through the desert was beginning to tell on his health. To make matters worse, his stock of medicines was already exhausted. And he had no instruments, which, he correctly pointed out, 'were of the greatest consequence in making a more extended tour intelligible'. For these reasons Richardson left Ghat in February 1846 on his return trip to Fezzan. After six weeks' stay at Murzuk as the guest of Gagliuffi, and having abandoned the idea of going to Bornu because of the raids of the Awlad Sulayman, he returned to Tripoli in May and to England in August 1846.

[1] F.O. 101/16, Account of Ghat, Richardson to Warrington, 1 May 1846.
[2] Richardson, *Travels*, vol. ii, pp. 10–11, 83, 86, 93–94.
[3] F.O. 101/16, Sultan of the Tuareg to Her Majesty the Queen, encl. in Richardson to Palmerston, 12 Aug. 1846.
[4] F.O. 101/16, Richardson to Aberdeen, 28 Feb. 1846; Richardson, *Travels*, vol. ii, pp. 109–10.

In conformity with his instructions, he submitted a detailed report on the slave traffic—its volume, how the slaves were obtained, how they were treated on their march to the coast, and how the traffic was to be abolished—to the Society and the British Government.[1] As his account of the traffic and those given by other travellers and consular agents have been dealt with already,[2] we shall confine ourselves here to the remedies which he suggested. He was realistic enough to see that abolition could not be accomplished overnight but only by stages. He therefore recommended two sets of measures for mitigating the evil and finally exterminating both the trade and slavery.[3] To accomplish the first, he suggested that Tripolitanian and Ottoman subjects should be allowed to buy and sell slaves only in the Regency of Tripoli, that a Government official should accompany slave caravans to see that slaves were humanely treated, and finally that for every slave who died *en route*, the owner was to be fined a sum equal to the duty paid on a slave to the Government. For the final extermination of the traffic and of slavery itself he suggested even bolder though unoriginal measures. The slave markets of Tripoli and Constantinople were to be closed down—a measure which he enthusiastically described as 'cutting off the branches and hewing down the trunk of the accursed tree of slaves'. Legitimate commerce was to be promoted and Christianity was to be propagated in the Sahara and Central Africa. 'Let any people imbibe the spirit of Christianity,' he asserted, 'and slavery cannot exist among them.' Some of these proposals which needed the co-operation of the local authorities were clearly impracticable, some were simply ridiculous (for example, the establishment of Christianity), while others (such as developing legitimate trade in the Sahara) were unrealistic at the time. But in spite of all this, he made every effort to see that his proposals were implemented. As soon as he returned to London he addressed a number of appeals to the missionary societies. He drew up, for instance, a 'project for the establishment of a Christian mission in Bornu' and distributed copies of it among the societies. In it he wrote with characteristic fanaticism:

---

[1] F.O. 97/430, Richardson to the Committee of the Anti-Slavery Society, 12 June 1846; F.O. 101/16, 'The Slave Traffic in Ghat and the Great Desert', encl. in Richardson to Warrington, 11 May 1846; The report was also published in three instalments in the *Anti-Slavery Reporter* of 1 Sept., 1 Oct., and 2 Nov. 1846.

[2] See above, pp. 128–9, 151.

[3] F.O. 84/648, Richardson to Warrington, 22 Apr. 1846, encl. in Warrington to Aberdeen, 23 Apr. 1846; Richardson, *Travels*, vol. ii, pp. 446–7.

The Christian Churches have left Central Africa now these twelve centuries in the hand of Mohammedans who in the countries have successfully propagated these false doctrines of the impostor of Mecca. If the Christian Churches wish to vindicate the honour of their religion, to diffuse its beneficent and heavenly doctrines and to remove from themselves the severe censure of having abandoned the Central African to the fake Prophet, I believe there is now an opening via Bornu to attempt the establishment of that faith in the heart of Africa.

The missionaries of the day were, of course, more realistic than Richardson and so concentrated their efforts on the more accessible regions on the west coast. For the abolition of the slave markets, the conclusion of treaties of trade with the chiefs of the interior, and the establishment of more consular posts, it was the Government that Richardson had to approach, and he sought and obtained an interview with Palmerston. It was as a result of this meeting that, as has been shown earlier, an appeal was made to the Porte and the vice-consular post at Ghadames was provisionally confirmed. More important still, a mission was organized and dispatched to the western Sudan.

It has been usual to regard the failure of the 1841 expedition as marking the end of the attempt by the British Government to develop legitimate commerce in the interior of Africa until the mission led by Richardson and Barth in the Sahara in 1850, and that of Baikie up the Niger in 1854.[1] Plumb has stated that after the failure of the 1841 expedition, 'it was natural that there should be a return to the desert routes and to the small expedition'. But according to him—and more recently to Flint—this return did not occur until the Richardson–Barth expedition of 1850.[2] However, from the approval of the establishment of the vice-consular posts at Murzuk in 1840 and Ghadames in 1847, from the missions of Richardson in 1845–6, and finally from the diplomatic negotiations that were going on simultaneously in Barbary and Turkey, it is evident that the return to the desert routes took place a decade earlier, not after the failure, but concurrently with the launching of the 1841 expedition. Buxton and the humanitarians did not confine their interest exclusively to the west coast but extended it to the whole continent of Africa. They drew attention not only to the 'Christian' or trans-

[1] Bovill, *Golden Trade*, pp. 216–17, 219; Burns, op. cit., p. 92; Mockler-Ferryman, *British Nigeria* (1902), p. 35.
[2] J. H. Plumb, *West African Exploration* (1951), p. 21; Flint, op. cit., p. 18.

atlantic but also to the 'Muhammadan' or trans-Saharan slave trade. And about the very time that the British Government agreed to implement Buxton's plans, they also approved the establishment of the first vice-consulate in the Sahara. The fact that no remuneration was originally attached to the post, but that first a subsidy and then later a fixed salary was granted, and that a second post was also set up, show that the failure of the 1841 expedition and the beginning of French expansion into the interior enhanced the importance of the northern approach to the interior.

Though it is true that the Vice-Consuls failed to establish any substantial trade—and no realist should have expected any other result—they did a great deal to popularize the British name and strengthen British influence in the Sahara and the Sudan. The rousing welcome given to Richardson and Dickson on their arrival at Ghadames and Ghat leaves no room for doubt about this. That the popularity and influence of the British in the region in the forties was known even to the French Government is evident from an application made by Guizot, the Prime Minister, to the British Consul-General in Tripoli in May 1847 on behalf of A. Raffenel, the French explorer. Guizot informed Crowe of Raffenel's project of crossing the African continent from the Senegal to the Nile. He referred to Crowe as 'l'agent European qui jouit du plus grand credit au Bornou', and asked him to allow Raffenel to draw a bill on him to the amount of 4,000 francs if he should need money during his journey. Crowe, of course, proudly and graciously granted his permission and promptly instructed Gagliuffi to recommend Raffenel 'to the protection and good offices of the chiefs' with whom he was in communication in Bornu and other districts of the interior.[1] The decade 1840 to 1850 was, quite clearly, the period of the most intensive British activity in the Sahara, an activity which the second Richardson expedition, otherwise known as the Central African Mission, was to bring to its culmination.

[1] F.O. 101/17, Crowe to Palmerston, 19 Aug. 1847, and encl., Guizot to Crowe, 19 May 1847. A. Raffenel set off from the Senegal but got only as far as Kaarta.

CHAPTER VIII

The Central African Mission, 1849-57

THE Central African Mission of Richardson and Barth was not, as we have seen, a bolt from the blue. It was the logical sequel to British activities in the Sahara in the forties and one of the belated results of Richardson's first mission in 1845-6. At the interview which Richardson had with Palmerston soon after his return to England from his 'philanthropic tour', he dwelt on the indispensability of a second mission to the interior. Palmerston showed positive interest in this and asked Richardson to draw up a plan for the mission. He readily submitted this in February 1847.[1] Though nothing was heard from the Foreign Office during the following eighteen months, Richardson never abandoned the project. In September 1848 he addressed another letter to Palmerston and asked for another interview. He lamented, in a characteristic tone, the neglect of the Sahara 'by the explorers and geographers of Christendom, the energies of mankind being directed either to other spheres and geographical discovery or absorbed in political changes and conventions'.[2] Richardson's perseverance eventually reaped its reward, for nine days later Palmerston asked him to state in writing the expense of the proposed tour, how long it would take, and the country through which he hoped to travel. It was in reply to this long-awaited request that Richardson submitted a lengthy memorandum entitled 'Projected journey of discovery and philanthropy through the great desert of Sahara to central Africa'.[3]

As one would expect, the project embodied his long-cherished views. The mission was to penetrate into central Africa via the Sahara instead of up the Niger. His main reason for choosing this route was that the Sahara was healthy and free 'from pestiferous maladies', while all expeditions from the western coast of Africa had failed to produce any permanent benefit, 'principally from the in-

[1] F.O. 101/19, Richardson to Bidwell, 3 Feb. 1847. This and many of the subsequent letters from Richardson to the Foreign Office bore the address and the stamp of the Anti-Slavery Society.

[2] F.O. 101/23, Richardson to Palmerston, 21 Sept. 1848.

[3] F.O. 101/23, Palmerston to Richardson, 30 Sept. 1848; F.O. 101/23, Richardson to Palmerston, 5 Oct. 1848, and encls.

salubrity of the climate'. This was undoubtedly a very telling argument for contemporaries whose memories of the 1841 expedition were still green. The object of the mission was to be 'the opening up of a regular and secure way of communication over the Sahara from the Mediterranean to the banks of the Niger'. To accomplish this, the tracks of the desert were to be delineated, and protection and security for European travellers and merchants obtained from the rulers. Richardson then went on to discuss the advantages that might be expected from establishing such direct relations between the peoples of Europe and Central Africa. The first would be the extinction of the slave trade and slavery through persuading the Africans to cultivate export products 'in order that they might have legitimate articles of trade and barter to exchange for our European goods and manufactures'. Secondly, information could be collected about the peoples of Africa which would promote 'the sciences of geography, language, ethnology, and general knowledge'. The final advantage, couched in typically humanitarian terms, was that the mission could 'by perseverance and pacific policy materially benefit and morally enlighten the African tribes and peoples, raising up degraded Africans to the standard of civilised Europe—and so expect in humility the favour and blessings of Almighty God upon us as a nation and the world at large'. These advantages were almost exclusively philanthropic and they do testify to the strength of the anti-slavery feeling, the crusading ardour, and the disinterested motives that inspired Richardson.

In spite of the lofty objects to be achieved, the mission was very moderately conceived as to personnel, cost, and duration. It was to be undertaken by a 'single individual' who was to 'feel the way'; it was to cost not 'more than £500', and to last 'either one or two years, this being regulated by the great heat of the desert'. In fact the mission left England with a personnel of three, it cost over £10,000, and lasted eight years.

Before the final instructions were issued, a new development had changed the nature and scope of the mission. This was the addition to its staff of two German scholars, Doctors Barth and Overweg. This was done, it is important to note, on the initiative neither of the British nor of the Prussian Government, but of Richardson himself, who confessed to his lack of 'a satisfactory education more especially the ability of making astronomical observations'.[1] If the caravan

[1] F.O. 101/23, Richardson to Bidwell, 11 Oct. 1849.

routes, wells, and oases were to be correctly mapped, accurate read-ings of latitude, longitude, etc., were absolutely indispensable. Richardson therefore wrote to Carl Ritter, the celebrated Professor of Geography at Berlin University, to ask whether he could find a 'well qualified scientific and literary man' who would be willing to accompany him.[1] In his lengthy reply,[2] the Professor heartily wel-comed the projected mission and suggested that it should not confine itself to the west of the Chad and the Sudan but should explore especially the quite unknown area eastward between the Chad and Abyssinia. With characteristic Teutonic love of detail, Ritter em-phasized that the explorers should take heights of mountains, ob-serve geological phenomena, and inquire into 'the languages and systems of writing used in those parts of inner Africa'. We find here the source of the highly scientific and academic bias which was to be given to this mission and was to make it one of the most important in the annals of exploration.

As a person with the requisite qualification, Ritter suggested Dr. Heinrich Barth. 'He is a young man about 33 years of age,' the professor wrote, 'a classical scholar, understanding modern languages and speaking besides French, Spanish, Italian, also English and Arabic.' While the Professor was certainly wrong about Barth's age, for he was born in Hamburg in February 1821 and was therefore only 28, his estimate of his merits cannot be challenged. Indeed Barth was not only a distinguished scholar and linguist but also an experienced African traveller. From 1845 to 1847 he had made a tour of North Africa overland from Tangier to Egypt and then by boat up the Nile as far as Wadi Halfa, visiting sites of ancient cities *en route*. He had just published the first volume of his journal entitled *Wanderings through the Punic and Cyrenine Shores of the Mediterranean* and had settled down as a lecturer on 'comparative geography and the colonial commerce of antiquity' at the University of Berlin. As Barth himself tells us in the preface to the journal of his mission to Central Africa,[3] while travelling along the Barbary coast he often 'cast a wistful look towards those unknown or little-known regions in the interior . . . and the desire to know something more of them acted on me like a charm.' He recounts how he met a Hausa slave in Tunis

[1] F.O. 101/23, Richardson to Bidwell, Paris, 22 Aug. 1849.
[2] F.O. 101/23, Ritter to Bunsen, 5 Oct. 1849, encl. in Bunsen to Palmerston, 12 Oct. 1849.
[3] Barth, *Travels*, vol. i, Preface, pp. vii–ix.

whose words, 'Please God, you shall go and visit Kano', kept constantly ringing in his ears on his return to Europe. It is not surprising, therefore that he 'volunteered cheerfully' on condition that he was paid a yearly indemnity of only £200 and was promised a professorship at the University,[1] and that the mission was allowed to return by a route east of Bornu.

Ritter's letter was forwarded to Lord Palmerston through Chevalier Bunsen, the Prussian ambassador in London and himself a distinguished linguist and Egyptologist. Bunsen showed keen interest in the mission and expressed his readiness to persuade the Prussian Government to join the British Government in sponsoring it.[2] Richardson also wrote to Palmerston recommending Barth and later Overweg, another pupil of Ritter and an eminent geologist and astronomer, whose addition to the mission was suggested by Barth himself. The services and terms of both Germans were accepted by the Foreign Office. But in return for a salary of £200 per annum, Barth was to submit a scientific report to the British Government at the end of the journey.[3]

It must be pointed out that Barth's main interest was not the Sahara and the Sudan but the exploration of the area to the east of the Chad and the elucidation of the long-discussed question of the connexion between the Nile and the Niger, the nature of the rising ground from the depression of the Chad to the table land of South Africa, and the course of the Upper Nile.[4] These differences in the objectives of Barth and Richardson generated a bitter quarrel between them. Richardson was certainly interested in the exploration of the area eastward, but to him this was of secondary importance. The mission was to him essentially philanthropic and diplomatic, and so necessitated interviews with the rulers *en route*. Barth, on the other hand, would not tolerate any interviews because they would obviously retard the speed of the mission, increase its cost, and prevent it from arriving at Ghat in time to join the last caravan bound for the Sudan. To stop negotiating treaties would have been tantamount to abandoning the main purpose of the mission, and naturally Richardson would not yield on that point. 'On no account,' he asserted emphatically, 'could I deviate from the necessities of this

[1] This was insisted upon by his father.

[2] F.O. 101/23, Bunsen to Eddisbury, 16 Nov. 1849.

[3] F.O. 101/23, Richardson to Palmerston, 12 Oct. 1849; Richardson to Palmerston, 17 Nov. 1849; F.O. 101/23, Palmerston to Bunsen, 23 Oct. 1849.

[4] F.O. 101/23, Barth to Palmerston, 20 Nov. 1849.

course of my mission for any merely scientific object, however important it might be for science, and . . . it will be necessary that he
[Barth] and Overweg absolutely submit to this.'[1] The Foreign Office
eventually worked out a compromise which was embodied in a
memorandum signed by the three travellers.[2] The route and the rate
of progress of the mission as far as Chad were to be decided by
Richardson in consultation with the two Germans. After the exploration of Chad, Richardson was to return via Tripoli while the Germans
could explore the area east of Chad at the expense of the British
Government. Before they separated, Richardson was to hand over
to the Germans all the scientific instruments except one thermometer,
one telescope, and one compass. Though this arrangement conceded
the basic object of each traveller, yet it was more in favour of
Richardson, as it did not quite adequately meet the Germans' fear of
delay. It is not surprising therefore that differences continued to exist
between them and Richardson, as Barth himself admitted. 'My way
of looking at things,' he noted as he stood by Richardson's grave in
March 1851, 'was not quite the same as that of my late companion,
and we had therefore often had little differences.'[3] Fortunately, however, the differences did not prevent the successful outcome of the
mission.

On the very day that the memorandum was signed, Richardson was
given his instructions. The purpose of the mission was stated in
unmistakable terms:

The countries which you are about to visit are as yet so little known to the
nations of Europe that every information of every kind respecting them
which you may be able to collect will be interesting and useful. But besides
those political and scientific subjects of investigation to which your attention will of course be directed, it is the wish of Her Majesty's Government
that you should specially endeavour to ascertain by what means the commercial intercourse between Great Britain and Africa might be extended
and developed; where are the districts and what the lines of communication in that country which offer the greatest facilities for commerce; what
are the European commodities which are most sought after by the natives;
and what are the main articles of African produce which could best be
obtained in payment for the production of Europe. You will not fail to
take advantage of every suitable opportunity to impress upon the minds
of the African chiefs with whom you may come into contact the great

[1] F.O. 101/23, Richardson to Bidwell, 22 Nov. 1849.
[2] F.O. 101/23, Memorandum, encl. in Bidwell to Bunsen, 30 Nov. 1849.
[3] Barth, op. cit., vol. ii, pp. 219-20.

advantage which they and their country would derive from the extension of legitimate commerce with the nations of other parts of the world.[1]

The political objects alluded to in these instructions were not clearly defined. But the fact that the whole expedition was financed from the Secret Service Fund instead of from the Civil Contingencies Fund, as had been the usual practice, and the reaction of the Foreign Office to Barth's diplomatic work, which will be discussed later,[2] make it not unreasonable to infer that they included the thwarting of French ambitions in the Sahara and the western Sudan.

The instructions were accompanied by a draft treaty which was a copy of the one given to the Commissioners of the 1841 expedition. The first three clauses, as one would expect, provided for the abolition of slavery, the slave trade, and human sacrifices; the fifth that Christians were to be allowed to exercise and propagate their religion freely and no person who embraced Christianity was to be molested or troubled in any manner whatsoever. The remaining clauses aimed mainly at ensuring security and freedom of movement for British traders. Richardson was also given a letter addressed to Sultan Shafou. In it the Sultan was asked to protect the travellers and was informed that if his fellow-rulers and their people wished to obtain European commodities for their use and enjoyment, the best way to do so was to increase by agriculture the products of the soil, to collect with care all those natural productions of their country valued in Europe, and to leave off the practice of buying and selling slaves 'which is incompatible with prosperous commerce'.

On the day that the instructions were issued, Richardson left England to join his two German associates in Tunis, and on 31 January 1850 the party arrived at Tripoli. After a delay there of nearly two months, Richardson, the Germans, and a caravan of thirty-six Arab merchants, sixteen freed slaves who were returning home, and thirty-one camels left in the last week of March. One of these camels was carrying a rather odd article, a boat specially built at the dockyard at Malta. It was to be used for the exploration and navigation of the Chad and other waters of central Africa, and was subsequently to be given to the Sultan of Bornu as a present from the

[1] F.O. 101/23, Instruction for Richardson, Palmerston to Richardson, 30 Nov. 1849, and encls., the Draft Treaty and Palmerston to Shafou, 30 Nov. 1849.

[2] F.O. 101/36, Clarendon to Hammond, 11 June 1854, and minute by Hammond; below, pp. 225-7.

Queen of England.[1] The party reached Murzuk on 6 May, and, escorted by Hateeta, the old 'friend of the English', and two sons of Sheikh Shafou, entered Ghat on 18 July. In both towns the reception given to them was, to the surprise of the Germans, exceedingly warm and friendly. In Murzuk the Ottoman flag was hoisted on the day of their arrival and an escort of twenty cavalry was harnessed to meet and welcome them to the capital; in Ghat many people came out to see them, 'some offering us their welcome', and the sheikhs received them 'with great kindness and politeness'.[2] The welcome accorded these travellers bears testimony to the success of the diplomatic work of Gagliuffi and the popularity of the British in these places. As Barth reported, the Governor of Ghat was 'really pleased to receive under his roof a mission of Her Britannic Majesty's Government, with whose immense influence and power: and the noble purpose of whose policy, he was not entirely unacquainted'.[3]

On 26 July the travellers left Ghat on their march into regions of the Sahara which no European had ever surveyed. Pushing across the rocky plateau of the country of the Azger and Hoggar Tuareg, they entered the district of Air (or Aheer or Asben), the home of the Kel Owi Tuareg.[4] After being robbed and blackmailed, they arrived at Tintellust on 4 September 1850, and pitched their camp on a hill on the outskirts of the town. They remained there for three months, for Al-Nur, the sheikh of the town, who was exceedingly friendly to the travellers and undertook to escort them, refused to leave before the departure of the annual Bilma salt caravan for Hausaland. Barth noted that the hill on which they camped 'will ever be memorable in the annals of the Asbenawa as the "English Hill" or the "Hill of the Christians".' History has proved this forecast true, for when F. R. Rodd, now Lord Rennell, visited Tintellust in 1922, he was shown the hill and the site of the camp, which was still remembered by the natives and was known as 'House of the Christians'.[5]

Led by Al-Nur, the travellers resumed their march on 12 December 1850.[6] The whole group went as far as the district of Damerghou, 'the

---

[1] Richardson, vol. i, pp. 4, 6; Barth, op. cit., vol. i, pp. x, 85-86; F.O. 101/26, Richardson to Palmerston, 28 Mar. 1853; F.O. 101/30, Overweg to Palmerston, 24 June 1851.

[2] F.O. 101/26, Richardson to Palmerston, 8 May 1850, Barth, op. cit., vol. i, pp. 162-3; Richardson, *Mission*, vol. i, pp. 160-1.

[3] Barth, op. cit., vol. i, p. 222.   [4] Barth, op. cit., vol. i, pp. 304-5.

[5] Barth, op. cit., vol. i, p. 334; Rodd, op. cit., pp. 311-13.

[6] Barth, op. cit., vol. i, p. 500; Richardson, *Mission*, vol. i, pp. 124-5, vol. ii, p. 97.

granary of Air' and the borderland between the Sahara and the fertile regions of the western Sudan. By this time their supplies had run very low. And since they would have had to pay heavy dues and tolls on the way if they had continued to travel in a large caravan, they decided to separate.[1] It was agreed that Barth was to go to Kano to sell his merchandise and make inquiries about the interior. Overweg was to proceed to Maradi and Gobir, and Richardson was to push on to Zinder (see Map. 4, facing p. 181); and all three were to rendezvous at Kukawa during the first week of April.

They took leave of each other on 10 January 1851. Richardson and Al-Nur went on to Zinder, the capital town of the westernmost province of the Empire of Bornu. The very enthusiastic reception given to him by the Governor and the sight of ten camels which had been sent there by Al-Hajj Bashīr, the Vizir of Bornu and friend of Gagliuffi, to convey the travellers and their baggage to Kukawa filled Richardson with hope. He reported confidently to Palmerston that he was 'safe, under the protection of Bornouese authorities and as secure perhaps as if domiciled in Tripoli'.[2] It was therefore in buoyant spirits that he left Zinder on 8 February 1851. But if the traveller had no thieves and robbers to contend with, he was now confronted with even more formidable adversaries, the heat and fever of the tropics. Barth tells us that at the time of their parting Richardson showed 'evident symptoms of being affected by the change from the fresh air of the mountainous district of Air to the sultry climate of the fertile lands of Negroland'.[3] He felt the heat so intensely that he was compelled always to carry an umbrella. It was obvious that he could not hold out much longer, and he fel a victim to fatigue and fever at Ungurutuwa, a place only six days' march from Kukawa, on Tuesday 4 March 1851.

Richardson is one of those men whom posterity has rather unjustly forgotten. His name is hardly ever mentioned among the famous abolitionists. In the history of the exploration of Africa he is never heard of except in the oft-repeated casual mention that he and Barth were sent out in 1850 and that he died in March 1851. But it is clear from this and the previous chapters that he was a man who devoted

---

[1] F.O. 101/30, Richardson to Palmerston, 18 Jan. 1851; Barth, op. cit., vol. i, p. 551, vol. ii, pp. 1–4; F.O. 101/30, Richardson to Palmerston, 16 Sept. 1850; Richardson, op. cit., vol. i, p. 245.

[2] F.O. 101/30, Richardson to Palmerston, 18 Jan. 1851; Richardson, *Mission*, vol. ii, p. 185.

[3] Barth, op. cit., vol. ii, pp. 3–4.

the last twelve of his life's short span of forty-five years (1806–51) to one cause, the abolition of the slave trade and slavery in Africa. He considered the traffic in slaves 'as the most gigantic system of wickedness the world ever saw'. Unlike many of his contemporaries, such as McQueen and Buxton, who stayed at home and wrote treatises on the subject, Richardson exposed himself to the dangers of the Sahara to report on the traffic and to take practical steps for its abolition. The sending out of the central African mission was the result of three years of remorseless pressure which he exerted on the Foreign Office. He described his expeditions not as journeys of exploration but as 'moral tours' or 'humane missions' undertaken 'to kill or cripple the monster slavery'. Richardson's ideas were certainly very unrealistic viewed against the background of the Sahara and the western Sudan. He was tactless, impatient, irascible, and indeed too fanatical to succeed. But he stood for a definite cause, and for this cause he died. His name is certainly worthy to stand beside those of Wilberforce, Clarkson, and Livingstone in the annals of the abolition of the slave trade and slavery in Africa.

Barth and Overweg parted company two days after leaving Richardson, and Barth pushed on to Katsina, where he arrived on 23 January 1851. He visited the once famous market of this town, which he found 'dull, showing the state of decay into which this once splendid and busy emporium of Negroland had fallen'.[1] He left Katsina a week later and on 31 January entered Kano, the celebrated entrepôt of Central Negroland. The spirited description which (like other explorers) he gave of the commercial and industrial life of Kano has already been noted.[2] He left Kano on 9 March, and, after passing through the thickly populated and very fertile regions to the east, sighted Kukawa on 2 April. It was with mixed feelings that he surveyed the town and with some hesitation that he entered its gates, since he was to come 'into contact with those people on whose ill or good-will depended the whole success of our mission'. All his doubts and fears were however soon dispelled by the amiable disposition of Bashir. 'He saluted me in a very cheerful way,' Barth noted with relief. To his pleasant surprise, he was shown the quarters, consisting of two immense courtyards, which had been expressly prepared for the mission. His reception by the Sheikh himself was no less reassuring.[3]

[1] Barth, op. cit., vol. ii, p. 60.   [2] See pp. 117–19.
[3] Barth, op. cit., vol. ii, pp. 240–4, 249.

Nevertheless, Barth was confronted with two immediate problems. The first was financial: he arrived at Kukawa 'without a dollar' and had to face a total debt of 1,570 dollars (£392) claimed by Richardson's servants. The second problem which agitated him was whether, now that Richardson was dead, the British Government would recall him. Barth promptly tackled these problems with hope. He first of all told the Sheikh and the Vizir about his financial difficulties and his wish to embark on exploration. The result was encouraging. The authorities soon restored Richardson's effects to him, and lent him money sufficient to enable him to liquidate the debt left by Richardson and to provide himself with urgently needed supplies. They also promised him every assistance and protection.

Thus assured, Barth turned to the second problem. In a letter to Palmerston, he informed him of the death of Richardson, which had paralysed the expedition, since the rest of them had 'no authority at all'. He then went on to advocate the continuation of the mission's work in spite of the death of its leader. Palmerston's reaction was favourable:

I think that Mr. Richardson's death ought not to make any difference as to the providing funds for the expedition [he minuted]. We do not want to save money by Richardson's death but to obtain notwithstanding that misfortune the same information by means of the two that we expected from the three.[1]

Addington, the Under-Secretary of State, therefore authorized Barth to take upon himself the future charge of the expedition. A copy of Richardson's instructions was enclosed for his guidance and he was told that a sum of £800 was being sent to him to defray any costs and debts. In this same letter it was suggested that he might either persist in his proposed eastward course towards the Nile after the completion of the exploration of the Chad or 'prefer a westerly one in the direction of Timbuctoo'.[2] Owing to the wars between the Tuareg and Tibu, which blocked the Fezzan–Bornu route for nearly a year, Barth did not receive this important letter and many others until nine months later. As it ended his anxiety about the mission and especially about his financial position, it is not surprising that he described the day he received it as 'one of the most lucky days of my life'.[3]

[1] F.O. 101/30, Barth to Palmerston, 21 Aug. 1851, and Palmerston's minute, 2 Sept. 1851.
[2] F.O. 101/30, Addington to Barth, 7 Oct. 1851.
[3] Barth, *Travels*, vol. iii, pp. 406-7.

Even before the pleasure of Her Majesty's Government was known, Barth and Overweg (who joined him at Kukawa in May 1851) undertook four exploring expeditions with the full financial assistance of the Sheikh and Vizir of Bornu. The first of these, with the primary purpose of solving the burning geographical question as to whether the 'Chadda', the Benue, and the Shari were different names of the same river, was begun on 29 May and lasted seven weeks.[1]

In the course of this expedition, Barth crossed the Benue near its confluence with the Faro and advanced as far as Yola, the capital of the Fulani province of Adamawa. In his absence, Overweg christened the boat *Lord Palmerston* and used it to explore the Chad and its islands.[2]

Escorted by the Awlad Sulayman, the people of Abd al-Jalīl, Barth and Overweg began the second expedition, largely financed by the Vizir of Bornu, on 11 September 1851.[3] They explored Kanem and the north-eastern shores of the Chad as far as the western frontiers of Waday. The wars between their escort and the people of Waday forced them to beat a retreat to Kukawa, where they arrived on 14 November. Eleven days later, the third expedition was undertaken in the company of a slave-raiding expedition sent out by the Sheikh of Bornu.[4] This enabled Barth to explore the districts of Logone and Mosgu as far as the River Logone, a tributary of the Shari. In the fourth expedition from Kukawa, which set out on 4 March 1852, Barth hoped to accomplish his long-cherished ambition of exploring the area east of the Chad. He crossed the Shari and after several delays entered Masena, the capital of Bagirmi, on 27 April. At this point, however, partly because his health and his means were 'entirely insufficient', partly because of the political instability in Waday following a civil war, and partly because of the age-long hostility between Waday and Bornu, which made it dangerous for any traveller to proceed from one kingdom to the other,[5] Barth reluctantly abandoned the eastern trip. He decided instead to implement the Government's suggestion that he might explore the area in the direction of Timbuctu.

[1] F.O. 101/30, Barth to Palmerston, 7 May 1847.
[2] Overweg died before he could write an account of this exploration—Barth, op. cit., vol. iii, p. 8.
[3] Ibid., vol. iii, pp. 20–21, 23.
[4] Ibid., vol. iii, p. 118.
[5] Ibid., vol. iii, pp. 422–3, vol. iv, pp. 1–2.

The timing of his departure, but not the change of his plans, as Mockler-Ferryman and other writers contend,[1] was determined by the death from fever of his only companion and friend, Dr. Overweg, on 27 September 1852. Barth had planned to make another attempt to visit the north-eastern shores of the Chad before moving westward. But after the death of his colleague, he found their house so 'desolate and melancholy and any longer stay in Kukawa so intolerable' that he determined 'to set out as soon as possible on [his] journey towards the Niger—to new countries and new people'.[2] After having settled all outstanding debts, which left him with very little means, he took his leave of the Sheikh and Vizir on 25 November 1852.

Traversing areas now familiar in their topography and vegetation, he stopped first at Katsina and then made for the Court of Aliyu Baba, the son and successor of Sultan Bello. He arrived within a few miles of Sokoto on 3 April to find, like Clapperton earlier, that the Sultan was campaigning against the people of Gobir. It was in a tense state of excitement similar to his mood in Kukawa exactly two years previously that he awaited the first palaver with Aliyu. Once more he was soon relieved. On the very day that he reached the camp, Aliyu received him with the utmost kindness and good humour and 'in the most cheerful and assuring manner' granted permission to pass through his dominions.[3] From the camp, Barth and his servants proceeded to Wurno, Aliyu's official residence a few miles north of Sokoto. A month later, with the best wishes of Aliyu and letters of introduction to the Emir of Gwandu and the Sheikh Al-Baka'i of Timbuctu, who was a personal friend of Aliyu, Barth resumed his journey.

After a fortnight's delay at Gwandu, he proceeded in a westerly direction through regions rendered unsafe by the conflicts between the Hausa and the Fulani. On 20 June 1853 he reached Say, where for the first time he set eyes on the Niger. Warned of the possible hostility of the Tuareg living along the Niger farther north, Barth gave up the idea of going to Timbuctu by river.[4] On 24 June he crossed the river and skirted the hilly country of Gurma to the north. Passing through a country 'well-wooded and intersected with a number of

[1] Mockler-Ferryman, *British Nigeria* (1902), p. 43.
[2] Barth, vol. iii, p. 478, vol. iv, pp. 1–2; F.O. 101/34, Barth to Malmesbury, 10 Oct. 1852.
[3] Ibid., pp. 133–4; F.O. 101/36, Barth to Clarendon, 3 May 1853.
[4] Barth, vol. iv, pp. 241, 248–9.

small water courses', he entered the commercial centre of Dore, the capital of Libtako, the most north-westerly district of the emirate of Gwandu, on 12 July. From here he soon entered Dalla, the eastern-most district of the Fulani Kingdom of Masina. As he was convinced that its fanatical ruler would not allow any Christian to enter his territory, and as he was not then under the protection of any chief or influential person, Barth assumed the dress of an Arab. Henceforth, until his arrival at Timbuctu, he was presented either as a 'Sherif from the East' or as 'the messenger of the Sultan of Stanbul'.[1] He managed to elude detection while passing through the districts inhabited by the Fulani, the Tuareg, and the Songhay, and hit on the Niger again at a place about 100 miles south-west of Timbuctu on 27 August. He and his servants sailed down the river and disembarked at Kabara, and shortly afterwards, on 7 September 1853, entered the far-famed city of Timbuctu.[2] Barth did not leave this city until March 1854. During this period he lived like a prisoner, partly in the town itself and partly in a camp belonging to Al-Baka'i five miles north-east of the town, always 'with a loaded gun in [his] hand, and a pair of loaded pistols in [his] girdle'.[3] He never had an opportunity to survey the whole town himself or to attend any of its markets. In the end, he had to be secretly sent out of the city on 17 March 1854.

This long stay, his close confinement, and the way in which he managed to leave Timbuctu alive, were all the outcome of the politi-cal situation, which was not unlike that at the time of Laing. The Fulani, who had conquered Timbuctu from the Tuareg a few weeks before Laing's arrival, were still wielding sovereignty over the town. Barth's disguise was therefore an absolute necessity, especially as he arrived at a time when Al-Baka'i was out of the city. Unfortunately, a day after his arrival information reached him that his identity had been disclosed by Hammadi, the nephew and 'the rival and enemy of El Bakay'.[4] As soon as this news reached Hamdallahi, the capital of Masina, 'a considerable troop of armed men mustering about 20 muskets' was dispatched with orders to drive Barth out of the city. They entered the city on 1 October. But unlike Laing, Barth had a protector in the person of Al-Baka'i, who had returned to the city

[1] F.O. 101/36, Barth to Malmesbury, 2 Oct. 1853; Barth, vol. iv, pp. 316–17, 356–7.
[2] Ibid., pp. 387, 391, 403–5.
[3] F.O. 101/36, Barth to Clarendon, 15 Mar. 1854, Timbuctu.
[4] Barth, op. cit., vol. iv, p. 438.

four days earlier and had guaranteed his security.[1] The Sheikh belonged to the famous priestly family recognized as the head of the
Qadiriyya order in the Sahara and the western Sudan and the
political head of the Arab Kunta tribe. Since the death of Laing's
benefactor, Sheikh Sidi Muhammad,[2] the family had moved into
Timbuctu and had been arbitrating in all disputes between the Moors
and the Tuareg and between the Songhay and the Fulbe of Masina.[3]
As the head of this family, Al-Baka'i was at the time occupying a
position in Timbuctu comparable to that of the Pope in Rome today.
He had such a large following in Timbuctu and among the Tuareg
and Kunta Arabs of the Sahara that he could and did defy the orders
of the Sultan of Masina and refused to hand over Barth,[4] although
the Arab and Moorish traders, as usual alarmed by the prospect of
losing their trade to Europeans from the coast, tried to induce him
to do so.[5] These intrigues made Barth's life in the city very precarious,
and he was periodically moved to the camp for greater safety.

Finally, in the middle of March 1854, the supporters of Al-Baka'i
heard of a conspiracy among the Fulani party to kill Barth, as well as
news of the approach of a large army sent by the Sultan of Masina to
arrest him, and they smuggled the explorer out of the town at night
and led him into the camp to join the Sheikh himself.[6] Even after this,
it was not until 15 May that Barth began his return journey. Al-Baka'i,
accompanied by his other nephew Muhammad ibn al-Khattar,
escorted him as far as Gao, the celebrated capital of the ancient
Songhay Empire, and then provided him with an escort of five people,
three to conduct him as far as Sokoto and the remaining two as far
as Kukawa.[7] But for the loyal support of Al-Baka'i, Barth would
most probably have suffered the same fate as Laing. His experience
supports the contention that once a traveller enjoyed the protection

---

[1] F.O. 101/36, Barth to Malmesbury, 2 Oct. 1853; Barth, vol. iv, pp. 453,
458–9.

[2] See above, p. 84.

[3] Felix Dubois, op. cit., p. 339; Barth, vol. iv, pp. 434–5; V. Monteil, 'Sur
quelques textes Arabes provenant du Soudan', *Bulletin du Comite D'etudes
Historiques et scientifiques de L.A.O.F.*, tome xxi, 1938, pp. 499–502.

[4] See Appendix IV for an extract from Al-Baka'i's letter to the Sultan in which
he advanced in very indignant and contemptuous terms his reasons for refusing
to surrender Barth to him.

[5] Ibid., vol. iv, p. 496, vol. v, p. 12; F.O. 101/36, Barth to Clarendon, 15 Mar.
1854.

[6] F.O. 101/36, Barth to Clarendon, 15 Mar. 1854, Timbuctu. This letter was
completed at Gao towards the end of June; Barth, vol. v, pp. 69–72.

[7] Barth, vol. v, pp. 235–6.

of a powerful and influential person in the interior, his religious convictions or his attire were relatively insignificant.

Continuing his journey along the Niger, Barth arrived at Say on 29 July 1854. He had contemplated the possibility of going farther down the river to Yauri, thus connecting by his own inspection 'the middle course of this noble river with the lower part, as far as it has been visited by the Landers'.[1] But he abandoned the idea because of his exhausted means, his weak health, and the advanced state of the rainy season, which made it necessary for him to reach Sokoto as soon as possible. On 2 August, therefore, he left the Niger, and without any difficulty arrived at Sokoto on 24 August, Kano on 17 October, and Kukawa on 4 December, after an absence of two years. As none of the letters which Barth wrote from Timbuctu arrived at Tripoli until about eighteen months later, rumours flashed through Tripoli and England in 1854 that he was dead. It was not until March 1855 that Herman, the Consul-General in Tripoli, reported to London that 'the rumour of Dr. Barth's death has most happily proved unfounded'.[2]

By the time he returned to Kukawa, Barth was feeling the effects of four years of continuous and strenuous travelling. As he became weaker, he found the weather correspondingly trying. 'Altogether my usual energy was gone, and my health totally undermined,' he wrote on April 1855, 'and the sole object which occupied my thoughts was to convey my feeble body in safety home.'[3] On 4 May he left Kukawa and, following Denham and Clapperton's footsteps, reached Murzuk on 14 July, Tripoli on 17 August, and England on 6 September 1855, after an absence of six years.

The Central African Mission did not end with the return of Barth to England, as is generally supposed. On his arrival in Kukawa in December 1854 he met a party sent out by the British Government and consisting of two Sappers, Corporal J. F. Church and Private J. Macguire, and two interpreters, Henry Warrington and Guiseppe (a Maltese), under the leadership of Dr. Edward Vogel, another German. Vogel has been asked to join the Central African Mission as 'an associate and scientific assistant', and his two sub-assistants were in

[1] Barth, vol. v, p. 299.
[2] F.O. 101/36, Herman to Clarendon, 24 Oct. 1854. Clarendon communicated this information to Bunsen, who was then in Germany, in December 1854. F.O. 101/37, Herman to Clarendon, 13 Mar. 1855; 101/45, Wodehouse to Bunsen, 7 Apr. 1855, telling him that Barth was alive.
[3] Barth, op. cit., vol. v, p. 406.

charge of the instruments that were to be delivered to the members of the mission.[1] He had been told to direct his attention in particular to 'botanical and zoological researches in the new and unknown parts of the country' through which he would pass. If he found on his arrival at Kukawa that Barth and Overweg had already left for the eastern regions,[2] he was to stay there and prosecute his scientific researches before returning to England via Tripoli. It is obvious that the party was more or less the natural-history wing of the Central African Mission and that it was sent out, like the Benue expedition which will be discussed in the next chapter, in response to requests from Barth and Overweg.

In the original instructions to the Mission no mention had been made of botanical collections. In a letter to Bunsen, however, both Barth and Overweg had urged that another scientific person should be sent out to devote himself entirely to the study and collection of the variety of new and interesting zoological and botanical objects they had come across in the western Sudan.[3] They also expressed an urgent need for a fresh supply of instruments, especially barometers and thermometers. Bunsen passed these requests on to the British Government with the suggestion that a supplementary mission might be sent out and that Vogel, who was then working as an astronomer at the Bishop Observatory in Regent's Park, London, might lead it. Bunsen's suggestion was fully supported by Captain Smyth of the Royal Geographical Society and Mr. Brown of the Botanical Department of the British Museum.[4] Brown recommended that a sum of £20 should be given to Vogel for the purchase of equipment for collecting, preserving, and transmitting specimens. In his minute on Bunsen's letter, Russell not only welcomed his suggestions but even recommended that two men from the Sappers should be selected to accompany Vogel. 'This,' he added, 'would give the scientific men more leisure and be also some security to their persons.'

This supplementary mission turned out a complete disaster. Of its five members only Church, whom Barth took with him on his home-

[1] F.O. 101/34, Instructions to Vogel, Addington to Vogel, 19 Feb. 1853.

[2] It was not known in England until five days later that Barth had abandoned his eastern project and at the time when these instructions were being drafted had reached Katsina on his way to Timbuctu. Vogel had just left London for Southampton when news of Overweg's death reached the Foreign Office.

[3] F.O. 101/34, Bunsen to Russell, 29 Jan. 1853.

[4] F.O. 101/34, Smyth to Bunsen, 28 Jan. 1853, and Brown to Bunsen, Jan. 1853, encl. in Bunsen to Russell, 29 Jan. 1853.

ward journey, returned alive to England. In February 1854, a month after their arrival at Kukawa, the Maltese died, and on his return to Tripoli five months later Henry Warrington was murdered at a place about 100 miles south of Bilma. Vogel and Macguire carried on the work, and by the time Barth returned from Timbuctu to Kukawa in December 1854, they had explored the Chad in the *Lord Palmerston*, visited the Mosgu country, and explored the regions south of Kukawa as far as Mora, the capital of Mandara.[1] In January 1855 Vogel left Kukawa again for the south and did not re-enter that town until almost a year later. During this long journey, about which little is known, he explored the south-eastern emirates of the Sokoto Empire—Bauchi, Gombe, Zaria, and Adamawa—and sailed on the Benue for three days.[2] He visited the capital towns of the first three emirates, and though he came within a day's march of that of Kano, an epidemic of cholera raging there at the time prevented him from entering it. Vogel must have been a man of inexhaustible energy, for in January 1856, only a month after his return to Kukawa, he left again for Waday and successfully entered Wara, its capital, where he was murdered by the Sultan.[3] On hearing of the death of his master, Macguire, who had been left behind at Kukawa, set off for Tripoli in January 1857. He too was murdered only six days' march north of Kukawa. Neither his own papers nor those of Vogel were ever recovered. Well did Clarendon, on reading of Macguire's death, minute: 'this is very melancholy'.[4]

As the records of Overweg, Vogel, and Macguire were never recovered, and as Richardson succumbed too early for his records, which were posthumously published, to contain much new information, we have to turn to Barth for an examination and assessment of the achievements of the Central African Mission. Fortunately for his contemporaries, and for scholars ever since, as well as reporting

[1] F.O. 101/36, Vogel to Addington, 22 Feb. 1854, Vogel to Addington, 14 July 1854; 101/37, Vogel to Herman, 15 Sept. 1854, encl. in Herman to Clarendon, 8 Feb. 1855; 101/35, Herman to Clarendon, 28 Nov. 1854.

[2] The only account of this remarkable journey, unfortunately a brief one which has so far never been mentioned by any writer, was that given by Vogel himself in his letter to Herman, 4 Dec. 1855, encl. in Herman to Clarendon, 19 Apr. 1856, F.O. 101/45.

[3] F.O. 101/41, Macguire to Herman, 5 Nov. 1856, encl. in Herman to Clarendon, 15 Feb. 1857; F.O. 101/43, Clarendon to Herman, 15 Jan. 1858; F.O. 101/43, Herman to Clarendon, 5 May 1858, and encls.; F.O. 101/46, Herman to Russell, and encls., 5 Nov. 1859.

[4] F.O. 101/41, Herman to Clarendon, 30 July 1857, and minute by Clarendon.

by letter to the Foreign Office, Barth presented his discoveries to the public in 1857 and 1858 in a monumental work in what the *Edinburgh Review* appropriately described as five 'portly volumes'.[1]

Geographically, Barth not only described in greater detail and more accurately areas already dealt with by earlier explorers; he also broke entirely new ground. In his description of the regions to the south of Kukawa and between Bornu and Sokoto already explored by Denham and Clapperton, Barth not only gives greater detail but also reveals and corrects the slips made by the earlier explorers. For instance, he pointed out that the Logone was not the same as the Shari, as Denham had reported, but only its tributary.[2] From the Logone to Masena to the east, from Mora to Yola to the south, from Ghat to Katsina and Kano to the north and from Sokoto across the Niger to Timbuctu, Barth solved a number of geographical puzzles. For instance, after having explored the Benue and the Shari, he asserted authoritatively that there was no connexion between the two rivers and correctly pointed out that 'the breadth of the water parting between the two basins at the utmost cannot exceed 20 miles'. When he crossed the Benue, he stated that there could 'no longer be any doubt that this river joins the majestic course [of the Niger]'.[3] This assertion was proved correct, as we shall see later, by the expedition of Baikie. An equally interesting, though less startling, contribution to geographical knowledge was his survey of the course of the Niger from the port of Timbuctu to Say. As positive evidence of his love of detail and accuracy, he brought back meteorological readings covering the areas he traversed, in which he not only showed the hour of the day and the reading of the thermometer but also added very useful comments.[4]

No less illuminating was the ethnographic survey of the western Sudan embodied in Barth's journals. In this respect he continued the work of Denham and Clapperton, but in his characteristic thorough manner. He endorsed the earlier explorers' picture of the complexity of the divisions of the peoples of the Sudan as compared with those

[1] The British Government generously contributed £2,000 towards the cost of publication. F.O. 101/45, Clarendon to Treasury, 7 Dec. 1855; F.O. 101/45, Treasury to Clarendon, 20 Dec. 1855; Clarendon to Barth, 26 Dec. 1855; *Edinburgh Review*, vol. 109 (1859), p. 338.

[2] Barth, op. cit., vol. iii, pp. 298–9, 313–14.

[3] Barth, op. cit., vol. iii, pp. 222, 468; F.O. 101/34, Barth to Malmesbury, 21 Aug. 1852.

[4] Barth, op. cit., vol. i, pp. 571–8, vol. ii, pp. 673–6, vol. iii, pp. 619–35, vol. iv, pp. 631–41; vol. v, pp. 655–6. For Barth's description of the political conditions in the western Sudan in the 1850's, see Appendix IV.

of the Sahara, showing that while the Sahara was the home of only two principal groups of peoples—the Tuareg and the Tibu, with a few Arab tribes especially along the Morocco–Timbuctu route—the Sudan was the home of over fifteen different peoples. The most important were the Mandingoes of Park (or as Barth calls them, the Wangarawa) and the Wolof in the west, the Songhay, Mossi, Fulani, and Hausa in the middle, and the Kanuri, Bagirmi, Mosgu, and Mandara in the east. Barth came into contact with most of these peoples and gave interesting and detailed accounts of their habits, standard of living, and especially their languages. The Fulani, he reported, 'evince great intelligence but do not exhibit much industry or disposition for trading'. He found the Hausas 'full of intelligence, liveliness and of cheerful social disposition and very industrious'.[1] With the exception of the tribes to the south of Bornu, he found most of the peoples of the western Sudan very decently clothed, the men in wide shirts and trousers mostly of a dark colour, and the women in large dark-coloured cotton cloths, called the *turkedi*, which they fastened under or above the breast.[2] But even the naked peoples, the Marghi, the Mosgu, and the Batta, until then considered as rude savages, had attained some standard of civilization, as Barth discovered to his utter surprise. The Masa of Logone, for instance, were familiar with the arts of weaving and dyeing. Among the Mosgu he found

that the ground was so carefully cultivated that even manure had been put upon the fields in a regular manner, being spread over the ground to a great extent—the first example of such careful tillage that I had as yet observed in Central Africa, both among Mohammedans and pagans.

He also discovered that the Marghi practised 'to a great extent inoculation for small pox, which in Bornu is rather the exception than the rule'.[3] Nudity in the western Sudan seemed, after all, not to be synonymous with savagery and barbarism.

Like some of his predecessors, Barth collected vocabularies of languages most of which had never been heard of in Europe. In his collection he displayed his usual meticulousness. For instance, he

---

[1] Barth, 'A general historical description of the state of human society in Northern and Central Africa', a paper read to the Royal Geographical Society on 10 May 1858—*Journal of R.G.S.*, vol. 30, pp. 112–28; Barth, *Travels*, vol. ii, pp. 163–4, 420–1.

[2] Barth, vol. ii, p. 25, vol. iii, pp. 451–2.

[3] Barth, vol. iii, p. 208, vol. ii, p. 399.

selected twenty-four of the languages and dialects spoken in Bornu, Bagirmi, and Adamawa, wrote down 196 words and phrases in each of those languages, and made some very interesting comments.[1] For example, he wrote:

It seems remarkable that the Musgu, as well as the Marghi, and several division of the kindred Kotoko, call the cattle by a name which closely approaches that given to it by the Hausa people, while the Batta call it by a name which is certainly derived from the Fulfude or the language of the Fulbe. Such linguistic relations are not without interest, as they afford some little insight into the history of the civilisation of these regions.[2]

Unlike his predecessors, however, he did not end with just a mere collection of vocabularies. As a philologist, he made a careful study of most of the languages, seven of which he learned to speak, and noted their peculiarities and the affinities they had with other languages, especially Bantu. He described the Hausa language as 'the most beautiful, sonorous, rich and lively of all the languages of Negroland; but it is defective in verbal tenses'. He noted some relation 'between the Hausa, the Berber, and the Coptic languages' and pointed out that though it had a few words in common with Kanuri, which he described as 'allied in grammar to the Mongolian languages,[3] Hausa was evidently distinct from it, as well in its vocabulary as in its grammar'. He showed for the first time that the Marghi language 'is nearly related to, or rather only a dialect of the Batta language, which is spread over a large part of Adamawa or Fumbina, and has many points of connection with the Mosgu language, while in certain general principles it approaches the great South African family'.[4] Most of Barth's conclusions have subsequently been accepted by linguists; others, such as the connexion between the Batta and Bantu languages, have been challenged by Homburger and other scholars.[5] But whether future research justifies, modifies, or

[1] F.O. 101/34, Bunsen to Clarendon, 23 Feb. 1853, and encls. These were published by Benton in his *Notes on some languages of the Western Sudan* (1912), pp. 78–129; see also his Temashight Vocabulary. Barth, vol. v, pp. 572–638.

[2] Barth, vol. iii, p. 235.

[3] Barth, 'A general historical description', op. cit., pp. 26–71, 121, 273 f.n.; Barth, *Travels*, vol. ii, pp. 385–6, 482, vol. iii, p. 309.

[4] Barth, op. cit., ii, 385–6.

[5] Schultze, op. cit., p. 192; Benton, op. cit., pp. 131–44; O. Temple, op. cit., p. 271; L. Homburger, *The Negro African Languages* (1949), p. 16. Barth started his great work on African languages on his return to Germany, but unfortunately died (1865) before completing it.

even rejects his conclusions, as pioneering work Barth's linguistic studies were certainly epoch-making.

But it is most of all the history they contain that has made Barth's volumes the treasure of scholars and unique in the annals of African exploration. Unlike almost all his predecessors, Barth did not confine himself to giving accurate and detailed descriptions of what he saw. His chief object was, as he said himself, 'to represent the tribes and nations with whom I came into contact in their historical and enthno-graphical relation to the rest of mankind as well as in their physical relation to that tract of country in which they live'.[1] From such sources as Ibn Battuta, Leo Africanus, and Bello, Barth investigated the past of the Azger Tuareg, noting especially how they came to Ghat.[2] Similarly, he studied the 'ethnographical relations of Air', pointing out that the Kel Owi, who formed the ruling aristocracy at the time, were 'traceable from the north-west and had conquered Air from the earlier arrivals at about 1740'. Of the Hausa nation he positively stated that it was not 'an indigenous nation or at least did not occupy its present seat from very ancient times', but had moved into the country from the north or from Bornu at a comparatively recent date. While he was quite certain that the Fulani had settled along the lower course of the Senegal and begun their march of conquest 'from west to east', he could not explain from whence they came or when they reached the Senegal.

He traced the histories of Agades, Kano, and Katsina from their foundations to the time of his visit. He also prepared the first chrono-logical lists of Bornu kings from about A.D. 850 to 1846, and of Songhay and Timbuctu rulers from A.D. 300 to 1855.[3] In his historical work, Barth used documentary sources in Arabic which he found in the western Sudan. His history of Bornu was pieced together mainly from the *Diwan*, a chronicle 'comprising the whole history of Bornu from the earliest time down to Ibrahim [1818-46]', two other short lists of Bornu kings, and a detailed history of the first twelve years of the reign of Edris Alawoma (1571-1603), written by the Imam Ahmed, a contemporary of the King.[4] In his work on Timbuctu and on the Mali and Songhay Empires, Barth drew heavily on the *Tarikh*

[1] Barth, op. cit., vol. i, xv.
[2] Barth, vol. ii, pp. 224–6, 228, 335–6; vol. i, pp. 335–59; vol. ii, pp. 69–73; vol. iv, pp. 103–51.
[3] Barth, vol. i, pp. 458–68, vol. ii, pp. 70–81, 117–20; vol. ii, pp. 633–71, vol. iv, pp. 579–630.
[4] Barth, op. cit., vol. ii, pp. 253–60.

al-Sudan, a copy of which he discovered in Gwandu.[1] He quarried the material for his history of the various states and empires of Hausaland mainly from the *Tazyīn al-Waragāt*, written by Abdullahi, the brother of Usman dan Fodio, and the *Infaq al-maysûr* by Bello. Not only did these sources enable Barth to write the history of states and kingdoms but—what is even more important—their discovery proved to the world for the first time the availability of written historical sources as well as the long tradition and high standard of literacy and learning in the western Sudan.[2]

Here, as in his linguistic studies, some of Barth's views have been challenged. Rodd, for instance, has suggested 'the latter half of the seventeenth century' rather than Barth's 1740 as the more probable date for the arrival of the Kel Owi in Air.[3] His list of Bornu kings has also been slightly revised by scholars such as Schultze and Urvoy. But the surprising fact is not that Barth has been proved wrong or challenged, but the great extent to which his conclusions have been

[1] Ibid., vol. iv, pp. 200–1.

[2] On several occasions in his wanderings, Barth came across many persons who were 'distinguished by a good deal of Mohammedan learning' and who had in their possession manuscripts of various sorts. A typical example was Faki Sambo, a Fulani whom Barth befriended in Masena, the capital of Baghirmi. Sambo, Barth discovered, was 'not only versed in all the branches of Arabic literature, but also had even read those portions of Aristotle and Plato which had been translated into, or rather Mohammedanized in Arabic'. As a young man he had been educated at the celebrated Muslim University of Al Azhar in Cairo and on his return home had become an influential courtier. Though he was completely blind at the time of Barth's visit, Sambo could still talk 'about the splendour and achievements of the Khalifat, from Baghdad to Andalos [Spain]— particularly of the latter country with the history of whose towns, kings, and literary men he was intimately acquainted'. Barth found that this blind man had numerous manuscripts in his possession and he recalled the day when he went to call on his friend and found him sitting in his courtyard in the midst of a heap of manuscripts which he could then only enjoy by touching them with his hands. This sight reminded Barth of a saying of J. G. Jackson that the time would come when the texts of the classics would be emendated from manuscripts brought from the interior of Negroland. Admittedly, this prophecy has not yet been fulfilled, but considering the large numbers of manuscripts that are being dug up now in Northern Nigeria, it may very well be in the near future. (Barth, op. cit., pp. iii, 373–80; for the Arabic documents that have recently been collected in Northern Nigeria, see W. E. N. Kensdale, *A catalogue of the Arabic manuscripts preserved in the University Library, Ibadan, Nigeria*; A. D. H. Bivar, 'Arabic documents of Northern Nigeria' (1955), *Bulletin of the School of Oriental and African Studies*, xxii, 2, 1959; H. F. C. Smith, 'Source Material for the History of Western Sudan', *Journal of the Historical Society of Nigeria*, i, 3 Dec. 1958; M. Hiskett, 'Material relating to the State of Learning among the Fulani before their Jihad', *SOAS Bulletin*, xix, 3, 1957.)

[3] Rodd, op. cit., p. 388.

accepted or justified by subsequent scholars and writers. A perusal of O. Temple, Mockler-Ferryman, Schultze, Burns, Bovill, Rodd, Urvoy, and Trimingham makes one marvel at the authenticity and accuracy of most of Barth's historical work.

Barth was not only a geographer, ethnographer, linguist, and historian, but also a diplomat, an aspect of his work that has so far been entirely ignored by historians. The death of Richardson conferred on him the responsibility for the diplomatic as well as the scientific aspects of the mission. Furthermore, by becoming an eye-witness to the brutalities of the slave trade, Barth became as passionately interested in its abolition and the civilization of Africa as he was in solving scientific problems. While fettered like a slave in a little village in Bagirmi, he reflected on this question and concluded:

It would be absolutely necessary . . . to colonize the most favourable tract of the country inclosed by the Kwara [Niger], the Benuwe [Benue], and the river Kaduna, and thus to spread commerce and civilisation in all directions into the very heart of the continent. . . . This is the only means to answer the desired end; everything else is in vain.[1]

He therefore considered himself as a herald preparing the way for future European activities by establishing friendly relations with the chiefs and obtaining what he called 'letters of franchise', which would guarantee freedom of movement and security of person to future traders and missionaries. Thus a cause which he repudiated while he was in Europe became, on his arrival in Africa, one of his main preoccupations. Throughout his wanderings, he paid as much attention to preparing for the future as to unearthing the past and studying the present.

The diplomatic work of the mission began in earnest soon after it left Fezzan. Two days after their arrival at Ghat, Richardson presented the draft treaty for consideration at a general meeting of the sheikhs. Although the clauses about the slave trade and religion were expunged as being obnoxious, the treaty was not signed. According to Richardson, final decision was postponed pending the winter *souk* (market) when all the chiefs of the Azger Tuareg would assemble. He was absolutely confident that it would be signed eventually. Barth, however, tells us that it would have been signed there and then had Richardson not produced, 'at the very moment

---

[1] Barth, op. cit., vol. iii, pp. 365-6.

when all the chiefs were ready to subscribe to the treaty', the letter to Shafou in which direct mention of the abolition of the slave trade was made.[1] Barth was certainly correct in stating that it was the letter to Shafou that wrecked the negotiations. Yet it is clear from the letters some of the chiefs wrote to Gagliuffi that what infuriated them was not the mention of the abolition of the slave trade but rather the fact that Shafou had been represented in the letter as the 'Sultan of the Azger Tuareg'. He was, in fact, not even a *primus inter pares* but, as Crowe pointed out, 'merely one of 14 or 15 Sheikhs independent of each other'.[2]

While at Tintellust, Richardson and his associates also discussed the draft treaty with Al-Nur and successfully persuaded him to sign it. After the usual two clauses dealing with the slave trade and religion had been excluded, the Sheikh appended his signature to the treaty on 23 November 1850. 'This is my first success in diplomacy', Richardson recorded, and it was celebrated in grand style. The British flag was hoisted, and no less than a hundred musket discharges were fired.[3] However, considering that Al-Nur was only a chief of one of the numerous divisions of the Kel Owi, it seems that Richardson exaggerated the importance of this achievement.

As in the field of exploration, so in diplomacy Barth began his work even before the pleasure of Her Majesty's Government was known. At one of his first interviews with the Sheikh and the Vizir, he delivered a speech which he was to repeat, with the relevant modifications, at all the courts he afterwards visited. Barth told the Bornu authorities that he had been sent by the Queen of England 'to renew the old friendship begun with the Sheikh el Kanemi ... partly to extend and to complete the inquiries made by the former mission, and partly to get liberty for their merchants to visit this country, and substituting legitimate commerce for that in human beings which we abhor, to trade in it with perfect security'. A copy of the treaty was then delivered with the usual omission of the articles respecting the slave trade, human sacrifice, and religion. Umar and Al-Hajj Bashīr, who were very enthusiastic about establishing commercial links with Britain, readily agreed on the terms of the treaty

[1] See above, p. 186; F.O. 101/30, Richardson to Palmerston, 24 July 1850; Richardson, *Mission*, vol. i, pp. 164–5; Barth, *Travels*, vol. i, p. 239.

[2] F.O. 101/30, Gagliuffi to Crowe, 4 Nov. 1850, and encls. in Crowe to Palmerston, 10 Jan. 1851.

[3] F.O. 101/30, Richardson to Palmerston, 25 Sept. 1850; Richardson, *Mission*, vol. i, p. 323.

and a copy was sent to the Foreign Office for approval.[1] Palmerston minuted that the treaty could be concluded and signed if the words 'that all Christians are subject to or tributary to the mussulmen' were left out. This amendment was, of course, accepted and the treaty was signed in Kukawa on 3 September 1852.[2]

Neither Barth nor the Bornu Government wanted the treaty to remain a dead letter. Barth spoke of 'the most ardent desire' of the Bornu Government that 'a consul should be sent out to their Court immediately in conformity with the terms of the treaty'. He emphasized the urgency of this request and pleaded that the consul would be a companion to him in his then lonely situation. He suggested that the person to be appointed should be a doctor or somebody with some knowledge of medicine. To prove their sincerity and anxiety, the Sheikh and Vizir also sent a present of specimens of Bornu manufactures to the British Government. This present was to be delivered by an envoy, who was instructed 'to visit the marvels of London and the other large towns of England, particularly the arsenal and manufactures in order to give full account of those things on his return'. To this Barth added that the Bornu envoy should be given free passage to England and every facility to attain the object of his visit.[3]

The information about the signing and ratification of the treaty, the impending visit of the Bornu envoy, and the request for a British consul reached England in February 1853, the very time when the envoy himself arrived in Tripoli. Backed by Chevalier Bunsen, who at the same time proposed the sending out of another mission up the Benue,[4] the suggestions met with prompt and favourable consideration. Addington's minute on the question of the envoy's visit is particularly significant. He wrote:

The Sheikh of Bornou has certainly behaved kindly and liberally to our African expedition, it may be of much use to secure a fast friend in the heart of Africa, which will now be attainable by stream from the Bight of

[1] F.O. 101/30, Barth to Palmerston, 24 May 1851; F.O. 101/30, Barth to Palmerston, 8 Aug. 1851; Barth, vol. ii, pp. 344–5.

[2] F.O. 101/34, Barth to Palmerston, 10 Oct. 1852. For the text of the treaty, see Appendix III.

[3] F.O. 101/34, Crowe to Palmerston, 20 Oct. 1851, and encls.; Barth to Crowe, 31 Aug. 1851 and Treaty between H.M. the Queen of England and the Sovereign of the Kingdom of Bornu and its dependencies; Palmerston's minute, 22 Dec. 1851, F.O. 101/34, Barth to Malmesbury, 10 Oct. 1852; Barth, vol. iii, pp. 412–13.

[4] See pp. 213–14.

Benin up the Quorra and the Tshadda . . . so as to bring our commerce within a moderate distance of Kouka on Lake Chad.

Addington therefore suggested that Reade, the Vice-Consul at Tripoli, should accompany the envoy to England and ultimately be posted to Bornu. He added, however, that a final decision on the consular post should not be taken until 'the arrival of the present bearer from Bornu and of Mr. Reade'. Both minutes were approved by Clarendon, Palmerston's successor, and Herman, the Consul-General in Tripoli, was accordingly instructed.[1] Unfortunately, on the arrival of the envoy, Herman found that he was 'simply a black slave'. In addition to this, the envoy himself soon fell seriously ill. For both reasons his visit was stopped by the Foreign Office. Herman was asked to inform the Sheikh of Bornu that since a slave became free on touching the soil of England, it was in his own interest that this envoy should not proceed to England.[2] With the cancellation of the visit, decision about the appointment of a consul to Bornu was postponed and then entirely forgotten.

While these exchanges were going on, Barth continued his scientific and diplomatic work. He took copies of the treaty with him on his missions to Adamawa and Bagirmi. Though he delivered the usual speech, he found neither the Emir of Adamawa nor the Sultan of Bagirmi friendly enough to enable him to bring up the treaty for discussion.[3] At the courts of Sokoto and Gwandu and in Timbuctu, however, his efforts were crowned with success. Barth's requests for the Sultan of Sokoto's help for his journey to Timbuctu and for a 'letter of franchise' were both granted. The letter of franchise which Aliyu gave Barth embodied all the clauses of the treaty signed with the Sheikh of Bornu. As a result Barth pleaded:

It is now certainly most desirable, that *an English merchant* who certainly must be a respectable as well as a clever man, should *without delay visit these countries* protected, and if necessary, even assisted by Government. . . . Let him establish himself in Kano . . . let him then have his merchandize forwarded to him by way of Nuffi [Nupe], and the nearer road by way of Kwara will be opened for English merchandize. . . .[4]

[1] F.O. Office, 101/34, Bunsen to Clarendon, 23 Feb. 1853, and minute by Addington; 101/34, Reade to Foreign Office, 23 Jan. 1853, and minute by Addington, 23 Feb. 1853; 101/34, Clarendon to Herman, 24 Feb. 1853.
[2] F.O. 101/34, Herman to Clarendon, 10 Mar. 1853; Addington to Herman, 6 Apr. 1853.
[3] F.O. 101/34, Barth to Palmerston, 21 July 1851; Barth, vol. ii, pp. 494-6, vol. iii, pp. 412-14.
[4] F.O. 101/36, Barth to Clarendon, 3 May 1853. The italics are Barth's.

In Gwandu, Sultan Khalilu also gave Barth a letter of franchise guaranteeing 'full security to any Englishman visiting his territories', and commanding the officers of the various provinces to respect their property and to facilitate their proceedings.[1] In Timbuctu, Al-Baka'i readily wrote a similar letter and persuaded two Tuareg Chiefs to do the same.[2]

On his arrival in England, Barth forwarded to the Foreign Office six letters written 'by native chiefs and stipulating security of commerce and intercourse to Her Majesty's subjects'.[3] The chiefs were Khalilu, the Emperor of Gwandu; Alkuttabu, the great chief of the Aulimmiden Tuareg, who dominated the banks of the Niger between Timbuctu and Gao; Awab, the chief of the Tadmekket Tuareg, who controlled the area north and north-west of Timbuctu; Sidi Ahmad Al-Baka'i, the religious chief of Timbuctu; Umar, the Sheikh of Bornu; and Aliyu, the Sultan of Sokoto. These letters provide clear evidence of Barth's success in forging close relations particularly with the rulers of Bornu and Sokoto and the religious chief of Timbuctu, and of the anxiety of these rulers to welcome English traders.

Barth not only prepared the way for future British enterprise by negotiating treaties with the African rulers; he also suggested a new highroad into the interior which was more suitable than the northern routes through the desert. 'A practicable high road, leading several hundred miles into the interior of the continent and passing to the south of Kano, the great commercial *entrepôt* of Central Africa, and only about two hundred miles in a straight line to the south of Kukawa', he wrote after his visit to Adamawa, 'had been found in the river Benuwe.' He also drew the attention of the British Government to the strategic importance of Nupe, a country, which, he hoped, would become of great importance in course of time 'for the civilisation of the whole of Central Africa'.[4]

It seems quite clear that Barth was the greatest of the explorers who scoured the western Sudan in the nineteenth century. The thoroughness and accuracy of his geographical work still stand unimpeached; his linguistic studies carried a stage further the practice begun by earlier explorers and continued ever since. The histories

[1] Barth, op. cit., vol. iv, p. 199.
[2] F.O. 101/36, Barth to Clarendon, 10 Nov. 1854; Barth, vol. iv, p. 507.
[3] F.O. 101/45, Barth to Clarendon, 18 Sept. 1855, and encls.
[4] F.O. 101/30, Barth to Palmerston, 7 Aug. 1851; F.O. 101/34, Barth to Foreign Office, 28 Jan. 1853; F.O. 101/36, Barth to Clarendon, 10 Nov. 1854; Barth, vol. ii, pp. 120, 465, vol. iii, pp. 13, 221, 365.

of the states and kingdoms which he so meticulously excavated and pieced together for the first time, as well as his revelation of the existence of written records and a high standard of learning, proved that Africa was not a 'Dark Continent', a continent with no history or civilization until white men came. Considering the light that it shed on the history and geography of the western Sudan, Barth's work was indeed, as it has been aptly described,[1] a work of exploration in a double sense—in time as well as in space. It was a fitting recognition of his accomplishments that he was awarded gold medals by the Geographical Societies of France, Germany, and England, and in England was created a Companion of the Bath and financially remunerated by the Government.[2]

But the question which has never been considered by any scholar is why Barth was so successful. The first answer is in his own inherent qualities. But for his sheer courage and dogged determination, he would have returned either immediately after his arrival at Kukawa because of lack of supplies, or after the death of Overweg because of loneliness and fear. As he told a friend of his in England, he was not 'a man who is afraid of death in such a cause'.[3] But while he was not afraid of death, he never courted it. When he realized that the regions farther east of Bagirmi were too unsafe, he promptly dropped his original plan of going eastward. Vogel rashly set out knowing well that Bornu–Waday relations were hostile, and inevitably lost his life. Again, when Barth saw that he could not pass through the domains of the Sultan of Masina undisguised, he tactfully adopted Arab dress. Even in his state of abject poverty, he did not fail to ingratiate himself with the people of Bagirmi with what little he could afford. As this consisted only of needles, he was nicknamed 'the Needle Prince'.[4] Whenever he could afford to be so, he was very liberal in his presents to the chiefs and people he came across because he was quick to realize that it was the best way of winning their friendship, keeping them in good humour, or laying them 'under lasting obligations'.

[1] T. Hodgkin, *Nigerian Perspectives* (Oxford, 1960), p. 16.

[2] F.O. 101/45, Barth to Clarendon, 28 Sept. 1855; F.O. 101/45, Clarendon to the Treasury, 7 Dec. 1855; Clarendon to Barth, 26 Dec. 1855; F.O. 101/45, Barth to Wodehouse, 10 Dec. 1855. In addition to the £2,000 grant-in-aid for the publication of his journal the British Government granted him a retrospective salary of £500 per annum from the date of Richardson's death to the return of the expedition.

[3] F.O. 101/34, Barth to Cooley, 20 July 1852.

[4] Barth, vol. ii, pp. 345-6.

But granting Barth's tact and courage, he could not have remained so long in the interior without the continued support of the British Government. Luckily every encouragement, moral and financial, was given to the intrepid traveller. As we have seen, instead of withdrawing the mission after Richardson's death, the British Government decided that it should continue. When Chevalier Bunsen, acting on behalf of the travellers, submitted a long list of goods which were to be sent out to be given as presents or shown as specimens of British manufacture, the Government promptly voted the required amount.[1] Finally, in September 1852, the Consul-General in Tripoli was authorized to meet any financial requests from Barth without even waiting for permission from the British Government.[2] For the first two years after his arrival at Kukawa and on many other occasions, Barth found himself, as we have seen, completely destitute. But this was not the result of parsimony on the part of the British Government but of the insecurity of the routes between Fezzan and Kukawa.

However, the Government's full support and Barth's tact and diligence cannot adequately explain his success. Barth and Overweg would have died of starvation in Bornu and Barth could not have explored the regions of the Chad and Bagirmi without the hospitality and financial assistance of the Sheikh and Vizir of Bornu. Without the co-operation of the Sultan of Sokoto, Barth could not have advanced to Timbuctu, and nobody can doubt that but for the protection of Al-Baka'i, he would there have suffered the same fate as Laing.

The question, then, is why were these rulers so hospitable and co-operative in their attitude towards Barth? The answer is that they had inherited a tradition of association with the British which they wanted to preserve and strengthen. Barth discussed Denham's mission with Sheikh Umar of Bornu, that of Clapperton with Sultan Aliyu of Sokoto, and that of Laing with Al-Baka'i.[3] There is nothing mysterious about this, because Umar, Aliyu, and Al-Baka'i were respectively the sons and successors of Al-Kānami, Bello, and Sidi Muhammad, who had entertained and assisted those explorers[4] and had received valuable presents, and in some cases letters, from the British Government. The Sheikh of Bornu and Al-Baka'i in par-

---

[1] F.O. 101/34, Bunsen to Granville, 1 Jan. 1852.
[2] F.O. 101/34, Addington to Herman, 15 Sept. 1852.
[3] Barth, vol. iv, pp. 134-5, 452-4.   [4] See above, pp. 60-63, 80-84.

ticular had other reasons in the early fifties to strengthen their contacts with Britain. As both Overweg and Barth reported, the Turks
in Tripoli and Fezzan were scheming to absorb Bornu into their
sprawling empire by persuasion or force or both. In August 1852
Overweg informed the British Consul-General in Tripoli that the
Sheikh and Vizir of Bornu wanted to enter into friendship with the
English for two reasons. The first was that they wanted to obtain such
English manufactures as the Arab merchants were not bringing into
the Sudan and the second was their belief that 'when the English
Government by making a treaty with Bornu is recognising the independence of this state, it will not suffer the Turks to make invasions'.[1]
Three weeks later and on the eve of his departure for Timbuctu,
Barth also drew the attention of the Foreign Secretary to this Turkish
threat and warned him that if the country fell 'under the desolating
hands of the Turks, all that has been begun would be destroyed in a
moment and the glorious kingdom of Burnoo . . . which has never
been tributary either to the Sultan of Constantinople nor to any
other power, would become the *demoralizing barracks of slave-
hunting barbarous soldiers*'.[2] The people of Timbuctu, as will be seen
in the next chapter, were facing a similar threat from the French.
But while the Crimean War saved Bornu, it combined with other
factors to be discussed later to seal the fate of Timbuctu.

   These political and commercial considerations irresistibly attracted
the rulers of the interior to England and made Englishmen most
welcome in their courts. On his return to England, Barth himself
informed Clarendon, the Foreign Secretary, that when Al-Baka'i
protected him he did not know 'that I was a German, but he thought
me an Englishman, and as such took me under his powerful protection, which he would scarcely have afforded me, had he known,
that I was not English and nothing but a foreign gentleman'.[3] That
Barth travelled as a British agent also enabled him to enjoy certain
facilities which would otherwise have been denied him, to his great
inconvenience and even peril. For instance, he could always call on
the commercial agents of the British vice-consuls in the Sudan for
financial and other assistance. Al-Hajj Bashīr, who was of such
inestimable help to Barth, was the agent of Gagliuffi. Barth also

   [1] F.O. 101/34, Overweg to Herman, 14 Aug. 1852, encl. in Herman to Malmesbury, 2 Nov. 1852.
   [2] F.O. 101/34, Barth to F.O., Nov. 1852; Barth, iii, 12. The phrase in italics was
underlined by Barth himself.
   [3] F.O. 101/45, Barth to Clarendon, 4 Oct. 1855.

reported that he borrowed 'enormous sums' from Muhammad Sfaksi, Gagliuffi's chief agent in the Sudan.[1] On Barth's first visit to Kano, in January 1851, it was Bawu, Gagliuffi's agent there, who introduced him to the Emir. When he came there a second time in October 1854, even more destitute than before, he was able to raise a loan of 200 dollars (500,000 shells) from the Ghadames[2] merchants who had 'English property in their hands'. Without these loans Barth's position in Kano would have been very precarious. Moreover, Barth could venture with every sense of security among the Awlad Sulayman, the people whom he himself described as 'the most lawless robbers in the world', because they still remembered and cherished the friendship and support of the British Government. At the first interview he had with their two leaders, who were the son and brother of Abd al-Jalīl, Barth recorded that they had 'commonplace talk about the English'.[3]

By his own able diplomacy and his long residence at the different courts, Barth increased even further Britain's reputation and popularity in the western Sudan. When Baikie visited Kano in 1862 he found the British so highly esteemed that he experienced no difficulty in raising loans and drawing bills on the Consul-General in Tripoli, whom he did not even know. He informed the Consul-General that he had 'obtained money at present the more easily in consequence of the punctuality with which an order of Dr. Barth was paid, and the civility which the messengers met with'.[4]

The Central African Mission, then, thanks largely to Barth, was a great success. It is not often realized, however, that this success was accomplished at a great cost both in life and money. Of the eight Europeans who took part in it, only two returned to England. The total cost in money, including payments to Barth and to Richardson's widow, amounted to £12,167. 11s. 5d. Yet the achievements more than justified this great amount. The mission, with its offshoot the Niger exploration of 1854, to be discussed later, brought to their culmination the British efforts to penetrate into the Sahara and the western Sudan begun in 1788. The mission cleared once and for all

[1] F.O. 101/34, Barth to Malmesbury, 10 Oct. 1852; Barth, vol. ii, pp. 100, 246, vol. iii, pp. 24, 473.
[2] Barth, vol. v, pp. 367–8. The property belonged to Gagliuffi, and Barth was given the loan after a palaver held before the Prime Minister of Kano.
[3] F.O. 101/30, Barth to Palmerston, 21 Aug. 1851; Barth, vol. iii, pp. 7, 68–69
[4] F.O. 84/1204, Baikie to the Consul at Tripoli, 4 Aug. 1862, and encl., Herman to Russell, 20 July 1863.

the mystery about Timbuctu and the areas farther south. It dispelled any doubts entertained about the populous and fertile nature of the regions south of the Sahara, the standard of civilization, and, above all, the attitude of the African rulers. It revived and strengthened British influence and prestige in the western Sudan. Finally, not only did it prepare the way for future enterprise by negotiating for 'letters of franchise', but it also pointed out once more the possibility of opening up a shorter and more practical route from the south to the rich markets of Hausaland and Bornu. Would the British Government follow up these discoveries and if so in what direction? Would the contacts with the rulers of the Sudan and the Sahara be maintained? We must turn to the next chapter for the answers to these questions.

CHAPTER IX

British Withdrawal from the Sahara

THE epoch-making work of the Central African Mission, like that of the Denham–Clapperton expedition, was indeed followed up. Even before the return of Barth to England, his pleas for assistance to the Bornu envoy and for a consular establishment were given serious consideration. Steps were also taken to follow up his main geographical discovery by the dispatch in 1854 of the Benue expedition— generally referred to in the records as the Chadda expedition. This expedition sparked off a chain of developments which profoundly affected the course of history in the Sahara and the western Sudan.

It is generally recognized that the expedition of 1854 was the direct outcome of the exploration of the Benue by Barth and that it was sent out by the British Government.[1] But it has not hitherto been appreciated that the idea of sending an expedition up the Benue was first mooted by Barth and that the person mainly responsible for its implementation was Chevalier Bunsen. In a private letter to Bunsen, Barth mentioned that he had established the identity of the Chadda and the Benue and suggested that a steam vessel should be sent up that river to examine the commercial potentialities of his discovery. In recommending this suggestion to the Foreign Office, Bunsen pointed out that a good steam vessel could make its way to the Benue in a fortnight and that this, with a month's voyage from England to the Gulf of Guinea, 'would bring in six weeks' navigation, the trade of Great Britain into the heart of Africa, to the central junction of the caravans going to Timbuctu or toward Darfur and the upper Nile'.[2] He added that the expedition might be sent in the summer and could include 'an English Physician and surgeon with zoological knowledge' to take the place of Overweg. The Foreign Office adopted this recommendation and passed it to the Admiralty for implementation. The Admiralty undertook to organize the expedition, but added that 'the melancholy loss of life, which so

---

[1] Burns, op. cit., p. 94; Plumb, op. cit., p. 22; Fage, op. cit., p. 118; A. F. Mockler-Ferryman, *British Nigeria*, p. 48.
[2] F.O. 101/34, Bunsen to Clarendon, 23 Feb. 1853.

fatally arrested the progress of that former enterprise makes it incumbent on them to act with more than common caution in organising a fresh expedition'.[1] The building of a special steam vessel for the expedition was entrusted to Laird, who was also permitted to take advantage of this to trade on the Niger and the Benue. Indeed, with such care was this expedition prepared[2] that it was not until May 1854, a whole year later, that it left England in the *Pleiad*, the steam vessel specially constructed for it.

Captain John Beecroft, the experienced African explorer who was then Consul for the Bights of Benin and Biafra, was selected to command the expedition; but he died before the *Pleiad* reached his own station of Fernando Po, and the command and instructions devolved upon William Baikie, a well-known zoologist and botanist.[3] He was first to explore the Benue or Chadda to the limit of naviga- tion and to meet and afford every assistance to Barth and Vogel. Secondly, he was to take advantage of every opportunity for opening up trade with the people on the banks of the river. For this purpose he was given £100 worth of suitable goods and presents. Thirdly, he was to make careful inquiries 'as to the political power of the several chiefs, as to the state of civilization among them, as to the existence of foreign slave trade, and if so, whether they would consent to put an end to it if lawful trade could be ensured to them and a market opened for ivory and other products of the country'. Finally, objects of natural history were to be collected. To assist Baikie in this collection were Dr. William Bleek, a German ethnologist, and John T. Dalton, zoological assistant.[4] Among the Africans on board the *Pleiad* was a Yoruba priest, the Reverend Samuel Crowther, who was asked by the Church Missionary Society 'to inquire into the apparent disposition, willingness or aptitude of the natives to evangelization'. The duties reveal the same scientific, commercial, and humanitarian aims as those of the 1841 expedition.

Leaving the mouth of the Niger on 8 July 1854, the *Pleiad*

[1] F.O. 101/34, Addington to Admiralty, 15 Apr. 1853; F.O. 101/34, Admiralty to Addington, 30 Apr. 1853.

[2] Among the people consulted by the Admiralty on various aspects of the expedition were Laird, the famous shipbuilder, the Admiral of the African station, the Director-General of the Medical Department, and Sir Roderick Murchison, the President of the Royal Geographical Society. F.O. 2/18, Laird to Admiralty, 7 May 1853; F.O. 2/18, Laird to Clarendon, 25 Jan. 1854.

[3] F.O. 2/18, Admiralty to Hammond, 19 May 1854, encl., Draft instructions for Captain Beecroft.

[4] Dr. Bleek was invalided home from Fernando Po.

anchored at the confluence of the Niger and the Benue on 4 August, two days after Barth had left Say on his return journey from Timbuctu. The *Pleiad* began its ascent of the Chadda on 7 August and went on till 29 September, when the exhaustion of the African labourers—mainly due to the crude instruments used in cutting firewood for the vessel—and the appearance of scurvy among the crew compelled Baikie to call a halt.[1] He himself continued up river in an iron boat for three days before starting the return trip. The *Pleiad* reached the confluence again on 20 October without much difficulty, and arrived at Fernando Po on 7 November and in England in February 1855.

In many respects this expedition did not fulfil the hopes of its sponsors. It failed to reach its main geographical goal, the confluence of the Benue and the Faro, and explored and mapped for the first time only that part of the course of the Benue that lies between Dagbo and Dulti, a distance of about 300 miles. Secondly, although Baikie was a good student of conditions and a prolific writer, and the information about the states and peoples of the Niger–Benue basin which he and two other members of his crew collected and published was copious and interesting,[2] it contained nothing entirely new. Like some of Barth's accounts, it merely confirmed the reports of earlier explorers about the dense population of the Niger and the Benue regions, the friendly disposition of the people, and the possibility of developing legitimate trade and British commerce. Thirdly, as a commercial venture it was a complete failure. Laird, who in spite of Government subsidy still shouldered the main expense of the expedition, lost so heavily that he appealed to the Foreign Office for immediate financial relief and declined to continue his efforts to develop British trade up the river unless he was granted a larger subsidy.[3] Worst of all, the expedition failed to get in touch with Vogel and Barth; Vogel was prevented from meeting Baikie by the revolution in Bornu, and Barth did not hear about the expedition until after its return to Fernando Po.[4] But for two achievements, this

---

[1] F.O. 2/18, Admiralty to Hammond, 9 Feb. 1855, encl., Baikie to Admiralty, 3 Jan. 1855.

[2] W. B. Baikie, *Narrative of an exploring voyage up the Rivers Kurora and Binne* (London, 1856); S. Crowther, *Journal of an Expedition Up the Niger and Tshadda Rivers* (London, 1855); J. T. Hutchinson, *Narrative of the Niger, Tsadda, and Binne Exploration* (London, 1855).

[3] F.O. 101/45, Laird to Clarendon, 8 Feb. 1855; F.O. 2/23, Laird to Clarendon, 18 Mar. 1856.

[4] Barth, op. cit., vol. v, pp. 141–2, 361–2.

expedition, like that of Gray and Dochard, might have been ignored by historians. The first was navigational. The surprising ease with which the *Pleiad*, an iron screw steamer 100 ft. long, of 24 ft. beam, and 260 tons burden, drawing 7 ft. laden and 6 unladen, ascended the Niger for the record distance of about 700 miles in the remarkably short period of eleven weeks proved beyond all reasonable doubt that if the right season, the right type of vessel, and the proper crew were chosen, the Niger could be used as a highway into the interior. In this way the expedition marks a very significant stage in the history of inland steam navigation in West Africa. It signifies the end of the experimental phase and the dawn of the era of practical exploitation of the Niger waterway. Well did Baikie describe the *Pleiad* as 'the *avant-courière* of European energy and influence'.[1]

The second impressive achievement was the preservation of the health of the crew of the *Pleiad* by Baikie and T. J. Hutchinson, the medical officer to the expedition. For the first time in the history of African exploration since 1788, not a single person of the entire crew of twelve Europeans and fifty-four Africans died. This achievement would have been astonishing in any part of Africa. In the Niger region, whose climate was generally believed to be deadly to Europeans, it was, to contemporaries, miraculous. This apparent miracle was achieved by a careful attention to diet, and especially by the use of quinine 'as a prophylactic or preventive'.[2] A dose of five grains was administered every morning to every man. Baikie dispelled all doubts about his achievement and refuted any imputation of it to mere chance by stressing the fact that there was nothing peculiar about the African fever and that it could not only be cured but even prevented. He asserted with authority:

The African fever has nothing specific about it; that it is certainly not *sui generis*, and that it is merely an aggravated form of the disease known in this country as ague. . . . The disease is what is termed by medical men *periodic*, and the remedies required are called *anti-periodics*, of which the best known and the most efficacious is quinine. This may be given as soon as the complaint shows itself, and the sooner the better, as it is the main-stay of the sufferer. . . . But the great modern improvement is the discovery that quinine not only cures, but that it actually prevents, and that by taking this invaluable drug while in unhealthy localities, persons may

---

[1] Baikie, op. cit., pp. 72, 399. For a detailed discussion of earlier navigational problems, see C. C. Ifemesia, *British Enterprise on the Niger*, 1830–1869 (unpublished Ph.D. thesis, London, 1959), pp. 27–145.

[2] Baikie, op. cit., p. 5.

escape totally unscathed. The best form for use for this purpose is *quinine wine*, of which half a glass should be taken early in the morning, and repeated if requisite in the afternoon.[1]

Contrary to the generally accepted view, the use of quinine both as a curative and a prophylactic was known in England long before the Baikie expedition of 1854. Cinchona (or Peruvian) bark, from which quinine was extracted, had been used in Britain ever since the seventeenth century, and as early as 1760 James Lind had recommended its use in wine as a prophylactic. It was not until 1820 that quinine was extracted from cinchona, and by 1830 it was in general use on the west coast of Africa as a substitute for the bark. The Niger expeditions of 1832 and 1841 certainly used quinine. From the high mortality rate of these expeditions, however, it was obvious that the prophylactic use of the medicine was still unknown and it was not until the 1840's that this was discovered by experiment. By the late 1840's the Admiralty and the Medical Department of the Army were instructing their officials to use quinine prophylaxis, and by the early part of 1848 'it had become common practice for Europeans on the Gold Coast to keep a bottle of quinine on the side table'. Some people were, nonetheless, still very sceptical about the new discovery, while others were afraid of its possible harmful effects. Baikie's victory dispelled these doubts and fears once and for all.[2]

One of the most telling arguments used against the Niger route and in favour of the Sahara had been 'the insalubrity of the climate' of the river basin. Richardson, as may be recalled, harped on this theme in 1848. Even as late as January 1853, Captain Smyth, the veteran Barbary Coast explorer, supported Bunsen's suggestion for sending out Vogel via the Sahara because 'the road across the desert is far more eligible for penetrating into Africa than the unwholesome rivers by which so many gallant men have perished'.[3] Laird expressed the current mercantile opinion when he said that 'the Chadda expedition may be considered to mark a new era in African discovery—the deadly climate having been fairly met and conquered by improved

[1] Ibid., pp. 453–4.
[2] This paragraph is based on the work of Professor P. D. Curtin and Dr. C. C. Ifemesia. For a detailed discussion of the question, see P. D. Curtin, ' "The White Man's Grave": Image and Reality, 1780–1850', *Journal of British Studies*, Nov. 1961, pp. 94–110: C. C. Ifemesia, *British Enterprise on the Niger, 1850–1869* (unpublished Ph.D. thesis, London, 1959), pp. 151–216.
[3] F.O. 101/34, Smyth to Bunsen, 28 Jan. 1853; encl. Bunsen to Russell, 29 Jan. 1853.

medical treatment and mechanical organisation the plausible objection to exploring Africa—the risk of life—is answered'.[1]

British penetration into the interior via the Niger having been proved possible, the question now was how it was to be financed. Both Laird and Baikie, like their predecessor Allen, made it quite clear in their long dispatches and memoranda to the Foreign Office that without the Government's financial support no ventures could be undertaken.[2] Laird pleaded that the continuation of activities on the Niger would not only enable the river systems of the central Sudan and the sources of the Nile to be fully explored; it would also facilitate the return home from the Americas and Sierra Leone of liberated Africans, who could serve as commercial agents for British firms and act as 'foci of civilisation' for other Africans. In July 1856 Baikie and his colleagues were joined in their campaign for the development of inland trade by Benjamin Campbell, the British Consul at Lagos. In a long letter to the Foreign Secretary,[3] he pointed out that the Fulani rulers and people took part in slave raids because 'they found no other commerce existing in the Sudan but that in slaves'; and that the small quantity of ivory exported across the Sahara was but a minute portion of the valuable commerce that the interior regions of Africa could yield. He then went on to suggest that the British Government should send an envoy to plead with the Fulani and that British firms should begin operations on the Niger. To the pressure of merchants, abolitionists, and consular agents was added that of the Royal Geographical Society and the British Association for the advancement of Science. In their letter to the Foreign Secretary[4] the British Association referred to the commercial and humanitarian arguments already advanced, and added the scientific ones. Further inland activities, they argued, would 'add vastly to our acquaintance with the Geography and physical and natural history of Africa'. The Association attached so much importance to the question that they followed this letter up with a deputation to the Foreign Office. All these appeals—a clear evidence of how widespread and national the question had once again become—brought home to the Government the great commercial, humanitarian, and scientific gains

[1] F.O. 2/18, Laird to Clarendon, 5 Mar. 1855.

[2] F.O. 101/45, Laird to Clarendon, 8 Feb. 1855; F.O. 2/18, Laird to Clarendon, 5 Mar. 1855; Baikie to Admiralty, 3 Jan. 1855, encl. in Admiralty to Hammond, 9 Feb. 1855; F.O. 2/23, Baikie to Foreign Office, 11 Oct. 1856.

[3] F.O. 84/1002, Campbell to Clarendon, 14 July 1856.

[4] F.O. 2/23, British Association to Clarendon, 29 Oct. 1856.

that could be won. It is not surprising then that a copy of Campbell's letter was sent to the Board of Trade with the Government's promise to 'countenance and support' any firm that wanted to start business on the Niger, and Laird was asked two months later for the terms of the contract which he had earlier proposed.[1] He promptly submitted his terms and in April 1857 the contract was signed. For five years from 1 January 1857 Laird was to keep a steam vessel on the Niger. In return, he was to receive an annual subsidy of £8,000 in 1857, diminishing annually by £500.[2]

The signing of this contract marks the third important turning-point in British penetration into the interior via the Niger. The Chadda expedition solved the navigational and health problems, and this contract surmounted, at least for the following two years, that of finance. With these impediments removed, attempts to develop British trade with the interior could proceed. In May 1857 the *Dayspring*, built by Laird under the terms of the contract, left England for the Niger. The commander was Baikie and his assistant was J. H. Glover, who later became the Governor of Lagos. Baikie was requested to explore the Niger and its tributaries, to develop British trade, 'practically to show the advantage of legitimate trade over the debasing and demoralising traffic in slaves', and to establish friendly relations with the rulers of the interior, especially the Sultan of Sokoto.[3] It is interesting to note that no definite mention of Bornu and Timbuctu was made in these instructions, a clear evidence that attention was now being focused on the Niger–Benue axis.

The *Dayspring* successfully ascended the Niger, passed the confluence, and started for Bussa, but was wrecked on a rock near Jebba. Its place was immediately filled by the *Sunbeam*, which was joined in the following year by the *Rainbow*. The outcome of the expedition, both commercial and diplomatic, was particularly encouraging. Between 1857 and 1859 the agents of Laird established trading stations at Aboh, Onitsha, and Lokoja, and their returns showed continuous increase. The value of produce collected at the stations was £1,800 in 1857, £2,750 in 1858, and £8,000–£9,000 in 1859.[4] Baikie, who was in charge of the diplomatic side, established

---

[1] F.O. 84/1005, Hammond to Board, 19 Sept. 1856; F.O. 2/23 Clarendon to Laird, 12 Nov. 1856.

[2] F.O. 2/23, Admiralty to Hammond, 28 Apr. 1857, and encl., being ten copies of the contract.

[3] F.O. 2/23, Draft instructions to Baikie, 1 May 1857.

[4] Dike, op. cit., p. 171; Flint, op. cit., p. 12.

himself at Lokoja as the unofficial British Consul. He succeeded in establishing very intimate relations with Masaba, the son of Mallam Dendo and the then undisputed Emir of Nupe, and soon became so popular in the area that he was nicknamed the 'King of Lokoja'. He did not leave Lokoja until 1864, and died at Sierra Leone on his homeward journey.[1]

The growing success which attended the operations up the Niger had two interesting effects. On the one hand, as Dike has convincingly shown, it aroused bitter opposition from the delta African traders and middlemen, who naturally objected to being by-passed. They attacked Laird's vessels and sacked his station at Aboh in 1859. It became obvious that a fourth impediment had still to be removed. On the other hand—a factor which incidentally facilitated the removal of this impediment—the British Government could no longer doubt the feasibility of a very lucrative trade via the Niger. 'The objects which Her Majesty's Government had in view in incurring the expense of the former exploring under Dr. Baikie have been attained,' the Foreign Secretary informed the Consul at Lagos in June 1860, '. . . it has been proved that the Niger can, at the proper season, be navigated freely for six months, and for a distance of 500 miles . . . and the natives of the countries visited on the expeditions have moreover shown a desire to engage in legitimate trade.'[2] At the same time the Foreign Secretary mentioned the Government's determination 'to establish and develop permanent commercial intercourse by this route with the interior of Africa'. The Consul at Lagos was asked to tell the delta people that the British Government 'have the means of punishing them for any outrage they may commit on the vessels engaged in peaceful commerce', and in the following year (1861) the *Espoir*, sent out by the Government, destroyed the delta towns which had attacked Laird's steamers in 1859. From that date till 1871, gun-boats were sent on annual punitive patrols up the Niger.[3]

With the removal of the four stumbling blocks, trade with the interior rapidly expanded, although the Government abandoned their policy of granting subsidies in 1866. What threatened to stifle this growing trade was the cut-throat competition that ensued among the five companies which were operating on the Niger by the late

[1] Dike, op. cit., pp. 172–4.
[2] F.O. 2/34, Russell to Brand, 19 June 1860.
[3] Robinson and Gallagher, op. cit., p. 40.

1860's. Through the foresight and energy of Mr. Goldie Taubman (later Sir George Goldie), this dangerous development was halted by the amalgamation of the companies into the United Africa Company in 1879. This company was incorporated as the National Africa Company in 1882 and chartered four years later as the Royal Niger Company. It played as decisive a role in the evolution of Nigeria as the discovery of the Benue and the victory over fever had played in the events leading up to its formation.[1]

In view of the rapid strides that were being made in the development of British trade via the Niger, British activities in the Sahara would have been continued only if they had shown similar progress. In fact there was a deterioration. The 80 per cent. mortality of the supplementary mission across the Sahara under Vogel stood in striking and agonizing contrast to the absolute safety of the contemporary Benue expedition via the Niger. The murder of Henry Warrington and Macguire in the desert revived memories of Laing's fate, while the Benue expedition buried those of the 1841 expedition. The failure of the Central African Mission to persuade the Awlad Sulayman to abandon their plundering propensities left the Bornu route as insecure as ever. Clearly, the boot was now on the other leg.

Moreover, such little trade as had been developed in and across the Sahara by the Vice-Consuls began to decline from 1854, when Gagliuffi left Murzuk owing to ill-health and Dickson quitted Ghadames for the Crimea. This decline was accelerated by developments farther south. Even if the routes across the Sahara had been secure, with the increasing penetration of European goods into Nupe and Hausaland most of the hitherto north-bound caravans from these areas began naturally to turn south. W. H. Wylde, the Head of the Slave Trade Department in the Foreign Office, drew the attention of the British Government to this in a long minute which he wrote in December 1861 on a letter from Barth. In this letter Barth asked for help for the German traveller Von Beurmann, who was going to Waday to look for Vogel and to open the Benghazi–Waday route to European trade.

Wylde minuted:

But I should doubt whether Mr. Von Beurmann will be enabled to re-open the caravan route to Waday or whether it would be expedient to do so. . . . The prohibition of the traffic in slaves by the Turkish Government, and

[1] See a stimulating study of this subject by J. E. Flint, *Sir George Goldie and the Making of Nigeria* (London, 1960).

our own influence being also brought to bear upon the traffic by destroying the market for slaves has almost entirely put a stop to the caravan trade by the old routes. . . . The result has been that Central Africa is now supplied chiefly from the *West* Coast of Africa, large caravans travelling now from Kano and Bornou to the regions recently visited by Lieutnant Glover and Dr. Baikie, from whence they obtain their European goods and supply their wants at a cheaper rate.[1]

Though Wylde's view that the caravan trade along the old routes had almost entirely stopped was inaccurate—the campaign against the slave trade did not affect the traffic along the Timbuctu–Morocco and Waday–Benghazi routes—yet this minute was well received. Russell's comment was simply 'I agree'. Wylde's statement, then, could be taken as the signal for the British Government's abandonment of their efforts to develop commerce and legitimate trade in the Sahara and to use it as a bridge into the western Sudan. The conquest of fever and the use of steam vessels made the Sahara and the camel blatant anachronisms.

Another reason for the eventual withdrawal of the British from the Sahara, a process signified by the abolition of their two vice-consular posts in 1860 and 1861, was the second French drive into the interior and the changed attitude of the British Government to it. On his accession to power in 1848, Napoleon III initiated a policy of militant colonial expansion in Africa aimed at uniting the French colony of Algeria in the north with that of Senegal in the west. Louis Faideherbe, the Governor of Senegal from 1854 to 1865, and Marshal Randon, the Governor-General of Algeria from 1851 to 1859, began the practical implementation of the emperor's schemes. Faideherbe pushed along the River Senegal and re-established the French forts at Bakel in Galam and Medina in Khasso. Crossing the Senegal, he occupied Dakar on the coast in 1857 and conquered the two neighbouring kingdoms of Futa and Cayor. In the sixties he sent out secret missions as far as Segu to survey the country.[2] Even more spectacular was the work of Randon in Algeria. The first drive into the interior, as may be recalled, was brought to a premature halt by the opposition of Abd al-Qadir.[3] In 1848, however, he was

---

[1] F.O. 84/1157, Barth to Laynard, 27 Dec. 1861, and minute by Wylde. Von Beurmann proceeded to Waday but was either killed or died there of illness in 1863.

[2] A. Bernard and M. Lacroix, *La pénètration Saharienne, 1830–1906*, Alger (1906), p. 55.

[3] See above, pp. 165–6.

decisively defeated by Marshal Bugeaud. This victory paved the way for the brilliant career of Randon. In 1852, a year after his arrival, Laghouat was effectively occupied. From there the French pushed south-eastward to the oasis of Wargla, which they conquered in 1853, and to Tuggurt in the district of Souf, which was occupied in 1854.[1] (See Map 4.) The occupation of these places brought the French to the edge of the desert, the home of the Tuareg.

Like Faideherbe, Randon was not a mere conqueror. He also set himself the task of developing the resources of the country, restoring Algeria's ancient commercial relations with the Sahara and the western Sudan, and diverting into the colony such caravan traffic as still trickled northward. To accomplish the first, he began the sinking of artesian wells in the southern regions of Algeria in 1856. This, even the British consuls admitted, proved a great success and gave a remarkable impetus to agriculture.[2] To divert the trans-Saharan traffic into Algeria he abrogated the ordinance of December 1843 which prevented the importation of products from the western Sudan and the Sahara into Algeria; he also remitted all duties on imports for twenty-five years in order to outbid the Turks, who were still charging import duties of 20–25 per cent. in Tripoli.[3] Furthermore, throughout the fifties and the early sixties, Randon and his successors sent out missions to the Sahara to establish friendly relations with the Tuareg of Tuat and Ghat, who held the key to the caravan trade. The most noteworthy of these missions was led by Sayyid Hamza, the Sheikh of the powerful Arab tribe of the Awlad Sayyadi al-Shaykh, and Henri Duveyrier, the famous French explorer. In 1854 Sayyid Hamza was sent to Ghat, where he was able to persuade the Azger Tuareg to grant the French the right to send caravans across their country without charging them any tribute and to guarantee their security. Under this agreement Randon sent out a caravan in 1856 which traded in Ghat with very encouraging results.[4]

With security between the south-eastern districts of Algeria and Ghat guaranteed, and with guides and guards provided by the Govern-

---

[1] F.O. 27/945, Bell to Malmesbury, 14 Dec. 1852; F.O. 27/1034, Bell to Clarendon, 12 Dec. 1854; F.O. 84/1054, Elmore to Hammond, 21 May 1858.

[2] F.O. 101/41, Herman to Clarendon, 24 May 1857; F.O. 84/1054, Elmore to Hammond, 21 May 1858.

[3] F.O. 101/41, Herman to Clarendon, 24 May 1857.

[4] F.O. 84/1054, Bell to Malmesbury, 29 Apr. 1858; F.O. 84/1054, Elmore to Malmesbury, 2 May 1858; Bernard and Lacroix, op. cit., pp. 35–42; P. Turnbull, *Sahara Unveiled* (London, 1940), pp. 97–98.

ment, the French soon succeeded in diverting such caravan traffic as there was on the Sudan and Fezzan routes into Algeria. In a very long memorandum in March 1858,[1] Herman drew the attention of the British Government to this development. He pointed out that the immediate effect of the laudable efforts of the Porte to suppress the slave trade and of the policy of the French had been 'the diversion of the trade from those channels which Herodotus first revealed to us, and through which it has continued to flow upwards of two thousand years into a new and exclusive direction'. He stated that the great caravans from Bornu and other parts of the Sudan which formerly found their way via Murzuk and Ghadames to Tripoli and Tunis and from Murzuk and Aujila to Benghazi and upper Egypt 'now move concentrically upon Ghat', which had 'suddenly become the entrepôt of the commerce of the interior ... between that place and the Algerian southern front a most extensive trade is at present in full operation'. This was confirmed by later reports from the Vice-Consul at Murzuk.[2] The fact that two-thirds of the traffic was in slaves did not affect the development. For though the French formally abolished the slave trade in their colonies in 1848, Africans were still allowed to enter Algeria under the spurious scheme of 'emigration' which was being enforced simultaneously in East Africa, Senegal, and the West Indies in spite of strong protests from the British Government.[3] According to Herman, they were either settled in the sparsely populated southern provinces or formed into large Negro or 'Tusco' contingents used in defensive and aggressive campaigns.[4] It was to strengthen the commercial links with the Tuareg that Henri Duveyrier was dispatched on a combined exploratory and diplomatic mission to Ghat in 1860.[5] So optimistic were the reports

[1] F.O. 84/1062, Memorandum on the new direction of the slave trade, Herman to Clarendon, 10 Mar. 1858.

[2] F.O. 84/1062, Fremaux to Herman, 26 June 1858, encl. in Herman to Malmesbury, 20 July 1858; F.O. 84/1062, Fremaux to Reade, 7 Aug. 1858, encl. in Reade to Malmesbury, 29 Sept. 1858.

[3] F.O. 84/1059, Malmesbury to Cowley (British Ambassador in Paris), 8 Jan., 5 Apr., 25 July, and 1 Aug. 1859.

[4] F.O. 84/1062, Herman to Clarendon, 10 Mar. 1858; F.O. 101/48, Herman to Russell, 28 Feb. 1861.

[5] Duveyrier left Biskra in April 1860 and passed through Ghadames to Ghat. After staying in Ghat for some time to discharge his duties he returned to Algiers via Murzuk and Tripoli in 1861. His expedition, an account of which he published in 1864, was the only really successful French expedition since that of Caillié. For further details, see Duveyrier, *Exploration du Sahara* (Paris, 1864), P. Villot, *L'exploration du Sahara* (Paris, 1895), pp.65–70; Bernard and Lacroix, op.cit., pp.46–48.

of the friendly disposition of the Tuareg brought back by Duveyrier in 1861 that in the following year Commander Mircher was sent out to conclude a formal treaty of commerce and friendship with them. The treaty was signed at a meeting held in Ghadames between Mircher and some of the Tuareg sheikhs in November 1862. Under its terms the Tuareg undertook to protect and facilitate the passage of any caravans sent by the French into the western Sudan and to assist the French in their endeavours to revive the caravan trade.[1]

Napoleon III himself watched these developments with keen interest, as is evident from his three weeks' official visit to Algeria in September 1860.[2] The reaction of the people in the desert and beyond was, of course, the very reverse of that of the Emperor. Barth was in Timbuctu when news of the capture of Wargla by the French arrived and he noted the universal commotion that ensued. He even attributed the difficulties he encountered there partly to the widespread belief that his journey had 'some connection with the expedition of the French'.[3] Among those in Timbuctu most disturbed by the French expansion was Al-Baka'i. In his letter which Barth delivered to the Foreign Secretary, the Sheikh appealed to the British Government to prevent their land, which according to him stretched 'from Ghadames as far as Tuat as far as Sudan as far as Timbuctu', from falling into the hands of the French.[4] Al-Baka'i followed this up with a mission to England led by his own nephew, Sayyid Muhammad ibn Khattar, an intimate friend of Barth, and his cousin and son-in-law, Sayyid Ahmad al-Baka'i. There were three other members, all of whom were described by the Consul-General of Tripoli as people who could read and write classical Arabic.[5] The mission arrived in Tripoli in June 1857.

What was the attitude of the British Government to these developments? This was first clearly revealed by the reaction of the Government to the news of the arrival of Al-Baka'i's envoys at Tripoli. In the Consul-General's letter of June 1857 informing the Foreign Office of the arrival of the mission and asking whether it should be

---

[1] F.O. 27/2455, Bell to Hammond, 9 Oct. 1863. For a full text of the treaty, see Vuillot, op. cit., pp. 83–84.

[2] F.O. 27/1358, Bell to Russell, 7 Sept. 1860.

[3] Barth, op. cit., vol. v, pp. 114–18.

[4] F.O. 101/45, Al-Baka'i to Her Majesty's Govt., encl. in Barth to Clarendon 18 Sept. 1855.

[5] F.O. 101/41, Herman to Clarendon, 7 July 1857.

allowed to proceed to England, he did not mention its real objects.[1] As Clarendon himself had only the previous year invited the Sheikh to send a messenger to England, preferably one of his 'own house and family, in order that he may take back such report as may contribute to the increase of mutual friendship',[2] his reaction to this request was as prompt as it was favourable. Not only did he instruct Herman to allow the mission to proceed to England if the leaders expressed a strong desire to do so; he also asked him to give the Sheikh's nephew 'the most friendly assurances on the part of the Queen and of Her Majesty's Government' and to acquaint him with the lively interest which they took in the welfare of the Sheikh and their desire to extend commercial relations.[3] Barth was also consulted about the best way in which the party could be entertained. He, of course, enthusiastically welcomed the news, emphasized the beneficial effects which intimate relations with the Sheikh's family might have on 'the influence of England along the whole course of the River [Niger]', and later even offered to arrange for accommodation for members of the party.[4]

In Herman's second letter, a month later, however, he reported that the object of the mission, which he had discovered only after his first dispatch, had reference to the French designs on Tuat and Timbuctu. He then went on:

That there are grounds for the apprehensions of the Sheik is not to be denied. Considerations of the soundest military and commercial policy appear to impose upon the French the occupation of Tuat and at no remote period. Thus to maintain her position on the Tell, she was strategically compelled to push her frontier to the northern edge of the Sahara. This line already extends from Wady Souf to Wargla; to round off her frontier, the prolongation of this line westward to In Salah in Tuat will be but the simple corollary of the military question. Once in the possession of France, this district would become a vast commercial entrepôt through which will flow into Algeria all the trade of the Sahara, and the basins of the Upper Niger and the Lake Tshad. Nor when the opportune moment for occupation shall have arrived do I see how it is to be prevented, for the bare idea of succour from without is an absolute chimera.[5]

[1] F.O. 101/41, Herman to Clarendon, 8 June 1857.
[2] F.O. 101/40, Clarendon to Al-Baka'i, 15 Apr. 1856. It was in this letter that Clarendon informed the Sheikh of the presents being sent to him in recognition of his hospitality and assistance to Barth and 'as proof of our friendship'.
[3] F.O. 101/41, Clarendon to Herman, 26 June 1857.
[4] F.O. 101/42, Barth to F.O., 24 June 1857; F.O. 101/42, Barth to Hammond, 25 July 1857.
[5] F.O. 101/41, Herman to Hammond, 26 July 1857.

He also expressed his suspicion that 'something must have passed on this subject between the Sheikh and Dr. Barth'. In view of the efforts that were being made by the vice-consuls to develop British trade in and across the Sahara, one would have expected that this letter would cause alarm in Government circles and set protests snowballing, or that definite measures would be concerted to thwart French designs. The letter did indeed cause a fluttering in the Foreign Office, as is evident from the minutes it elicited,[1] though for reasons entirely contrary to all expectations. 'Will you see Dr. Barth?' Clarendon minuted in an obvious state of perturbation, 'and ask him what has passed and whether he has given any encouragement ... the notion that *we can interfere with the French Government would be quite out of the question. . . . We must escape from it if we can do so decently.*'[2] Hammond, the Under-Secretary, hurriedly had an interview with Barth. But this only confirmed the suspicion of the Foreign Office and intensified their alarm. 'I have seen Dr. Barth,' Hammond minuted, 'I cannot but fear that he may have given the Sheikh of Timbuctu more reason to expect the support of Great Britain against French encroachment than he admits to have done.' Conscious of the political objects of the mission and in particular of Palmerston's opposition to French expansion into the Sahara, and, as he confessed on his return to England in 1855, then 'not fully aware of the intimate alliance which had been entered into between the French and the English',[3] Barth must have given the Sheikh such an assurance. In actual fact he did promise the Sheikh that an English consul would be sent to Tuat if he could guarantee that the official would be respected. Furthermore, he appended his signature to the Sheikh's letter to the French forbidding them from penetrating any farther into the Sahara except as single explorers.[4]

In these circumstances the only way out of the dilemma was for the Foreign Office to stop the mission from proceeding from Tripoli to England. The most easy and 'decent' way of discouraging any African from coming to Britain is, of course, to impress upon him the coldness of the English climate. Herman was therefore asked to

[1] Minutes by Clarendon and Hammond on Herman to Hammond, 26 July 1857 (F.O. 101/41).
[2] The author's italics.
[3] Barth, op. cit., vol. v, p. 124.
[4] Barth, op. cit., vol. v, p. 125. Barth said that he signed the letter under pressure, but it seems that this was only an excuse to placate the dignitaries of the Foreign Office.

expound to the leaders the lateness of the season, which 'will expose them to serious and painful inconvenience on their arrival in England'.[1] Providence also interceded on behalf of the British Government. On the very day that Lord Clarendon signed the dispatch instructing Herman to find an excuse to stop the mission, Herman also completed one informing him that Ibn al-Khattar and all his people had been attacked by a skin disease which would be aggravated in a colder climate. This dispatch was of course received with a heavy sigh of relief by the Foreign Office. Herman was instructed again by return of post to emphasize the probable effect on their health of the 'severe northern climate which we have to encounter in this country in the late autumn and winter'. To make the escape even more 'decent', Herman was further asked to inform Ibn al-Khattar that the Government would be glad to see him in the ensuing spring, when the weather would be more congenial to him.[2] Needless to say, the mission was given up, and al-Khattar and his suite began their homeward journey on 30 October 1857.

Encouraged by the promise of the British Government to entertain another envoy at a more suitable time, and greatly disturbed by news of the progress of the mission under Commander Colonieu and Lieutenant Burin dispatched by the French Government to Tuat in 1860, Al-Baka'i again sent a courier to Tripoli in October 1860 with letters to the Queen of England, Lord Clarendon, Barth, Herman, and the Emperor of the French.[3] In his letter to the 'Sultana of England', the Sheikh entreated Her Majesty to ask the French not to enter Tuat. 'I consider Tuat as my own and myself as your devoted servant. Take measures therefore,' he pleaded, 'before the advent of winter, as the French have already left for the eastward.' In his letter to Clarendon, the Sheikh asked him to obtain a favourable answer from the *Sultana* and informed him of his intention to send another mission to England. In forwarding these letters, Herman asked for instructions about the impending mission. Though Clarendon had been replaced as Foreign Secretary by Russell, his policy was maintained. Herman was in fact asked to dissuade the Sheikh from carrying out his intention by using 'the same arguments' about the inconvenience of the climate which he was instructed to use in 1857.

---

[1] F.O. 101/41, Clarendon to Herman, 15 Aug. 1857.
[2] F.O. 101/41, Herman to Clarendon, 15 Aug. 1857; Clarendon to Herman, 10 Sept. 1857.
[3] F.O. 84/11/44, Herman to Russell, 4 Oct. 1861, and encls.

Moreover, he was to inform the Sheikh that though he could send an envoy to England 'after next April', the cost of his passage as well as his maintenance there must be borne by himself and not by the British Government as promised in 1857.[1] The latter condition was added obviously with the aim of severing all connexion with the Sheikh, and this was achieved.

That Al-Baka'i's religious power and influence was recognized all the way from Timbuctu to Tuat by most of the Tuareg and Arab tribes of the western Sahara was admitted even by Duveyrier. From the information which he gathered during his travels and from his visit to Tuat, the French explorer also confirmed that it was the people of Tuat and Hoggar themselves who appealed to the Sheikh to use his influence in London and Constantinople on their behalf.[2] The Sheikh, then, was not an impostor, and if Britain had accepted his appeals and granted him protection, if through him she had negotiated treaties of amity and protection with the Tuareg and Arab tribes of the western Sahara, and if she had established consular agents in Tuat, Azawad, Timbuctu, Kano, and Kukawa, the tides of French expansion could have been stemmed. But by staving off the envoys of Al-Baka'i and refusing to make representations on his behalf, the British lost their advantage in the Sahara and made French expansion there simply a question of time. Moreover, it is quite clear from the consternation caused by Herman's letter, from the subterfuges resorted to, and from Clarendon's refusal even to approach the French Government on the Sheikh's behalf, that the British attitude to French expansion into the interior had undergone a revolutionary change by the late fifties. Whereas in the forties the Foreign Office under Palmerston shuddered at the thought of French expansion, the same Office under Clarendon and Russell gave the movement their blessing and refused to raise a finger to prevent it.

This fundamental change in the British attitude was the outcome of political exigencies in Europe and of the general spirit of mid-Victorian imperial policy. Had news of the correspondence between the Sheikh and the Foreign Office reached Paris, it would undoubtedly have alienated Napoleon III and weakened the recently re-created Anglo-French *entente*. However, since the terms of the Treaty of Paris concluded at the end of the Crimean War and the pressure of Italian affairs, which were mounting to a crisis, necessi-

---

[1] F.O. 101/48, F.O. to Herman, 14 Nov. 1861.
[2] H. Duveyrier, *Les Toureg du Nord* (1864), pp. 292–3, 310–11.

tated close Anglo-French collaboration, the Foreign Office could risk alienating the Emperor only when vital British interests were at stake.[1] And by the late fifties the Sahara had ceased to be of any commercial or strategic interest to Britain. Indeed, to keep France out of Morocco and Tunis and thereby prevent her from turning the Mediterranean into a French lake—one of the traditional canons of British foreign policy—and at the same time to preserve the *entente* it was definitely in rather than against Britain's interest to allow the French a free hand in the Sahara and other parts of Africa where Britain had no political or economic stake. This policy, as Schwitzer has shown, continued from the fifties to the seventies, when Britain regarded French penetration into Senegal and the upper reaches of the Niger 'with tolerance and sometimes with encouragement' while she persistently excluded them from the Gold Coast and the Bights of Benin and Biafra.[2]

Furthermore, had the Sheikh's request been granted, it would have meant a direct involvement of Britain in the affairs of the Sahara and the western Sudan. And, as Gallagher and Robinson have shown, British policy in the late as in the mid-Victorian period 'preferred informal means of extending imperial supremacy rather than direct rule'.[3] Admittedly, direct intervention would have been resorted to—as it was in Lagos in the 1850's and 1860's—if it had been deemed absolutely necessary. But Britain's very limited interests did not necessitate the abandonment of the preferred policy.

It was obvious that Britain would soon withdraw from the Sahara. The first step in that direction was taken in January 1860, when the Foreign Office sent out a circular letter to the consuls in Barbary asking them to report on 'the necessity of keeping up the various vice-consular posts'.[4] In his reply, Herman, the Consul-General in Tripoli, recommended the closing down of the Ghadames post since the only British interests there were 'the very limited commercial operations of the vice-consul himself'. Significantly enough, Lord

[1] J. P. Schwitzer, 'British attitude to French colonisation, 1875–1887' (unpublished London Ph.D. thesis, 1954), pp. 16–26; *Cambridge History of British Foreign Policy* (1923), pp. 391, 401, 447–51; E. Ashley, *Life of Viscount Palmerston* (1877), vol. ii, pp. 125–6, 166–7.

[2] Schwitzer, op. cit., pp. 224–5.

[3] J. Gallagher and R. Robinson, 'The Imperialism of Free Trade', *Economic History Review*, vol. 6, 1953–4; *Africa and the Victorians* (1961), pp. 1–11.

[4] F.O. 27/1358, F.O. to Bell, 7 Jan. 1860; F.O. 101/47, F.O. to Herman, 7 Jan. 1860; F.O. 101/47, Herman to Russell, 7 Mar. 1860.

Wodehouse, Under-Secretary of State, minuted that the post should be abolished when 'a vacancy occurs', and Russell, the Foreign Secretary, readily concurred. When therefore a vacancy occurred in Greece in December 1860, Freeman, the then Vice-Consul at Ghadames, was transferred to that post, and Russell informed Herman that he had 'taken advantage of this arrangement to abolish the agency at Ghadames'.[1]

As to Murzuk, though Herman pointed out that British commercial interests there, as at Ghadames, were confined to those of the Vice-Consul, and that the great trade formerly carried on with the Sudan had almost ceased 'since the prohibition of the trade in slaves', he nevertheless doubted the expediency of abolishing the vice-consulate because of the trade in slaves that was still going on in Ghat and Tuat. He contended that:

From the advanced position in the interior of Murzouk, it is from that point that the direction and extent of the illicit traffic in Negroes can be best determined. Once relieved from the active surveillance of a British vice-consul, the local authorities themselves would seize the initiative and impart a development to the contraband trade. Whether the advent of such a contingency may be considered to furnish an adequate reason for retaining a vice-consul at Murzouk, is a point that Your Lordship's superior judgement will best decide. I will only take the liberty of observing that should it be withdrawn, it is extremely probable that France would establish there a consular agent.[2]

Again Wodehouse accepted Herman's view and therefore recommended that the post should be retained. Russell, on the other hand, felt so unconvinced that he asked for Wylde's opinion. Although Wylde had already written off the Sahara as an area for the development of British commerce and legitimate trade, he nevertheless strongly supported Herman and Wodehouse. He argued that 'it is only by strict supervision that we have any chance of keeping the Turkish authorities up to the mark as regards the suppression of the slave trade', and that if the vigilance of the British agents was relaxed, the Turks were 'too wedded to their old associations to be at once weaned from a traffic which is both profitable and in accordance with the tenets of their religion'. On the question of French expansion inland, Wylde pointed out that since the French had

[1] F.O. 101/47, Minutes by Wodehouse and Russell on Herman to Russell, 7 Mar. 1860; F.O. to Herman, 15 Dec. 1860.
[2] F.O. 101/47, Herman to Russell, 7 Mar. 1860.

succeeded in diverting a considerable portion of the trade in slaves into Algeria, it might 'be worthwhile politically to keep an agent for the present at Mourzouk until we see the ultimate effects of the stoppage of the slave trade at Mourzouk'.[1] Russell endorsed this minute. It is evident that the reason for the retention of the Murzuk vice-consular post was not the fear that France would move in, but rather Britain's old interest in the abolition of the trans-Saharan slave trade.

For that reason if for no other, the post would not have been closed down when it was but for the ill-health and consequent retirement of Fremaux, who had been acting for Gagliuffi for the last five years, and the refusal of Gagliuffi to return to his post because of old age (he was then sixty-five).[2] It is interesting to note that even then Russell did not immediately order the liquidation of the post, but instead wrote to Herman to find out whether it should be filled, and if so whether he would recommend 'a British subject' for it.[3] It was in reply to this that Herman passed a death-sentence on the Murzuk vice-consulate. He first of all referred to his memorandum of March 1858.[4] He then drew attention to the fact that the system of emigration was still in full force in Algeria and could not be stopped from Murzuk or Tripoli, that large Negro or 'Tusco' contingents had been formed which had recently supplied escorts for a large caravan from Geryville to In Salah in Tuat 'en route for Timbuctoo' and another from Souf in the direction of Ghat, and finally that their superior organization enabled these caravans to march in almost any direction, so that they would speedily attract to the Algerian frontier all the commerce of the interior. 'It is under these circumstances,' he concluded, 'that I venture to question the necessity of appointing a successor to Mr. Gagliuffi.' He added that if the Government wanted information about events in the Sahara, it could be easily obtained 'through native agencies'. If therefore he could be authorized to spend a small sum of money annually for that purpose, 'the vice-consulate at Mourzouk, as we have no longer a scientific mission in the interior may without detriment to the public service be abolished'.[5] Russell, who had never been particularly

[1] Minutes by Russell and Wylde on Herman to Russell, 7 Mar. 1860.
[2] F.O. 101/47, Herman to Russell, 3 Sept. 1860, and encl., Gagliuffi to Herman, 1 Sept. 1860.
[3] F.O. 101/48, Russell to Herman, 30 Jan. 1861.
[4] See pp. 223–4.
[5] F.O. 101/48, Herman to Russell, 28 Feb. 1861.

enthusiastic about the Saharan posts, readily accepted Herman's verdict. In his reply in May 1861, he therefore asked Herman to establish a native agent at Murzuk at the ridiculous cost of £30 to £40 per year—this was never done—and ordered the immediate closing down of the post.[1]

With the withdrawal of the British, the major impediment to ultimate French control of the Sahara and Timbuctu was removed. It is significant that the meeting between Commander Mircher and the Tuareg sheikhs of Ghat took place at Ghadames only two years after the British had pulled out of that town. The tides of French expansion were stemmed in the later sixties. This, however, was caused not so much by events in Africa as by those in Europe. The increasing bankruptcy of Napoleon III's government in the late sixties, followed by the Franco-Prussian War of 1870-1, buried all colonial and imperial dreams—but only for a brief moment. For after their incredibly rapid revival in the following decade the French recommenced their drive into the interior from Senegal and Algeria. This continued, with checks and reverses, till the nineties, when the two tides met at Timbuctu and swept across the northern boundaries of the Sokoto Empire, inundating both Bornu and Waday before the end of the first decade of the present century.

The closing down of the Murzuk vice-consulate was also a tacit admission by the Foreign Office of their inability to abolish the slave traffic in the Sahara. But considering the immense expanse of the area, which greatly facilitated the illicit trade even in Tripoli, only a total abolition of slavery in the Ottoman Empire and Barbary could have made the attempt successful. And given the reluctance of the British Government to enforce this, the fight in the Sahara was bound to be lost.

The extinction of the last vice-consulate provides a dramatic conclusion not only to British activities in the Sahara but also to this study. It marks the end of a series of events that were first touched off by the formation of the African Association in 1788, events which reached their climax in the famous Central African Mission. It has not been generally known that the first serious attempts to tap the reputed riches of Timbuctu, Hausaland, and Bornu were made from Tripoli, thanks to Colonel Warrington, the brilliant British Consul-General from 1814 to 1846. The records of the two vice-consular posts at Murzuk from 1843–61 and Ghadames from 1850–

[1] F.O. 101/48, Russell to Herman, 18 May 1861.

60 provide clear evidence of the scope of British interests and activities in the Sahara. Though the vice-consuls failed to promote British commerce, develop legitimate trade, or abolish the trans-Saharan slave trade, they succeeded in reviving and extending British influence; and it was further enhanced by the work of Richardson, and especially by that of Barth. Throughout the forties and fifties the British name was well-known in the Sahara and the western Sudan; British credit stood so high in Bornu, Hausaland, and the Sahara that loans could easily be raised by the explorers; and British power was so well known and trusted that some of the African rulers repeatedly attempted to strengthen their relations with the *Sultana*. Indeed, had Britain decided to remain in the Sahara and keep out the French, she could most probably have done so by close collaboration with the Sheikh of Timbuctu and the Tuareg of the western Sahara, the Sultan of Sokoto, and the Sheikh of Bornu. But the discovery of the prophylactic use of quinine made the Niger rather than the Sahara the obvious route to the Sudan. The failure of attempts to develop British commerce, the fear of alienating the French, and the ineffectiveness of the Murzuk vice-consulate in the crusade against the Saharan slave trade—all these factors brought about the withdrawal of the British from the Sahara and the region of Timbuctu, and the concentration of their efforts on the Niger–Benue axis. This withdrawal paved the way for the birth of what came to be known as the French Sahara and French West and Equatorial Africa on the one hand, and of British Nigeria on the other.

APPENDIX I

Arabic Names Assumed by the Explorers

Hornemann	Yūsuf ibn 'Abdallah
Denham	(Al-) Ra'īs Khalīl
Clapperton	'Abdallāh
Laing	Al-Ra'īs
Richardson	Ya'qūb
Barth	'Abd Al-Karim
Vogel	'Abd Al-Wahhād

APPENDIX II

The Consular Agents in Tripoli and the Sahara

Tripoli; Consuls-General

R. Tully	1780–1804
W. W. Langford	1805–13
H. Warrington	1814–46
F. H. Crowe	1846–52
G. F. Herman	1853–65
R. Hay	1865–71

Murzuk; Vice-Consuls

G. B. Gagliuffi	1843–54
Frederick Warrington	1854–5
Gaetano de Fremaux	1855–60

Ghadames; Vice-Consuls

C. Dickson	1849–54
H. S. Freeman	1858–60

Treaty Between H.M. the Queen of England and the Sovereign of the Kingdom of Bornoo and its Dependencies

(1) English subjects are permitted to enter the capital of Bornoo and any part of the kingdom to travel or establish themselves therein and English residents shall be treated by the inhabitants of the country as friends, their person and properties shall be respected; and in case they wish to depart, no impediment shall be offered, either as regard their persons or their property.

(2) British subjects may always trade freely without hinderance by the people of Bornoo, in all kinds of merchandise of lawful commerce, which they may desire to sell or buy in every part of the country. The sovereign of Bornoo himself to grant to English subjects all the commercial privileges which may be enjoyed by the subjects of any other Christian nation.

(3) The communication between the country of Bornoo and other places shall be safe, so that English merchants may without obstacle import their merchandise of whatever kind and bring them for sale in Bornoo or elsewhere; and it shall be equally free for them to export from Bornoo such merchandise as they wish to sell in other places. Merchants of other countries shall not be prevented from bringing their merchandise of lawful commerce to Bornoo and its Dependencies, or from passing through to Soudan or elsewhere, when their purpose is to trade with English subjects.

(4) The Queen of England may appoint an agent to reside in the Capital of Bornoo and of its Dependencies, to protect the interests of British subjects, and to see that the present treaty is fulfilled. The said agent shall be respected and protected throughout Bornoo and its Dependencies. The sovereign will attend to his representations, will treat him with respect, and guarantee his person and goods.

(5) The Soveriegn of Bornoo El Amir Amor El Kanemi promises to do all he can to facilitate the passage of couriers carrying dispatches of the English national within his territories and to provide for their security.

(6) The sovereign of the Kingdom of Bornoo will put in execution the present treaty; will make it public, and cause it to be observed, and it shall not be violated from the day for ever.

(The treaty was signed by Barth and Vogel on behalf of the British Government and the Sheikh and Vizir of Bornou on 3 September 1852.)

Political Conditions in the Western Sudan in the First Half of the Nineteenth Century

BARTH'S accounts throw a good deal of light on the political conditions in the kingdoms and empires of the western Sudan by the middle of the nineteenth century and on the changes that had taken place since the visit of the earlier explorers. In the basin of the Chad, it was clear from the reports of Lucas, Park, and Hornemann, based mainly on information supplied by Arab and Tuareg traders, that Bornu and Bagirmi were the dominant states.[1] By the time of the visit of Denham and Clapperton, Waday had joined these states and the three of them were engaged in a bitter struggle for the mastery of the basin. Bagirmi was then courageously challenging Bornu, and in December 1823 even invaded her.[2] When Barth visited the basin, the three states were still predominant though a significant shift had occurred in the balance of power. Bagirmi's offensive of December 1823 would appear to have been her last determined effort in the protracted struggle for the control of the Chad basin. For in a later engagement, of which Denham and Hillman were eye-witnesses, the Bagirmi army was decisively defeated and nearly annihilated. Bagirmi never recovered from this defeat, for Barth discovered that she was paying tribute to both Bornu and Waday. 'Ruined by a most disastrous civil war and trodden down by its neighbours,' Barth reported, 'the country of Bagirmi seems to linger till it is destined either to rise again or to fall a prey to the first invader.'[3] Bagirmi did not in fact rise again but lingered on till, like Waday and Bornu, she fell a prey to Rabeh, the adventurous Arab warrior, formerly of the Khalifa's army, in 1892-3. Until the conquests of Rabeh altered conditions in the Chad basin in the 1890's, Waday and Bornu remained the main powers.

It was, however, in the area west of Bornu that political conditions underwent a fundamental and revolutionary change in the nineteenth century. By the beginning of the century, as is evident from the reports of Lucas,

[1] Proceedings, op. cit., vol. i, pp. 74-196; Park, Travels, op. cit., p. 214; Hornemann, Journal of Travels, op. cit., pp. 110-15; D.T.C. 11/265-74, Hornemann to Banks, 19 Aug. 1799.

[2] Denham, op. cit., pp. 214-15, 240-1, 244.

[3] Barth, vol. iii, pp. 369-70.

Park, and Hornemann as well as the research of Barth, Hausaland was divided into about fourteen separate and independent states. Hornemann sent home a rough map sketched for him by a *marabout* on which Kebbi, Nupe, Noro(?), Daura, Kano, Katsina, Gobir, Zamfara, and Solan(?) were shown (see Map 5). Of these states Katsina was certainly the most powerful, the most prosperous, and the best known in the Sahara and the Barbary states.[1] But when Clapperton visited Hausaland, he found that in place of the Hausa states was a single Fulani Empire stretching from the Niger in the west to the borders of Bornu in the east and to Adamawa on the Benue in the south-east. The Empire was at that time divided into two: the area from the Niger to Katsina, including Nupe and Ilorin in the south,

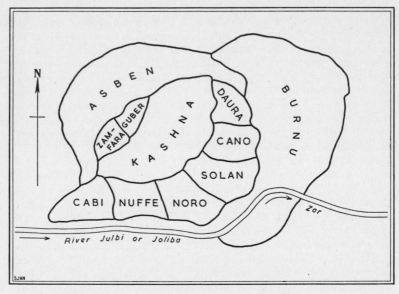

Map 5.   The Muslim Priest's sketch map of the interior

was under the Emir of Gwandu, and the area from Katsina to the western border of Bornu was under the Sultan of Sokoto.[2] Clapperton also found that Kano and not Katsina was the main commercial emporium of Hausaland. As he and Denham gathered from people who had actually taken part in the wars, the phenomenal change was the outcome of a predominantly Fulani rebellion led by Usman dan Fodio, the great Fulani scholar and ascetic, against the Hausa rulers.

The Fulani had been infiltrating into Hausaland and Bornu from the Senegal and the Futa Jallon regions since the thirteenth century. Some of

[1] Hornemann, p. 111.
[2] Denham and Clapperton (Clapperton's journal), pp. 1–80; Clapperton, *Journal of a Second Expedition*, pp. 107–68, 205–7.

them, the *Bororoje* (Cattle Fulani) were wandering about in the rural areas; while others, the *Fulani Gida* (Town Fulani) had settled in the towns, where their higher education soon won for them positions of influence as *mallams*, secretaries, and political advisers at the courts of princes. Usman dan Fodio, the leader of the rebellion, was one of the Fulani Gida and had lived for some years at the Court of Gobir, where he acted as a tutor to the princes Yakuba and Yunfa. The increasing pagan practices at that Court forced dan Fodio to leave his job and to settle in the village of Degel, a few miles west of the modern town of Wurno. There he began to preach against the prevalent unorthodox practices with ascetic zeal and devotion and gradually won a large following. Alarmed by the growing strength of this zealot, his former pupil Sarkin Yunfa was alleged to have given secret orders for his murder. This leaked out and led to the flight of Fodio and his followers from Degel on 23 February 1804, an event whose anniversary is still celebrated in Northern Nigeria. From now on, assisted by his son Bello, afterwards Clapperton's host, and his brother Abdullahi, Usman planned the revolt, and letters were written by Bello to the Fulani *mallams* in the other Hausa states.[1] Having gathered a large following, Usman raised the standard of revolt about May 1804 by attacking the neighbouring Gober-awa towns. Proclaimed *amir al-mu'minin* (Commander of the Faithful), he gave his blessing in the form of flags to various Fulani *mallams* who initiated similar rebellions in the states and kingdoms in which they lived. For instance, *Mallams* Bauchi and Adama began the Jihad in the pagan states of Jacoba and Fumbina respectively, and their conquests were named after them. Whatever the true nature of this rebellion—and from modern research it is clear that it was a complex one[2]—its successful outcome cannot be doubted. By 1831 the various independent Hausa and other states had superimposed on them the Fulani Empire of fourteen emirates owing allegiance to the Commander of the Faithful, who resided in Sokoto, the new town founded by Usman dan Fodio. Before his death Usman divided the Empire into two Sultanates, Gwandu for his brother and Sokoto for his son, who was recognized as the religious head of the whole Empire.

When Barth visited Hausaland in the 1850's, the twin Fulani Empire of Sokoto and Gwandu still held sway. But from his observations of the state of the Empire he concluded: 'it cannot be denied that the Empire of Sokoto if going on in the present way, will soon be dissolved and thrown into pieces.'[3] Barth's fears were unfounded, for in fact the results of the rebellion have lasted to this day. The present Northern Nigeria is more or less coterminous with the Fulani Empire, the Sultan of Sokoto is still a direct descendant of Usman dan Fodio, he bears to this day the title of *amir*

---

[1] Westermann, op. cit., pp. 629–30; F. Daniel, 'Shehu Dan Fodio', *Journal of the African Society*, vol. 25, pp. 279–80; Muhamad Bello, *Infaq al-maysur*, translated by A. J. Arnett, Introduction, pp. 14–15; Bello, op. cit., pp. 49–50.

[2] See Appendix V.

[3] F.O. 101/34, Barth to F.O., 28 Jan. 1853; Barth, op. cit., vol. iv, pp. 154–6.

al-mu'minin, and is recognized as the religious head of Muslim Nigeria. Most of the present emirs of the region are also the direct descendants of the founders of the emirates.

That Barth's forecast did not come true is not at all surprising, since the picture he painted of the whole Empire as a Hobbesian state of nature, a picture which many historians, especially those of the 'Lugard' or 'Pax Britannica' school of thought, have only too readily accepted, is grossly misleading. There is no doubt that in the provinces of Yauri, Gwari, and Nupe to the south-west, as well as in the former Hausa states of Gobir, Kebbi, and Zamfara, wars and revolts continued throughout the century. Clapperton and Lander found that the people of Yauri and Gwari had revolted against the Fulani and were maintaining their independence.[1] Though nearly all these regions were conquered and formed into the Fulani emirate of Kontagora by Umoru Nagwamache, one of the sons of the fifth Sultan of Sokoto, they still remained exceedingly restless and insecure in the fifties.[2] In Nupe, too, the struggle between the Fulani and the former rulers continued intermittently, as the Landers, Laird, and Baikie saw, until the fifties, when the issue was finally decided in favour of the Fulani. Farther north in Sokoto, Barth arrived in 1853 to find that the Sultan was campaigning against the same people, the Goberawa and Kebbawa, who had revolted during Clapperton's visits of 1823 and 1826.[3] During his travels in this neighbourhood Barth often met troops on the move and heard echoes of war drums. He once had to wait in Katsina for seven weeks because of a threatened invasion of the district by the Goberawa.[4] Undoubtedly these wars and revolts must have caused some devastation and insecurity.

This situation should not, however, be exaggerated. In the first place, these wars and revolts were usually sporadic and of short duration. Secondly, they were mainly limited in the north to the area immediately north of Katsina and west of Sokoto and in the south to Nupe and Gwari. In other words, they were chiefly confined to the Emirate of Gwandu and should not therefore be taken as a reflection of the state of the Fulani Empire as a whole. Thirdly, Barth was certainly wrong—and so of course are Lugard, Meek, Bovill, Trimingham and other scholars who follow him—in describing these wars either as raids for slaves or as the 'struggle carried on between paganism and islamism'.[5] What he observed was no

[1] Clapperton, *Journal of a Second Expedition,* pp. 149–55, 307–10.
[2] E. C. Duff and W. Hamilton-Browne, *Gazetteer of the Kontagora Province* (1920), pp. 8–16.
[3] Denham and Clapperton, Clapperton's Journal, pp. 65–83; Clapperton, *Journal of a Second Expedition,* pp. 178–87; Barth, op. cit., vol. iv, pp. 132–6; F.O. 101/34, Barth to F.O., 28 Jan. 1853.
[4] Barth, op. cit., vol. iv, pp. 110–20, 200–38; Barth, op. cit., vol. ii, p. 37.
[5] Barth, op. cit., vol. ii, p. 37; C. K. Meek, *The Northern Tribes of Nigeria* (1928), vol. ii, p. 25; Bovill, *The Golden Trade,* pp. 245–6; J. S. Trimingham, *The Christian Church and Islam in W. Africa* (London, 1955).

less than a struggle for independence by the Hausa, the Gwari, and the Nupe. Far from reconciling themselves to their fate, the Courts of Gobir and Kebbi moved to Argungu and Matadi and from there spasmodically continued the struggle, with the assistance of some of the other dethroned Hausa dynasties and some of the Tuareg tribes, until the British occupation.

Whatever may have been the situation in the areas under Gwandu, it was different in those under Sokoto. During his travels through the emirates of Kano and Zaria in 1826, Clapperton did not notice any rebellions or civil wars. On his return journey after the death of his master, Richard Lander proceeded, to use his own words, 'on my way unmolested' and with a perfect sense of security through the southern districts of Kano and the northern and eastern parts of the emirate of Zaria, and through the emirate of Bauchi to within a day's march of its capital; nowhere in these districts did he come across any rebel armies.[1] Nor had Vogel, who travelled through the emirates of Gombe, Bauchi, Zaria, and the southern part of Kano, any story of wars, revolts, and insurbordination to tell. If anything, especially in Bauchi and Adamawa, it was the Fulani who were on the offensive. Instead of attempting to regain their independence, most of the people of the south-eastern emirates merely emigrated across the Benue or sought refuge in the almost inaccessible reaches of the hills and plateaux.[2] From Barth's own observations, as well as from the information he collected about the Sokoto Sultanate, it was only in the emirate of Hadeija, in the northernmost districts of Katsina, and in Zamfara that he found disturbances. In Hadeija the deposed governor, Bukhari, was still carrying on the campaigns for the reconquest of his post which he began in 1851. By 1853 he had killed his successor, had retaken his emirate, and was still attacking the districts of Gumel and Katagum.[3] The disturbances in Katsina and Zamfara were due, as we have seen already, to the people of Gobir and Kebbi. These districts were all on the fringe of the Sokoto Sultanate. Indeed, when, in order to avoid the Goberawa, Barth had to proceed southward instead of westward from Katsina to Sokoto in March 1853, he himself was astonished to find that the country within a single day's journey south of Katsina was 'populous and well cultivated', with extensive cotton and tobacco fields and large plantations of indigo.[4] Of the other provinces of the Sokoto Sultanate, Barth informed the Foreign Office in January 1853 that 'there was nothing particularly to be said'.[5]

In the regions of Timbuctu and the upper reaches of the Niger, conditions were also entirely different from those that Houghton and Park

[1] Clapperton, *Journal of a Second Expedition* (Lander's Journal), pp. 287–305.
[2] F.O. 101/45, Vogel to Herman, 4 Dec. 1855, encl. in Herman to Clarendon 17 Apr. 1856.
[3] Barth, op. cit., vol. ii, pp. 154–77, vol. iv, pp. 154–6; F.O. 101/45, Vogel Herman, 4 Dec. 1855, encl. in Herman to Clarendon, 17 Apr. 1856.
[4] Barth, op. cit., vol. iv, pp. 106–8.
[5] F.O. 101/34, Barth to F.O., 28 Jan. 1853.

had portrayed. The area did not consist of a series of independent Tuareg and Songhay principalities. As may be recalled, in the days of Barth as in those of Laing and Caillié the whole stretch from Timbuctu to Jenne formed part of the Fulani Empire of Masina.[1] This empire was founded at the same time as that of Sokoto and would seem to have been a product of the same movement—the Jihad of Usman dan Fodio. Though Shehu Ahmadu, the Fulani *mallam* and founder of Masina, may not have actually taken part in the Hausa wars as Westermann thought, he was influenced by the puritan ideals and fanatical zeal of Usman dan Fodio.[2] About 1813, while the wars in Hausaland were still raging, Ahmadu raised the standard of revolt against what he considered the idolatrous and semi-pagan rulers of Masina. He soon overthrew these rulers, attacked and conquered Jenne, the important trading centre, and from there invaded Bambara at the time when Dochard was waiting a few miles from Segu for a reply to his request for freedom of passage.[3] From Bambara Ahmadu again turned his attention eastward, overran the petty Tuareg and Songhay principalities, and in 1826 only a few weeks before Laing's arrival, conquered Timbuctu. Like Usman dan Fodio, Shehu Ahmadu founded a capital for his new empire which he characteristically named Hamdallahi (God be praised). Ahmadu ruled with fanatical zeal till his death in 1844, and his empire lasted until it was overthrown by the Tuculor Tijani, Al-Hajj Umar, between 1855 and 1862. Undoubtedly it was the religious fanaticism of Ahmadu and his successor, a feeling which had not burned itself out even by the time of Barth's visit, which made the regions of the Niger bend so dangerous for European explorers after 1826.

The relations between these various empires and kingdoms of the western Sudan as revealed by the accounts of the explorers are also noteworthy when compared with the ideas of the 'Pax Britannica' School. As we have seen, Bagirmi, Waday, and Bornu were in the days of Denham and Clapperton bitterly struggling among themselves.[4] The warlike spirit of Bagirmi declined after 1823, but Waday and Bornu continued the struggle in the thirties and forties. During the stay of Barth and Vogel, however, while relations were not at all friendly, the two states were not in armed conflict. Farther west, Bornu and Sokoto were also far from being permanently at war with each other. Relations between the two would even appear to have been quite friendly at the time of the Denham–Clapperton mission, mainly because Al-Kānami had his hands full with the Waday–Bagirmi wars. When at one of their palavers in 1823 Clapperton told Bello that Al-Kānami would seize any guns and presents sent to him through

---

[1] See above, pp. 88 and 193–4.
[2] H. C. F. Smith, 'A neglected theme of West African History; The Islamic Revolutions of the Nineteenth Century' in *Historians in Tropical Africa* (Salisbury, 1962), pp. 145–58; C.O. 267/49, Dochard to Gray, 21 Feb. 1820, encl. in MacCarthy to Bathurst, 15 Sept. 1820; Westermann, op. cit., pp. 625–6; Dubois, op. cit., pp. 134–5.
[3] See above, p. 42.   [4] See above, p. 239.

Bornu, the Sultan replied confidently, 'Oh no, he will never do that, he will never do that, he is my friend.'[1] But, as may be recalled, Clapperton arrived in Kano the second time only to meet an invasion of Sokoto by the army of Al-Kānami.[2] This invasion was successfully beaten back, and from then on till Al-Kānami's death in 1837 peace prevailed between the two states. His son and successor, Umar, revived his father's aggressive policy towards Sokoto and during the first five years of his reign launched a number of attacks on that state. These were mostly unsuccessful, and in 1842 he concluded peace with the Fulani.[3] During Barth's long stay he found that the two states were still officially not at war, that the rulers were 'professing to be on the best terms with one another' and that messengers were going to and fro. But he did discover that covertly Bornu was aiding Bukhari as well as Gobir, that clashes between the governors of the border provinces were not infrequent, and that both states were giving asylum to each other's political refugees. Indeed, when he was leaving Bornu for Timbuctu, Barth was specifically asked by the Government of Bornu not to go to Kano, because that would 'interfere with their policy'.[4]

This hostile attitude particularly on the part of Bornu towards Sokoto dates from the *Jihad* of Usman dan Fodio, which was not confined to Hausaland, for two Fulani *mallams*, Ibrahim Zaki and Gwani Mukhtar, led the Fulani of Bornu in 'sympathetic risings' against the Sultan in about 1808 and were in fact later given flags by Usman dan Fodio.[5] By 1812 the Fulani had conquered most of the western provinces of Bornu and completely burnt down Birni Ngazargamo, its capital since its foundation in 1470.[6] However, under the inspired leadership of Muhammad Al-Kānami, another celebrated scholar and ascetic who was called in from Kanem by the helpless Sultan, the Bornu army reconquered most of the lost provinces except Katagum.

Al-Kānami became so indispensable to the Sultan that he was invited to stay permanently in Bornu. He accepted the invitation, built a new capital, which he named Kukawa, in 1814, and became from then till his death in 1837 not only the king-maker, but, as Denham and Clapperton observed, the effective ruler of Bornu.[7]

[1] Clapperton, *Journal of First Expedition*, op. cit., p. 95; C.O. 2/13, Denham to Bathurst, 20 Sept. 1822.

[2] See above, pp. 81–82.

[3] Barth, op. cit., vol. ii, p. 666; Y. Urvoy, *Histoire de l'Empire du Bornu* (1949), pp. 110–11.

[4] There was a clash at that time between the Governors of Kano and Zinder. Barth, op. cit., vol. ii, pp. 175–7, vol. iv, pp. 5–6, 84, 96; F.O. 101/34, Barth to F.O., 28 Jan. 1853.

[5] H. C. F. Smith, 'A neglected theme of West African History, the Islamic Revolutions of the Nineteenth Century', a paper read at the Leverhume History Conference, 2 Sept. 1960; a letter by H. C. Smith to the author, 2 Aug. 1961.

[6] For a description of its present ruins, see A. D. H. Bivar and P. L. Shinne, 'Old Kanuri capitals', *Journal of African History*, vol. iii (1962), No. 1.

[7] Bello, op. cit., pp. 99–101; Denham, op. cit., p. 28; Barth, vol. ii, pp. 661–4.

On Barth's arrival he discovered that the office of Sultan had been entirely abolished and that sovereign power in theory as well as in practice was exercised by Umar, the son and successor of Al-Kānami. This change took place, Barth informed Palmerston, in 1851, 'in consequence of an attack from Waday'. The invasion of Bornu in 1846 by the Sultan of Waday had been undertaken at the request of the people of Bornu, who wanted to rid the country of the Kānami family and restore Sultan Ibrahim 'to the authority of his forefathers'. The Sultan of Waday defeated Umar at the first encounter and went on to raze Kukawa to the ground. He then appointed Ali, the last surviving member of the Sefuwa dynasty, as Sultan in place of Ibrahim, who had been executed by Umar. During the second battle, however, Umar defeated and killed Ali, whose death ended the Sefuwa dynasty which had been reigning in Bornu since the tenth century. From that time till today the descendants of Al-Kānami have continued to rule Bornu under the title of Sheikh or Shehu.[1]

The Jihad then had very far-reaching consequences in Bornu, including a legacy of hostility and jealousy towards Sokoto owing to the loss of Katagum, Kano, Katsina, and Daura, all of which owed Bornu nominal allegiance before the Jihad. But from the visit of Barth and Vogel to the death of Umar in 1880 this feeling of jealousy and hostility did not lead to any invasions or wars.

Equally strained in the fifties were the relations between the Gwandu–Sokoto and Masina Empires. When Barth was leaving for Timbuctu, the Sultan of Sokoto repeatedly asked him not to visit the ruler of Masina. According to Barth, this was due to the insulting message which Shehu Ahmadu had sent to the rulers of Sokoto to the effect that unless they reduced the number of their wives to two and renounced their effeminate dress, he would 'pay them a visit'.[2] The two sister empires, however, never took the field against each other.

From this brief survey of the observations of the explorers, it seems that during at least the first half of the nineteenth century, the states of the western Sudan were not permanently at each other's throats. As between the states of contemporary Europe, jealousies, animosities, and rivalries existed and these led occasionally to wars and invasions. Indeed the Fulani wars were contemporaneous with the Napoleonic wars in Europe. But as in Europe, there were long periods of peace between states in the western Sudan. During the fifties, while Europe was in the throes of the Crimean War, the states and kingdoms of the area from Timbuctu to Chad were at peace with each other: the area was in a state of 'cold war' not dissimilar to what we are experiencing today.

[1] F.O. 101/28, Barth to Palmerston, 30 Apr. 1851; 101/30, Overweg to Palmerston, 9 Aug. 1851; Barth, vol. iv, pp. 666–9. Barth's account of this war has been confirmed or accepted by later scholars. See A. Schultze, *The Sultanate of Bornu*, translated with additions by P. A. Benton (London, 1913), p. 22; Urvoy, op. cit., pp. 92, 110–11.

[2] F.O. 101/36, Barth to Malmesbury, 2 Oct. 1853; Barth, vol. iv, pp. 188, 257.

Another interesting aspect of political life on which the accounts of the explorers shed some light was the structure of government of the states and kingdoms of the western Sudan. As Denham and Clapperton discovered, at the head of each was a sultan who, either by himself, as in Bagirmi, or assisted by a council of ministers, as in Sokoto and Bornu, governed the kingdom or empire. Provincial administration was in the hands of governors or emirs who were appointed and could be deposed by the sultan. Except in Bornu the structure remained unchanged at the time of Barth, and indeed as a result of the system of indirect rule adopted by the British, the traditional arrangement has continued as the framework of local administration in Northern Nigeria to this day.

APPENDIX V

The Nature of the Fulani Rebellion

THE true nature of this rebellion has been the subject of a literary battle which began with the rising itself and has been raging ever since. The first round was led by two contemporaries of Usman dan Fodio, Bello, his son, and Al-Kānami, the Sheikh of Bornu, in the letters which they exchanged while the war was going on. Al-Kānami admitted that the Bornu kings were indulging in certain pagan practices, that women went about unveiled and that the judges were corrupt. He, nevertheless, contended that those evils did not justify a *jihad* against Bornu, and that the Fulani were concealing political ambitions behind a cloak of religious reform. In his replies, Bello disowned all political ambitions and argued that though the Hausa people and their kings had once been converted to Islam, they had lapsed into paganism and that to make war on such people was a duty. Each of these generals has since had his own supporters. Arnett, Daniel, Mockler-Ferryman, and Bovill have accepted Bello's interpretation of the rebellion. 'The story of Usman dan Fodio,' Daniel wrote in an article on him, 'is the story of the religious war or *jihad*'; and it ended, according to Mockler-Ferryman, 'in the complete overthrow of the pagans and the establishment of Mohammedanism in that part of Africa'. Opposed to them are the Kanamites, including Hogben and M. G. Smith, who see the rebellion simply as a national rising of the Fulani against Hausa domination, with religion as a mere transparent pretext. 'It had as its confessed object the purification of the Muslim religion and it was directed against the corrupt rulers of Hausaland. . . . In reality,' Hogben contends, 'it was originally a national fight of the Fulani both Muslim and pagan against the forces of Yunfa, the King of Gobir.' There is yet a third school which sees in the rising both religious and political motives. 'To his [Dan Fodio's] religious nature filled with the zeal for the purity and supremacy of Islam and enriched by literary education,' argues Westermann, the leading exponent of this school of thought, 'the oppressed condition of his countrymen who were devoted adherents of their religion must have been as humiliating as the heathen conduct of the royal court at Gobir was offensive.' The latest round in this age-long battle was begun by the Russian scholar D. A. Olderogge in a paper read at the 24th International Congress of Orientalists in Munich in 1957. In this paper he rejected all the views outlined above, and came to the conclusion that the rebellion was neither a religious nor a national rising but a class war, a conflict between the Hausa nobility on the one hand and the poor Fulani cattle-breeders and the downtrodden Hausa commoners (*talakawa*) on the other. In his recent book

Black Mother (1961) Davidson follows this wise man from the east and states categorically that 'the origins of this Fulani invasion had lain in revolt against a gross social inequality'.

Most of these historians did not use any of the Arabic materials that have been recently accumulating in the archives and libraries in Nigeria mainly as a result of the work of W. E. N. Kensdale, H. F. C. Smith, Hiskett, and A. D. H. Bivar, with the full backing of the Nigerian Government and the University College of Ibadan. The only person who has so far tapped this new source is Mr. H. F. C. Smith, and his conclusions, in which he emphasizes the intellectual aspect hitherto ignored, are noteworthy. While admitting the complex nature of the rebellion, he has given prominence to the intellectual and religious aspect of it. 'The movement,' he contends in a paper presented at the Leverhume Conference in Salisbury in September 1960, 'represented much more than the attempt of a few under-privileged and determined men to seize political power for their own benefit. In origin it was also an important intellectual movement, involving in the minds of the leaders a conception of the ideal society and a philosophy of revolution.' He points out that perhaps the most remarkable characteristic of the leaders was their great learning, that their thought followed a classical pattern of Islamic revivalism, and that their aim was to 'recreate in the western Sudan the society of the Rightly-guided Caliphate'. In a letter to me, he pointed out that in classical Islamic social theory, there is no distinction between 'Church and State', that Islamic movements for what we should call religious reform are *ipso facto* movements for political reform; therefore the political activities of Usman dan Fodio do not destroy his position as a Jihad leader. In this letter Smith is even more categorical in his conclusion: 'The movement was properly speaking a Jihad because it was aimed at the establishment of Islamic government.' I find Smith's arguments quite convincing and his conclusions acceptable. Thomas Hodgkin, who has like myself come under the spell of Smith, but who at the same time cannot abandon his friends from the east, has in his brilliant introduction to his work *Nigerian perspectives* (Oxford 1960) reconciled both views. According to him, 'while its deeper causes remain obscure, the revolution itself can be regarded in three ways'. First it can be regarded as a religious reform movement and in that respect 'can be compared with reforming movements in other parts of the Muslim world during the late eighteenth and nineteenth centuries—the Wahhabiya in Saudi Arabia, the Sanusiyya in Cyrenaica, Hajj Umar al-Tall's movement in the eastern Sudan'. Secondly, it can be regarded as 'an expression if not of Fulani "nationalism" at least of the sense of common purpose which a group with ties of education, culture, and ideology, as well as language and kinship, is liable to generate'. Thirdly, at least in its early stages, the movement had a genuine popular basis and 'also represented a protest of the Hausa Commoners (*talakawa*) against the old Hausa dynasties—against the oppression of the ruling class as much as against its "paganism" or lack of orthodoxy'. According to Hodgkin, the type of state which the leaders of the revolution were pledged to establish was a state 'in which social justice, administered in the light of the *Shari'a* by God-fearing rulers, took the place of the arbitrary decisions of irresponsible despots'.

These conflicting views are enough to show that the history of the Fulani movement has as yet to be written. This, however, cannot be done until the collection and translation of Arabic sources has been completed. For further reading see:

M. Bello, '*Infak al-maysur*' translated by Arnett (a new translation is in preparation).

F. Daniel, 'Shehu dan Fodio', *Journal of the African Society*, vol. 25, 1925–6, pp. 279–80.

E. W. Bovill, *The Golden Trade*, op. cit., pp. 220–32.

S. J. Hogben, *The Muhammedan Emirates of Nigeria* (London, 1930), p. 73.

D. Westermann, *Islam in western and central Sudan* (London, 1920).

D. A. Olderogge, Foedalism v. Zapadnous Sudane, in *Sovietskaya Etnografia*, 4 Nov. 1957, pp. 91–103.

(Summarized in *African Abstracts*, vol. x. 1, Jan. 1959, pp. 11–12.)

H. F. C. Smith, 'A neglected theme of West African History: The Islamic Revolutions of the nineteenth century'. Paper presented at the Leverhume History Conference in Salisbury, September 1960, and published in *Historians in Tropical Africa* (Salisbury, 1962), pp. 145–58.

B. Davidson, *Black Mother* (London, 1961), pp. 35–36.

J. S. Trimingham, *A History of Islam in West Africa* (Oxford, 1962), pp. 193–207.

T. Hodgkin, *Nigerian Perspectives* (Oxford, 1960), pp. 38–43.

Extract from Al-Baka'i's Letter to the Sultan of Masina[1]

'You must know that I would not have thought that a man such as you could be ignorant of the rules relating to the *jihād*—and to him who conducts and him who suffers it—nor that it could escape a Muslim, or even an Infidel, that it is not permitted to be unjust towards an Infidel, whoever he may be, whether soldier or private person, who has penetrated into *dar al-Islam* with a safe-conduct (*āmān*) provided by the Muslims.

'If your are ignorant of this prohibition, it is none the less well-known to jurists of a ripe age, and to the chiefs associated with you. And if they themselves know nothing about it, and if the jurists of your country are ignorant of it (although it is a Muslim country that it takes ten days march to cross), well then, so much the worse. We belong to God and it is to Him that we shall return.

'In any case this Christian, he is not ignorant of the Law concerning the *jihād*. Perhaps that is why he has travelled in the *dar al-Islam* as a solitary foreigner, trusting in the good faith of Muslims, in the prescriptions of their God, in their Book, and in the *Sunna* of their Prophet.

'For ten years while he has been travelling through the countries of the Muslims, he has clearly seen that he has no one to fear but the ignorant Tuareg, who have abandoned the rules of Islam, or the Pagans of the Sudan, who are outside Islam.

'He is not afraid of you, neither you nor your people: he doesn't even think of it. For you belong to those who claim to know the rules of the Law; and the Muslims do not trouble one who is either a *dhimmi* or a Christian authorised to move about in their territory and enjoying good relations with them. On the contrary his person and goods are secure. . . .'

'I disapprove of your having given the order to arrest him and having wished to appropriate that which belongs to him. You have committed a sin (*harām*), and, as for him, he is the victim of injustice. Has he not arrived under the protection of the Muslims? All the tribes of the Christians are at the present time on good terms and at peace with us. Only the Muscovites (*al-mūsk*), we have been told, are at war, this year, with Sultan 'Abd al-majīd [Ottoman]. And, in any case it is not for you to declare the state of *jihād*: you, anyway, are not the *Imam* of the Muslims. At the

[1] Vincent Monteil, 'Quelques textes arabes provenant du Soudan (region de Tonbouctou)', *Bull. Com. Et Hist. de l'AOF*, vol. xxi (1938).

present time the *Imam* of the Muslims is either Moulai 'Abd al-rahman [Sultan of Morocco] or Sultan 'Abd al-majīd. By right it should be Moulai 'Abd al-rahman, but in fact 'Abd al-majīd is the greater and more powerful of the two. As for you, living five days' march from Hamdullahi to Timbuktu, away—you are only a simple *Amiru*, a ruler of huts at the extremity of West Africa, and at the same time the *Imam* of a fraction of the *Muslims* of this country. You have not the right to break this agreement and this peace with the Christians, which the two Sultans—of whom one is the *Imam*, to the exclusion of the other, and yourself—have made with them.

'Besides, I never said that this Englishman was a *dhimmi*; I never said that, and if I wrote it, well, that was a slip. For the English are not *dhimmi*. They have simply been in peace and alliance with us for a long time; for 500 years and more, according to this Englishman. . . .'

'If all the world had said that he [Barth] had not passed through the territories of the Sultans in order to come to Timbuktu, I would not have believed otherwise; and, even if this Christian himself had affirmed this, I would have regarded him as a liar. For that which must be the case imposes itself necessarily on the mind, while the improbable is necessarily rejected. At least, as far as I am concerned, it is so.

'But you others, you think all this is false, and you suppose that, from Timbuktu, this man could harm you at Hamdullahi. The English—would they cross the whole of the Gharb, the whole of Africa, Syria, and Constantinople, and come and raid Timbuktu? Really, my astonishment is unlimited when I consider the intelligence of those who are not Arabs. . . .'

'Finally, this Christian is not a warrior—as I have already said—and he does not belong to a warlike nation. There is no *jihād* against him. Keep your *jihād* for warriors and prepare it against them. For, I tell you, if your *jihād* was of divine origin, it would be in conformity with the *sunna* of the Prophet; and, if you were following the *sunna* of the Prophet, you would have consulted me on this subject. . . .'

Bibliography

PRIMARY SOURCES

I. *In the Public Record Office*
C.O. 2 and 392: These contain correspondence about the exploration of the interior of Africa from 1794–1844.
C.O. 267 and 268 deal with Sierra Leone.
F.O. 8—Barbary, General.
F.O. 76, 101—Tripoli. They contain the correspondence of the explorers sent from Tripoli and of the vice-consuls at Murzuk and Ghadames.
F.O. 335—Tunis.
F.O. 52 and 99—Morocco.
F.O. 84—Slave Trade Papers (Turkey, Tripoli, Tunis, Algeria, Morocco).

II. *Private Papers*
1. Papers of Sir Joseph Banks in the Museum of Natural History (D.T.C.).
   Kew Gardens (Kew, B.C.).
   British Museum (B.M. Add. MSS.).
2. Papers of Major Laing in the Royal Society Library (R.S. 374 (La)).
3. Papers of the British and Foreign Anti-Slavery Society in Rhodes House, Oxford (Br. Emp. MSS.).

III. *Reports of Societies*
1. Proceedings and Minutes of the African Association, 2 vols. (London, 1810).
2. Transactions of the Linnaean Society.
3. Annual Reports of the African Institution.
4. Annual Reports of the British and Foreign Anti-Slavery Society.

IV. *Parliamentary Papers*
1840 XXXIII (57)—Correspondence relating to the Niger Expedition.
1847–8 XII (273, 366, 536, 623)—Reports of Select Committees on the Slave Trade.
1865 V (1)—Report of the Select Committee on the State of the British West African Settlements.

V. *Journals of Explorers*
BATTUTA, IBN, *Travels in Asia and Africa*, translated by H. A. K. Gibb (London, 1929).
AFRICANUS, LEO, *History and Descriptions of Africa*, Hakluyt Society, 3 vols. (London, 1896).

PARK, M., *Travels in Africa* (London, 1799);
The *Journal of a Mission to the Interior of Africa in the year 1805* (London, 1815).

HORNEMANN, F., *The Journal of F. Hornemann's Travels from Cairo to Murzuk, the capital of Fezzan* (London, 1802).

LAING, A. G., *Travels in the Timannee, Kooranko and Soolima Countries in Western Africa* (London, 1825).

GRAY, W., *Travels in Western Africa* (London, 1825).

TUCKEY, J. K., *Narrative of an expedition to explore the River Zaire usually called the Congo in South Africa in 1816* (London, 1818).

LYON, G. F., *A narrative of the Travels in Northern Africa, 1818–1820* (London, 1821).

DENHAM, D., and CLAPPERTON, H., *Narrative of Travels and Discoveries in Northern and Central Africa in the Years 1822, 1823, 1824* (London, 1826).

CAILLIÉ, R., *Travels through Central Africa to Timbuctoo and across the Great Desert to Morocco, performed in the years 1824–1828*, 2 vols., English translation (London, 1830).

LANDER, R., *Records of Captain Clapperton's last expedition to Africa with the subsequent adventures of the author*, 2 vols. (London, 1830).

LANDER, R., and LANDER, J., *Journal of an expedition to explore the course and termination with a narrative of a voyage down the River to its termination*, 3 vols. (London, 1832).

LAIRD, M., and OLDFIELD, R. A. K., *Expedition into the interior of Africa*, 2 vols. (London, 1837).

RICHARDSON, J., *Travels in the Great Desert of Sahara in 1845–6*, 2 vols. (London, 1848);
Narrative of a Mission to Central Africa in 1850–1, 2 vols. (London, 1853).

BARTH, H., *Travels and Discoveries in North and Central Africa*, 5 vols. (London, 1857–8).

BAIKIE, W. B., *Narrative of an exploring voyage up the Rivers Kworo and Binue—commonly known as the River Niger and Tsadda—in 1854* (London, 1856).

CROWTHER, S., *Journal of an expedition up the Niger and Tshadda Rivers* . . . (London, 1855).

HUTCHINSON, T. J., *Narrative of the Niger, Tsadda and Binue Exploration* (London, 1855).

DUVEYRIER, H., *Exploration du Sahara: les Touareg du Mord* (Paris, 1864).

LENTZ, O., *Timbuctou*, 2 vols. (Paris, 1886).

DUBOIS, F., *Timbuctoo the mysterious* . . . translated from the French by D. White (London, 1897).

HASANEIN BEY, A. M., *The Lost Oasis* (Cairo, 1926).

VI.   *Contemporary Memoirs*

BARROW, J., *Sir Joseph Banks* (London, 1845).
An autobiographical Memoir of Sir John Barrow (London, 1847).
Sketches of the Royal Society and the Royal Society and the Royal Society Club (London, 1849).

JACKSON, J. G., *An Account of the Empire of Morocco* (London, 1820).

MACQUEEN, J., *A Geographical and Commercial View of Northern Central Africa* (Edinburgh, 1821).

BUXTON, T. F., *The African Slave Trade* (London, 1839);
The Remedy (London, 1838).

BUXTON, C., *Memoirs of Sir Thomas Fowell Buxton* (London, 1848).

BANDINEL, J., *Some account of the Trade in Slaves from Africa as connected with Europe and America, especially with reference to the efforts being made by the British Government for its extinction* (London, 1842).

MACKENZIE, D., *The Flooding of the Sahara* (London, 1877).

SECONDARY SOURCES

ASHLEY, A., *Life of Palmerston*, 2 vols. (London, 1877).

BATES, O., *The Eastern Libyans* (London, 1914).

BENTON, P. A., *Notes on some languages of the Western Sudan* (London, 1912).

BOVILL, E. W., *The Caravans of the Old Sahara* (London, 1933);
The Golden Trade of the Moors (London, 1958).

BROWN, R., *The story of Africa and its Explorers*, 4 vols. (London, 1892–5).

BERNARD, A., and LACROIX, N., *La Pénétration saharienne, 1830–1906* (Alger, 1906).

BODELSEN, C. A., *Studies of mid-Victorian imperialism* (Copenhagen, 1924).

BURNS, A., *History of Nigeria*, 4th Edition (London, 1948).

CAMERON, H. C., *Sir Joseph Banks* (London, 1952).

COUPLAND, R., *East Africa and its invaders from the earliest times to the death of Sayyid Said in 1856* (Oxford, 1938).
The exploitation of East Africa, 1856–1890 (London, 1939).
The British Anti-Slavery Movement (London, 1933).

DELAFOSSE, M., *Haut-Sénégal-Niger, Le Pays, les peuples, les languages, l'histoire, les civilisations*. 3 tom. (Paris, 1912).

DIKE, K. O., *Trade and politics in the Niger Delta* (Oxford, 1956).

DARCY, J., *France and Angleterre, Cent années de rivalité colonial* (Paris, 1904).

DUVEYRIER, H., *La Confrérie musulmane de Sidi Mohammed ben Ali Es-Senous et son domaine géographique* (Paris, 1884).

EVANS, J. L., *The British in Tropical Africa* (London, 1929).

FLINT, J. E., *Sir George Goldie and the making of Nigeria* (London, 1960).

FLOURNOY, F. B., *British policy towards Morocco in the age of Palmerston, 1830–1865* (London and Baltimore, 1935).

FRIES, R. E., *A short history of Botany in Sweden* (Uppsala, 1950).

GAUTIER, E. F., and CHUDEAU, R., *Missions au Sahara, par E. F. Gautier et R. Chudeau.* 2 tom. (Paris, 1908–9).

GRAY, R., *A History of the Southern Sudan, 1839-1889* (Oxford, 1961).

GREENIDGE, W. W., *Slavery* (London, 1958).

GWYNN, S., *Mungo Park and the Niger Quest* (London, 1890).

HEWITT, W. H., *Mungo Park* (London, 1923).

HOWARD, C., and PLUMB, *West African Explorers* (Oxford, 1951).

HOGBEN, S. J., *The Muhammadan Emirates of Nigeria* (London, 1930).

JOHNSTON, H. H., *The Opening Up of Africa* (London, 1911).

JULIEN, C. A., *Histoire de l'Afrique du Nord* (Paris, 1951).

MINER, H., *Timbuctoo* (Princeton, 1953).

MILL, H. R., *The Records of the Royal Geographical Society* (London, 1933).

MAUNOIR, C. H., and SCHIRMER, H., *Journal de route de Henri Dureyrier* (Paris, 1905).

BONNEL DE MÉZIÈRES, A., *Le Major A. Gordon Laing* (Paris, 1912).

MAIDEN, J. H., *Sir Joseph Banks, the father of Australia* (London, 1909).

MARTIN, B. G., 'Five Letters from the Tripoli Archives', Journal of the His. Soc. of Nigeria, Vol. II, No. 3, 1962.

MEEK, C. K., *The Northern tribes of Nigeria* (London, 1925).

NADEL, S. F., *A black Byzantium* (London, 1942).

PRITCHARD, E. E., *The Sanusi of Cyrenaica* (Oxford, 1949).

RODD, F. R., *People of the veil* (London, 1926).

SCHULTZE, A., *The Sultanate of Bornu*, translated with additions by P. A. Benton (London, 1913).

SELIGMAN, C. G., *Races of Africa* (London, 1957).

SMITH, E., *The Life of Sir Joseph Banks* (London, 1911).

SCHIFFERS, H., *The Quest for Africa*, English translation (London, 1957).

THOMSON, J., *Mungo Park and the Niger* (London, 1889).

TRIMINGHAM, J. S., *The Christian Church and Islam in Africa* (London, 1955);
Islam in West Africa (Oxford, 1959).

TURNBULL, P., *Sahara Unveiled* (London, 1940).

URVOY, Y., *Histoire de l'Empire du Bornou* (Paris, 1949).

VUILLOT, P., *L'Exploration du Sahara* (Paris, 1895).

WEBSTER, C., *The Foreign policy of Palmerston, 1830–1841*, 2 vols. (London, 1951).

WESTERMANN, D., *Islam in western and central Sudan*, English translation (London, 1920).

WILLIAMSON, J. A., *Great Britain and the Empire* (London, 1944).

WOLF, A., *A History of Science, Technology and Philosophy in the eighteenth century* (London, 1938).

UNPUBLISHED THESES

MADDEN, A. F., 'The attitude of evangelicals to the Empire and imperial problems, 1820–1850', D.Phil., Oxford, 1950.

RAYMON, A., 'British policy towards Tunis', D.Phil., Oxford, 1954.

SCHWITZER, J. P., 'The British attitude towards French colonisation, 1875–1887', Ph.D., London, 1954.

IFEMESIA, C. C., 'British enterprise on the Niger, 1830–1869', Ph.D., London, 1959.

Index

Printed in Great Britain by Richard Clay and Company, Ltd.,
Bungay, Suffolk

DATE DUE